EARLY GREEK STATES
BEYOND THE POLIS

EARLY GREEK STATES BEYOND THE POLIS

Catherine Morgan

Routledge
Taylor & Francis Group
LONDON AND NEW YORK

First published 2003
by Routledge
2 Park Square, Milton Park, Abingdon, Oxon, OX14 4RN

Simultaneously published in the USA and Canada
by Routledge
270 Madison Ave, New York NY 10016

Routledge is an imprint of the Taylor & Francis Group

Transferred to Digital Printing 2008

© 2003 Catherine Morgan

Typeset in Garamond by Exe Valley Dataset Ltd, Exeter

All rights reserved. No part of this book may be reprinted or reproduced or utilised in any form or by any electronic, mechanical, or other means, now known or hereafter invented, including photocopying and recording, or in any information storage or retrieval system, without permission in writing from the publishers.

British Library Cataloguing in Publication Data
A catalogue record for this book is available from the British Library

Library of Congress Cataloging in Publication Data
Morgan, Catherine, 1961–
Early Greek states beyond the polis / Catherine Morgan.
p.cm.
Includes bibliographical references and index.
1. Greeks–Ethnic identity–History–To 1500. 2. Group identity–Greece–History–To 1500. 3. Greece–Politics and government–To 146 B.C. I. Title.

DF135.M67 2003
321′.00938–dc21   2002032623

ISBN10: 0–415–08996–4 (hbk)
ISBN10: 0–415–48671–8 (pbk)

ISBN13: 978–0–415–08996–8 (hbk)
ISBN13: 978–0–415–48671–2 (pbk)

CONTENTS

List of figures   vii
Acknowledgements   xi

1 **Introduction**   1

   Ethnos and polis 4
   Ethne, ethnicity and tribalism 10
   Archaeology and early Greek ethne 16
   Thessaly 18
   Phokis 24
   East Lokris 28
   Achaia 31
   Arkadia 38

2 **Big sites and place identities**   45

   Big sites or urban entities? 47
   Questions of scale 54
   Place identities 69
   Economics, subsistence and production 71
   Political statements in big sites 73
   Symbols of authority 76
   Thessaly 85
   Larisa 89
   Pherai 92
   Dimini, Sesklo and Volos 95
   Thessalian geography and the Catalogue of Ships *102*
   Conclusion 105

3 **Communities of cult**   107

   The cult systems of Phokis 113
   The spread of cults 135

Temple buildings 142
The economic roles of sanctuary authorities 149
Arkadia 155
Conclusion 162

4 **Territory, power and the ancestors**   164

Ethne in the landscape 168
Community of territory? 171
Marginal areas and routes of communication 176
The territory of our ancestors? 187
Penestai 190
Burial and the past in Thessaly 192
Beyond the boundaries 196

5 **Beyond the polis: political communities and political identities**   206

Regional interconnections: the case of the Corinthian gulf 213
Envoi 222

Notes   226
Bibliography   278
Index   322

FIGURES

1.1	Greece: regions and principal sites mentioned in the text (C.L. Hayward)	19
1.2	Thessaly (C.L. Hayward)	20
1.3	The western Thessalian plain from the acropolis of Kierion (photo: author)	21
1.4	Volos and the head of the Pagasitic gulf from south of Portaria (photo: author)	21
1.5	Phokis (C.L. Hayward)	25
1.6	Kephisos valley: looking east from outside Amphikleia (photo: author)	26
1.7	The Chrysaean plain from modern Delphi (photo: author)	27
1.8	The bay of Itea and the lower Pleistos valley from the coast outside Chaleion (Galaxidi) (photo: author)	27
1.9	The cemetery at Elateia (photo: author)	28
1.10	East Lokris (C.L. Hayward)	29
1.11	Achaia (C.L. Hayward after Yvonne Rizaki)	32
1.12	Aegira acropolis, looking east (photo: C.L. Hayward)	33
1.13	Aegira: erosion inland from the acropolis (photo: C.L. Hayward)	34
1.14	Coastal plain near Diakofto: view inland to Panachaikon (photo: author)	34
1.15	Aigion (photo: author)	35
1.16	Pharai valley: south west from Platanovrysi (photo: author)	35
1.17	Pharai valley: looking south from east of Chalandritsa (photo: author)	36
1.18	Arkadia (C.L. Hayward)	40/41
1.19	Alipheira acropolis: looking south (photo: author)	42
1.20	Lousoi: valley bottom from the Hellenistic settlement (photo: author)	43
1.21	Lousoi: Mt. Helmos from above the temple site (photo: author)	43
1.22	Tegean plain: southern end showing flooding after Spring snowfalls, April 1998 (photo: author)	44

FIGURES

2.1	Eretria (courtesy of the Swiss School of Archaeology at Athens)	51
2.2	Aegira 'Temple A' (author, after Alzinger, *ÖJh* 1983)	52
2.3	Aegira acropolis (photo: C.L. Hayward)	53
2.4	Late Bronze Age and eighth-century settlement in the Corinthia (C.L. Hayward)	56
2.5	Corinth (C.L. Hayward after C.K. Williams II)	58
2.6	Corinth: Acrocorinth from above the west end of the Roman forum (photo: author)	59
2.7	Temple Hill from the Acrocorinth road (photo: author)	60
2.8	Oolitic limestone quarry at Mavrospelies (photo: C.L. Hayward)	61
2.9	Principal quarries for building material in the main lithologies of the Corinthia (C.L. Hayward: reproduced from *Corinth* XX by permission of the American School of Classical Studies at Athens)	62
2.10	Early Iron Age Argos (reproduced by courtesy of the École française d'Athènes)	63
2.11	Modern Argos from the Larisa (photo: author)	64
2.12	Classical Argos (reproduced by courtesy of the École française d'Athènes)	65
2.13	Athens agora: Submycenean to early Archaic (American School of Classical Studies at Athens: Agora Excavations)	66
2.14	Athens, agora *c*.500 BC (American School of Classical Studies at Athens: Agora Excavations)	67
2.15	Early Athens (American School of Classical Studies at Athens: Agora Excavations)	68
2.16	Mantineia: the Ptolis acropolis (photo: author)	70
2.17	Olympia: Classical bouleuterion (photo: author)	75
2.18	Thessaly, mint group 1, obverse showing figure of Thessalos (© The British Museum: reproduced by courtesy of the Trustees of The British Museum)	82
2.19	Early Arkadikon issue (© The British Museum: reproduced by courtesy of the Trustees of The British Museum)	83
2.20	Eastern Thessaly (C.L. Hayward)	86
2.21	Pherai	93
2.22	Modern Velestino looking north-east from the Ag. Athanasios acropolis (photo: author)	94
2.23	Pherai: temple of Zeus/Enodia looking south-west towards Magoula Bakali (photo: author)	95
2.24	Principal sites around the head of the Pagasitic gulf (C.L. Hayward)	97
2.25	The acropolis of Dimini (photo: author)	99

FIGURES

2.26	Mycenaean tholos beside the acropolis of Dimini (photo: author)	100
2.27	Pefkakia promontory: looking north towards Volos (photo: author)	101
3.1	The Corinthia in LHIIIC (C.L. Hayward)	110
3.2a	Boot figurines: Morgan 1999a, F38 (left, Corinthian), F36 (bottom right, Attic), F37 (top right, Attic) (University of Chicago Excavations at Isthmia: photo: Ioannidou and Bartzioti)	111
3.2b	Attic closed vessel shoulder sherd with part of prothesis scene: Morgan 1999a, cat. 370 (University of Chicago Excavations at Isthmia: photo: Ioannidou and Bartzioti)	111
3.3a	Isthmia: bronze tripod, c.750 (Morgan 1999a, M14) (University of Chicago Excavations at Isthmia: photo: Ioannidou and Bartzioti)	112
3.3b	Isthmia: bronze tripod attachment, second half eighth century (Morgan 1999a, M18) (University of Chicago Excavations at Isthmia: photo: Ioannidou and Bartzioti)	112
3.4	Kalapodi (Prof. R.C.S. Felsch)	115
3.5	Kalapodi: sanctuary looking south to Mt. Chlomos (photo: author)	116
3.6	The environs of Kalapodi (C.L. Hayward)	117
3.7	Coastal Phokis (C.L. Hayward)	120
3.8	Delphi: Apollo sanctuary from above the Marmaria (photo: K.W. Arafat)	123
3.9	The bay of Itea: looking towards the Chrysaean plain and Delphi from the headland due north of Galaxidi (Chaleion) (photo: author)	126
3.10	The Corycaean Cave (photo: C.L. Hayward)	127
3.11	Upland plain: looking south-east from the Corycaean Cave (photo: C.L. Hayward)	128
3.12	Principal sanctuaries in Thessaly (C.L. Hayward)	136
3.13	Pherai: sanctuary of Enodia /Zeus Thaulios (Béquignon 1937a)	137
3.14	Bassai: limestone outcrop close to the Classical temple, showing bedding planes (photo: C.L. Hayward)	145
3.15	Bassai: architectural use of local limestone (photo: C.L. Hayward)	145
3.16	Isthmia: temple of Poseidon during the 1989 University of Chicago Excavation season (Archaic temple postholes seen at right) (photo: author)	146
3.17	Isthmia: Archaic temple of Poseidon showing area of excavated deposits (reproduced by courtesy of E.R. Gebhard, plan by Pieter Collett)	147

FIGURES

3.18	Isthmia: temple of Poseidon, plainware juglet (photo: K.W. Arafat)	148
3.19	Isthmia: temple of Poseidon, sealstone IM 581 (University of Chicago Excavations at Isthmia: photo: Michiel Bootsman)	148
3.20	Isthmia: oolitic limestone block from the Archaic temple of Poseidon (photo: C.L. Hayward)	151
3.21	Isthmia: rooftiles from the Archaic temple of Poseidon (photo: author)	151
3.22	The acropolis of Pallantion (© Scuola Archeologica di Atene)	156
3.23	Pallantion Temple A (photo: author)	158
3.24	Pallantion Temple C (photo: author)	159
3.25	Asea acropolis: looking on to the line of the main route north (photo: author)	160
3.26	Ag. Ilias Kantrevas (photo: C.L. Hayward)	161
3.27	Alipheira: Classical temple (photo: C.L. Hayward)	162
4.1	Pharees and northern Azania (C.L. Hayward)	178
4.2	Achaian Late Geometric figure decoration (drawing: author, after *PAE* 1952 and 1956)	182
4.3	Northern Azania: the area of Manesi (photo: author)	185
4.4	Principal burial sites in Thessaly (C.L. Hayward)	193
4.5	Achaian western colonies (C.L. Hayward)	200
5.1	Perachora (photo: author)	216
5.2	Polis bay (photo: author)	218
5.3	Rhion–Andirrion crossing: from the north (photo: author)	221

ACKNOWLEDGEMENTS

This book has been many years in preparation – certainly much longer than its commissioning editor, Richard Stoneman, would have envisaged (or wished) when he first asked me to write an account of the early history of 'those parts of Greece that tend to be ignored'. I thank him for his patience, and hope that I have gone some way to producing what he wanted.

I am most grateful to John Davies, Birgitta Eder, Jonathan Hall, Thomas Heine Nielsen, Erik Østby and Maria Stamatopoulou for comments on earlier versions of the text, and to Thomas and John in particular for invaluable critique of the final manuscript. Mogens Herman Hansen has played a major role in shaping my approach – the volume of work on related subjects emerging from the Copenhagen Polis Centre has been a constant stimulus (as have many informal conversations during Centre meetings), and I owe to Mogens the initial impetus to return to my doctoral research on Achaia.

Many scholars have been generous with unpublished work, and I have endeavoured to thank them all at the appropriate points. I am acutely aware that, largely for reasons of space, there are far too many references to my own syntheses on Achaia and Arkadia, and it is therefore a particular pleasure to reiterate my thanks to Athanassios Rizakis, Michalis Petropoulos, James Roy, Yanis Pikoulas, and Björn and Jeannette Forsén for their advice and help over many years, and for sharing with me the fruits of their own original research. The counsels of Sigrid Jalkotzy and Fanouria Dakoronia on central Greece have been invaluable. Remaining errors are, of course, my own.

I gratefully acknowledge financial support under the British Academy Research Leave scheme which funded much of my fundamental research in Greece. The book was largely written in the library of the British School at Athens, and as ever, it is a pleasure to thank the School staff, and especially the librarians, Penny Wilson Zarganis and Sandra Pepelasis, for their help and good humour. Without the School, my task would have been immeasurably more difficult. At Routledge, I thank Catherine Bousfield, and for overseeing the smooth passage of the book through production, the staff of Swales & Willis.

ACKNOWLEDGEMENTS

Last but not least, my thanks to Chris Hayward for his patience in seeking out small sites up mountain roads, his geological and cartographical skills, tolerance of my mental (and physical) absences, and so much more. This book is dedicated to him with love and apologies for the shortage of rocks.

All dates pertaining to antiquity are BC unless otherwise noted.

1

INTRODUCTION

'εἴ τις τάδε παραβαίνει ἢ πόλις ἢ ἰδιώτης ἢ ἔθνος)'.
Amphictyony law of c.590: Aischines 3.110

This book is an exploration of the different tiers of identity by which mainland Greek communities constituted themselves during the Early Iron Age and Archaic period. Just as individuals' social identities consisted of a palimpsest of inherited and ascribed traits (such as age, gender, different forms of wealth, work and profession) which were more or less important under different circumstances, so too the political identity of each community was constructed of a complex of associations, including relationship to a polis, an ethnos or groups within these, which could be differently weighted to the perceived advantage of that community. Far from being distinct and alternative forms of state, poleis and ethne were thus tiers of identity with which communities could identify with varying enthusiasm and motivation at different times. And to these may be added extra-community class or interest bonds (for example the ties of *xenia*), in doing so emphasising that while patriotism is praised as a public virtue in Archaic martial elegy, it is notably absent from the contemporary funerary epigrams of the elite.[1]

Understanding the chronological development of, and balance between, often highly localized ties of place and broader notions of people and/or geography in the construction of political identities is a particularly important challenge. As will be seen in the following chapters, when politically significant indicia like coinage and certain usages of city or regional ethnics do appear, generally in the late sixth or fifth century, there is no significant time lag between the occurrence of instances related to individual cities and to regions. There are certainly cases where one appears marginally earlier than the other – federal coinage appears first in Phokis yet city coinage in Achaia, for example[2] – but this discrepancy appears closer to a weighting of options than to the kind of chronological progression that would inform any evolutionary sequence of political organization. The archaeological record therefore offers the only prospect of gaining chronological depth, but it has its own difficulties and limitations, and requires more nuanced exploration than hitherto attempted.

This book moves both literally and metaphorically beyond the polis. In focusing on the different kinds of identities to which communities could attach political salience (i.e. the circumstances and manner of group closure), it sets the polis within a fuller and rather different political context than do traditional analyses. Geographically, the regions which provide most of the case material discussed in the following chapters (Thessaly, Phokis, East Lokris, Achaia and Arkadia) lie on the margins of what has been considered to be the polis world. Despite the richness and complexity of their material records, they have not featured to any great extent in synthetic accounts of Early Iron Age and Archaic state formation, and the perspective adopted here offers a good opportunity to redress the balance.

Certain aspects of my approach are not wholly original,[3] but since the book as a whole builds on relatively recent discoveries and arguments, it is worth pausing to reflect on the coincidence of scholarly trends which makes it so timely. Particularly striking is the radical transformation in the nature and extent of the material record of most parts of Greece, with new data which often challenge current assumptions and preconceptions. The discovery or renewed excavation of sites in areas of known importance has proved extremely fruitful (Skala Oropos in northern Attica and Euboian Kyme are notable such cases),[4] as has the impact of regional projects in recontextualizing known sites (such as Praisos and those in the Kavousi region of East Crete),[5] and the reappraisal of earlier finds which radically alters our understanding of site chronology or function (as, for example, at Isthmia, Olympia, and the area of the later Athenian agora).[6] Furthermore, syntheses of data from regions such as Achaia, previously thought to be backwaters, have revealed bodies of information sufficient to sustain at least preliminary reconstruction of local organization.[7] Rarely, new research, such as that undertaken in East Lokris or western Macedonia, has revealed an early record in regions where previously almost nothing was known.[8] Perhaps most striking, however, is the shift in the balance of the archaeological record, as evidence from supposedly 'peripheral' areas comes to complement and challenge that from the 'great poleis' of traditional scholarship (such as Athens, Argos and Sparta). When much of the evidence used to trace the emergence of the polis as traditionally conceived (i.e. as an independent city-state combining *astu* and *chora*) is clearly not peculiar to it, it is time for reappraisal.

Related to this is a more balanced appreciation of the Mediterranean context of different 'Greek' communities and the nature of their 'Greekness'. This issue has long been highlighted by a number of scholars from different perspectives and with sometimes conflicting agendas (noting, for example, the longstanding debate over the role and identity of the Phoenicians among other eastern peoples, or the impact of Greek settlers in colonial circumstances),[9] but one does not need to subscribe to any particular view to recognize the importance of the overall critical thrust. Underlying these arguments is recognition that the construct of Greekness, which owes as much to nineteenth-century Europe as to the Greeks themselves, is an anachronism in this early period. While the nature and development of Hellenic identity is a major problem in its own right, it largely falls later than our period and will not concern us here.[10] It could be claimed to have a pre-Herodotean existence as early as the sixth century, and one should not overlook traits like the geographical extent of the common alphabet used to *write* Greek by this date (emphasizing the written language, with all that the act of writing entails, and setting aside regional distinctions in script).[11] But, emphasizing our mainland perspective, there are clear differences (not least in its degree of political salience) with the post-Persian war world of the fifth century, let alone with the fourth, when Isokrates' comment (*Pangyrikos* 50), that 'the name of Hellene should be applied to persons sharing in the culture rather than the ancestry of the Greeks' readily encompassed the rapid geographical spread of Hellenistic culture.[12]

Perhaps more significant from an archaeological point of view is recognition that in the open, interconnected Early Iron Age and Archaic Mediterranean, geographical proximity and common points of social reference could transcend what from a later, Hellenocentric standpoint seems to be greater ethnic distance. Under such circumstances, claims of autochthony (let alone 'racial purity') were rendered weak by their inability to play any useful role in articulating the associations and differences which defined different forms of group and kinds of contact. It is easy to see how, for example, an eighth- or seventh-century Ithakan could have had at least as many and varied contacts with any number of the (sometimes multi-ethnic) communities surrounding the bay of Naples, or a Corfiote with Illyria and the Salento, as either had with Corinth, even though in the former case Corinthian settlement has been claimed (chiefly on the basis of pottery style) and in the latter, colonization is attested in the late eighth century.[13] Precisely whom one credits with the initiative for establishing and maintaining particular contacts, and how the interests represented in each case may fluctuate, are controversial, and in many cases unresolvable, questions. Lefkandi, for example, like Athens and Knossos, has Cypriote, Phoenician and Syrian luxuries in its graves (here from the tenth and ninth centuries), but did Euboians actively seek them out?[14] The extent to which the dispersal of Euboian pottery, especially along the Levantine coast and at Pithekoussai in the west, represents Euboian settlement or trade by Euboians and/or others is equally debated, even though these are not always the most interesting questions to ask of such material.[15] In the case of ethne, a small but significant body of epigraphical evidence points to long-distance activity by inhabitants of the regions considered in this study. At Kommos, where there was intense Greek mercantile activity during the late eighth and seventh century, graffiti on local pots (presumably written *in situ*) include examples in the scripts of Lokris or Phokis as well as Euboia and Boiotia.[16] And in regions like Achaia which have extensive coastal territory, the extent and nature of their implication in trade and colonization are important issues, emphasizing that the role played by the choice and utilization of imports in different local systems is as revealing as production, shipping or other mercantile activity in assessing the degree and nature of a community's involvement in trade.[17]

It is no accident that most analyses of the material correlates and consequences of mobility of goods and people within and beyond the Greek world have been directed towards regions such as Crete and Cyprus, whose geographical position, if nothing else, made such contacts routine.[18] Even under these circumstances, as Gail Hoffman has concluded in considering Early Iron Age Crete,[19] identifying the processes operating in any individual case can be extremely difficult, and her study highlights the limitations of typology-driven methodology in addressing this kind of problem. Nonetheless, the exercise highlights the basic point that mobility and interaction are the base line against which issues of identity must be assessed, and this in turn has profound implications for our understanding of the material records of old Greece and of the colonial world (indeed, the scholarly divisions between the two are of dubious validity).[20] The other side of this problem, however, is the question of social closure. How, and under what circumstances did different kinds of community constitute and define themselves, and on what level were they salient to their members? There are (admittedly few) cases, of which, perhaps paradoxically, Early Iron Age Corinth is one,[21] where surviving material evidence from the region itself shows very little sign of outside contact other than with immediate neighbours. In Corinth, what seems to be a combination of a lack of interest in imported goods (or at least those liable to leave any trace in the archaeological record) combined with considerable care and conservatism in the disposition of material wealth, and especially of recyclable resources such as metals, suggest that degrees of openness or closure may not always be expressed in the material record in ways which are readily traceable. Overall, however, if one takes too broad an approach to the question of interaction, mobility and especially eastern influence, there is a danger of losing sight of the complexity and variety of community ordering across Greek lands. Achieving balance in understanding local patterns of development without resorting to wholly particularist arguments demands focus on the nature of each level of identity and its point of closure.

Ethnos and polis

One of the central themes of this book is the failure of the political terminology in general use (or perhaps rather our interpretations of ancient terminology) adequately to describe and explain the variety of situations evident in the record.[22] Re-examination of the Archaic and Classical Greek understanding of the terms polis and ethnos has long been needed, and here the research programme undertaken since 1993 by the Copenhagen Polis Centre is of key importance. The Centre's agenda is deceptively simple: to compile an inventory of Archaic and Classical Greek poleis so named in contemporary sources, and via consideration of the full range of attestations to see how the term polis was understood at the time and thus to make comparison with modern perceptions.[23] There have naturally been many points of criticism and refinement in the course of the development and execution of this programme,[24] but these do not concern the present argument. I would emphasize the value of the perspectives opened up by the work of the Centre for the study of ethne and the role of poleis within them. A basic point of principle is that whatever is called a polis in an Archaic or Classical source must be one: such a polis may depart from some ancient or modern ideal,[25] but it is impossible to have a polis which is not a true polis. Although the 'typical' polis is highly elusive (if not a modern fiction),[26] much scholarly attention has been devoted to its characterization, and it has been perceived in a wide variety of sometimes contradictory terms, ranging from constitution to citizenship and physical development (especially urbanization, per se or in terms of the seat of government institutions).[27] The Copenhagen investigation, however, rejects emphasis, implicit or explicit,[28] on abstract models of state types, with their implications of timelessness, in favour of the polis as an historical concept identified and characterized through enactment.

The work of the Centre has ranged widely over issues related to Greek perceptions of the polis, including Greeks' conceptions of their own settlement patterns, and what a polis did (examining each named site's record of, *inter alia*, inscriptions, known actions, building features and institutions).[29] Many of the insights arising from this work will be discussed in the following chapters. Here, I focus on two points of more general importance. The first is the observation that certain features correlate so strongly with named polis status that they are effectively indicative of it. Perhaps the clearest, and most useful for our purposes, is the appearance of city-ethnics, since these occur early in regions like Arkadia where other evidence for community status can be hard to find.[30] Second, it has been demonstrated that *autonomia* was not a prerequisite for polis status.[31] This is a point of central importance here, since the previous contrary assumption led to the conclusion that the polis was incompatible with any higher or parallel form of political organization. As a result, controlled abandonment of *autonomia* was seen as a key step in the creation of the great federations of the late Classical and Hellenistic periods, which in turn were forced to look to some primeval but politically dormant sense of ethnic ('tribal') identity to bind their members. Hence the ethnos, while primitive, was seen as the more

INTRODUCTION

durable form of political organization. Yet as the Copenhagen investigation has shown,[32] poleis could be dependent on other poleis (as the perioikic poleis in Lakonia, Messenia, Elis and Crete),[33] or exist within the territory of ethne (as those in Achaia, Arkadia or Boiotia).[34] In other words, whatever their precise form of internal organization, political communities called poleis were entities with which their members could identify in a different (complementary or conflicting) way than with the ethne to which they might simultaneously belong. As the quotation at the head of this chapter shows, it was prudent to legislate for all such eventualities.

As emphasized at the start of this chapter, one important consequence of the abandonment of *autonomia* as a defining characteristic of the polis, and the acceptance that tiered identities were more common than not,[35] is to reopen the question of the relative chronology and context of the attribution of political salience to these different identities (polis and/or sub unit, ethnic of various forms, and localized ethnos, or tribe as it is usually called) in different regions. The priority accorded to the polis as conceived in much nineteenth- and twentieth-century scholarship as (to echo Victor Ehrenberg) the most dynamic, creative and influential form of political organization in the Archaic and Classical world, is no longer sustainable.[36] It is certainly true that some Archaic poleis have produced no evidence for any other politically salient forms of identity: Corinth is perhaps the most striking case (see p. 57). But there are no grounds for prioritizing these comparatively few cases over political systems like those of Achaia and Thessaly which had more complex levels of identity, were active internationally in, for example, trade, colonization and warfare, and maintained complex social interconnections with other state systems. Indeed, they may have much to teach us about the political evolution of internally complex poleis like Athens (how, for example, did patronymics like Eupuridai and Kuantidai come to be associated so closely with places that they could form part of the Kleisthenic deme structure?)

Clearly, reappraisal of the role of the polis as a focus of political identity begs the question of our understanding of the term ethnos prior to the formation of wider political leagues in the later fifth and fourth century. Until quite recently, interest in early ethne centred on the search for the 'primeval' roots of later federal states, following from the belief that ethne were more durable, or at least more capable of transformation and adaptation to the changing circumstances of the post-Classical world, than poleis.[37] A particularly influential model, most fully developed by Fritz Gschnitzer, distinguishes between the 'tribal' or 'stem' community (*Stammesgemeinde*) or state (*Stammstaat*), and the *Ortsgemeinde*, a community defined by place, linked with the *Stadtstaat* or polis.[38] According to this view, *Stamm*- communities, named after their constituent 'tribes' (i.e. ethnics, see below), formed the basis of city-states when parts broke away and established local groups with their own place-identity.[39] *Stammstaaten*, geographically focused

INTRODUCTION

in northern and western Greece, were conservative, whereas the advanced *Stadtstaaten*, mainly in southern and central Greece, were responsible for such later developments as colonization.[40] As an indication of the chronology of this transformation, Gschnitzer cites Homer's reference to early city-states (poleis) in the Greek east, as well as his use of ethnic plurals which are taken as evidence of *Stammstaaten*.[41] The model is explicitly evolutionary, and since the tribe, as the origin of later developments, is by definition primeval, it must require some exceptional cause (usually migration) to put it into place. Precise details of the evolutionary progression have been debated, and in particular, an intermediate stage of demes or *komai* is sometimes invoked.[42] However, the fundamental principle of social evolution embodied here has received less attention (with notable exceptions, as in the work of Kurt Raaflaub and Denis Roussel),[43] and as will be argued, I too perceive it as fundamentally flawed. Two particular objections may be raised here briefly and will recur in different ways throughout this book. First, *ethnika* do not reliably denote any particular form of *political* order, and, as constructed statements of group identity, are subject to change in nature and meaning.[44] Second, the archaeological records of many ostensibly very different regions indicate that the construction of localized place and wider regional communities was a dynamic, parallel and continuing process. Indeed, in several cases (Arkadia, for example) it is possible to reverse the sequence of development implied by Gschnitzer's model, and see the *politicization* of regional-ethnic identity as a relatively late, post-city phenomenon.[45]

Ancient discussions of ethne as political organizations are rare and generally date from the latter part of the fifth century onwards, a fact which creates significant historiographical difficulties in basing generalizations upon them. The earliest comments are two brief passages in Thucydides' *History*, which appear in very different rhetorical contexts. In his report of the Messenian attempt to persuade the Athenian general Demosthenes to attack the Aetolians, Thucydides (3.94.4) has the Messenians describe them as warlike but using only light armour and living in widely scattered villages, and thus easy to defeat before they could unite for defence. The special pleading involved in persuading Demosthenes is perfectly plain: the Aetolians are presented as a worthy, warlike enemy, but one whom the Athenians could easily defeat (and to add further colour, at 3.94.5 the Eurytainians are described as 'according to report, eaters of raw flesh').[46] Second, Thucydides (1.5.2) makes the general observation that the old-fashioned conditions whereby men went armed and communities plundered the weaker at will still pertained in certain ethne, mentioning specifically the Ozalian Lokrians, Aetolians and Acarnanians. This passage in particular is cited by Larsen[47] as evidence of the weakness of domestic government in ethne, with the city seen as the agency which filled the gap arising from the defence needs of the inhabitants of scattered and unfortified villages. While this reading clearly fits Larsen's broader picture, here too it is important to

INTRODUCTION

emphasize the context of the passage. In Book 1 of his *History*, Thucydides sets the scene for what he believed to be the greatest war among the Greeks since the Trojan war, and attempts to establish why a war fought between two particular poleis, Athens and Sparta, and in a particular manner, should deserve such attention. He thus gives a brief quasi-evolutionary account of Greek warfare after Troy, and inevitably given this structure of argument, methods of warfare that are not 'modern' and regions that do not match up to the ideal of the adversaries that are his focus can only be subsidiary at best. Thucydides may have been perfectly accurate about the level of violence in Lokrian or Aetolian society during the fifth century, but his remarks do not add up to analyses of these regions, let alone to assessments of the factors underlying the phenomena he observes.

It is Aristotle, however, who provides the basis of most modern discussion of ethne. This rarely rests on detailed discussion of specific cases. Almost all of the 158 or so constitutions which Aristotle wrote or commissioned in preparation for the *Politics* are lost, but there are indications that they included accounts of the Arkadian federation plus Tegea and Lepreon, of Thessaly, and of Achaia as well as the Achaian polis of Pellene. Surviving fragments of the Thessalian constitution mention the division of the region into tetrads, and references in the *Politics* to the government of, for example, Pharsalos (5.5.7) and Larisa (5.5.9) imply detailed knowledge of individual cities.[48] The loss of these works clearly leaves a major gap. By contrast the romantic, quasi-historical works produced during the third century, notably Rhianos of Bene's epics, *Thessalika*, *Achaika*, *Eliaka* and *Messeniaka*, and Euphorion's prose work *On the Aleuads*, fit a contemporary fashion for heroizing local histories reflected also in 'historical' sculptural dedications (as discussed in Chapter 3 in the case of Delphi), and had they survived would surely have been problematic sources with which to reconstruct the early societies they purported to describe.[49]

Instead, scholars have tended to rely on certain general statements made in the *Politics*, but at considerable risk of misinterpretation. As Mogens Hansen has recently restated, consideration of the full context of Aristotle's analogy between symmachies and ethne at *Politics* 2.1.4–5 suggests that he recognized that most Greek ethne were in effect collections of poleis. Since for Aristotle the distinction between the two was quantitative (compare his much-quoted observation at *Politics* 7.4.7 that ethne may be distinguished by their large populations), the polis was, in Hansen's words, 'the atom of political science' beyond which it was unnecessary to move.[50] Aristotle very likely had a view of what an ethnos was, but it was not his purpose here to explain it. Aristotle does highlight certain contrasts between the Greek political orderings of his day, be they primitive ethne or advanced state constitutions, in terms of, for example, political inequality, synoikism (physical and/or political, for instance 7.4.7), the role of trade versus primitive barter (1.3.10–12), and kingship (1.1.7–8). How 'true' these were is debatable, but given the variety of circumstances they encompass, and Aristotle's overall attitude as outlined above, they cannot be taken as a consistent set of characteristics with which to approach even later fifth- and fourth-century Greek ethne.[51] Most importantly, Aristotle writes of a different world from that considered in this book and the dangers of retrojection are considerable.[52]

The evolutionary perspective and the negative observations which can be read into Thucydides and Aristotle come together in approaches to Early Iron Age and Archaic state evolution which treat ethne almost by default as negative images (or even precursors) of the polis,[53] despite mounting evidence for the nature of their physical development and political engagement which make any such propositions readily testable (and in most cases flatly refute them). This is true of historical writing such as that of Victor Ehrenberg, Giovanna Daverio Rocchi and Frederick Larsen as much as archaeological work like Anthony Snodgrass' 1980 *Archaic Greece*, which, while inevitably overtaken over the past twenty years in points of fact and argument, rightly remains influential as the first programmatic integration of archaeological data into the historical analysis of polis formation.[54] Thus, for example, Ian Morris cites Aristotle (*Politics* 2.2.29–30) in arguing that the crucial difference between a polis and an ethnos is that the latter was not a political society even though, as he acknowledges, the two show strong similarities in material development (for example, in subsistence bases, settlement patterns, monumental public building and writing), and an ethnos could do most of the things that a polis did, from waging war to raising taxes and concluding treaties.[55] Morris' observation has force to the extent that different tiers of identity operative within particular geographical areas probably acquired political salience at different times, and politicization of regional ethnics (or as they will be termed here, *ethnika*) was often later than that of city-ethnics or *politika*. But this is not the sense in which it was offered, since he seems rather concerned with poleis and ethne as geographically distinct state forms. It must be noted that analysis is not aided by the Athenocentrism of much discussion of early Greek political structures – as McInerney rightly emphasizes, Athens came to be seen as normative when it was not even normal.[56]

Paradoxically, therefore, although the term ethnos has received scant analytical attention in ancient or modern scholarship, modern usage often carries a range of associations, from tribalism to migration, which are not inherent in the Greek.[57] Archaic and early Classical sources from Homer onwards use the word in a wide variety of contexts to refer to almost any form of group of beings, human or animal, with none of the consistency evident in contemporary usage of the term polis. This is well illustrated by the examples chosen to support the dictionary entry in Liddell-Scott-Jones, where ethnos is shown to apply to peoples in general (*laon*, as *Iliad* 13.495), specific named peoples (as the Lycians, *Iliad* 12.330), people of a certain condition (such as the dead, *Odyssey* 10.526) or gender (women, Pindar *Olympian* 1.66), animals or birds (such as bees, *Iliad* 2.87).[58] There are thus no political (let alone organizational) connotations to the term as attested during these periods, and none should be assumed unless specifically introduced by qualification or context of use.[59] Again, this is not to suggest that those in antiquity who used the term to classify any particular people as a group lacked a clear view of why they were doing so, but it is precisely such specific qualification that should be the subject of enquiry rather than assumption. Indeed, taking the innocent definition of an ethnos as a group – the product of the discourse that is ethnicity – it implies a flexible and widely applicable form of classification as an important aspect of Early Iron Age and Archaic *mentalité*.[60] Ethne were thus socially and often politically real outcomes of a process of definition, not fixed (let alone immutable) entities to be analysed, demarcated and explained. Plainly, Archaic Greeks could and did think in terms of ethnic identity when considering their own political organization and status, and recognition of this fact has given rise to renewed interest in the real nature of those regions characterized as ethne and often dismissed as backward (at least during our period). Jeremy McInerney's 1999 study of Phokis is such a case, as is the collective work of the Copenhagen Polis Centre on Arkadia.[61]

Ethne, ethnicity and tribalism

Intimately implicated in any discussion of Greek ethne along these lines is the concept of ethnicity. Until relatively recently it would have been necessary to argue the case for viewing ancient Greek ethnic groups not as primordial, reified entities, but as social constructs which are the outcomes of ongoing processes of identity negotiation, real to those who claimed and experienced them but nonetheless elective and constantly open to reconfiguration. Fortunately, the nature and role of ethnic expression in Greek antiquity have been among the most debated topics of recent years among both archaeologists and historians, and the key issues for the present discussion are well covered in the resulting literature.[62] Working from this basis, I shall therefore treat ethnicity as, to quote Orlando Patterson, 'that condition wherein certain members of a society, in a given social context, choose to emphasize as their most meaningful basis of primary, extrafamilial identity certain assumed cultural, national or somatic traits'. In other words, it is a matter of continuing choice, manipulation and politicization, highlighting traits accorded active importance in the structuring and expression of sociopolitical relations within the community and in relation to outsiders[63] Emphasis is thus placed on the strategy of definition according to context rather than on the precise criteria chosen (indeed, it is commonly noted that ethnically salient criteria are rarely objectively definable) – on process rather than outcome.[64] While Patterson's approach has been criticized for its instrumentalism, including the fact that ethnic identity could be claimed or exploited to mask some other (political and/or economic) purpose, it seems self-evident that people sometimes consciously or unconsciously conceal their intentions to obtain their goals (and 'real' purpose is unlikely to be the only benefit or consequence of any assertion of ethnicity). More seriously, it is misleading to distinguish and privilege explanations rooted in, for example, economics or gender, since an effective ethnic claim will draw on whatever is seen (by insiders or outsiders) best to articulate the distinctive nature of the group concerned in the social context in which it operates.

Overall, I differ in emphasis (rather than substance) from both Hall and McInerney in distinguishing ethnicity, the *process* of choice by which a tier of identity is constructed or prioritized for perceived group advantage, from ethne, the observable *outcomes* of such processes and thus entities rooted in place and time. The latter come close to what Anthony Smith terms ethnic communities, or *ethnie*, which when politicized may share some of the same structural and material characteristics of nations. Unsurprisingly, therefore, the six characteristics of such an ethnic group identified by Smith bear striking resemblance to the areas of analysis highlighted in Snodgrass' analysis of Greek polis formation.[65] They thus reveal the existence of a politicized entity, but not its precise nature in any given case. Ethnicity in the sense followed in this book has to do with the acquisition, exercise or subversion of power. This is not always a matter of achieving complete dominance of a society or geographical area. Claims of shared ethnicity did help to sustain otherwise fragile power structures, as for example, the politically unequal relationship between Sparta and her *perioikoi*, poised between Spartiates and helots.[66] Perceived with hindsight, expressions of ethnic identity traceable in the material and historical record may be transitory or long-lived, but to insiders they are equally real. Indeed, it would be wrong to treat traits which recur over a long period as by definition more important, let alone as part of some ethnic 'deep structure', since they are products of the same cognitive processes operating throughout. Each generation takes its own decisions about what to forget and what to repeat according to its own standards of salience, let alone accuracy, thus introducing both conscious and unconscious variation from the inherited norm.[67]

Clearly, it would be desirable to observe ethnic behaviour at the level of the individual participant, but the evidence at our disposal rarely permits this. In reading the archaeological record, we generally observe the average of assumed social identity in any given context – in Clifford Geertz's term the 'actor', a conscious individual interpreting through his behaviour his membership of different social groups, yet driven by broader community norms and values.[68] Yet what is this 'community'? I have so far used the term as a neutral description for groups which may define themselves in one or more ways (including in relation to a polis or an ethnos), yet this in itself raises questions. As Anthony Cohen notes, 'community is one of those words

– like "culture", "myth", "ritual", "symbol" . . . apparently readily intelligible to speaker and listener, which, when imported into the discourse of social science . . . causes immense difficulty'.[69] My approach will be to treat a community as a complex of relationships rather than a single organic entity, which has the advantage of demanding investigation of the nature and operation of such relations in each case (an essential first step if we are to understand how and where ethnic expression might be directed). 'Political community' covers the variety of common relations implied in, for example, residence arrangements, adherence to laws, warfare, cult and subsistence strategies – areas which Greek sources themselves identified as key to the expression of shared identities, and which will be investigated in the following chapters. It is not, however, a synonym for the polis, even though it has been treated as such, implicitly or explicitly, by a diverse range of scholars from Weber to Meier,[70] and the plurality of local systems and trajectories within Greek lands remains a problem to be researched in its own right.[71]

It is tempting to enquire why only some ethne achieved a high level of political identification over a large area. Were all ethne potentially equal, or did some have characteristics which favoured their long-term political success? Clearly, the Early Iron Age and Archaic Greek situation does not fit the nationalist view that ethnic boundaries should be coterminous with the political boundaries of the state, and that it is the ethnic group, with its common culture and territory, that defines a nation.[72] Posing the problem in this way ignores the discursive nature of ethnic identification, a constant process of creation, ascription and reascription of those entities with which communities and groups identified. Indeed, some 'tribes' or ethne subordinated themselves either to their own advantage or though succumbing to *force majeure*, and from time to time accepted the kind of formal dependence exemplified by that between the communities of the Thessalian heartland and the *perioikoi* who surrounded them (an issue discussed further in Chapter 4).

This last point brings us to the problem of what is usually, for want of a better English term, called the tribe.[73] This is sometimes treated as effectively coterminous with the ethnos (the so-called 'tribal state'), not least because of the kinship terms in which ethnic ties tend to be expressed. Yet as noted, larger ethne can themselves contain other ethnic groupings as well as poleis. Arkadia, for example, contained at different periods groups explicitly identifying themselves via the use of an ethnic name (or *ethnikon*) as Eutresians, Kynourians, Mainalians, Parrhasians and Azanians (Strabo 8.8.1).[74] In some instances the terminology used in Greek sources is wholly different (the Athenian *phylai* are an obvious example, although the date and circumstances of their creation must always be borne in mind), but the majority (including the Arkadian tribes) are also called ethne. The modern translation 'tribe' may help to distinguish these usually smaller ethne from those which achieved pan-regional political salience, but it has the greater disadvantage of concealing the conceptual similarity behind their creation and maintenance,[75] as well as perpetuating the problematic modern association between Greek ethne and tribalism as constructed in nineteenth- and twentieth-century anthropological thought. It is perhaps hardly surprising to find that, Athens apart, where tribes have been explicitly considered (in Arkadia, for example), discussion has focused less on broader theoretical issues than on local circumstances, and on questions which largely mirror those asked of the great pan-regional ethne. Which came first, city or tribe, for example, how do the two relate socially and politically, and is there is a consistent and/or characteristic settlement organization associated with tribes?[76]

Tribe is a troublesome word, however, and although I have occasionally used it in association with ethnos to reflect common practice, I prefer to avoid it as far as possible. Yet since its use nowadays has implications beyond the ancient meaning of ethnos, and the nature of so-called tribal states has received scant critical attention, it is worth pausing briefly to explore both the historiography of the connection in modern scholarship and the distinct but related issue of the extent to which tribal political systems as we understand them in the modern record may be compatible with social institutions constituted in other ways. The idea of opposition between community organizations constituted through kinship (the essence of tribalism) and states where roles and statuses are determined using other criteria, goes back to the mid-nineteenth century, for example in Henry Sumner Maine's discussion of tribalism as a primitive stage in the comparative evolution of political society.[77] Theoretical problems surrounding models of social evolution will be considered presently; here, I focus on what is usually meant by 'tribal society' and how it relates to our understanding of the ethnos.[78] While a few scholars have moved beyond treating ethnics in ancient sources as descriptions of tribal groups pure and simple, there is a significant difference between broadly archaeological/historical and historical/philological approaches. Archaeologists tend to use the term tribe with no particular political sophistication, to characterize regions where the material record lacks traits that would suggest other interpretations. Thus, for example, Anthony Snodgrass suggests that the geographical extent of pre-eighth-century artefact styles and distributions reflects the existence of extensive political units in areas where the only other hint of a tribal system of sorts is the use of ethnics (for example to name the groups listed in the *Catalogue of Ships* in *Iliad* 2), and where we have scant direct information about local political systems.[79] By contrast, literary/philological discussions have focused more closely on the terminology of kinship and thus relate more directly to anthropological approaches to tribalism: Walter Donlan's reconstruction of early kinship organization based on the meaning of *phylon* and *phretre* in Homer is a case in point.[80] This distinction essentially corresponds to that drawn by Patricia Crone between the use of the term tribe for a cultural unit and for a political entity (effectively a classificatory versus an ethological usage). Clearly, in terms of the material record, identification of the two phenomena requires different criteria; the latter demands recognition of the politicization of material traits, a flexible strategy of selection, whereas the former merely observable similarity (a point to which we will return in Chapter 4).[81]

One approach which has been so heavily (and rightly) criticized that it now has few advocates attempts to identify as by definition primitive, 'tribal' traits 'preserved' within later polis structures. It is, however, worth exploring the grounds for its rejection as they have implications for the study of ethne as tribes. The citizen bodies of many Classical poleis were divided into *phylai*, a term broadly translated as tribes, often with forms of subdivision (phratry and *genos*) which are rarely evident outside poleis. In Athens, for example, radical as Kleisthenes' reforms were, it was long held that since the previous, 'primitive' tribal order needed to be accommodated, traits could thus be traced through later structures. The Classical Athenian tribal system, as a hangover from an earlier form of state, was thus taken as a general model applicable both to 'pre-poleis' and to contemporary 'primitive' states, i.e. ethne.[82] The resulting evolutionary models are susceptible to the same criticisms as those long directed against social evolution in anthropology, not least for the way in which they place in a hypothetical series socio-political orders observed as independent entities in an ethnographical record which itself has no real time depth. Not only is this seriation untestable, but, by contrast with Darwinian evolution which (however applied in archaeological contexts) focuses on the mechanisms of change, it is impossible to understand these mechanisms from observation of the data themselves.[83] Indeed, a social evolutionary approach of any kind may bias readings of the evidence. Such was the case in Athens, where both Roussel and Bourriot demonstrated that the Kleisthenic system, far from echoing a primitive order, was a new, if sometimes archaizing, creation.[84] More pertinently, Roussel was joined by Finley (and most recently Hans-Joachim Gehrke) in emphasizing that *genos*, phratry and *phyle* cannot be treated as kinship terms in the strict anthropological sense, and one should therefore be wary of reconstructing tribal organization on the basis of meaning so inferred. In terms of the present argument, perhaps the most valuable aspect of this critique is the implicit rejection of evolutionary links between the polis and the 'primitive' tribal ethnos, which fits well with the reappraisal of Archaic and Classical perceptions of the term polis already noted.[85]

Clearly, the contribution of anthropological studies of tribalism should merit closer examination, but here too, following the critique of Roussel and Finley, we should consider the potential circularity arising from the well-documented and in many ways formative contribution of nineteenth-century Classical scholarship to kinship analysis in social anthropology.[86] Thus, for example, George Grote's work on the kinship structure of historical Greek society[87] was a major influence on Henry Sumner Maine's development of the concept of the phratry in his *Ancient Law* (1861). Maine's treatment of the phratry within ancient and modern tribal systems went beyond analogy, as he claimed to have identified tribal organizations in ancient Greece and Rome identical to those in the modern record. Similar lines of thought are evident in the work of his scholarly adversary, Lewis Henry Morgan (in *Systems of Consanguinity and Affinity of the Human Family* [1871] and *Ancient Society* [1877]). Not only did Morgan make direct structural comparison between ancient tribes and what he called the modern Iroquois, 'warrior democracy', where kin roles structured a multiplicity of functions (including war, cult and subsistence), but he placed this tribal organization within an evolutionary sequence, thus forming part of a long history of interplay between evolutionism and the use in ancient history of Greek kinship terms with their acquired anthropological meaning.[88]

It is therefore necessary to consider afresh what is meant by 'tribal' society, and how this may be evaluated against growing bodies of data from early ethne. Disputed and problematic as tribalism is,[89] in essence it involves the use of real or ascribed kinship, age and gender, as the basis for structuring the political community.[90] To some extent this is a question of degree, since kinship is used politically in other forms of society also, but where the majority of roles are defined by other criteria, a system cannot be truly tribal. Hence at least one potential difference between true tribal systems and the 'tribes' of states such as Athens, at least from the time of Solon's establishment of economic criteria for political office.[91] Equally, although references to blood ties are pervasive in Greek literature, as for example Herodotos' claim (8.144) that the kinship of all Greeks was as much part of Hellenic identity as shared language and religion, the rhetoric of kinship employed as a means of claiming or reinforcing ethnic ties is not coterminous with the practical ordering of a society.[92] In practical terms, kinship principles are capable of adaptation to a wide variety of roles, and discrepancies with social needs can be concealed by invention, selection, or suppression. In defining a system as tribal, the nature of roles and factors like territoriality are thus less important than the organizing principles involved in filling and sustaining them. As Patricia Crone points out,[93] kinship, gender and age in general most sharply differentiate roles in societies where people are in other respects very similar (for example, in terms of access to subsistence resources or political influence). But theoretically, there is scope for considerable political and socio-economic differentiation, and an important question is therefore the degree of organizational complexity and dissent tolerated (allowing, for example, the centralization of power in the hands of leaders), before other criteria start to augment and replace kinship principles. Ethnographical evidence seems to suggest that a high degree of specialization and interdependence within the community is more characteristic of other forms of state, and indeed, it may be hard to envisage kin relations dealing satisfactorily with certain kinds of complex problem. Conflict resolution is such a case, as shown by the extent to which regulation or accommodation of the potentially disruptive effects of self-help solutions may come to dominate communal activities such as ritual (a point further explored in Chapter 3).[94] Yet just how complex tribal societies can become, and thus the limits applicable in analysing ancient data, has not been fully investigated.

Overall, it is clear that such theoretical discussion of tribalism as there has been in anthropological scholarship has not really entered into Greek studies, and critical interrogation of early Greek sources has not kept pace with work in other fields.[95] Perhaps surprisingly, the same is true of much of western European Late Bronze and earlier Iron Age prehistory. Hallstatt evidence, contemporary with the Greek cases considered here, has largely been evaluated in terms of the development of chieftainships centred on hillforts, polities whose emergence is sometimes treated as analogous with Greek poleis.[96] Issues of ethnicity, and detailed discussion of the development of tribal or group identity have not been foremost in discussion of this earlier period.[97] Subsequently, during La Tène, while priority is still sometimes given to Roman epigraphical and historical sources (especially Caesar and Tacitus) for initial identification and characterization of 'tribal' systems, ethnicity as an active strategy is now being discussed, chiefly in the context of the process of 'Romanization'.[98] The perspectives taken in individual studies vary considerably,[99] but we lack more general theoretical evaluation of the meaning of tribalism and its material expression.[100] The key point is that ethne are not self-explanatory: they may be politically structured in the manner of tribes or they may not, but the terms are not identical and should not be assumed to be so.

Archaeology and early Greek ethne

The combination of trends in archaeological and historical research so far outlined offers rich scope for the analysis of the political organization of early Greek societies as tiered complexes of identities. Since this book is written from a primarily archaeological perspective, it is important to consider the place of material evidence alongside other sources within this broader analytical framework. It is often suggested that ethnic identity is ultimately constructed through written and spoken discourse, and that other common cultural forms (artefact styles, and aspects of performance, such as mortuary and cult rituals, many of which can be expected to leave material traces) served to bolster that identity.[101] For much of our period there are clear difficulties in reconstructing written and spoken discourse other than by retrojection. Such inscriptions as we have reflect the particular place of writing within a predominantly oral context, and are thus both rare and specific – and while we may recognize the place of the oral, we can hardly retrieve the mass of information thus conveyed. Homer apart, literary sources referring to our regions are all retrospective, and whatever local sources may have predated them are lost.[102] This is not to deny the worth of later sources, merely to highlight the historiographical issues which surround them.[103]

INTRODUCTION

Plainly therefore problems arise both from the loss of written sources and from the fact that so little was conveyed in writing during our period. Yet the resulting focus on material evidence is no mere pragmatism. Indeed, it would be wrong to assume that written text, or any other single source, will give anything like a rounded view, or that different kinds of evidence will necessary support each other. Language and material behaviour comprise multiple channels of communication which may be deployed within various discourses, and some of the most interesting insights arise from the dissonance, as well as consonance, between them.[104] On one hand, language use is a creative process which often results in multiple (successive and contemporary) group 'traditions'. The deployment of *ethnika*, for example on coinage (together with visual devices), was an important means by which individuals and communities expressed their perceived existence as a group with a shared history. Rather than being remnants of genuine historical memories of migrations at the end of the Bronze Age, multiple and sometimes conflicting versions of particular myths therefore reflect the manipulation of group identity through time and according to viewpoint.[105] While one might expect these myth-histories to bear some relationship to groupings traceable in the material record, this is unlikely to be straightforward and there is a risk of searching for material correlates by convenience, according to what happens to be known of the archaeological record of a particular region at the right time. Conversely, thinking one's identity is as much a visual as a verbal process. Monuments such as cemeteries, shrines or other public buildings were physically lasting tools for thought, the meaning of which could shift or be deliberately altered over time (as is clear in the case of Kalapodi, discussed in Chapter 3). Since perceived communal tradition, 'ethnic heritage', is an important element in establishing and maintaining group identity, the meaning and ownership of such monuments are likely to be important and open to dispute (as the sacred wars over Delphi well illustrate).[106] It is, however, necessary to determine which elements of a society's material culture are selected to convey meaning in any given context and time, and from whose viewpoint.[107]

The Early Iron Age and Archaic archaeological record offers fertile ground for the exploration of material discourse, especially in view of the comparatively close spatial and chronological control often available.[108] From Protogeometric times onwards, the styles of most types of artefact, and the behaviour patterns involved in, for example, mortuary and cult practices, are highly localized. Emphasis has long been placed on the identification of regional traits, especially in Early Iron Age ceramic styles and burial practices, yet intra-regional variation in artefact styles (including the impact of external influences and imports) exists in many regions.[109] Furthermore, especially during the eighth and seventh centuries, differences in the pattern and extent of circulation of metalwork and fine pottery styles appear far greater than one might expect on the basis of resource distribution alone.

17

INTRODUCTION

Overall, the style choices involved, notably those affecting artefacts in daily use (pottery for example), or the selection and manipulation of prestige goods (especially those using scarce resources), probably reflect communication strategies of some form, including individuals' conscious or unconscious perceptions of group loyalties. However, problems of reconstructing the strength, complexity and register of the social messages conveyed to whom, under what circumstances, and with what degree of conscious intent, are much debated.[110] Combined with statements made via cult, mortuary practices,[111] and the construction of communal myth-history, they form part of an interconnected web of identity statements operating at different levels and changing through time (a fact which may in turn help to explain apparently sharp discontinuities in individual categories of material evidence, as will be further discussed in Chapter 4 in the cases of Achaia and Arkadia). It cannot be too strongly emphasized that the existence of artefacts per se is no basis for inferring their role as social or political indicia. Not only is the range of possibilities in most archaeological assemblages too limited to give much scope, but the fundamentally discursive nature of the creation and expression of group and personal identity should lead one to consider first and foremost the selection, manipulation and juxtaposition of different forms and style of artefact in different contexts over time (as is further discussed in the cases of the Achaian *mesogeia*, northern Azania, and Thessaly in Chapter 4).[112]

In the following chapters, I shall explore some of the conceptual difficulties involved in reading and interpreting the diverse range of political structures in the Greek world prior to the Persian wars with particular reference to the material record of some of the less-often considered regions. (Figure 1.1) While the evidence cited is drawn from many parts of Greece, my emphasis on the central and northern Peloponnese (Arkadia and Achaia) and central Greece (Phokis, Lokris and Thessaly) reflects idiosyncrasies of personal interest and archaeological research. Most of these areas have been the subject of recent synthetic studies drawing together key parts of the necessary information in accessible form, and they also represent a variety of physical and social circumstances which offer scope for fruitful comparison. We will therefore conclude this introduction with a brief outline of the geography, state of research and areas of special interest relevant to each region.

Thessaly

Throughout our period, Thessaly was clearly defined both as a social and as a geographical entity. (Figure 1.2) Its extensive territory, bounded by mountains (Olympus to the north, Pindus to the west, and Othrys to the south) and the sea to the east, is divided into two large plains, both renowned throughout antiquity for supporting grain cultivation and horse rearing.

INTRODUCTION

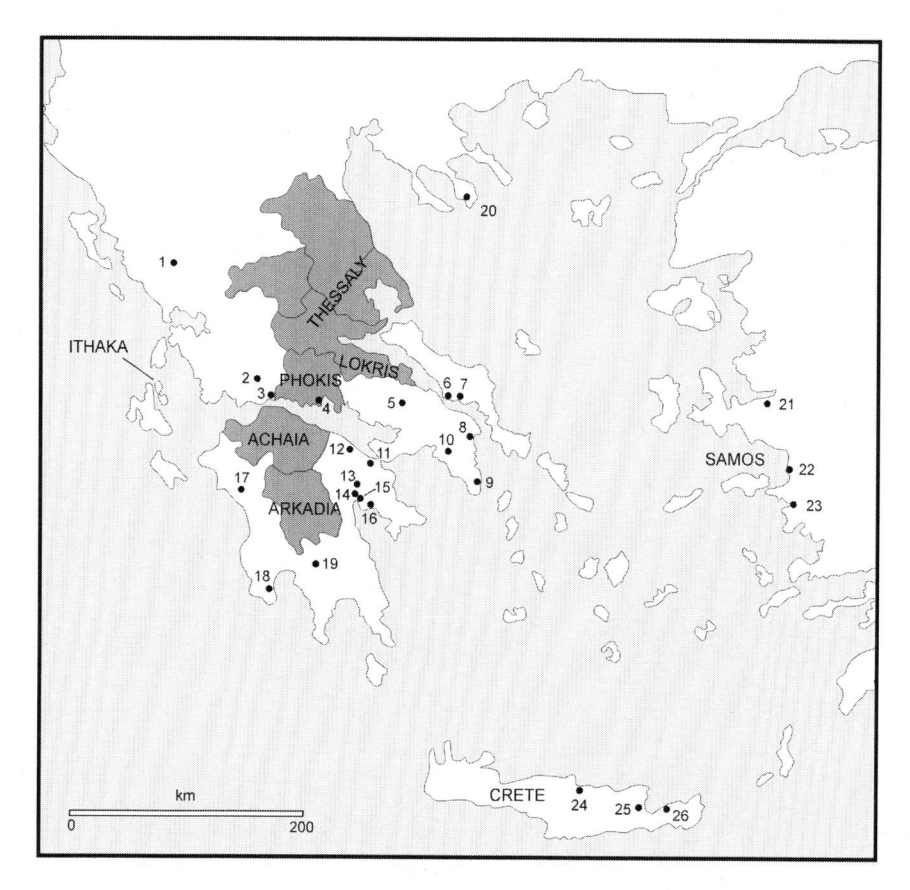

Figure 1.1 Greece: regions and principal sites mentioned in the text (C.L. Hayward).

Key:	Argos	14	Miletos	23
	Asine	16	Mycenae	13
	Athens	10	Naupaktos	3
	Corinth	11	Nichoria	18
	Dodona	1	Old Smyrna	21
	Ephesos	22	Olympia	17
	Eretria	7	Sikyon	12
	Galaxidi/Chaleion	4	Sparta	19
	Kavousi	26	Thebes	5
	Knossos	24	Thermon	2
	Lato	25	Thorikos	9
	Lefkandi	6	Tiryns	15
	Marathon	8	Torone	20

INTRODUCTION

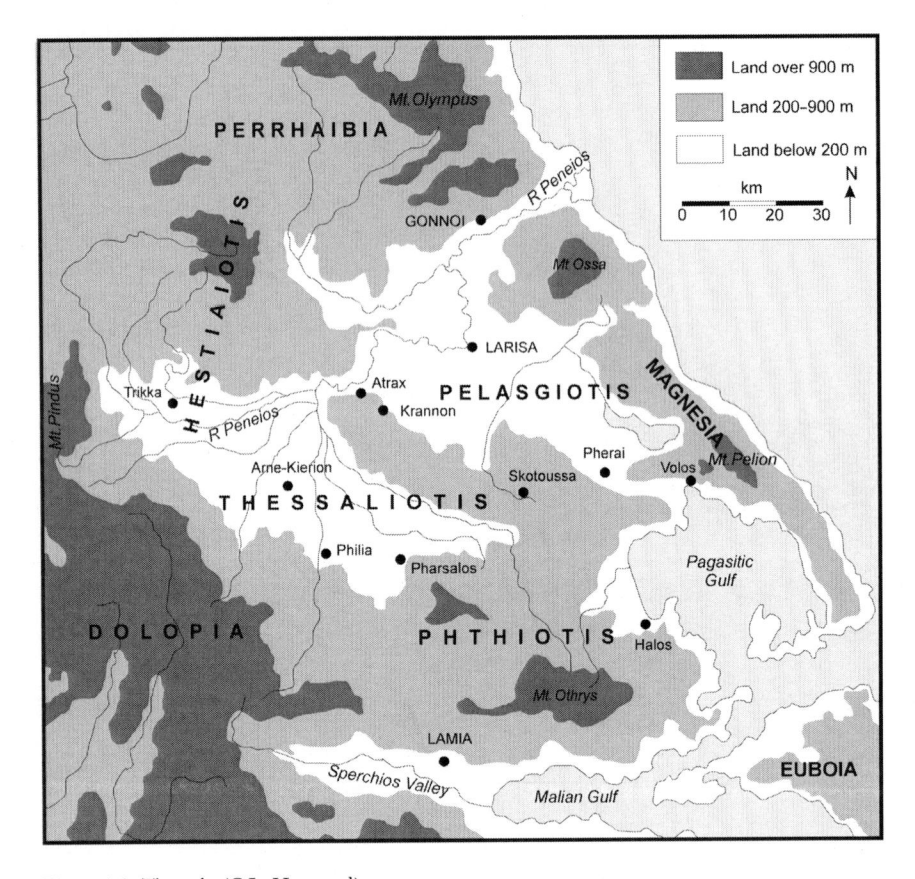

Figure 1.2 Thessaly (C.L. Hayward).

(Figure 1.3) The western plain was larger but more liable to flood (often being swampy in winter and hardpan in summer), whereas that in the east was dryer and cooler. To the south, Mt. Othrys divided these plains and the area of the Pagasitic gulf from the Sperchios valley which extended inland from Lamia. Major routes of communication cut across both plains (that with Macedon, for example, via the Europos valley). (Figure 1.4) The region's harbours lie along the east coast and were mostly separated from the eastern plain by mountains (Othrys, Pelion and Ossa) and thus readily accessible only to part of the population. The narrow route inland from Volos via Pherai was the major link between the cities of the eastern plain and the sea, but overall there is a marked distinction between the more outward-looking communities of the east within reach of the sea (although including Pharsalos), and notably those around the head of the Pagasitic gulf, and the landward orientation to the social, economic and political life of those communities further west.[113]

Figure 1.3 The western Thessalian plain from the acropolis of Kierion (photo: author).

Figure 1.4 Volos and the head of the Pagasitic gulf from south of Portaria (photo: author).

Archaeological data of our period derive from over a century of intense activity, chiefly on the part of the Greek Archaeological Service, combined with the extensive explorations of individual travellers (notably Stählin)[114] in the early twentieth century. While rescue work has predominated (escalating in pace over the past thirty years), and has provided substantial bodies of

INTRODUCTION

data from sites such as Pherai,[115] systematic excavation has taken place at a number of key settlements, including, for example, Volos-Palia and Gonnoi.[116] In addition, the work of the CNRS Thessaly project, established in 1979 and centred on the Maison de l'Orient at Lyon, has added immeasurably to our knowledge of the epigraphy and topography of many parts of the region (although research has tended to focus on later periods than those considered here), and intensive survey and excavation conducted by the 13th Ephoreia and the Dutch Archaeological Institute in Achaia Phthiotis has produced important early material.[117] An indication of the extent of the transformation of our knowledge of Early Iron Age and Archaic Thessaly since the mid-1970s may be gained by comparing the publications of three conferences devoted primarily to Thessalian archaeology, that held in 1975 in Lyon, that in memory of Dimitrios Theocharis held in 1987, and finally, that held in Lyon in 1990.[118] More recently, synthesis of Early Iron Age burial data has revealed not only the extent of accumulated knowledge, but the degree of intra-regional variation present in tomb forms and offerings.[119] Survey data are also beginning to contribute to our understanding of the evolution of city territories and to broader historical-geographical studies of Thessalian settlement,[120] although to date they have been confined to relatively localized projects in, for example, the Enipeus valley[121] and the Pherai area,[122] and have mostly employed extensive rather than intensive strategies.

While the basic outlines of Thessalian political history appear clear, much debate surrounds issues of detail and chronology, not least since Aristotle's account of the Classical Thessalian constitution is almost completely lost and surviving sources are generally fragmentary.[123] The division of Thessaly into tetrads or *moirai* was, at least by the fifth century, regarded as one of the oldest aspects of Thessalian organization (Hellanikos of Mytilene, *FrGHist* 4.51). Together with other reforms, such as lawgiving, it is thus credited to the quasi-legendary *basileus* Aleuas the Red of Larisa,[124] whose rule is conventionally dated around the second half of the sixth century.[125] Each tetrad contained cities (occasionally described as poleis) dominated by leading families. Pelasgiotis in the east had as its leading cities Larisa (seat of the Aleuads),[126] Krannon (home of the Skopads) and Pherai; Phthiotis in the south-east contained, for example, Pharsalos, Hestiaiotis in the west, Trikka and Aiginion; and Thessaliotis in the south-west, Arne-Kierion among others.[127] Historically, the Thessalian ethnos was a form of confederation of poleis. By the fifth century, Archibald has argued that the basis of this cohesion was primarily social, sustained by what was effectively a caste of leaders with bases in different cities.[128] The extent to which this was also true in earlier times, the role of place communities and the process by which big sites emerged as physical centres of power are thus key questions which will be investigated in Chapter 2.[129] Evidence for overarching institutions is lacking at this stage since, as Helly has argued, although the titles *tagos* and *basileus* were used almost interchangeably for local leaders or magistrates, the idea of an early federal *tageia* lacks support in the surviving sources.[130] Thessaly as a whole is described as a polis on a very few (generally later) occasions, but always in contexts which fit the established sense of polis as the smallest political entity relevant to the discussion at hand, with no necessary implication of a unitary state.[131]

During the sixth century in particular, the engagement of the Thessalian aristocracy with their peers in other regions can be traced in a number of ways. Patronage of the arts, for example, by which the Thessalian elite associated themselves with, and helped to shape, an initially fragile new framework of shared panhellenic culture, or the ties of *xenia* which probably underpinned events like the offer to the exiled Hippias of the Magnesian city of Iolkos as reported by Herodotos (5.94). In the latter case, the existence of a tie is presupposed by Peisistratos' choice of the name Thessalos for one of his sons (Thucydides 1.20.2; 6.55.1) although here as elsewhere, Herodotos merely names the would-be donors of Iolkos as 'the Thessalians' without further qualification.[132] Most striking is the extent of engagement of Thessalians in military activity abroad, as also the renown in which Thessalian forces were held. Military aid to *xenoi* is again prominent, as exemplified by Herodotos' reference (5.63–64) to the force of one thousand cavalrymen sent under *basileus* Kineas (probably of Gonnoi) to aid the Peisistratids against their Spartan attackers. Thessaly was not, of course, the only source of manpower (paid, loaned or 'volunteered') in Archaic Greece; even if Thessalian activities are unusually well documented, among our chosen regions, Arkadia and perhaps also Achaia were almost certainly involved. Considered as a wider phenomenon, such activity raises complex questions concerning the social and economic principles upon which forces were constituted and causes chosen, and also the impact (again both political and economic) of military activity abroad. These issues will be further considered in Chapter 4, questioning especially the extent to which the exercise of military force during the Archaic period can truly be seen in the old polis-focused terms of defining and defending state territory.

Consideration of territory raises one final issue relevant to Thessaly of all our chosen regions, namely the role and impact of groups which were to varying degrees socially and/or economically dependent. The Thessalian tetrads were surrounded by *perioikoi*, including the Perrhaiboi to the north, the Dolopes to the west, and the Magnetes and Achaian Phthiotai to the east and south, all of whom were in some way subject probably to their closest Thessalian neighbours. That their dependence was economic rather than political (at least from the time that reliable sources begin in the fourth century) is implied by, for example, their separate representation in the Delphic amphictyony. A similar economic case may be made for another subject group attested in Thessaly, the *penestai*, which will be further considered in Chapter 4 in the context of assessment of comparative approaches to territorial and demographic definition.[133]

INTRODUCTION

It is clear that the complex picture of Thessaly now emerging from decades of historical, archaeological and epigraphical research overturns previous notions of a simple progression from tribal to federal to polis organization.[134] According to these older models, the federal state had its origins in the shared interests of large Archaic and Classical 'baronies', an almost feudal system of warlords, reinforcing the (erroneous) impression of war as the natural basis for national unity, and to a significant extent resting on the assumption of a federal *tageia* (see above). In turn, federation gave rise to a construct of Thessalian unity derived from a notion of ethnos, a primitive condition which held back the development of poleis. It seems an unwarranted step to move from evidence which shows that particular families were prominent in, or dominated the affairs of, individual cities (the usual state of affairs in Archaic Greece) to inferring feudalism. But nonetheless, this leaves open the question of how the actions of individual families and their leaders fitted within the overall context of socio-political relations at Thessalian big sites and in their territories. As Archibald rightly stresses, in Thessaly as in Macedon and Thrace the relationship between power, territory and urban centres is likely to have been particularly complex.[135]

Phokis

Phokis, divided by Mt. Parnassos into distinct northern and southern parts, is highly diverse in its topography and climate. (Figure 1.5) The resulting lack of cultural unity is clear in many aspects of its archaeological record. (Figure 1.6) During the early centuries of the Early Iron Age, for example, north-eastern Phokis (the upper Kephisos plain) was in many ways culturally closer to East Lokris than to the southern Phokian sites by the coast of the Corinthian gulf (a pattern further discussed in Chapter 3). Mountains also divide Phokis from Lokris (with the principal pass running via Hyampolis) and punctuate the southern coast, in particular defining the Chrysaean plain south of Delphi, the only significant area of lowland plain in the region.[136] (Figures 1.7, 1.8) The implications of this diversity, both in terms of the pattern and pace of the politicization of regional identity, and the way in which Phokians engaged with wider regional networks (with Lokris and Euboia and in the ambit of the Corinthian gulf) will be further considered in Chapters 3 and 5.

Perhaps through chance of excavation, there is for much of our period a marked difference in the nature of the archaeological records of northern and southern Phokis. In the north, evidence comes mainly from cemeteries, many of which (like that at Elateia, Figure 1.9) were extensive and reached a peak of wealth during the Late Bronze Age/Early Iron Age transition, a period of decline in many other areas.[137] The sanctuary of Artemis at Kalapodi was also founded at this time (in LHIIIC).[138] By contrast, the south coast has produced settlement evidence from both major areas of plain, notably from Delphi,

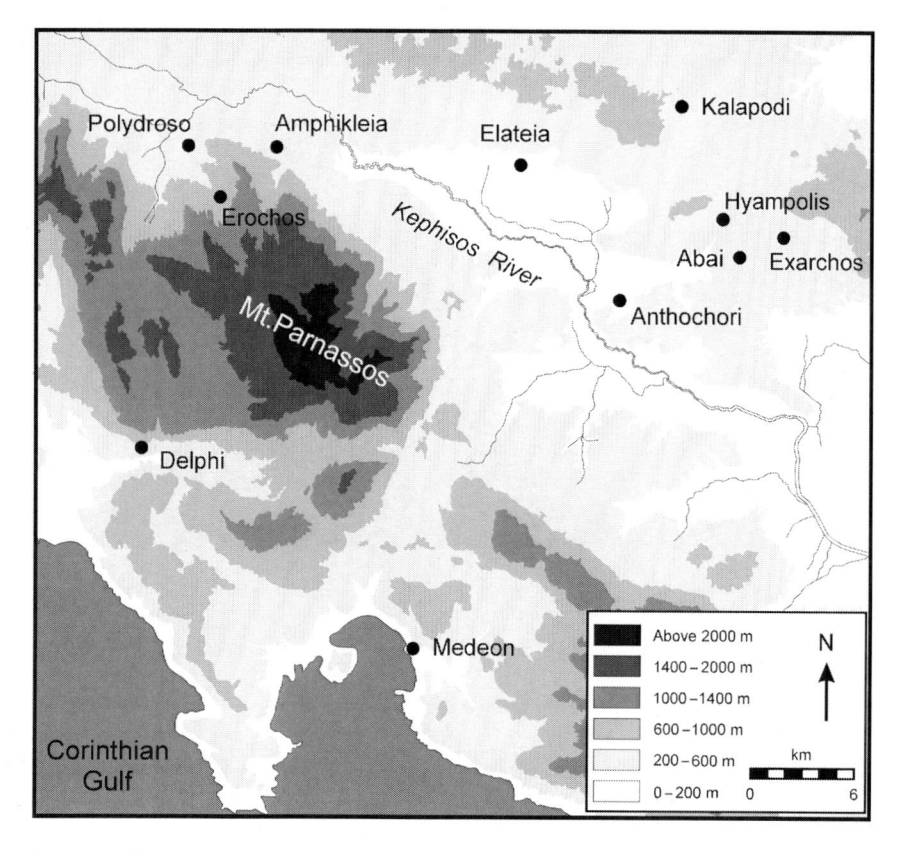

Figure 1.5 Phokis (C.L. Hayward).

where a substantial village lying over a Mycenaean settlement dates back at least into the tenth century and probably earlier.[139] To the east, prospection on the acropolis at Medeon and rescue excavation in the associated cemeteries has revealed almost continuous activity from Mycenaean to Roman times, although with a marked decline from the end of the eighth century at least until the Hellenistic period.[140] No systematic survey has yet been undertaken in Phokis, but Photios Dasios' 1992 gazetteer of data from Archaeological Service records and personal fieldwork offers a particularly valuable overview for our period.[141] By the end of the eighth century, it is possible to trace activity at or near most of the settlements destroyed by the Persians in 480. This network, which began to link physically the northern and southern parts of the region, was consolidated through the seventh and sixth centuries when a series of local shrines was also established, a process which will be further explored in Chapter 3. I would, however, stress that the archaeological record directly contradicts the idea of early cohesion, let alone tribal unity, and thus an unproblematic progression to an ethnically homogeneous federation.[142]

INTRODUCTION

Figure 1.6 Kephisos valley: looking east from outside Amphikleia (photo: author).

Most Phokian centres were destroyed by the Persians in 480, and the settlement pattern established thereafter differed markedly.[143]

There is no evidence for any formal pan-Phokian political organization before the late sixth century. Thereupon, the issue of federal coinage (probably *c*.510) was followed probably within a generation by the construction of a building to house the federal meetings of the Phokikon.[144] As McInerney has stressed, the sudden and comparatively early appearance of such clear evidence for the emergence of the Phokian *koinon* highlights the impact of two particular forms of outside intervention through the sixth century, namely the Thessalian occupation and the rise of international involvement at Delphi. The broad implications of both are easy to see, if hard to assess in detail. The Thessalian occupation is surrounded by often conflicting traditions reported in late sources and is only vaguely dated, chiefly by Herodotos' reference (8.27) to the events of its ending as occurring a few years before the Persian expedition. It is clear that anti-Thessalian sentiment remained a strong force behind subsequent Phokian policy, as for example, in the decision to take the opposite course to the Thessalians and resist Mardonius (Herodotos 8.30), which brought about a second, highly destructive, occupation (Herodotos 8.32–39).[145] As in the case of Thessaly, therefore, military activity played a major social (and probably also economic) role, but in the rather different terms of resistance and liberation, acting as a catalyst for ethnogenesis and the oppositional definition of Phokian identity. Quite apart from the cohesive effect of resistance to outside occupation, the events of its ending (the so-called 'Phokian despair') offered rich scope for the creation of a communal

26

INTRODUCTION

Figure 1.7 The Chrysaean plain from modern Delphi (photo: author).

Figure 1.8 The bay of Itea and the lower Pleistos valley from the coast outside Chaleion (Galaxidi) (photo: author).

history for the new *koinon*, in turn reinforced by the symbolic reconfiguration of the principal Phokian sanctuaries into a national network, as explored in Chapter 3. In the case of Delphi, the steady growth in foreign involvement with the shrine and oracle though the latter part of the eighth and seventh century created not only an increasingly varied and complex collection of vested interests, but also considerable economic demand for services and consumables. Here too, the resulting conflict had lasting implications for the economic and territorial development of Phokis as a whole.

Figure 1.9 The cemetery at Elateia (photo: author).

East Lokris

Our third study region, East Lokris, is significantly smaller and more homogeneous than either Thessaly or Phokis, being in essence a series of coastal plains looking out onto the Euboian straits and divided by mountains from Phokis to the west and Boiotia to the south (Figure 1.10). According to Strabo (9.4.2), it extended from Halai in the south to Thermopylae in the north, and historically, Opountian Lokris (and at times all of East Lokris) had as its centre the city of Opous, which may be identified with modern Atalante where continuous activity can be traced back to the Bronze Age.[146] The area in the north around Daphnous was perhaps the most vulnerable to separation as and when Phokis sought a northern outlet to the sea (thus separating Opountian and Epiknemidian Lokris). Equally, Opountian Lokris was on a number of occasions subsequent to our period subsumed into the Boiotian league. Historically, therefore, the communities of East Lokris were on one hand united by their access to the sea, and on the other to varying extents vulnerable to the interests of their larger neighbours. However, by contrast with relationships such as those between Thessaly and Phokis, or in the case of Arkadia, Tegea and Sparta, where hostility underpinned oppositional claims of regional identity, these interests could offer certain important advantages (for example, in access to trade networks). Indeed, the effect of external contacts during our period, principally with Euboia and Phokis, is of particular interest.

In this sense, and despite its small area overall, there is a less obvious rationale behind East Lokrian political integrity than that of many other

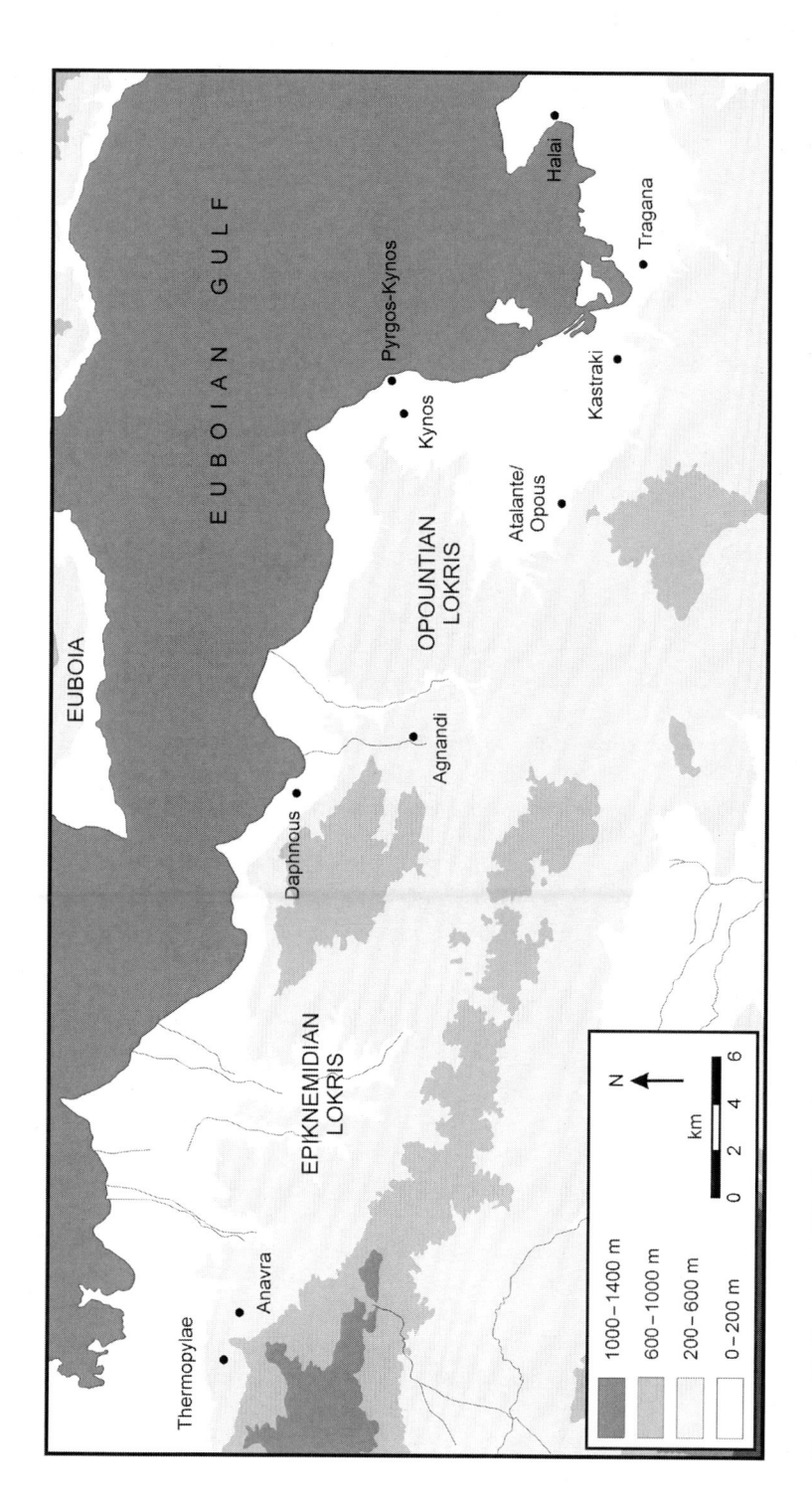

Figure 1.10 East Lokris (C.L. Hayward).

regions. Indeed, we have no direct evidence of any formal supra-regional organization before the fifth century. On probably two occasions Opountian Lokris participated in colonizing expeditions. While we lack information about the exact origin of the 'central Greek' (i.e. eastern or western) Lokrian colonists who founded Epizephyrian Lokri in 679 or 673 (according to Eusebius), later sources hint at East Lokrian involvement.[147] Somewhat later, direct evidence of East Lokrian settlement at Naupaktos is provided by an inscription which may date as early as 500–475, in which the relationship between the motherland and those East Lokrians who left as colonists is defined. As Meiggs and Lewis suggest, some West Lokrian involvement is implied by the use of West Lokrian script and by the findspot of the surviving copy at Chaleion (modern Galaxidi). Nonetheless, its provisions relate directly to the east, and it constitutes the principal source of evidence for the organization of East Lokris by this time.[148] It is clear that the city of Opous played a dominant regional role, and reference is also made to an assembly of the Opountian Thousand which Larsen believed to have been a federal organization (a view recently questioned by Heine Nielsen);[149] specific mention of the Perkothariai and Myascheis implies families or clans with some specific (perhaps priestly or ritual) role. The implication of a dominant city among the several known in the region, combined with what seems to be an overarching assembly or at least pan-regional acceptance of certain rules of conduct, is interesting, but it is impossible to determine the date and process by which this came into being. That a maritime region like East Lokris should be involved in colonization is hardly surprising (Achaia offers close parallels), yet while such activity of itself holds no implications for the level and nature of regional organization, it does raise questions of strategies for managing demographic and economic change which will be considered more fully in Chapter 4.

Of all the regions to be considered, our understanding of early settlement in East Lokris has been most strikingly transformed by archaeological research during the last twenty years. Before the establishment of the 14th Ephoreia of Prehistoric and Classical Antiquities, Halai was the only site to have been systematically excavated. The flood of information which has followed is especially welcome as ancient writers rarely mention, let alone discuss the region. Early Iron Age and Archaic finds have come from extensive survey conducted by John Fossey,[150] renewed systematic excavation at Halai (where settlement, cemetery and sanctuary evidence dates from Archaic times onwards),[151] and in particular, from a series of major rescue and research excavations conducted by the Ephoreia from the mid-1970s onwards. These include extensive settlement sites at Atalante and Kastraki, the Late Bronze Age/Early Iron Age port and settlement at Kynos, inland cemeteries of the same period (for example Agnandi), and the rich Protogeometric and later cemeteries nearer the coast, notably that at Tragana.[152] Our knowledge of almost all periods has been greatly enhanced, but particularly important in the context of this study is the extent of Protogeometric evidence, reinforcing a trend clear through most of the Greek world that wherever specific interest has been directed towards this period, substantial new evidence has been found. Despite this wealth of new information, however, the extent of coastline change (largely due to seismic activity) complicates reconstructions of the historical geography of the region.[153]

Achaia

Achaia spans much of the north coast of the Peloponnese, from its easternmost city, Pellene which borders Sikyon, to Dyme in the west (Figure 1.11). To the south lie land borders with Elis towards the west and, south of Mt. Panachaikon, with the territory of the Arkadian Azanes (an ethnos further discussed in Chapter 4) in the area of modern Kalavryta. Environmentally and culturally, the Achaian territory divides into four sub-regions.[154] (Figure 1.12) Along the narrow, punctuated, coastal plain running from Pellene to Neos Erineos, major settlements were located mainly on a series of headlands or plain extensions surrounding the outflow of rivers. As is clear in the case of, for example, Aegira (Figure 1.13), extensive erosion has substantially reduced the amount of cultivable upland close to certain sites. Indeed, assuming the process at Aegira to have been more or less continuous, the resources available to its inhabitants by the eighth century must have been considerably impoverished in comparison with the situation when the settlement was founded in Neolithic times. The coastal area is divided from the upland plains inland (the Pharai valley and Arkadian Azania) by a chain of mountains (Panachaikon, Aroania and Kyllini) which limited access south to Arkadia and the central Peloponnese. (Figure 1.14) Of the coastal cities, Aigeira in the east and Aigion further west (perhaps the finest natural harbour along the Corinthian gulf, Figure 1.15) seem to have had substantial inland territories, indicated by the locations of Phelloe (Seliana), a *kome* of Aigeira, and by Aigion's control of the shrine of Artemis at Ano Mazaraki (Rakita) in the Meganeitas valley. The second sub-region comprised what was to become the *chora* of Patras, which in Classical times extended from Drepanon perhaps as far as Tsoukaleika, and consisted of a broader plain with few natural divisions as well as the northern foothills of Panachaikon. The third area is that west of the river Peiros, around Dyme (modern Kato Achaia), which comprises perhaps the largest area of coastal plain (including the marshy lowlands around Cape Araxos) plus the lower and more undulating uplands west of Mt. Erymanthos.[155] Finally, there is the Pharai valley, a funnel-shaped valley extending inland south of Panachaikon, punctuated by well-watered plains.[156] (Figures 1.16, 1.17) As Jonathan Hall and I have argued, these divisions, while primarily topographical, are echoed in the material record via site groupings and the distribution of artefact types and styles, and serve to highlight the degree of diversity across the region, reflected in the pace and pattern of local development. This sharp

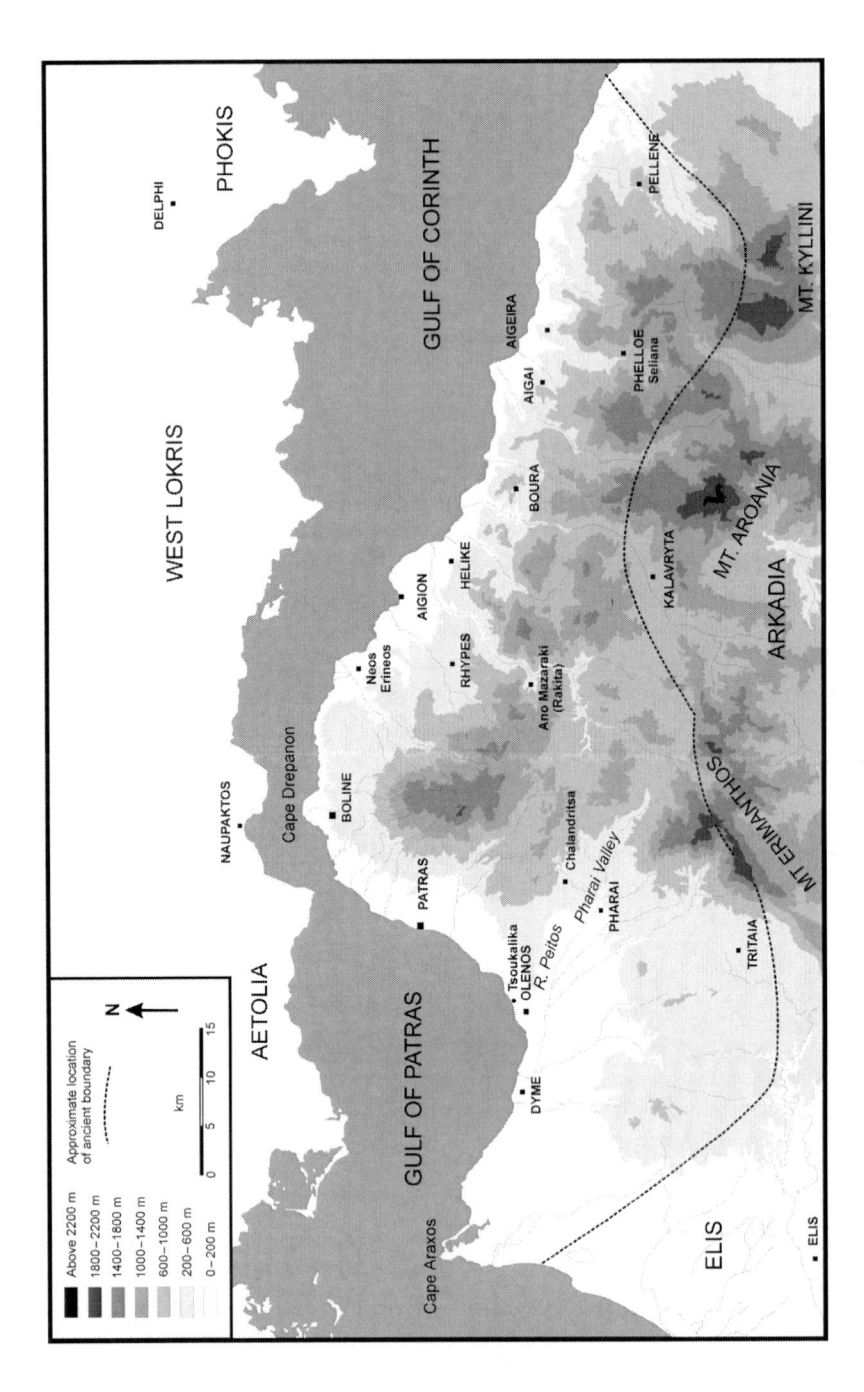

Figure 1.11 Achaia (C.L. Hayward after Yvonne Rizaki).

INTRODUCTION

Figure 1.12 Aegira acropolis, looking east (photo: C.L. Hayward).

Figure 1.13 Aegira: erosion inland from the acropolis (photo: C.L. Hayward).

Figure 1.14 Coastal plain near Diakofto: view inland to Panachaikon (photo: author).

juxtaposition of different settlement trajectories in different environments is a distinctive feature echoed also in Arkadia as discussed below.

Until relatively recently, studies of early Achaian history, while fully exploiting the meagre literary sources, have suffered both from a shortage of

Figure 1.15 Aigion (photo: author).

Figure 1.16 Pharai valley: south west from Platanovrysi (photo: author).

archaeological data and from an analytical concern to trace the roots of the later post-280 league, retrojecting assumptions about the form of regional organization.[157] Over the past two or three decades, however, renewed exploration has transformed our understanding of the archaeological record.[158] A

Figure 1.17 Pharai valley: looking south from east of Chalandritsa (photo: author).

programme of extensive and intensive surface survey instigated in 1986 by the 6th Ephoreia of Prehistoric and Classical Antiquities (Patras) and the Centre for Greek and Roman Antiquity (KERA) of the Greek National Research Foundation (EIE) has so far covered the Dyme area and the *chora* of Patras, and is scheduled to continue.[159] At Dyme itself, rescue excavation has produced traces of a small settlement established in the Archaic period. Along the north coast, renewed systematic excavation of the settlement and sanctuary on and around the acropolis of Aigeira has been conducted by the Austrian Archaeological Institute,[160] excavation has resumed (following survey) at what may be the site of Rhypes (Trapeza hill),[161] and rescue work been undertaken on many occasions, notably accompanying the construction of two national roads and the Athens–Patras railway. In two other major settlements, Aigion and Patras, rescue excavation over many decades has produced substantial bodies of information. At Patras, early levels lie deeply buried and much damage has been caused by later construction, but in the case of Aigion, we have a basic understanding of the formation and expansion of the city during our period.[162] In the Pharai valley, significant periods of research during the late 1920s and the mid-1950s produced a series of Early Iron Age and Archaic burials, although despite the discovery of extensive Mycenaean and Submycenaean settlement at Chalandritsa, relatively little later material has come to light in recent years.[163] Clearly, therefore, existing evidence from all parts of Achaia is only the tip of the iceberg and negative arguments should be treated with caution. However, the picture is not uniform across the region, since a higher proportion of known sites along the north coast and in the Patras area have been excavated to some extent, producing a clearer picture of the nature of artefacts, burial customs, and architecture than is currently available for the western and inland areas.

The earliest indication of a perception of Achaia as a geographical entity with internal subdivisions comes in the much-cited passage in which Herodotos (1.145) records the division of Achaia into twelve *mere*, which he names as Pellene, Aigeira, Aigai, Boura, Helike, Aigion, Rhypes, Patrees (Patrai), Pharees (Pharai), Olenos, Dyme and Tritaiees (Tritaia). These divisions are also cited, with minor and explicable changes, by later authors, certain of whom appear to have drawn directly upon Herodotos' account.[164] The import of the term *meros* is unclear, however, other than in the accepted mathematical sense of being the product of an act of division. Herodotos offers no explanation (although this is hardly to be expected in a discussion focused on the origin of the twelve poleis of Ionia), and its use in other regions (Boiotia, for example) suggests no consistent or readily transferable purpose.[165] It does, however, imply a perception of a whole, and so the relationship between the twelve-fold division of Achaia implied by a literal reading of Herodotos' account and the broader geographical and cultural divisions evident in the Early Iron Age and Archaic record requires further investigation (not least as a point of comparison for the contemporary treatment of the social geography of neighbouring Arkadia).[166] It is, for example, interesting to note a contrast between those *meros* names which appear as ethnic plurals and are located inland, or in the case of Patras relate to a polis with a complex history of synoikism and dioikism,[167] and those in the singular which seem more tied to place and are generally to be found along the north coast. The one exception, Dyme, probably reflects its geographical relationship to the older heartlands (Strabo 8.7.5) and is thus an interesting reflection on contemporary topographical perceptions.[168]

The date of the earliest overarching regional political structure, and thus the active politicization of the regional ethnic, has been the subject of considerable debate. While it is almost certain that an Achaian league existed prior to the refoundation of 280, its date and nature are harder to establish. Polybius' discussion of Achaia focuses on the post-280 league and shows no real knowledge of any regional organization other than city-states.[169] Earlier evidence is more fragmentary, but as Jonathan Hall and I have argued, while there may have been a growing sense of collective identity, there seems to be little to indicate the existence of any overarching political structures much before the end of the fifth century.[170] From the late eighth century onwards, Achaian colonization of Sybaris (which in turn founded Poseidonia), Kroton (which may have been the *metropolis* of Kaulonia if it was not founded directly from Peloponnesian Achaia) and Metapontion, mark her out as one of the regions most actively involved in the west (and as will be argued in Chapter 4, there is growing evidence for earlier western and north-western contacts too). Larsen's

INTRODUCTION

suggestion that colonization constitutes evidence for eighth-century Achaian political unity is hard to sustain, however, and as will be argued in Chapter 4, a variety of factors in different parts of Achaia may have given rise to demographic mobility of various kinds and colonization should be understood within this wider comparative context (echoing earlier comments on Lokrian colonization and Thessalian military mobility). It is hardly surprising to find that a regional ethnic could be as effective as the *politikon* of a mother city as the prime point of reference for the creation of colonial political identity. More interesting in the case of Achaia (as also in Phokis as noted) is the question of the extent and nature of engagement with neighbouring political communities, and the specific role of the Corinthian gulf as a focus of communication and interaction, noting in particular the dialectic between insider and outsider perceptions in defining group identity.[171]

Arkadia

The Arkadian landscape is perhaps the most distinctive of all those considered here. (Figure 1.18) Much of the region consists of high plains surrounded by mountains; the lowest valley bottoms (in western Arkadia, Figure 1.19) are some 400 m above sea level, rising to c.950 m in the north (Lousoi, Figures 1.20, 1.21) where the mountains reach some 2,300 m. While the richest agricultural land lies in the east, there is no substantial variation in the quality or nature of resources available across the region as a whole, and thus environmental constraints on economic strategies were felt across the region, as was the necessity of co-operation between communities on a wide range of issues from drainage (especially in the east, Figure 1.22) to road maintenance and the exchange of labour, commodities and resources (metals for example).[172] Issues of demography (the level of sustainable permanent population and optimal group size) are also particularly pertinent in this region. It is perhaps predictable that common concerns of this kind fostered complex perceptions of territory and territorial marking, and also from time to time the temporary dominance of larger poleis over their smaller neighbours. More problematic is the emergence of any overarching perception of regional identity.

In Arkadia, as in most of the other regions considered, synthetic work has drawn together often extensive bodies of information from many decades of research.[173] These, combined with the results of more recent large-scale excavation and survey projects (notably at Asea, Tegea and the Pheneos valley)[174] and continuing extensive exploration (in particular, the continuing work of Yanis Pikoulas),[175] provide a substantial, if inevitably uneven coverage of the region and certainly adequate information to address basic issues of local and regional development. The nature of the record is, however, somewhat different from those of the other regions so far considered. Despite a long tradition of extensive surface prospection, early evidence from sites other than sanctuaries remains limited and graves in particular are rare.[176] There is clearly a problem of surface visibility of pre-sixth-century pottery, and the resulting shortage of survey data is also an important factor behind the lack of early settlement excavation, as it is hard to identify locations for detailed research. That most Early Iron Age evidence comes from eastern Arkadia largely reflects the concentration of excavation of sites of all periods. The greatest bodies of Early Iron Age and Archaic evidence come from sanctuaries,[177] and as will be discussed in Chapter 3, variation in the contents of early votive deposits and the physical form of shrines (including built temples) constitutes important evidence for the evolving interests of cult communities through time, the ability to mobilize resources, and the relationship between local systems and regional consciousness from the sixth century onwards.

As Thomas Heine Nielsen has argued, while the primary level of identification for most inhabitants of Arkadia probably remained place communities which were in many cases explicitly called poleis, a sense of Arkadian identity was present by the late sixth century even while the regional borders were changing.[178] Indeed, Arkadia was fundamentally a human construct, the land inhabited by Arkadians at any given time, and this sense of rolling geography and of a complex dynamic between people and places, between the creation of community territories and their politicization as Arkadian, is present in early treatments of the region, notably those of Homer and Herodotos.[179]

It is clear that by the fifth century at the latest, Arkadian identity had real political salience (whatever the origin(s) and function(s) of the Arkadikon coinage, for example, the exploitation of the name is striking), although there is no evidence for formal federation before 370 (also named the Arkadikon).[180] But a survey of the archaeological record makes it plain that this wider identity emerged from great diversity, and that the complexity of the underlying place and sub-regional structure was not lost. Arkadia has no natural feature which could draw communities together over a larger area in the same way as, for example, the Corinthian gulf helped to bind together northern Achaian communities or the Euboian gulf those of East Lokris within wider systems of exchange and communication. On the contrary, the existence of powerful and sometimes hostile neighbours like Argos and Sparta (and from the sixth century onwards, Elis) promoted rather localized responses in terms of self definition, defence, interaction and accommodation with non-Arkadians. The image of Arkadia as the enclosed and mysterious heart of the Peloponnese presented in, for example, Pausanias Book 8, simply does not fit the Early Iron Age and Archaic evidence.[181] And to this picture of competing and co-operating place communities operating within the overarching construct of Arkadia we should add the sub-regional groupings commonly called tribes, although as noted, effectively smaller-scale ethne. These did not extend uniformly across the region: with the exception of the Azanes in the north, preserved tribal names, Mainalians, Parrhasians (attested in the *Catalogue of Ships*; *Iliad* 2.603–9), Eutresians and Kynourians,

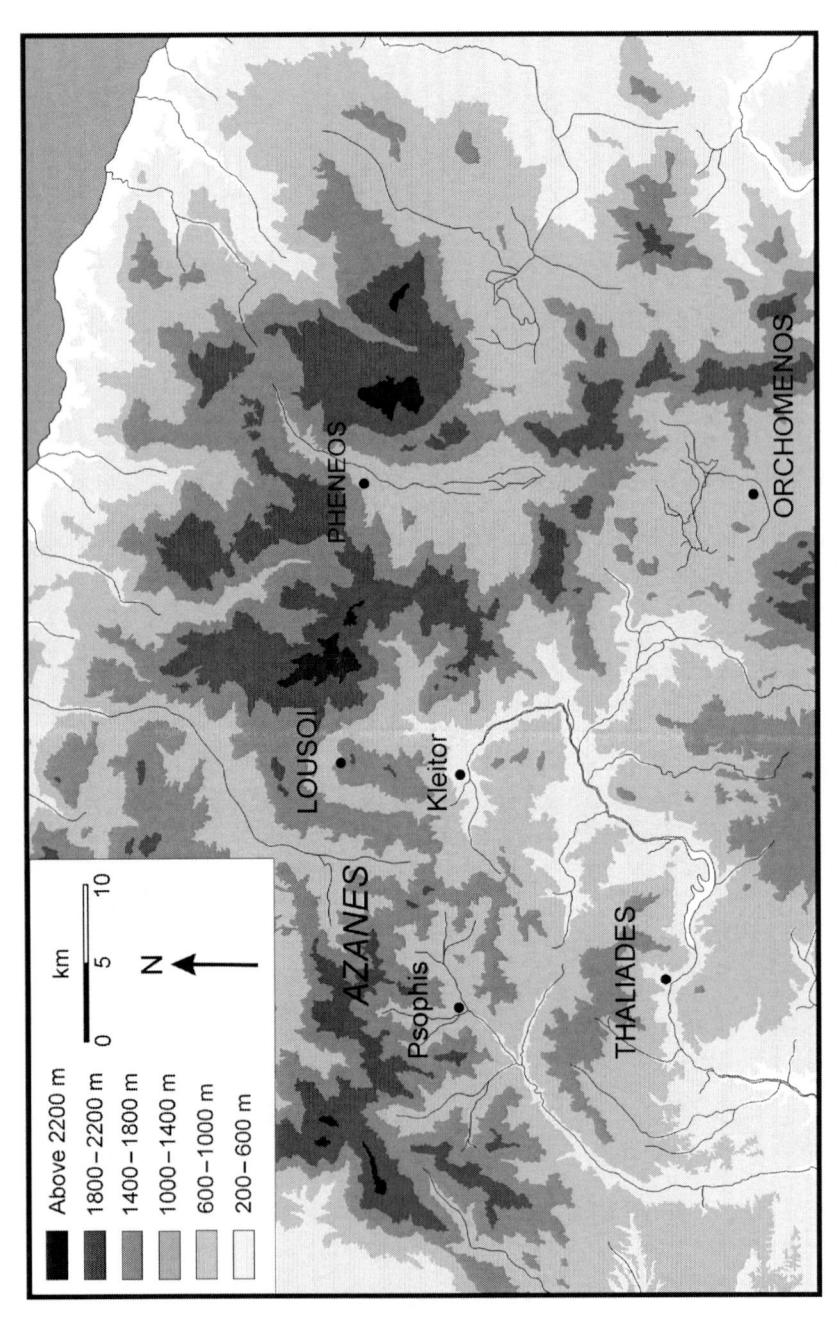

Figure 1.18 Arkadia (C.L. Hayward).

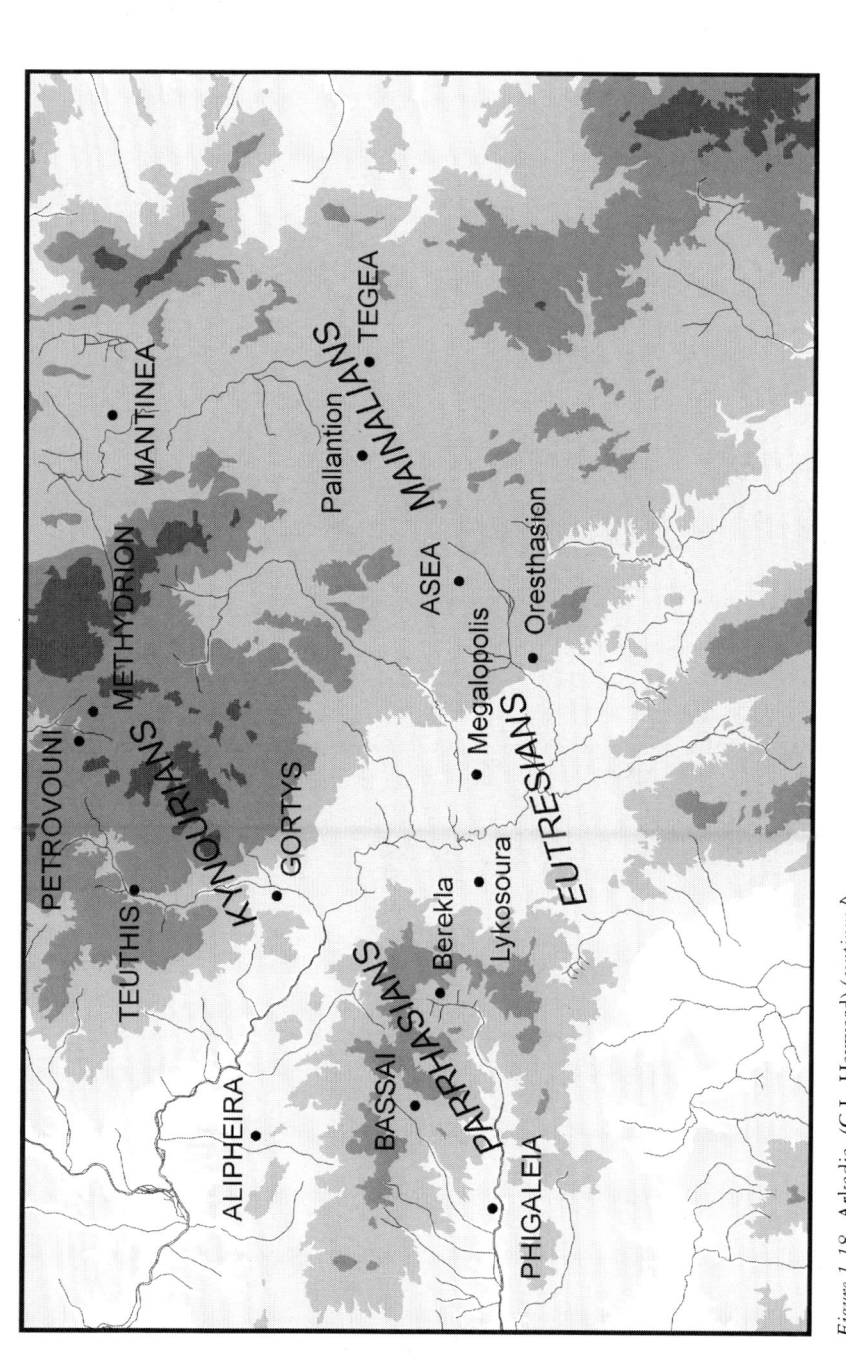

Figure 1.18 Arkadia (C.L. Hayward) (continued).

Figure 1.19 Alipheira acropolis: looking south (photo: author).

pertain to south-west Arkadia, although this may reflect the fact that much information derives from accounts of the synoicism of Megalopolis. James Roy has argued that the tribal system predated polis organization and broke down with the growth of urban centres by the fifth century. Conversely, Thomas Heine Nielsen prefers to see tribes as later phenomena, developed in the context of inter-city rivalry. The balance between tribe and community was therefore problematic and probably variable.[182]

The case of the Azanes raises the important additional issue of the fate of an ethnos that lost political salience. Although well attested in the eighth-century and Archaic material record and treated as group with a distinct identity in descriptions of Archaic events (for example, Herodotos 6.127), the Azanes had effectively ceased to exist as a politically salient group by Classical times. The name appears in later sources, but more as a construct of historical memory (as, for example, Strabo 8.8.1) than as a living force in contemporary social politics. While analytical attention has concentrated on the phenomenon of ethnogenesis, the Azanes of Arkadia constitute one of the most striking cases of the opposite circumstances, the death of an ethnos.[183]

All of these case studies show a range of characteristics and problems in common, including internal variation in social development and complex structures of tiered localized and regional identity. More specific problems, such as the effects of demographic pressures, seasonal mobility or warfare on the construction of regional identity, can be highlighted in each case.

INTRODUCTION

Figure 1.20 Lousoi: valley bottom from the Hellenistic settlement (photo: author).

Figure 1.21 Lousoi: Mt. Helmos from above the temple site (photo: author).

INTRODUCTION

Figure 1.22 Tegean plain: southern end showing flooding after Spring snowfalls, April 1998 (photo: author).

Furthermore, their geographical grouping in central Greece and the north and central Peloponnese gives scope for considering interaction between them, and with neighbouring poleis, in relation to major routes of communication (especially those associated with the Corinthian gulf). With these issues in mind, we will move to consider the specific ways in which identity could be articulated, beginning with the role(s) played by localized settlement and especially big sites, before turning to cult communities and the construction of territory.

2

BIG SITES AND PLACE IDENTITIES

The social, economic and political implications of urban development are among the most widely discussed aspects of early polis formation on the Greek mainland. They are also among the most controversial, since the manner of relating social and power relations to physical behaviour and thence the material record remains a much debated issue. The importance of the main town is highlighted by the Copenhagen Polis Centre's observation that the two predominant usages of the term polis, for a political community and the main town associated with it, correlate so strongly that they were probably indistinguishable.[1] The origins of city life, consistently highlighted by ancient sources as central to the polis as a political community,[2] have been sought in the emergence or expansion of nucleated settlements (often collected around an acropolis), in the creation of public space, and in certain (mostly colonial) cases, in systematic town planning with perceived implications for an underlying decision-making process.[3]

On the Greek mainland, attention has concentrated on the eighth and seventh centuries.[4] Inevitably, therefore, discussion tends to centre on issues of settlement morphology, since the existence and location of public buildings are not sufficiently consistent to be reliable indicators of site status (although clearly the context of any such investment within a settlement must be considered). Even fortifications, strikingly present on Early Iron Age Crete and in the islands, as well as at Old Smyrna, were not common on the mainland until the late seventh or sixth century and, as Anthony Snodgrass points out, once constructed they are likely to have outlived any changes in the political status of the site concerned.[5] Attention has therefore focused on the fact of settlement expansion and/or agglomeration rather than on specific building types, noting especially the emphasis placed on synoikism, political if not physical, and the material consequences of the resulting acceptance of a political centre.[6] Such nucleation was rarely at the expense of rural settlement, however, and as we will see, the eighth century was a period of expansion of settlement of all kinds.

In this chapter, we will consider the nature of mainland big sites during the Early Iron Age and the Archaic period, the social and economic implications of their development, and the ways in which they operated as focal points for the expression of identity. It must be stressed from the outset that there is no archaeological support for a contrast between the polis as an urbanized state form and the generally unurbanized and thus politically backward Archaic and early Classical ethnos.[7] Most ethne have produced eighth–sixth century evidence of sites which can be classified (usually subjectively) as big by contemporary local standards, or of occupation of unknown extent at centres of later importance. Indeed, wherever substantial bodies of evidence permit even basic reconstruction of site size and/or morphology, it is hard to drawn any meaningful distinction between settlements in ethnos territory (such as Pherai or Aigion) and the centres of traditional poleis such as Argos or Megara.[8] It is therefore better to recognize fundamental similarities in the nature and potential meaning of the evidence than to presuppose separate explanations (as for example, Victor Ehrenberg's suggestion that local groupings or unions of villages shared citadels for use in time of danger).[9]

Given the volume and geographical spread of evidence for communities explicitly called poleis in Archaic and Classical sources, it is hardly surprising to find that there is at least as strong a case for the importance of settlement-focused place identities within what were to emerge as ethnos territories as within states constituted purely as poleis. In Achaia, for example, sixteen settlements are included in the Copenhagen inventory as certainly or probably poleis during these periods, and in almost all cases where there has been significant research, the archaeological record of these sites dates back into the Early Iron Age.[10] We will return to the question of retrojected political status; here I merely emphasize that big sites as focuses of group identity are a phenomenon of almost all political communities by the eighth century at the very latest (and often substantially earlier). The rare (and relatively short-lived) exceptions are considered in Chapter 4.

Yet there is a further and potentially more complex sense in which place in the wider sense (i.e. subsuming, even if focused by, particular big sites) has been perceived as fundamental to ethnic expression. Central to the collective myth-history of most ethnic groups is the manner in which they lived, migrated and settled together. As Anthony Smith comments,[11] this 'togetherness' incorporated myths of common descent, shared history and cultural practices, as well as association with a specific territory. As emphasized in the previous chapter, such collective myth-histories were the products of continuing discourses of identity which could be created, adapted and forgotten as needed (to bind together cohabiting groups, for example, or to distinguish those who moved away), although recognition of their mutability should not be taken to imply that they were necessarily less real to those whose situations they described and justified. Of particular interest here is the role of place in defining group identity. According to Smith, this may be territory in the sense of the actual area of group residence, or it may be an aspired-to 'homeland', the aspiration being justified by some form of sacred or commemorative association or by external recognition of the connection between the group and the place.

From the perspective of the Early Iron Age and Archaic Greek mainland, such emphasis upon the symbolic role of homeland aspirations seems anachronistic. In most of our regions, the complex process by which different perceptions of territory relating to different kinds of group activity were hardened into external borders with groups recognized as distinctively 'other' was slowly unfolding throughout this period (as discussed in Chapter 4). The probable exception is Phokis, where the genesis of the ethnos as a political entity owed much to Phokian responses to outside military intervention. As has been emphasized, most of the ethne considered in detail in this book were not self-evidently natural or cultural unities. In the case of Achaia, for example, Dyme, in the far west of the Classical ethnos territory, does not appear to have been settled to any notable extent during the Early Iron Age.[12] Equally, Arkadia's western frontiers with Elis and her dependencies were probably not significant until the sixth century, when we have the earliest epigraphical evidence for the long process by which Elis defined her borders and her relationship to (often perioikic) neighbouring communities.[13] Defining and binding together what were to become the territories of Classical ethne was usually a complex process, and it therefore seems hard to find much of a role for symbolic homelands before the sixth century at the earliest (the possible exception, Achaia as perceived by her western colonies, is discussed in Chapter 4).

In more general terms, however, Smith's formulation raises the important question of the balance between different kinds of place identities (territorial, specific settlement, or other forms of community with a geographical focus, such as cult communities centred on a specific sanctuary) within the social geography of any group which recognized a common identity, even if this identity was not yet perceived as politically salient. The role of big sites within this picture in comparison with sanctuary constituencies and the territories of subsistence, law and kin-ties is thus a particularly challenging area of enquiry. In this chapter we will focus on big sites themselves, moving to address interrelated issues of cult communities in Chapter 3, and the nature and role of territories, as embodied in the broader Aristotelean discussion of community of place (*Politics* 7.4–5), in Chapter 4.

Big sites or urban entities?

The problem of defining urban entities arises in the interpretation of the archaeological settlement record of almost all regions, and is hardly confined to the Early Iron Age, even if concentration on the rise of the polis has given it particular prominence.[14] One does not have to accept the extreme formulation implied in Fustel de Coulanges' treatment of the city in relation to the civic community to recognize the strength and pervasiveness of the conceptual opposition between cities and supposedly primitive social structures, families and phratries.[15] Implicit is the notion of the city as the social, and eventually physical (and often monumental), context for political and religious activity distinct in nature or scale from that performed elsewhere in the territory. Yet modern scholarly emphasis on urbanism as central to complex political development is not always accompanied by explicit definition of the term or consideration of its identification in the archaeological record.[16] Should this be a relative judgement depending on regional context (stressing that the Early Iron Age is a particularly difficult period for recognition of surface evidence in many areas) or should assessment of the material record rest on abstract criteria reflecting the nature of those activities perceived as 'urban'?[17]

The debate surrounding the essential nature of the ancient city and the nature and validity of comparison between ancient and later European urbanism is one of long standing.[18] Without wishing to imply an evolutionary perspective, it may be that different approaches and emphasises are more appropriate to different periods. Effective assessment of the likely status of a particular site according to any set of abstract criteria not only depends on the choice of those criteria, but is complicated by diachronic changes in the built form favoured for Greek settlements. The shifting ideals which lay beneath these changes were rarely made explicit in contemporary sources and are usually modern judgements of hindsight, based on often limited research at a small proportion of sites (at best a 10 per cent sample of those defined as poleis according to the Copenhagen criteria).[19] In other words, the application of abstract criteria, while imposing a certain clarity, is a complex exercise which inevitably involves a degree of bias, normative judgement and circular argument. Furthermore, such criteria are very hard to formulate for the Early Iron Age and early Archaic period (at least without resorting to hindsight), since the epigraphical record is comparatively slight and patchily distributed, and a significant range of public activities had yet to acquire their own formal settings.

It therefore seems more realistic to consider the growth of big sites in the context of a developmental process than as a phenomenon linked to any ideal concept of the city. Not only does this focus attention on the human dynamics of settlement development and thence the wider contemporary context of the available data, but it also avoids the pitfalls inherent in selecting a model of urbanism against which to measure specific cases. Too narrow and restrictive an ideal may exclude evidence which does not seem to fit, while too inclusive and vague a definition gives rise to continualism which conceals more than it reveals.[20] This should not be taken to imply an absence of underlying processes which transcend regional context. As is clear from the comparisons already drawn, evidence from sites across the Early Iron Age and Archaic political spectrum is closely similar, and there is much to support the idea of a punctuated process whereby changes within settlement concentrations accumulated to the point where key decisions about the physical form and role of such sites became inevitable.

In this chapter, we will consider the various standpoints from which one might assess how Early Iron Age and Archaic big sites focused, created and reflected the expression of different kinds of identity. First, though, we should clarify terminology, since the notion of urbanism, while commonly if controversially applied, has potentially misleading connotations especially when linked to ideas of political progress in the rise of the polis.[21] These connotations are perceived not only in physical terms (stressing the large extent of ethne and the size of their populations) but also in political ones, emphasizing as a negative image the absence of government in 'unurbanized' societies like ethne, with resulting reliance on self-defence, kinship ties, and unrecorded law (a very Thucydidean image, see pp. 7–8). The model of the *Stammstaat* thus places as much emphasis upon urbanism as a dynamic force for change as do most analyses of the emergence of the polis.[22] In its original nineteenth-century formulation (in Ildefonso Cerdá's 1868–71 *Teoría general de la urbanización*), the term urbanism encompassed planning for a variety of newly fashionable issues, ranging from public health to the efficiency of transport and circulation. This concern with the relationship between the conduct of life and the built environment as a holistic entity marked a real departure from the previously prevalent Vitruvian ideals of good building per se, and was conceived in more detailed and concrete terms than the Aristotelean discussion of place. Urbanism, in the sense of the city as an organic whole and life within it as an issue of moral and physical public health, was thus intimately linked with ideas of social progress. Similar overtones are evident in attempts to assess the relative date of 'planned' towns in early Greek colonies and their mother cities as a sign of political development, as also in ethnic readings of building forms and settlement layout in colonial or contact situations (Morgantina being a case in point).[23] Indeed, as I will argue, such preconceptions about the role of urban centres in the polis have biased interpretations of developments even in supposedly paradigmatic mainland cases, as Athens, Corinth and Argos. The eighth–sixth century structural changes which occurred at many mainland settlement sites were of an order which, if our present record is not hopelessly skewed, was unparalleled since the Late Bronze Age (and then with major organizational differences). The decisions taken on key management issues had consequences not only for the contemporary conduct of community life but also for future problems and options for their solution. But if we are to view such developments with the benefit of hindsight, let alone from perspectives current only from the nineteenth century onwards, we should be explicit about the implications involved.

Many studies of early settlement planning are heavily dependent on evidence from the western colonies, the Cyclades and Crete. The difficulties of transposing the needs underlying colonial town planning to the interpretation of mainland evidence are well known. In the case of some Cretan and island sites, topographical constraints combined with the extensive use of stone for construction have resulted in relatively good preservation of what appear to be close and well-planned population agglomerations.[24] On Crete, sites like Karphi and Kavousi belong within complex strategies of upland settlement,[25] although as is shown by the very different pattern of continuing occupation in the area of former palaces like Knossos,[26] there was a wide variety of strategies across the island. The Cyclades and neighbouring islands, the distinctive character of settlements like Zagora, Xombourgo, Minoa or Emborio, characterized by, for example, fortification and at least in some cases dense yet brief occupation, reflects the particular topographic, demographic, economic and security factors which affected island life over centuries.[27] The prominence of these regions in general discussions of Early Iron Age architecture and planning, and especially in the identification of social differentiation in housing (such as 'rulers'' houses) therefore skews the picture.[28] In particular, the relatively swift appearance and disappearance of certain sites whose plans are sufficiently preserved to read in them hierarchical distinctions may create an overall impression of greater physical (and perhaps social) instability than is justified.[29] James Whitley's distinction between stable and unstable settlement (setting aside the question of whether the latter should be taken as evidence for rule by 'big-men') essentially describes the geographical divide between much of the mainland and certain island sites (with Crete falling in between, depending on the particular local system).[30]

This is not to imply a lack of interest in the planning of mainland sites and its relation to social structure. Considerable attention has been paid to those few settlements, notably Nichoria, Eretria and, in a rather different manner, Lefkandi, that have been sufficiently excavated to reveal archaeological traits that could be claimed to differentiate the residences and social roles of the elite from those of the commons, and most particularly, of a chief from the wider aristocracy. This is usually a matter of building size and location, but factors such as proximity (in life or death) to cult areas, or control of resources (for example, the storage of agricultural produce), can also be relevant.[31] In terms of the contribution of such residence relationships to the construction and expression of individual or group identity, predictably enough they highlight the attraction that may be exerted by a particular oikos, and the way in which maintenance of a hierarchy could in turn impact upon the construction of group ideology and the conduct of group activity (something that will be pursued further presently). But in no case do they reveal the particular nature of power, nor does any single model adequately describe all cases (few as they are for the mainland).

Furthermore, the three examples cited illustrate the disparate dates of the available evidence and the varying time-depth of the hierarchies indicated (where this can be estimated). At Eretria, for example (Figure 2.1), arguments have focused on architectural evidence which mostly dates to the second half

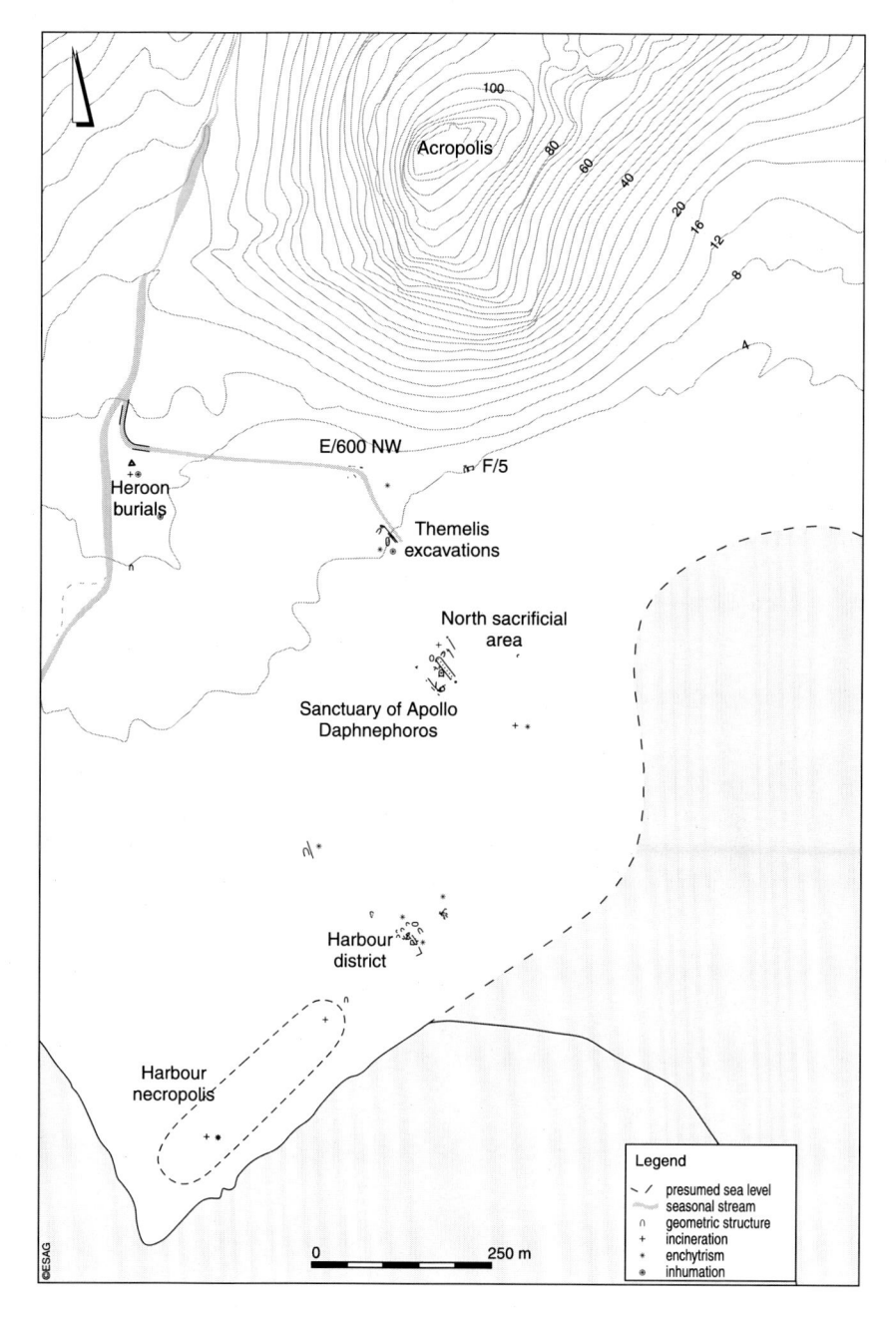

Figure 2.1 Eretria (courtesy of the Swiss School of Archaeology at Athens).

of the eighth century, and on this basis, Alexander Mazarakis Ainian has distinguished an elite residential area in the north from the more crowded mass settlement by the shore, and the elite West Gate cemetery from the main burial ground. As he acknowledges, the state of the evidence precludes any useful discussion of the relationship between this spatial ordering and that of the earlier eighth century, let alone the ninth when evidence is very fragmentary indeed.[32] Discussion of the northern settlement area around the so-called Daphnephoreion has focused on the connection between elite residence and control of cult, and especially on the process of transfer of ritual from the residence of a priest-chief to a formal temple. Yet renewed excavation and ongoing reappraisal of previous work in this area suggest that we may have been too quick to draw conclusions, and until these new results are published, it would be unwise to rely on older interpretations.[33] Unfortunately, very few other sites in southern and central Greece have produced sufficient evidence to address such problems.[34] Of our study areas, only Achaia has produced one controversial case, the so-called Temple A on the acropolis of Aegira. (Figures 2.2, 2.3) Following Anton Bammer and Alexander Mazarakis, I believe this to be a large domestic structure within a settlement rather than a temple per se, as there is no direct evidence for associated cult. A ninth- or early eighth-century massif-style tripod would imply some form of cult activity in the area, but it lacks secure context. Overall, the extent of excavation, the scoured state of the Aegira acropolis

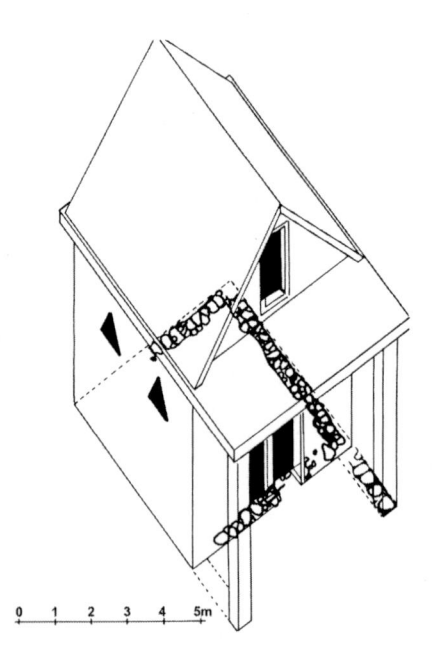

Figure 2.2 Aegira 'Temple A' (author, after Alzinger, *ÖJh* 1983, p. 38, fig. 2b).

Figure 2.3 Aegira acropolis (photo: C.L. Hayward).

and the poor chronological resolution make it unwise to attempt reconstruction of the settlement and the place of the 'big house' within it.[35]

Elsewhere, it is impossible to move beyond the basic inferences derived from often gross and impressionistic reconstructions of the scale of permanent sites (since estimation of population per hectare or per roofed area founders on ignorance of site extent and building density, especially under the circumstances of rescue excavation). Ian Morris has estimated that the largest communities, i.e. large stable sites like Argos or Athens, probably never dropped below 500 members and perhaps not below one or even two thousand, although he views smaller village sites with members in the hundreds as more common.[36] At this gross level one can draw the rather obvious conclusion that most big sites had some form of chief, and in the largest cases a hierarchy of authority. An inhabitant of a particular big site would therefore have as an aspect of his political identity his personal relationship and/or that of his family to that of a chief and other aristocrats, however rule was constituted and maintained in any particular case. Given the quality of data at our disposal and the large potential error factor, it would be rash to try to relate site size to level of complexity to officials involved in individual cases. Yet other questions can be asked of the archaeological record of big sites which may highlight ways in which individual and group responses to changing settlement dynamics promoted cohesion, fission or at least a need for practical decision making, often with long-term consequences for insider and outsider perceptions of the site. As already emphasized, there is scant evidence for major public construction at most mainland big sites much before the sixth century. But from the eighth century onwards it is often possible to detect both growing density of occupation and the settlement of new areas around old nuclei, and the practical impacts of such changes were potentially far reaching.

Questions of scale

It is often argued that a true city should be defined by the functions concentrated within it, rather than being a mere agglomeration of population.[37] Yet especially in this early period, these two aspects are not clearly separable. Characterization based on size alone may seem simplistic, but one should not overlook the implications of changes of scale and the decisions thus demanded, not least because in most cases they were occurring for the first time since the Bronze Age. Settlement size is both a geographic and a demographic issue, and demands consideration of a range of factors including territorial extent, the number and density of occupied buildings, and the size and density of population.[38]

In the simplest terms, the residence of comparatively large numbers of people in relatively close proximity creates basic problems, the solutions to which affect the circumstances of succeeding generations – access to water and land, for example (balancing near and far resources), disposal of waste, proximity to kin or social equals, and the impact of new building on notions of privacy and access.[39] As Roland Fletcher has emphasized,[40] the material world of a settlement is not a mere representation of human social strategies, but is an active force in shaping conduct. Indeed, recognition of these practical implications underpins the emphasis on site size (i.e. in most cases extent) as a basic criterion for the interpretation of survey data on a regional level, even though establishing site-type thresholds is a more controversial matter.[41] There is, of course, a variety of models with which to assess the role(s) of individual sites in their contemporary regional contexts, in relation to site hierarchies based on factors such as size or function, resources or transport.[42] In the case of the Early Iron Age and early Archaic mainland, however, the state of preservation and excavation of early levels in most continuously occupied centres (Patras or Larisa being good examples)[43] makes it impossible to determine absolute area (and in later times the best guide is often the wall circuit). Even where sites were abandoned with only limited reoccupation, as Nichoria, constraints are imposed either by post-depositional processes or the resources available for research.[44] Yet it is usually possible, allowing for different regional contexts and research strategies, to make a subjective identification of big sites, and focusing on broad-brush issues of scale permits the inclusion of a more extensive body of evidence from all parts of the Greek world, rather than just the few better preserved or more fully excavated cases.

Nonetheless, it is worth stressing that insights gained from this line of enquiry can enhance our knowledge even of supposedly well-known sites, as the case of Corinth shows. Despite the wealth of physical evidence from the city centre from the sixth century onwards,[45] our knowledge of settlement in earlier centuries is as patchy as at most of the other sites considered here, and the location of certain key features (notably the Greek agora) has yet to be determined.[46] (Figure 2.4) Corinth is the only settlement in the Corinthia to have been continuously occupied from the Late Bronze Age onwards, although to judge mainly from the evidence of isolated and usually single period grave groups, other (probably small) sites must have existed at various times. Indeed, while little of the region has been intensively surveyed, Geometric surface finds from both intensive and extensive research are rare, and it seems that contrary to the general principle that the expansion of big sites was accompanied by increased evidence from the countryside (see Chapter 4), in the Corinthia the eighth century saw perhaps the strongest concentration of settlement at one main site.[47] There can be little doubt that, by contrast with the Late Bronze Age pattern of plural local centres, Corinth was the focus of regional settlement from Submycenaean times onwards, although it was centrally located neither in relation to previous, Bronze Age settlement (a role which may have been filled by the Isthmian shrine) nor to the territory of the Corinthia and its road system (the centre of

BIG SITES AND PLACE IDENTITIES

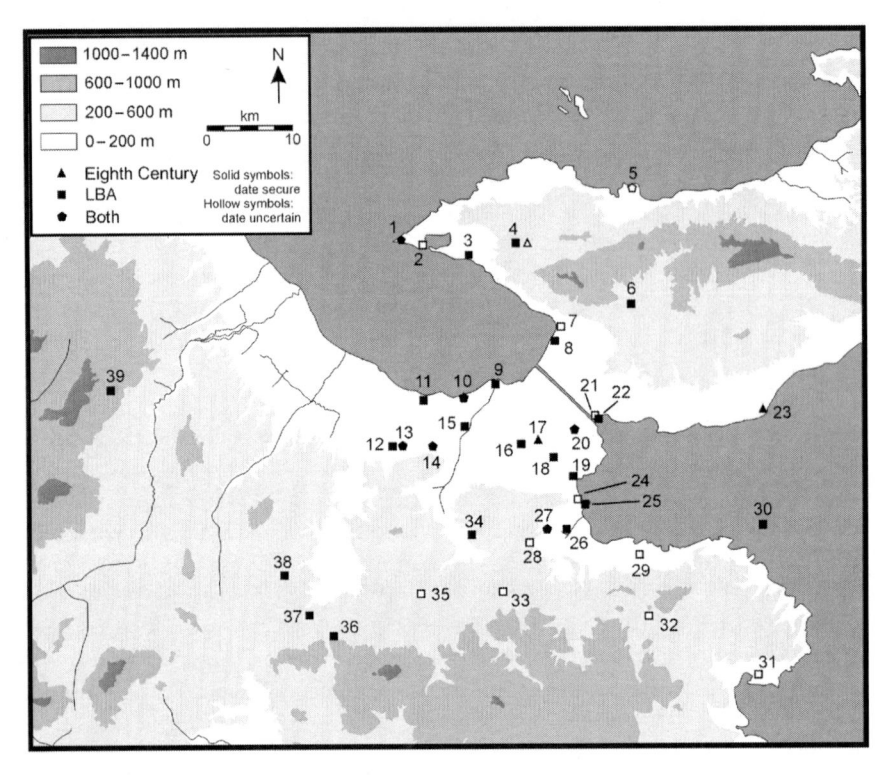

Figure 2.4 Late Bronze Age and eighth-century settlement in the Corinthia (C.L. Hayward).

Key:
1. Perachora Heraion
2. Vouliagmeni
3. Perachora Skaloma
4. Ag. Dimitrios
5. Schoinos
6. Ag. Kyriaki
7. Loutraki
8. Aspro Chomata
9. New Corinth
10. Korakou
11. Ag. Gerasimos
12. Aetopetra
13. Mylos Cheliotou
14. Corinth
15. Arapiza
16. Gonia
17. Perdikkaria
18. Kromna
19. Kenchreai
20. Isthmia
21. Diolkos
22. Kalamaki
23. Ag. Theodoroi/Krommyon
24. Loutra Elenis
25. Chersonesos
26. Kato Almyri
27. Solygeia
28. Brielthi
29. Katakali
30. Evraionisos
31. Korphos
32. Tourla
33. Athikia/Ag. Nikolaos
34. Alamannos
35. Chiliomodi
36. Ag. Triadha
37. Zygouries
38. Kleonai
39. Gonoussa

which lies closer to Kromna, settled perhaps from Geometric times onwards).[48] Even following the foundation or expansion of other substantial settlements through the Archaic period, such as those at Kromna and Krommyon,[49] there is no clear evidence, in the form of other ethnics, that Archaic and Classical inhabitants of the region as a whole saw themselves as other than Corinthians. The earliest reasonably secure local ethnic (Agathon Kromnites) dates to the second half of the fourth century. The only possible earlier example, an inscription naming Timos Teneos on the lip of an Attic black-figure band cup of *c*.540–530 from Sellada on Thera, could be a genitive patronymic, and the identification of the script as Corinthian is controversial.[50]

The development of the settlement at Corinth is therefore of some interest. (Figure 2.5) Compared with Late Bronze Age activity, pre-eighth-century settlement, represented by graves, sherd scatters and wells, contracted into key nuclei of long-term significance. These followed the lines of long-established roads and the scattered springs created by the limestone geology of the area, on to the marine terrace, around the so-called Lechaion Road valley and up towards Acrocorinth and the area of the later sanctuary of Demeter and Kore.[51] (Figure 2.6) Not only did the level of activity at these locations increase during the eighth century, with the provision of facilities such as terracing in the area of the Sacred Spring and below Peirene which created new building space, and drainage at the head of the so-called Lechaion Road valley, but settlement expanded into areas such as the Potters' Quarter and the Panayia Field.[52] Even allowing for limits of excavation, it seems clear that residential zones were being created either completely anew or after long gaps in activity. And here the choice of the relatively northerly but prominent Temple Hill for a new shrine and probably also the first temple is interesting (the earliest votives here date to the late eighth century, with temple construction *c*.680).[53] (Figure 2.7) The settlement thus consisted of localized clusters of activity, physically closer to each other than to any other Corinthian site and therefore likely to be interrelated, and presumably with some principles governing proximal residence. This is hardly a primitive or random agglomeration, even though Corinth does not conform to the supposedly advanced levels of planning inferred at certain of her colonies – indeed here as at most early colonizing centres, both topography and inherited social conditions make such comparison inappropriate.[54] The eighth-century expansion raises questions of the processes by which new residents came to be accepted or rejected in particular areas, or existing groups came to divide. The old kin ties of the traditional village may thus have become increasingly important and controversial points of residential closure.[55]

In seeking signs of supra-communal organization attention has focused on the expanding network of Corinthian sanctuaries (at Corinth itself, Perachora, Isthmia and Solygeia). While stress has been placed on shrine location as an

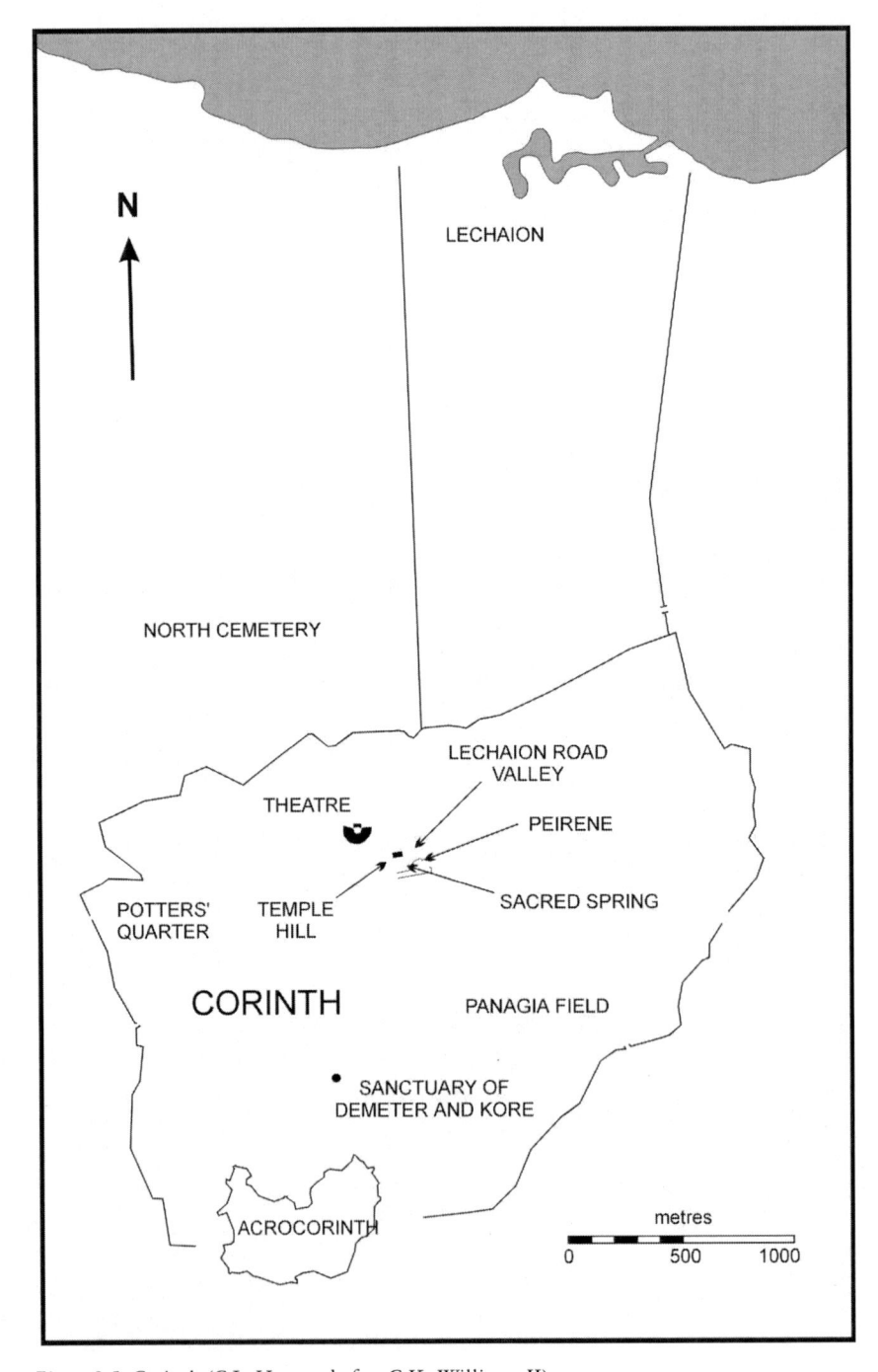

Figure 2.5 Corinth (C.L. Hayward after C.K. Williams II).

Figure 2.6 Corinth: Acrocorinth from above the west end of the Roman forum (photo: author).

Figure 2.7 Temple Hill from the Acrocorinth road (photo: author).

aspect of the social and political definition of Corinthian territory, it is interesting to note that settlement expansion at Corinth coincided with the clearest expression of social roles, by gender, wealth and status, in the votive record of each shrine.[56] Considering the burial record, while the evidence does not support the idea that from MGII onwards Corinthians chose to bury their dead in new extra-mural 'citizen' cemeteries, within the North Cemetery the grouping of graves around a Middle Helladic tumulus which was respected into the Classical period may suggest focus upon an 'ancestral' monument.[57] In short, while we have only outline evidence for settlement structure and lack the architectural evidence with which to make comparison between nuclei, the basic dynamics of settlement expansion raise complex social questions which could easily be overlooked were one to focus simply on formal planning and monuments.

One further aspect of the growth of big sites concerns their impact upon the surrounding countryside. As noted, this can be perceived in terms of scheduling access to subsistence resources, and at Corinth the position of the settlement on the marine terraces, between the coastal plain and the uplands around Acrocorinth, left ample scope for this. The case of Corinth, however, highlights the further demands that a big site may make on the local landscape. Clay, woodland, water and other basic resources will be considered later in this chapter, but increased building activity raises the question of control of, and access to, stone for public construction, at least from the second half of the eighth century and the earliest surviving sarcophagi and worked architectural members.⁵⁸ On one hand this is a basic resource, but on the other, it is potentially exceptional in its ability to raise the prestige of those who could mobilize it for the enhancement of the main settlement and sanctuaries (Figures 2.8, 2.9). Arguably, stone in eighth-century and Archaic Corinth had the highest social and economic conversion value of any natural resource, in turn highlighting the depth and variety of ways in which settlement expansion was embedded in control of the land. As has often been stressed, the 'urban' and the 'rural' were poles of a continuum,⁵⁹ but for much of our period, the interconnection between the two was greatly affected by site size, being potentially more complex at a larger site like Corinth than a smaller like Krommyon.

Corinth, although considered here in some detail, is hardly untypical. Early Iron Age Athens is largely reconstructed from burial evidence, with clusters of graves mostly focused along the lines of main roads, notably those through the Classical agora and Kerameikos, and that leading out from modern Syntagma Square towards Evangelismos.⁶⁰ (Figures 2.10, 2.11) At Argos too, a mixture of rescue excavation and systematic exploration of the Classical agora has revealed a pattern of distinct Early Iron Age house clusters and associated graves over an area of some 50 ha at the foot of the Aspis and Larisa hills. A few of these date back to Protogeometric times, but evidence for complete continuity of occupation either of individual structures or clusters is rare, perhaps because, with the exception of the Charadros to the north and east which floods seasonally, there were no major

Figure 2.8 Oolitic limestone quarry at Mavrospelies (photo: C.L. Hayward).

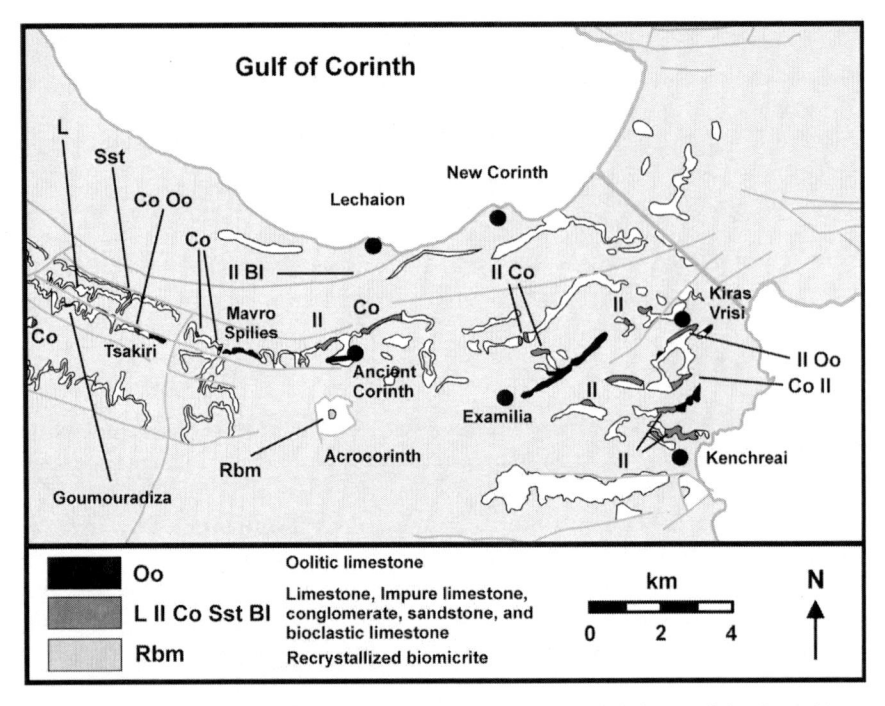

Figure 2.9 Principal quarries for building material in the main lithologies of the Corinthia (C.L. Hayward: reproduced from *Corinth* XX by permission of the American School of Classical Studies at Athens).

constraints on localized movement. The settlement expanded markedly during Late Geometric, and here both the greater quantity and quality of (notably architectural) evidence in comparison with Corinth permits two additional observations. First, while there was an overall growth in settlement density, this appears to have been significantly greater in central than in southern areas, and it seems likely that social factors may have had a marked effect in determining desirable residence location. Second, there was a complex relationship between burial and settlement history. By the Late Geometric period, Argos had at least three organized cemeteries plus individual tombs and tomb clusters within settlement areas. The latter are particularly interesting, since while some plots were consistently used for burial (sometimes surrounded by periboloi), others were successively used through the Early Iron Age for burial and settlement, a complex situation which raises questions concerning perception and 'ownership' of the dead. Were the dead who were buried close to, or even under, particular structures the 'ancestors' of later residents, and if not, how were they perceived?[61]

Whatever changes in complexity and managerial needs took place within the expanding big sites of the later eighth and seventh centuries, mainland

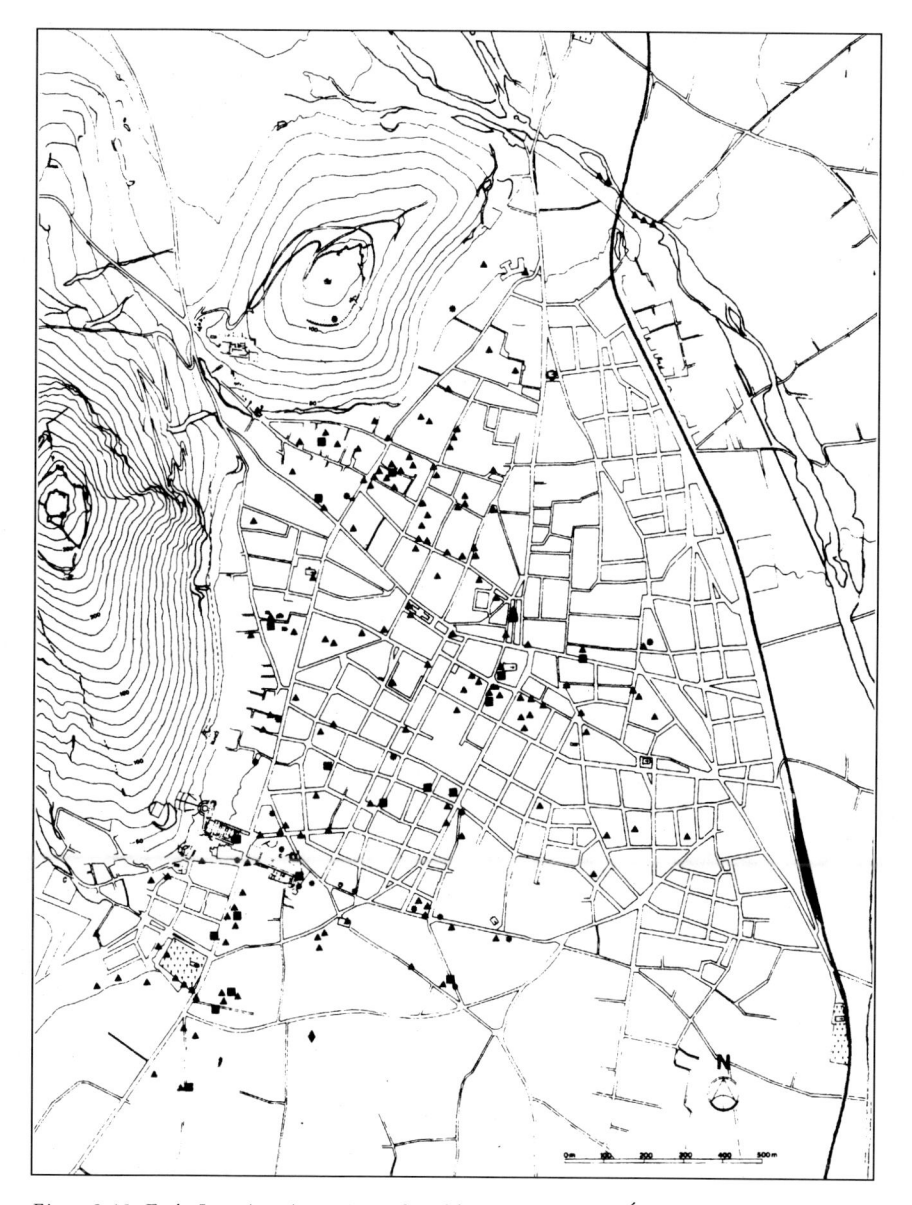

Figure 2.10 Early Iron Age Argos (reproduced by courtesy of the École française d'Athènes).
Note: triangles=tombs, squares=settlement traces.

settlements at least have produced strikingly little evidence for organized public space before the late seventh or sixth century (and even much-cited cases elsewhere, such as Lato on Crete, are susceptible of alternative interpretations).[62] In many cases (Corinth, Sparta and Pherai included),[63] we are

Figure 2.11 Modern Argos from the Larisa: with the exception of the agora area, seen close to the centre of the image, the information conveyed in Figures 2.10 and 2.12 comes from the rescue excavation of individual plots within this conurbation. (photo: author).

hampered by a lack of excavation in key areas. But in the rare instances like Argos and Athens where evidence is relatively plentiful, there is nothing to suggest that early activity in those areas later developed as agoras was public in character. (Figure 2.12) At Argos, for example, the agora area, flanking an important crossroads in the heart of the early settlement, was surrounded by houses and wells into the seventh century,[64] and workshops remained concentrated in this area in Archaic and Classical times, a situation akin to that of the Athenian Kerameikos/agora. The first evidence of public activity in the area comes in the late seventh or early sixth century with the beginning of activity at a number of shrines (the Aphrodision in the southwest, for example), followed during the sixth century by the laying of a thick fill to consolidate the agora surface, a strong hint that it was intensively used. Even so, there is little evidence for public building before the late sixth or early fifth century, thus fitting the wider mainland pattern for all but temples.[65]

In Athens, Early Iron Age burials in the area of the late Archaic and Classical agora are well known, and the long sequence of wells containing debris of pottery production and metalworking points to a focus of manufacturing activity[66] (Figure 2.13). The pace and nature of the process by which this area acquired public functions remains ill-understood. Attention has focused on the decline in burials and the closure of wells *c.*700 as

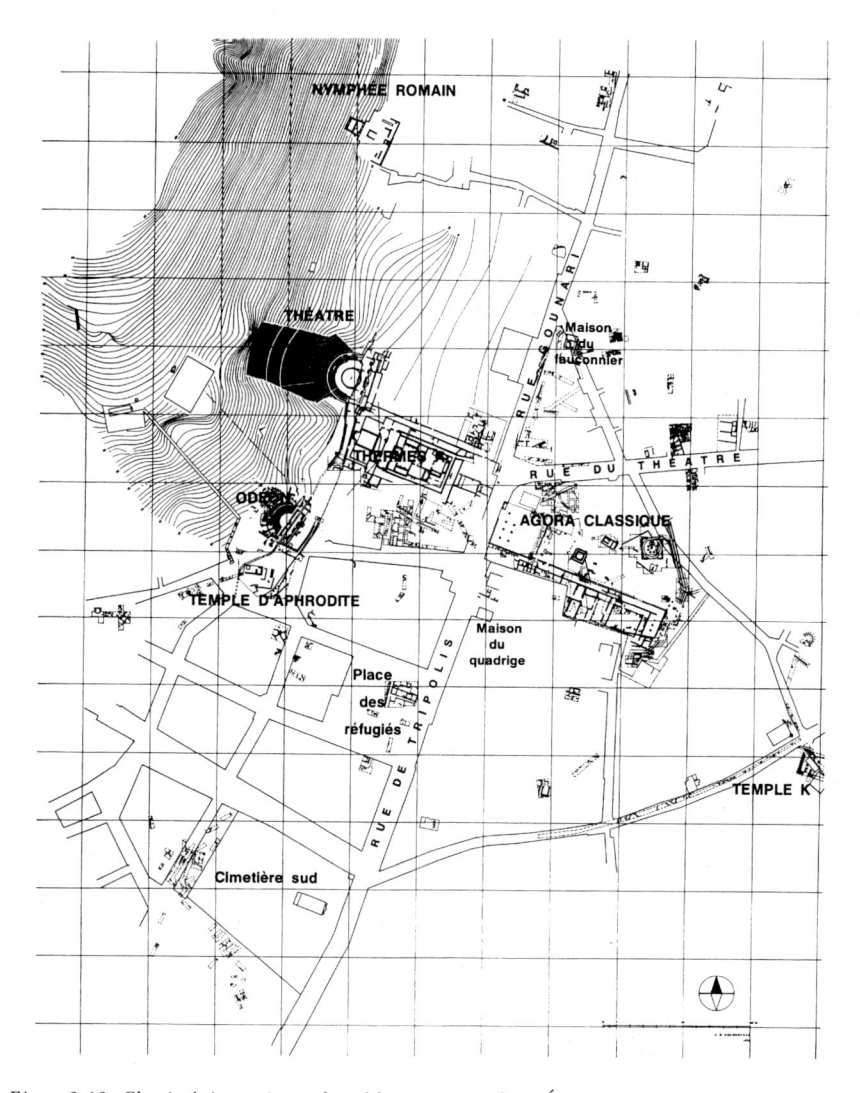

Figure 2.12 Classical Argos (reproduced by courtesy of the École française d'Athènes).

evidence for a shift in settlement and the creation of public space,[67] and in most cases the deposits of potters' debris do not continue into the eighth century (although a seventh-century kiln has been found in Building A).[68] Yet overall this change is less abrupt than sometimes implied, and should be considered in the wider context of settlement morphology and the location of workshop activity. Indeed, the growing importance of the road system through the Eridanos valley following the systematic development of the port of Piraeus and Athenian domination of Eleusis has been highlighted as

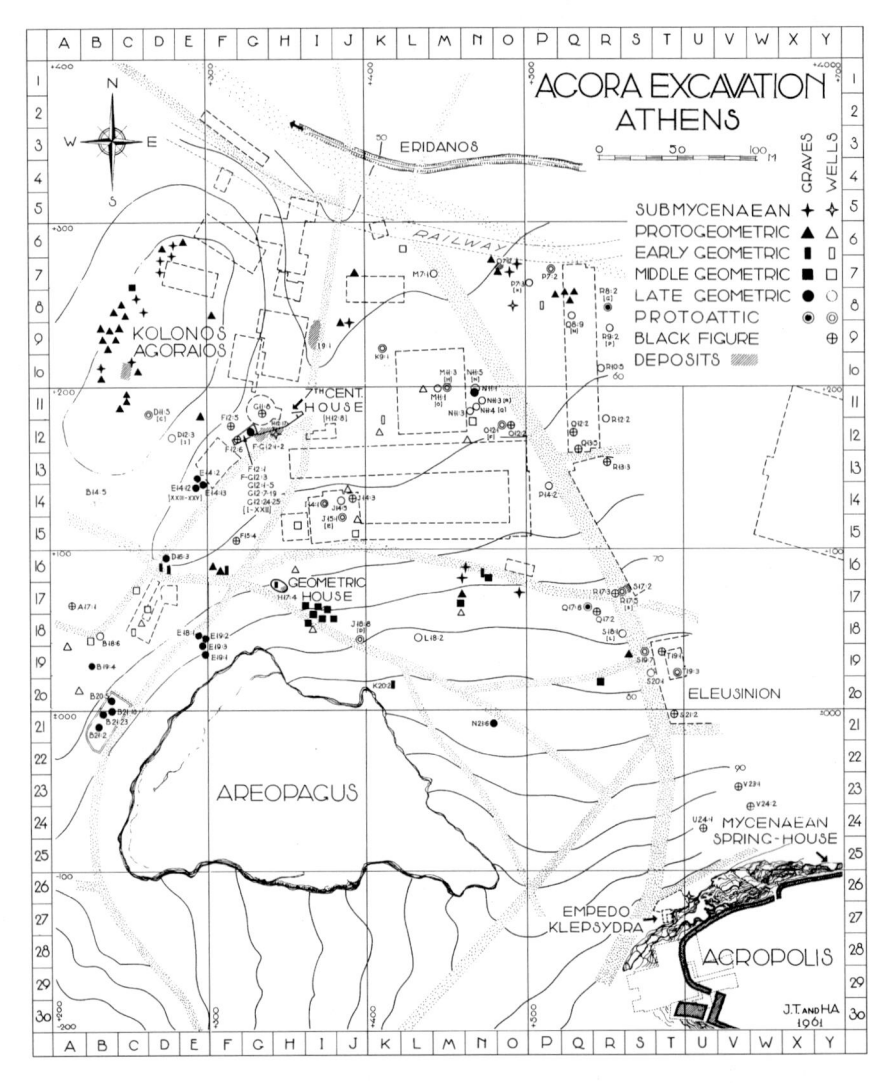

Figure 2.13 Athens agora: Submycenean to early Archaic (American School of Classical Studies at Athens: Agora Excavations).

an important factor.[69] Current evidence points to the second half of the sixth century as the likely date of the canalization of the Eridanos and the filling of the valley in the north-west corner of the later agora to increase the space available for public gatherings. This was a major undertaking, paralleled in date and nature at Argos and perhaps also the forum romanum, and preceded by similar treatment of open assembly areas at Greek sanctuaries (see for example, pp. 119, 122, 132).[70] Especially in the flatter southern part of the agora, activity continued at least to c.600, although remaining evidence consists largely of what may be private well shafts.[71] (Figure 2.14) Indeed, both John Camp and T. Leslie Shear treat the emergence of the agora as a civic centre as a gradual process, while emphasizing the sixth century as the key phase of monumentalization. The Southeast Fountain House was constructed during the second half of the century, although claims of public status for Building C (of the first quarter of the century) followed by Building F (soon after 550) have been disputed (with greater force in the former case). The benchmark for the existence of formal public space must be the erection of boundary stones (at the earliest c.500) and the establishment of the Altar of the Twelve Gods by the younger Peisistratos in 522–521 (Thucydides 6.54–5), which implies a clear perception of the agora as the physical heart of the political community.[72]

Figure 2.14 Athens, agora c.500 BC (American School of Classical Studies at Athens: Agora Excavations).

BIG SITES AND PLACE IDENTITIES

Debate about the location of an earlier agora in Athens, predating that of Classical times, as of many key Archaic public structures, has raged for decades. (Figure 2.15) The Aglaureion inscription is often taken as confirmation that the old agora lay somewhere to the north-east of the acropolis,[73] but we lack direct evidence to assess by how far it may have predated the formalization of its Classical successor. Setting aside this debate, however, and focusing simply on the wider issue of perceptions of public space within the community, the present record indicates a gap of between one and two centuries between large-scale settlement expansion and the provision of built facilities for at least some of the institutions that emerged, a gap which echoes the physical development of sanctuaries discussed in the next chapter. Indeed, in the case of Athens, it seems clear that the acropolis (which, unlike those of Corinth and Argos, was both well watered and readily accessible) served as the earliest physical focus of the community. There is evidence of continuous occupation here in the form of Submycenaean graves

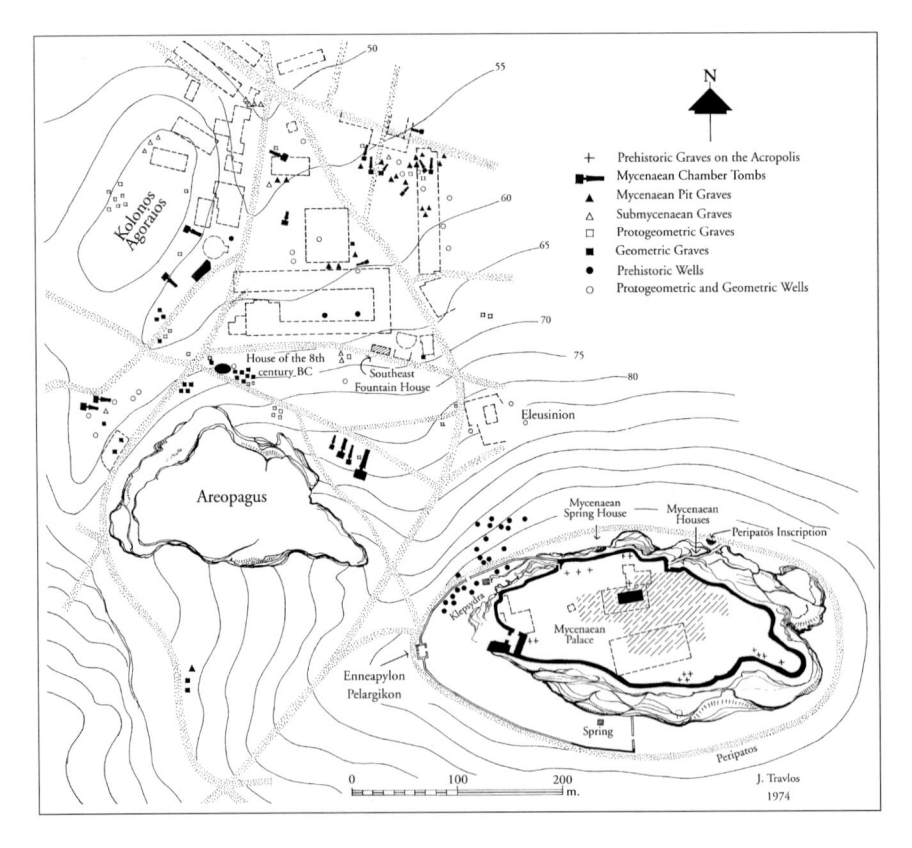

Figure 2.15 Early Athens (American School of Classical Studies at Athens: Agora Excavations).

followed by a pottery sequence which (during the eighth century) includes a number of distinctive Dipylon style vessels with funerary scenes; cult activity is securely attested (notably by tripod dedications) by the second half of the eighth century.[74] A seventh-century cult building has been suggested, largely on the basis of a metope-like plaque by the Nettos Painter and less precisely datable stone column bases, but a more secure date for the beginning of monumental religious construction is provided by the earliest, sixth-century, tiles and architectural terracottas.[75] The construction and repair of the Dromos is recorded in three inscriptions from the acropolis beginning in 566–565,[76] and in general, there are parallels to be drawn between the chronology of monumental building and sculpture on the acropolis and in the Classical agora.[77]

While the nature and date of agora development may seem a rather specialized argument in the context of the broader framework advocated so far, I dwell on it to emphasize that there is no reason to assume that categories of evidence of later importance are being missed within our more inclusive approach. Indeed, while one might see a chronological benchmark in the view attributed by Herodotos to Cyrus of Persia (1.153) that, 'I have never yet feared men who have a place set apart in the midst of their city where they perjure themselves and deceive each other', there is little physical evidence to suggest that such formal space was of any great antiquity by Cyrus' time.

Place identities

In most of our chosen regions, archaeological evidence for a relatively stable structure of big settlements long predates politicized supra-regional consciousness. That Arkadia should be perceived as the weakest case[78] is ironic given that Aristotle (*Politics* 2.2) distinguished the Arkadian ethnos with its poleis from ethne settled *kata komas*. (Figure 1.11) In Achaia, with the exception of the two inland *mere* of Pharaees and Tritaees (discussed further in Chapter 4), there is more or less continuous occupation at most major settlements which have been investigated to any significant extent, notably Aigion and Aegira, Boline which was later a deme of Patras, and perhaps also Rhypes (although excavation here has until recently been limited).[79] Here too, expansion into major centres with monumental public building was a feature of the sixth century and later. We lack direct evidence for the polis identity of Achaian communities before the later fifth century at the earliest,[80] but the existence of these settlements raises the interesting and problematic issue of the relationship between perceived political status and the earlier communities of place which may be inferred from the archaeological record. To what extent is it legitimate to retroject the later significance of particular settlements as polis centres when faced with continuity of occupation though the Early Iron Age,[81] especially given the well-documented changes in the physical form of known polis towns between the Archaic and Hellenistic periods?[82] From a philological point of view, Hansen has suggested that certain rarer meanings of the term 'polis' in later sources are likely to be of some antiquity (polis as a stronghold, for example, noting its survival as a place name, as that of the Ptolis acropolis in Mantineia, Figure 2.16).[83] But whether this remained a constant (let alone widespread) usage is impossible to assess. Taking a more general view of the relationship between poleis and ethne however, it is clear (as emphasized in the previous chapter) that far from being primeval systems within which poleis developed relatively late, the vast majority of Greek ethne developed around a pre-existing structure of local centres. It is therefore highly likely that these big sites were important focal points for individual and group identity. Whether such identification also operated at lower levels, focused on lesser communities in local hierarchies, raises the problematic question of the nature of the politicization of residence patterns, and especially the reality of the widespread deme and *kome* organizations described by later sources (notably Strabo), a point to which we will return in Chapter 4.[84]

It is also worth noting a related point in the longstanding and much wider debate about the chronology and nature of polis development. It is hardly controversial to observe that understanding the long-term process and effects of interactions between the Greek world and the Near East relies upon bridging the artificial divide between the Bronze and Iron Ages, and moving beyond a focus on eighth-century change.[85] Various local political communities within these wider areas show mid to long-term patterns of social development which differ in pace and nature, yet were interlinked by contacts operating at different levels with different degrees of frequency and answering to different needs. There is thus huge scope for the transmission, reception and transformation of cultural and political ideas by whatever

Figure 2.16 Mantineia: the Ptolis acropolis (photo: author).

means at different times and in different places, depending on immediate conjunctions of circumstances. Yet it is harder to argue that the polis should be seen as a phenomenon of the immediate post-palatial period (or even earlier) without strong qualification.[86] Many of those who place the origins of the polis in the eighth century rightly emphasize the necessity of understanding attendant changes in the context of preceding circumstances.[87] But whether one chooses to place poleis in the twelfth or eighth century (or neither – perhaps on the grounds that 'the birth of the polis' is itself a red herring), any communities which it is deemed appropriate on whatever grounds to call poleis in 1200 are inherently unlikely to be the same by 700. One cannot 'explain' a phenomenon by pushing back its perceived roots and making time alone a causal variable.[88]

Economics, subsistence and production

The expansion of settlement at often pre-existing big sites from the eighth century onwards clearly had the potential to enhance their role as focal points for the construction of personal or group identity. But is it possible to go further and detect specific functions or activities conducted within big sites which could complement the place identity constructed by residence? An obvious starting point is the economic base, especially in relation to agricultural production. The expectation that the whole community, including those living in settlement centres, would, barring crop failure, be able to feed itself from its territory is well documented and at least during our period uncontroversial. This is not to imply the Weberian economic model of the consumer city (as opposed to the Medieval/Early modern producer city) where the hinterland serves merely as supplier, since, as has often been pointed out, even in the case of Athens this argument cannot be sustained until the latter part of the fifth or fourth century at the earliest.[89] Assessing the proportion of the working population engaged in primary economic activities is equally anachronistic. Indeed, as Foxhall has highlighted, the problem should rather be approached from the agricultural 'bottom' up, considering big sites as developments within the productive landscape exploited by all its residents. And as she among others notes, by the Archaic period land divisions based upon what could be ploughed by a household in a day were used across a spectrum of exploitation, from settlement plots to agricultural holdings.[90]

Considering the hierarchy of services provided in relation to other settlements in a region may seem more promising, but here too this cannot be an absolute judgement since there is no evidence that big sites should be regarded as *the* primary units for economic discussion during our period. While Finley emphasized the divide between the economic and political functions of the ancient city and questioned whether the city was an appropriate category of economic analysis in antiquity, his attempts to identify urban types in relation to their economic role largely draw on later evidence.[91] His ideal ancient city was the fifth-century polis, and he dealt neither with the origins and earlier development of cities nor with 'urban' development as a process.

In pre-Classical times it is clear that specialist craft activities were not *exclusively* located within big settlements. The activities of itinerant metalworkers are well documented, notably at shrines (see Chapter 3), and there are also early literary hints of rural workshops. The physical setting of the smithy which Hesiod describes as a wintertime *lesche* (*Works and Days* 493–4) is not described, but the fact that the countryman is instructed to pass by and forego its pleasures implies that it was readily accessible, perhaps sited to satisfy continuing needs for fuel and water. More explicitly, the iron offered as a prize at the funeral games of Patroklos (*Odyssey* 23.826–35) is praised as providing five years' supply for the victor, however remote his fields, thus saving his shepherd or ploughman the journey into town. This picture of craftsmen based on or near rural landholdings complements that of itinerant working not merely in rounding out the more limited impressions gained from archaeology, but in reinforcing the point that, depending on the technology involved, craftsmen had some choice about where they worked. The decision to locate workshops in or near big settlements thus reflects a form of identification with the nature and demands of large communities that could have a long term reflexive effect upon perceptions of the role of such sites.[92]

Even allowing for the biases generated by the nature of excavated sites, it is clear that the physical concentration of consumers concomitant with settlement expansion (and indeed, building activities themselves) did affect the location of certain production sites where choice was possible. With the exception of activities such as metal or stone extraction which were governed by the location of resources (although in the latter case at least, optimal conjunction of use and resource location must have been desirable), evidence from the mainland as a whole shows that potters' kilns and metalworking establishments were regularly found at major settlements, even if they are located on their fringes (alongside roads or by cemeteries, for example).[93] There is no clear geographical or chronological trend to be detected, although admittedly the quantity of evidence is small. Instances include a potters' kiln from Dodona dated to the Protogeometric period by Dakaris and associated with a pre-sanctuary settlement, the eighth-century kiln on Terrace V at Torone which lies on the edge of a disused cemetery and constitutes important evidence for settlement continuity, and the seventh-century kilns from the settlements at Miletos (Kalabaktepe) and Ephesos.[94] There are indeed sites, notably in central Athens, where substantial areas were given over to workshops, usually located close to water and major roads, and housing more than one type of production (the symbiosis of pottery and metalworking, for example, reflects shared needs). But production centres almost certainly existed in relation to other population concentrations in Attica too (e.g. at Thorikos and Marathon), even though these tend to be defined on the basis of style and/or distribution rather than production debris.[95] Within the Euboian sphere, evidence from Oropos is particularly striking, but Early Iron Age metalworking is also attested at Lefkandi and Eretria.[96] In Messenia there is good evidence from Nichoria, and a Geometric 'industrial area' (perhaps for silverworking) lies within the main settlement area of Argos.[97] If direct mainland evidence for the location of production is slight, there is a notable increase through the Archaic period, and in the context of this present study it is interesting to note the existence of bronzeworking at Pherai by the sixth century and a potters' kiln at Aigion of $c.600$.[98]

Overall therefore, there is nothing to suggest that towns played a dominant, let alone an exclusive role as specialist production centres, and as will be discussed in the next chapter, Early Iron Age sanctuaries were major centres of production and consumption. Nonetheless, with the expansion of often long-established settlements and a shift in the focus of markets, the articulation of production within individual regions almost certainly became more complex through our period, and producers' responses to the growing needs of population concentrations probably enhanced the interrelated perceptions of production as an urban phenomenon and big sites as centres of manufacturing. Clearly, this will merit closer investigation case by case as more evidence becomes available.[99]

Political statements in big sites

Central to perceptions of the role of big sites within the changing political circumstances of the eighth to sixth centuries is the extent to which they served as 'political' entities, either in terms of the location of government or of ideological institutions like communal cults. Max Weber's discussion of the city, which sets the polis as an ideal into the context of the development of occidental cities, emphasizes the separation of state organization and political discourse from the traditional skills of community life, and thus places great emphasis on distinctive developments within city centres.[100] Emile Durkheim, by contrast, saw no absolute divide between public and private activity, and argued that the political institutions of the ancient city should be understood in terms of the totality of forms of social interaction.[101] These two approaches give rise to very different expectations of city centres as political arenas, and thus the pace and form of their physical development. From an archaeological viewpoint, Weber's approach implies the existence of cities capable of being studied as entities in their own right (or even in isolation, although comparison has the advantage of highlighting the focus of functions in relation to the whole community). Durkheim's approach, however, demands consideration of the entire spectrum of sites within a region.[102] The latter may seem better suited to the Early Iron Age and Archaic data available from most regions, but whichever model one prefers, our understanding of the process of physical adaptation to certain functions (i.e. monumentalization in the widest sense) inevitably rests on the much smaller data set which results from the chances of urban excavation.

As noted, present evidence suggests that the monumentalization of civic space on the mainland, be it via formal levelling and demarcation of assembly areas or the construction of city walls,[103] was largely a sixth-century phenomenon. Such constructions may serve as benchmarks for the ideas which they embody, but how much further back those ideas go is usually unclear. As with the location of workshops, however, the emergence of other forms of public monument may suggest a growing attraction exerted by the expansion of population concentrations. In the case of temples, location inside or beyond major settlements depended entirely on the emphasis placed on the sanctuary in question (and rare as they were on the mainland before the very end of the sixth century, stoas too tend to be associated with shrines, as at Argos or on the Sparta acropolis).[104] Here it is interesting to note both the different locations chosen for monumental building (a rural shrine in the case of Aigion's sanctuary at Ano Mazaraki, for example, whereas at Corinth, the temple at the newly established shrine on Temple Hill slightly, but significantly, predates that at the long-established sanctuary of Poseidon at Isthmia), and the range of functions served by temples over and above their existence as votives. These issues will be pursued in greater detail in the following chapter, and here I merely note that there is no obvious geographical pattern to the choices made, and much seems to depend on where the dedication would make the most conspicuous point about group values and the wealth consumed in their expression. One might follow François de Polignac in concluding that this presupposes the existence of a political community which perceived, in however haphazard a fashion, all the urban and rural shrines within its territory as forming a system within which priorities for, and modes of, investment were determined.[105] This certainly implies a form of expression of social power which could produce monumental construction at those big sites which held relevant shrines, but it is not necessarily a direct reflection of the perception of big sites per se in the eyes of those who exercised that power.

In this light, it is worth digressing briefly to note two instances where a state-political function has been claimed for mainland Greek shrines. At Pallantion in Arkadia, Temple A (one of a very unusual complex of four cult buildings on the acropolis discussed in the following chapter, Figure 3.22) has been likened to a bouleuterion temple chiefly on the grounds of its internal hearth and the large capacity of its undivided cella. Yet if the association with cult implies a perception of the main communal sanctuary as the proper place for political meetings, the position of the complex as a whole on the acropolis is interesting, and at the risk of speculating on slight evidence, may bring together the aspects of religious sanction and the politics of big settlement in an evocative and unusual fashion for the mainland (and here compare the discussion of legal inscriptions later in this chapter).

At the vast majority of sites where they have been identified, bouleuteria, as other buildings designed to house specific political institutions, are later than our period.[106] The two likely exceptions both belong in sanctuaries. In the case of Delphi, the construction of a bouleuterion, if it is indeed to be dated to the first half of the sixth century, would relate directly to the establishment of the new polis.[107] At Olympia, by contrast, the erection of what is usually termed a bouleuterion during the second half of the sixth century (rapidly followed by the prytaneion early in the fifth) has been taken together with the display of Elean inscriptions at the sanctuary, the fact that Olympian Zeus received fines levied by the Eleans, and the location of production of the supposedly Archaic coinage of Elis, to indicate that the sanctuary was the political centre of the Elean state prior to the synoikism of 471 and the creation of a polis town.[108] (Figure 2.17) This is problematic in many respects. It is hardly surprising that the most prominent regional deity effectively guaranteed laws, among which sacral laws and treaties between Elis and the communities surrounding the sanctuary feature prominently (see p. 80, below).[109] In the case of coinage, as Kraay highlights, the date of the earliest Elean issue (and its very existence before synoikism) is far from clear.[110] The function of both the bouleuterion and the prytaneion is inferred by analogy with later evidence: it may have changed with synoikism, but there is no direct evidence that any political function fulfilled during the late Archaic period went beyond sanctuary administration (a major undertaking in its own right).[111] Most striking, however, is evidence for the Early Iron

Figure 2.17 Olympia: Classical bouleuterion (photo: author).

Age and Archaic development of the settlement at Elis accrued from the limited excavations conducted to date.[112] Elean bronze legal inscriptions were displayed in the city as well as at Olympia, and the earliest debris of monumental public building (the first of four sima sections recovered) dates back to the first half of the sixth century. In other words, by the time that the Olympia 'bouleuterion' was constructed, the city centre of Elis already boasted one monumental public building probably in the agora area, and others followed soon after the Olympia construction. By the sixth century, the variety of close links with a prominent regional sanctuary such as Olympia is perhaps predictable, as this period saw the beginning of Elean territorial expansion and the subordination of a variety of other communities as *perioikoi* (something which, as Roy has highlighted, may have been most effectively articulated through the sanctuary).[113] In short, the identification of Olympia as the pre-synoikism administrative centre of the Elean state looks increasingly fragile, and it should be emphasized that there is as yet no stronger case to be made elsewhere on the mainland.

Symbols of authority

As the discussion so far has shown, there are several possible approaches to tracing the physical location of different kinds of authority and the contribution of big sites to creating and sustaining individual and community identity. These in turn highlight the complex, and even ambiguous, role played by such sites in relation to, for example, sanctuaries and the authority of deities, or the territories over which different forms of community decision and activity were enacted. Two particular problems draw us directly into these areas of overlap, namely the nature and location of public inscriptions and the issue of coinage. Both were outcomes of a process of elite decision making, and in the case of inscriptions, the strong link with the polis as the issuing authority is present from our earliest extant law on stone, that from the wall of the temple of Apollo Delphinios at Dreros, *c*.650–600.[114] It is very likely that this decision making took place in big sites, but what role did those sites subsequently play in the enactment and display of these decisions? The problem is posed in this way to avoid the anachronistic implications of 'seats of government'. Indeed, it is worth stressing that when one surveys the quite substantial literary and epigraphical record for public offices across the Greek world by the end of the sixth or the early fifth century, relatively few can be securely located as operating within specific settlement centres. At Arkadian Thelpousa, for example, an early fifth-century inscribed sceptre attests to the office of public herald,[115] but other than the obvious need for an audience, we do not know where and how he exercised his duties.

In considering the location of expressions of political power and the constituencies which they governed, law and public decrees and treaties offer significant if complex evidence. Our sample is largely conditioned by the specific role of writing, which was deployed to reinforce the authority of decrees and treaties or to record particular (usually procedural and perhaps contentious) provisions which enhanced or complemented the customary, oral law of a community.[116] Whoever actually administered it, the continuing importance of this customary law is plain. The terms in which Pindar (*Pyth*. 10.69–72) praised the values and conduct of the fifth-century Aleuads are strongly reminiscent of the Homeric *basileis*, part of whose role was to administer justice,[117] and the existence of a formal office of legal remembrancer is first attested on a late seventh-century inscription recording a sacred law from Tiryns.[118] As Rosalind Thomas has emphasized, at least in Archaic times there is no good evidence to suggest that written law was perceived as different in a legal sense. The 'added value' given by writing was rather as a source of power in the face of contention, a point reinforced by the frequency with which sanctions against offenders are left to the gods.[119] In this respect, the act of writing law may be equated with consulting an oracle over a proposed course of action,[120] or bringing in an outside lawgiver (see p. 78, below).

The preserved sample of legal inscriptions is therefore likely to reflect the differing degrees to which contentious issues arose region by region. And while the issues per se are secondary to the argument, they may well have affected the choice of location for the display of a particular inscription. Conversely, it is clear that the absence of this kind of evidence does not imply a simple level (let alone a lack) of legal provision or government agency. It may simply be that such issues did not arise at this time, that they were handled by other means, or that the relevant types of site have not been sufficiently excavated. In the case of Achaia, for example, all three explanations are possible. The diverse and quite small-scale local systems, combined with the ability to relocate implied both by internal movement into Dyme and by western colonization, may have reduced the need for the kind of stabilizing of new and/or newly problematic situations and political relationships that written law provides. In the one likely activity where wider cooperation may be assumed (albeit somewhat early for written agreements), that of western colonization (discussed in Chapter 4), the Delphic oracle was consulted. One might therefore argue that Achaian communities coped perfectly well using customary law and divine sanction. The exception that may prove the rule consists of two fragments of a bronze tablet dating *c*.500–475, on which two extant lines record a fine(?) of one hundred drachmae payable to the temple of 'E. . . . .' (Hermes?), and twenty talents to (or by?) the polis.[121] Jeffery interprets this as the section in a treaty between Lousoi and a neighbouring Achaian city which deals with sanctions against violation. A provenance in such a frontier area would help to explain the Arkadian and Achaian traits of the script, but the attribution specifically to Lousoi rests on a report given when the tablet was seen and copied in

77

Kalavryta, and cannot be regarded as secure. In historical terms, the appearance of a written law concerning relations between communities across what seems to have been the one strongly marked Achaian border, that with Arkadian Azania (see pp. 184–6), would not damage the overall picture. Nonetheless, it must be emphasized that there is an overall shortage of early Achaian inscriptions of any kind, and one likely reason for the lack of public texts is the limited excavation of major settlements and especially sanctuaries.

Given the common attachment of divine sanction to written law, it is worth digressing briefly to consider the figure of the lawgiver, since he embodies enhanced authority conceptually similar to that of a deity, albeit on a lesser scale.[122] Traditions concerning individual lawgivers, occasionally local kings or magistrates (as Solon) but usually outsiders, date back at least to the seventh century.[123] While the greatest number of 'importers of law' are found in Magna Graecia, and Crete in particular was renowned as a source of legal knowledge, individual cases of both kinds are widespread, and involve a number of poleis within important ethne. Aristotle, for example, in his notes on early lawgivers and their actions (*Politics* 2.9.5–9), focuses on the history and training of the lawgivers at Epizephyrian Lokri and the Chalcidian colonies in the west, but also relates the story of the Bacchiad Philolaos of Corinth who was lawgiver in Thebes. Aristotle notes that Philolaos' lover Diocles was an Olympic victor in 728, and thus by implication dates Philolaos to the late eighth or early seventh century (although he bemoans the lack of chronological coherence of early traditions). On at least one and possibly two occasions, Arkadian Mantineia provided lawgivers to other communities. Herodotos (4.161) reports that the Cyrenians, on the advice of Delphi, had Demonax of Mantineia reform their state, re-organizing their tribes and reassigning some of the domains and priesthoods of King Battos III to the people in common. The basis on which the Mantineians chose to send Demonax is not stated; he may have been *basileus*, but Herodotos merely describes him as their most esteemed townsman.[124] The possibility that Mantineians were involved in arbitration closer to home is raised by three fragments of a bronze decree from Olympia dating before 450, written in Elean dialect and perhaps part of a Triphylian law.[125] This set out procedures for the treatment of rebellious Skillountians (with penalties guaranteed by Olympian Zeus), as well as dealing with an issue arising from homicide, and reported that the magistrates involved, the *damiourgoi*, were acting on a Mantineian plan. The implication would seem to be an arrangement to end a period of stasis, put in place perhaps as a result of Mantineian arbitration and guaranteed by the Eleans via Olympia.

To return to the issue of written law, discussion of early evidence has inevitably been dominated by those few regions, Crete in particular (and especially Dreros and Gortyn), which have produced the largest and earliest collections of inscriptions.[126] Yet while there is less evidence from other regions, including the major ethne, and such as we have tends to be late, with all the caveats noted above interesting observations can still be made. Excavation in Arkadia has favoured temple sites, but it is nonetheless interesting to note that the subjects covered in Arkadian inscriptions are not merely the religious issues that one would expect to find at a polis shrine (as, for example, the regulation of c.525 enforcing proper dress for women at a sanctuary of Demeter Thesmophoros, probably at Kleitor or Lousoi),[127] but also show sanctuaries administering what are in some respects civil matters. At Tegea, for example, a bronze inscription of c.450 records the deposit at the sanctuary of 400 minai of silver by a foreigner, Xouthias son of Philachaios, setting out who could reclaim it and when, and naming 'the Tegeans' and the *thethmos* as ultimate arbitrators (the latter presumably the magistrate competent to adjudicate on issues of inheritance).[128] It is hardly surprising that this kind of record should be kept at the place of transaction, but the procedures involved show a close engagement with civic authorities over practical issues.

Conversely, two inscriptions from the city centre of Mantineia show oracles intimately involved in the administration of civil law. The first, found on a column of the bouleuterion and dated c.460–450, refers to the problem of fines for 'blood right' and lists among the authorities involved the oracle of the Horkomotai.[129] At around the same time, an inscription found built into a Byzantine church by the south-east entrance to the ancient agora records the judicial procedure used to try thirteen men involved in a case of murder.[130] The blend of divine and civil authority involved in the actual sentencing here is complex and on present evidence unique. The thirteen indebted to Athena Alea are listed, and the sentence (loss of property and banishment from the sanctuary) is noted as given by divine oracle and by human judgement, and reinforced by a curse. The equal and parallel nature of divine and human judgement is explicit, as for example in lines 14–15 'whoever the oracle may condemn or whoever may be condemned by judgement', or lines 18–19 'if we, the goddess and the judges have judged in the following way' (transl. H. Taeuber), although how this operated in practice is unclear. We know of no sanctuary of Athena Alea at Mantineia and cannot therefore tell whether a copy of the decree was also displayed there, but at the risk of relying on sparse and late information, the location of these two inscriptions in the city centre does suggest a clear perception of the place of civic justice, whatever the role of the divine within it.

In Thessaly, early public inscriptions are few and focused in the eastern part of the region.[131] For at least one, a sacred law of the first quarter of the fifth century believed to be from Atrax,[132] we lack contextual information, but in two other instances, both from Magnesia, the information recorded relates directly to the context in which it is displayed. The earlier, on a stele of the mid-sixth century or slightly later from the precinct of Apollo at Korope, is interpreted by Jeffery as prohibiting removal or misuse of temple utensils.[133] By contrast a stele of c.550 from the acropolis at Nevestiki (perhaps ancient

Orminion or more probably Methone) is a straightforward commemoration of an action (perhaps connected with construction) by one Androkides, plus the provision by one Qolouros during his tenure as judge of a 'roof' (either literally or shorthand for the whole structure) of a (presumably public) building.[134] That such a record should be erected in the city and presumably close to the building in question is predictable.[135] It is more interesting to find legal inscriptions, like the East Lokrian legislation in relation to the settlement of Naupaktos (discussed in the previous chapter), copied and displayed in Lokrian city centres (the extant copy coming from Chaleion).

In short, while the evidence is slender and widely dispersed, the issue of written law highlights the complex relationship between human and divine authority, and a resulting ambiguity concerning the appropriate place(s) of display. It is, however, interesting that mainland communities did not tend to follow the Cretan practice of writing on religious buildings, adding direct physical association to the moral ties given by the broader sanctuary context. A rare exception, Corinth, proves the rule in that the law inscribed on the first temple of Apollo (some while after construction but probably by c.580–570) may be part of a religious calendar.[136] Plainly, therefore, the straightforward notion of the city as the seat of government fails to take account of the way in which the most complex and contentious community issues required a particular construction of authority.[137]

Nowhere on the Archaic mainland is this clearer than at Olympia. While the sanctuary has undoubtedly produced one of our largest collections of late Archaic and early Classical legal inscriptions, the role of the sanctuary in relation to the city of Elis before 471 was, as argued, complex. It is clear that Olympia guaranteed the treaties of foreign states (notably in Magna Graecia), and that several decrees concerned matters specific to the sanctuary (for example, protection of the *theoroi*,[138] treatment of *xenoi*,[139] and the conduct of the Olympian festival, noting that in one late sixth-century decree concerning the festival the political guarantor was probably Elis).[140] Yet issues of direct or indirect concern to the Elean state also feature prominently, including the definition of her borders and those of communities which may have become part of an Elean 'alliance' around 500,[141] and state decisions, some of which were guaranteed by Olympia.[142] And as noted, the discovery of an Archaic legal inscription at Elis shows that at least some public documents were displayed in the city centre. The very different scale of excavation at Olympia and Elis and the corresponding discrepancy in the quantities of evidence available make it impossible to assess the nature of overlap between the two sites, but the very fact of its existence is significant. It is tempting to speculate that the sanctuary might have had two particular, discrete but overlapping, uses for the Eleans, namely to guarantee sanctions in the way widely attested elsewhere, and as a means of helping to articulate relations with other local communities, especially when they entailed implicit or explicit acceptance of Elean dominance.[143]

If the epigraphical record reveals a complex relationship between place communities centred on major settlements and their sanctuaries which reflects the perceived inability of human authority to ensure the effective enactment of public policy in difficult areas, the picture that emerges from the other major state-political creation of the Archaic period, coinage, is also ambiguous. The notion that the right to coin reflects the right to rule, and is thus a statement of sovereignty (noting that this is usually expressed in polis terms) is, as Thomas Martin highlights, both anachronistic and simplistic. Coin issues were rather the direct consequences of political decisions, and since one of their main functions was to guarantee value, they *may* reflect a need to deal with those who were in some way outsiders in the immediate context of the transaction concerned.[144] Coinage therefore reflects sovereignty only in the more limited sense of the ability (not the right) to establish and/or fulfil goals in certain areas of government. In cases of tiered political identity, and especially of poleis within ethne, it is therefore interesting to trace the political level on which the response of coinage was made, and how this may reflect the initial purpose of a particular issue. In some cases, the answer is relatively straightforward. In Achaia, for example, only the issue of *c*.500 attributed to Aigai definitely predates that of the fourth-century league.[145] But in considering the more complex relationships, Thessaly is an obvious starting point, since even though Thessalian issues begin rather later than those of neighbouring regions,[146] there is a substantial body of evidence which suggests a balance between city and wider regional needs (and a range of scholarly views on the nature of that balance).

Coin dates are notoriously difficult to establish, but it seems clear that the earliest issue in Thessaly was that of Larisa (sometime after 500) on the Persian standard. It may be, as Colin Kraay has suggested, that this standard was simply the most convenient, since the Persian empire already encompassed Macedon and Thrace.[147] Thomas Martin, however, goes further in seeing it as evidence that this issue was struck to pay tribute, since Persian custom was to pay in coin, and according to Herodotos, the Aleuads first invited Xerxes into Greece (7.6) and were the first Greeks to surrender themselves to the King (7.130).[148] After the Persian wars, a number of Thessalian cities coined on the Aiginetan standard, and setting aside the unrelated coinage of Pharsalos, two mint groups can be identified: while these have been seen as sequential, we have, as Martin points out, no independent means of establishing their relative chronology.[149] Mint group one, which included Larisa, Krannon (at least initially), the Perrhaibians, Pharkadon, Trikka (perhaps later than the rest of the group), Pherai and Skotoussa, covered much of Thessaly, and produced issues with the same obverse and reverse types.[150] Mint group two, which also produced a uniform type, again included Skotoussa (hence Kraay's suggestion that the city had defected from group one on the establishment of this 'rival'), Methylion and the mint(s) which struck the issue of 'the Thessalians'.[151] In both cases, Kraay saw the shared types as direct evidence that the coinage was federal (with a certain political rivalry between the mint groups): in the latter case, the legend seemed self-explanatory, and in the former, he identified the youth on the obverse as Thessalos. (Figure 2.18) Martin, by contrast, held that neither group's issues need be federal in the political sense, but that their shared appearance and standard reflect their role as a convenient, common medium with which to meet wider regional needs, such as army pay if it was necessary to demonstrate equality of treatment of contingents raised from different cities. Neither Martin nor Peter Franke accept the second group's issues, including the 'Thessalian' coins as by definition federal – Franke on the grounds that we know too little of Thessalian history to answer such questions, and Martin emphasizing that we do not know whether this issue replaced city coinage or supplemented it for certain common needs (although he suggests that its short duration may favour the latter, on the analogy of the Arkadikon coinage discussed below).[152] Clearly, the difference between these approaches lies in the extent to which coinage is seen as a political indicator in own right, rather than as a form of response to a range of possible needs. In the case of ethne, the latter approach offers greater potential for understanding both the level at which decisions to coin were taken and the register of the problems which coinage was intended to solve.

Similar issues arise in the much-discussed case of the Arkadikon coinage. Despite the strength of localized place communities in Arkadia and the relative lack of regional coherence highlighted in the previous chapter, the only securely sixth-century city coinage is that of Heraia, where a series of triobols (or hemidrachms) and obols was minted from c.510–470.[153] The issue of a large series primarily of triobols, plus fewer obols, with the legend Arkadikon and a depiction of Zeus Lykaios on the obverse, followed soon after the Persian war (Figure 2.19), and was interpreted by Williams and

Figure 2.18 Thessaly, mint group 1, obverse showing figure of Thessalos (© The British Museum: reproduced by courtesy of the Trustees of The British Museum).

Figure 2.19 Early Arkadikon issue (© The British Museum: reproduced by courtesy of the Trustees of The British Museum).

subsequently Kraay as a federal Arkadian issue which largely replaced city coinage for much of the fifth-century (until the type ceased soon after 420).[154] Two principal objections to this case may be highlighted. First, as Thomas Heine Nielsen has argued, there is no other sound evidence for a fifth-century Arkadian confederation.[155] Second, as Selene Psoma has stressed, several cities minted their own coinage during the life of the Arkadikon series (namely Psophis, Kleitor, Thaliades and Mantineia – the last from the early years of the fifth century, probably just predating the Arkadikon series), and so the Arkadikon coinage was in some areas a complement to, and not merely a substitute for, city issues.[156] It is therefore interesting to consider how the two categories of coinage might have related, in terms of purpose and/or geography (bearing in mind that the two are not mutually exclusive). The location of the earliest cities to coin independently raises some interesting questions. Heraia, for example, lies in the north-west on the border with Elis, and while it is probably not the city named in the Elean treaty inscription of *c*.500 noted above, it was very likely engaged in cross-border dealings at a time when political relationships and divisions in this wider area were evolving rapidly.[157] Psophis, Kleitor and Thaliades, whose issues were relatively short-lived, all lay in the western part of Azania, a region with a distinct ethnic identity through the Archaic period, and only Mantineia among the prominent and powerful eastern Arkadian cities coined at this stage (most eastern city issues date from *c*.420 at the earliest, after the Arkadikon series).[158] The precise motivation for the Mantineian issue remains unknown, although it is easy to speculate about factors such as trade obligations that might have made coinage advantageous. The imagery used, however, reflects an interesting balance between pan-Arkadian identity and the purely local. On the obverse is a bear, representing Kallisto, mother of Arkas, as transformed by Hera, whereas on the reverse the images of a dolphin or acorn(s) allude to the city's oracular shrine of Poseidon Hippios and the oak forest (Pelasgos) which surrounded it.

If we accept that there was no Arkadian federation in the fifth century and that political power essentially lay in individual cities, the Arkadikon coinage becomes a crucial piece of evidence for the nature of cross-regional collaboration, in that it implies a widely shared need to make a large number of payments at standard rates over a reasonably long period of time. Excluding the earliest and latest phases of the issue, Williams' conclusion that three mints produced the coinage independently (with no traceable die links) has been generally accepted. Yet while it is clearly important to know how these mints relate to those producing city coinage, the question of their location remains unresolved. Williams proposed Kleitor, Tegea and Mantineia on the grounds of iconography and especially these cities' supposed historical importance (reflecting his political interpretation of the coinage), but I concur with critics who have regarded the evidence overall as insufficient and Williams' case as biased by his political-historical standpoint.[159]

We are therefore left with two principal interpretations. The notion of an issue somehow connected to the major festival at the shrine of Zeus on Mt. Lykaion (as implied by the iconography of the obverse) dates back to Head and was recently revived by Heine Nielsen.[160] Such an issue would have been struck either by the sanctuary authorities (although this leaves the problem of the three unconnected die sequences which would have to have operated within a single mint) or, more plausibly, by different cities aspiring to gain *kudos* from the festival. The latter certainly merits consideration since it reflects the coincidence of expansion at the sanctuary and the growing aspirations of individual cities.[161] The second possibility, that of mercenary payment, was proposed by Williams, who saw the coinage as a means of guaranteeing a standard payment for military aid between Arkadian cities.[162] It has been revived most recently by Selene Psoma, who sets the origins of the coinage in the complex military collaborations between Arkadian cities (usually against Sparta) in the period immediately after the Persian Wars, followed, after the battle of Dipaia, by the inclusion of Arkadians (Mantineia excepted) within the Spartan symmachy until the Peace of Nikias.[163] As with the festival hypothesis, individual aspects of the case can be questioned. For example, while triobols fit what we know of mercenary payment (Thucydides 5.47.6), they also complement the denominations of neighbouring Olympia, as Heine Nielsen stresses, and such mutual adjustments between neighbours are not unparalleled; equally, we simply do not know how many (if any) Arkadian city hoplites were paid.[164] Both cases, while attractive, have weaknesses which cannot be addressed on present evidence, but together they serve to highlight the two areas of collaboration most commonly seen as drawing together place communities within ethne before formal federation.

Comparisons are often made between the Arkadikon coinage and other 'ethnic' issues, notably the Phokikon coinage which dates from *c.*510 onwards. Yet here too, caution is required. On one hand, as noted in the previous chapter, the Phokian state is unusual in having a clearly defined ethnogenesis linked to military action, and the generally accepted view that the decision to issue federal coinage was one of the first acts of the new state puts the Phokikon issue on a different political level from the Arkadikon. Indeed, with the exception of a short-lived issue of $c.480$ controversially attributed to Lilaia (and explained by Williams as the result of medizing by a city isolated on the borders of pro-Persian Doris, especially after the Persians had reduced much of Phokis), the fact that it was the only coinage issued for a long while illustrates the dominance of the ethnos as the primary level of identification for most Phokians.[165] On the other hand, as with the Arkadikon coinage, it is important to see the Phokikon issues in terms of their likely practical function and in the context of neighbouring regions. Economic connections with Delphi are likely to have been of particular importance to Phokis, and it is interesting to note that while the first coins of the polis of Delphi date from $c.520$, after $c.480$ they also bear the comparably structured legend 'Dalphikon'.[166]

So far, we have examined the potential of big sites for creating and promoting the forms of association that could add up to a strong place identity. We have also considered the way in which certain phenomena, like written law and coinage, which are often seen as characteristic of the polis if not of urban life, instead highlight problems which could not be managed by city elites in isolation, yet during our period were only rarely handled on a formal federal level. Solutions to these problems thus reveal a complex interconnection of interests between individual cities, peer settlements and religious authority. To conclude this chapter, we will consider a further set of issues surrounding the definition of place identity, making particular reference to evidence from Thessaly which highlights the complexity of potential relationships between a community's social geography and its big sites. Here comparison of the development of big sites with the sociogeography of the *Catalogue of Ships* and archaeological discussion of the long-term evolution of settlement structure and city territories, raises the issue of the physical location of social power, and draws attention to an issue which will be explored further in Chapter 4, namely community territory as a palimpsest of group interests.

Thessaly

In a comparative review of settlement and political ordering in Thessaly, Macedon and Thrace,[167] Zosia Archibald has highlighted the particular problem in these regions of understanding the relationship between large settlements and local and regional power structures. Until relatively recently, it was widely argued that Thessaly was late to develop big sites, with the expansion of most city centres and governmental systems dating to Classical times.[168] But whereas criticism of this position used to rest on the dangers of negative argument from a limited archaeological record, nowadays a more positive approach is based on Early Iron Age and Archaic evidence from a number of major sites which enables us to assess long-term changes in settlement structure, and to relate the physical record to literary evidence for the power structure of Archaic Thessaly.[169] (Figures 1.2, 2.20)

An important strand running through the literary sources is the strong connection between ruling families and particular cities, with big sites like Larisa for the Aleuads or Krannon for the Skopads serving as seats of power and regional centres.[170] The link between aristocratic families, the proper exercise of traditional law, and the city is plain in Pindar's praise for the family of his Aleuad patron, Thorax: 'bearing on high the nomos of the Thessalians they increase it. Ancestral and trusty governance of cities belongs to the aristocrats'

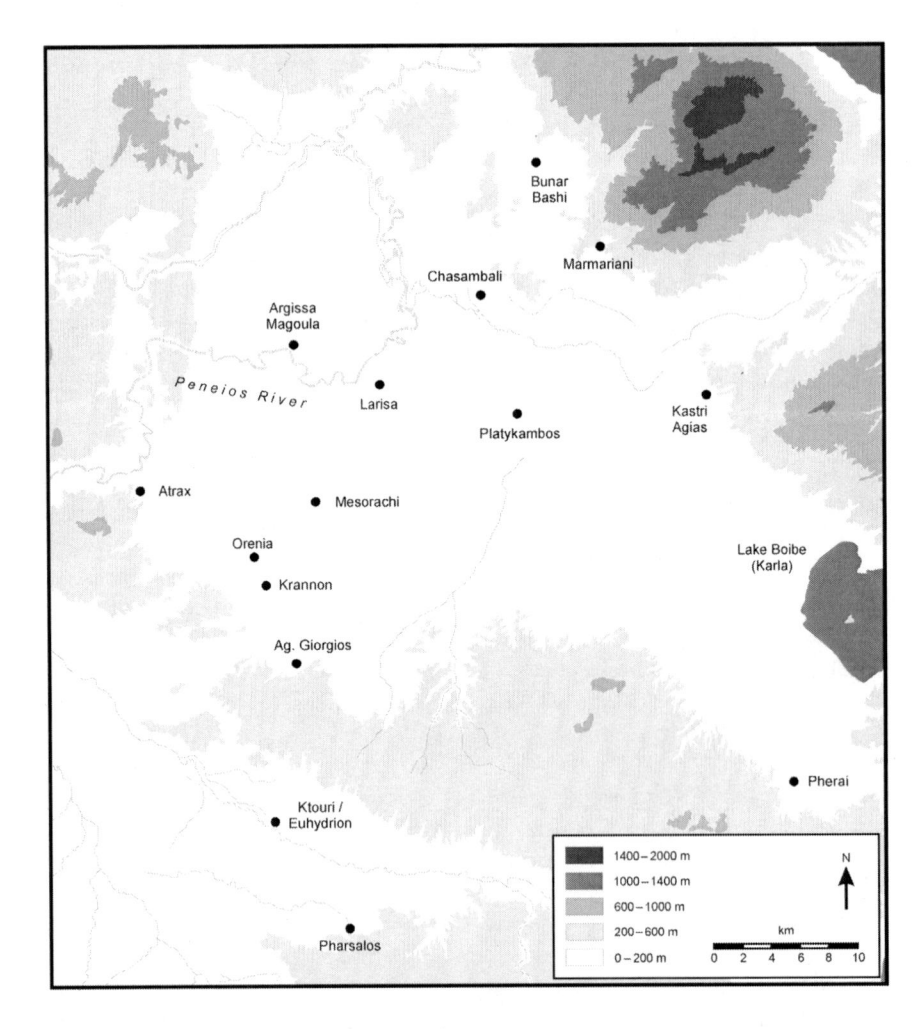

Figure 2.20 Eastern Thessaly (C.L. Hayward).

(*Pyth.* 10.69–72, transl. Sandys). Pindar's reference to poleis in the plural may imply peer systems, in Archibald's words 'a caste of leaders with bases in different cities'.[171] Yet this should not be taken as evidence of strong regional coherence. Sources from the fifth century onwards (as Thucydides 4.78, or Aristotle *Politics* 5.5.9) highlight factional strife between and within aristocratic families, and during the Archaic period a complex network of feuds and alliances frequently transcended the boundaries of Thessaly (most strikingly involving the Peisistratids) and reached its logical conclusion with the Aleuad submission to Persia.[172] Distinctions between cities went beyond the level of aristocratic conduct, with, for example, striking differences in the nature and organisation of cult activity (as discussed in Chapter 3). In short, variation in the long-term development of local centres, and their relationships to their territories and to each other, are key issues for investigation.

By the Archaic period, evidence that Thessalian big settlements were favoured contexts for investment in monumental building or art is as uneven and suggestive as the evidence for political conduct (inscriptions and coinage) discussed above. Temple building will be reviewed in the following chapter. Here I merely note that at least in eastern Thessaly (which has been more thoroughly investigated), while it is not a universal phenomenon and only rarely predates the second half of the sixth century, the choice of locations within large settlements may be more consistent than in much of southern Greece (or indeed in western Thessaly to judge from the sanctuaries at Philia and Metropolis which lie in the *chorae* of their patron cities). To the catalogue of temples may be added two 'Archaic' public structures (temples or stoas) within the shrines at Ktouri (see p. 89 below) and Korope,[173] and the stele of *c*.550 from the acropolis of Nevestiki, (probably ancient Methone) mentioned earlier, which records the actions of Androkides and Qolouros in public building.[174] Furthermore, traces of a possible mid-sixth-century wall round the acropolis at Pharsalos (erected soon after the Echekratidai were established as the ruling family)[175] are a further sign that where fortification was undertaken during the Archaic period, it almost always dates to the sixth century (and in this case one should also note the neighbouring walled site at Palaiokastro Deregkli, ancient Palaipharsalos).[176]

Considering the spread of monumental art, especially sculpture, it is worth emphasizing that although Archaic and early Classical Thessaly was renowned for its wealth (Plato *Meno* 70a-b), surviving evidence suggests that Archaic aristocratic patronage of the arts did not extend in any great measure to sculpture, since neither freestanding nor relief is common until the fifth century. Securely Archaic (rather than Archaizing) pieces tend to date from the latter part of the sixth century onwards and are at present also concentrated in the east, although the likely effects of biases in research are well illustrated by the recent discovery of a sixth-century bronze cult statue of Apollo at Metropolis.[177] Even though Thessaly cannot be compared with Attica or Boiotia, it is interesting to note the existence by the end of the sixth century of a distinctive regional style of (chiefly freestanding) sculpture produced for a relatively localized clientele.[178] The most popular type is the kouros, of which single finds have been made at Latomion (between Velestino and Volos), Skotoussa, Trikka (a kouros or warrior figure) and the area of Volos, and two come from Larisa. The only kore yet found comes from Latomion, although a seated female figure was found by chance at Mataranga near Karditsa.[179] Thereafter, finds become more common, one of the earliest fifth-century pieces being a marble head of a youth (stylistically akin to the Blond Boy) from Skiatha, east of Larisa.[180] Animal statuary is represented by a bull head from Pherai, a lion from Aetolophos-Desianis to the north, and from Demetrias an inscribed base which probably held a sphinx. Unfortunately, few of these pieces have any useful context, and while we have a general idea of their provenance and the location of the workshop's clientele, it is impossible to determine where and why they were erected. Relief sculpture is very rare: funerary stelai are mostly Archaizing rather than Archaic (and increasingly popular through the fifth century),[181] and architectural relief is limited to the mid-sixth-century boar and panther frieze from Dendra near Larisa.[182] As Ridgway has noted, however, this is of considerable interest since its proposed early date would set it near the start of the mainland frieze sequence, highlighting its island and Ionian connections.[183] The earliest examples of smaller-scale work are the sixth-century terracotta relief pinakes from the shrine of the Nymphs at Koukouvaia west of Pharsalos.[184] Clearly, caution is required in drawing conclusions from a slight and poorly preserved record, but relatively few mainland Greek poleis have produced large quantities of Archaic sculpture of any form, and some otherwise notable centres, such as Corinth, have surprisingly little.[185] The Thessalian evidence bears close comparison with that of, for example, Arkadia in terms of volume, bias towards freestanding sculpture with a similarly skewed distribution, yet occasional striking examples of temple decoration which reveal interesting external connections (see pp. 159–60).[186] There is no reason to regard Thessalian cities as atypical in the nature and chronology of their public building or artistic adornment – a more interesting question is the rationale for the production of sculpture where it occurs.

If the record of public building and perhaps sculpture tends to support the focus on investment connected with big sites by the end of the sixth century, it is interesting to work backwards and assess their earlier physical development. Architectural evidence rarely predates the Geometric period, although one should not underestimate the problems posed by the depth of stratigraphy under modern city centres and the fact that in many places ancient building materials are still being reused. This situation is hardly unique to Thessaly, but the resulting variations and limitations of the record should nonetheless be recognized. It is worth stressing from the outset that while there is a strong bias towards eastern Thessaly in both excavation and survey (on a regional and city level), even here few sites have been systematically excavated down to early levels. Gonnoi is a rare exception,[187] but elsewhere, evidence for early activity at many sites of later importance (Krannon for example)[188] consists largely of graves. Rescue excavations at sites such as Larisa and Pherai have revealed substantial bodies of evidence for Early Iron Age and Archaic settlement and Archaic public construction which will be discussed presently, although the layout and extent of settlement are hard to reconstruct.[189] Only occasionally does limited research combined with poor preservation effectively eliminate a site from discussion: Atrax (Aliphaka-Palaiokastro), for example, has produced little more than Protogeometric sherds, although outlying sites are beginning to fill out the picture.[190] More typical is the situation of Euhydrion (modern Ktouri, north of Pharsalos), where the main settlement has produced LHIIIC, Protogeometric, Archaic and Classical sherds, a stone building which Béquignon regarded as a temple and a possible Archaic circuit wall.[191] Evidence for early domestic architecture is very rare: excluding the substantial evidence from Volos-Palia discussed below, one of the best preserved cases is the foundation of a Submycenaean-Protogeometric house in the upper levels of the so-called Argissa Magoula near Larisa, a site which has also produced Archaic and Classical buildings on the north side of the mound plus a possibly Archaic circuit wall. Yet even here, the strongest evidence for continuous occupation through our period is ceramic.[192] In short, while the available evidence is clearly insufficient to sustain any broad analysis of the role of big sites across Thessaly, there are sufficient signs of variation to merit a comparative study of one or two better preserved cases. Thus we may at least draw attention to the variety of routes by which Thessalian place communities developed and established territories, and emphasize the likely complexity of the human ties and points of identification which they incorporated above and beyond the level of aristocratic interaction.

Larisa

Among the better preserved sites, Larisa and Pherai (both later to feature among the main cities of Pelasgiotis) show striking differences in their form and local circumstances. At Larisa (Figure 2.20), it is clear that activity continued throughout our period around the Phrourio hill, one of a number of Mycenaean settlement locations within the modern city, although no secure evidence for public building has been found.[193] Protogeometric evidence comes mainly from tombs, including those located by the second theatre, on the banks of the river Peneios and on the south slopes of the Phrourio. In Geometric times, traces of settlement continue on the Phrourio in the form of pottery and part of an apsidal mud brick house, probably with a thatched roof, on the east slope. Archaic and Classical buildings in the same tradition have also been found on this site. Yet by contrast with the apparent Early Iron Age focus on the Phrourio, Archaic evidence, especially from the sixth century onwards, indicates a significant expansion on to the surrounding plain accompanied by a more formalized planning of the centre. Rescue excavation has produced evidence of a street layout with aligned houses, architectural changes including the use of Lakonian rooftiles, and imports (notably Attic black and red figure) suggesting wider external contacts.[194]

Athanasios Tziaphalias has suggested that during the Early Iron Age the Larisa acropolis may have served as a stronghold for the area, and that the real change from Geometric village to city occurred from the seventh century onwards, and was discernible not only in the expansion and formalization of the city itself, but also in its control of neighbouring villages and territory.[195] This is a plausible scenario, although there is always the danger of hindsight in reconstructing an 'early' regional role for what was to become the leading city of Pelasgiotis.[196] The chief difficulty, as Tziafalias among others acknowledges, lies in tracing the extent of Larisa's territory at any particular time, let alone her influence over other settlements scattered around the large and fertile eastern Thessalian plain. During the Early Iron Age and Archaic period, Larisa was surrounded by communities which were in later times poleis in their own right, albeit not always such prominent ones.[197] Atrax and Argissa Magoula have already been mentioned, and Krannon too has a particularly rich record. Here the Protogeometric and Geometric cemetery (at Girlena), which lies over a prehistoric settlement, contains forty-one cist graves (a common form in the region) and a peribolos surrounding the cremated remains of four adults, plus a child just outside the entrance. This is a distinctive structure in the immediate context of the plain (though paralleled at Kastri Agias to the east on the foothills of Mavrovouni). Tziaphalias and Zaouri liken it to the idea of a tholos, and its central position in the cemetery is suggestive.[198] Geometric burials have also been located at Sarmanitsa west of the acropolis of Krannon and within the village of Ag. Georgios some 6 km to the south, and given the partial nature of rescue work in this region, it is possible that these various sites orginally formed part of one or more much larger cemeteries.[199]

During the Archaic period there is surface evidence from Orenia (Eleuthero) 1.2 km north-west of modern Krannon, and from Ag. Georgios (both within the village close to the Geometric burials and at nearby Palaiochoria),[200] but perhaps the most spectacular discovery is the settlement and extensive tumulus cemetery of the late seventh and sixth centuries surrounding Ag. Georgios. Two tumuli from this cemetery have been partially investigated, at Xirorema (late seventh century) and Karaeria (first half of the sixth century). Both contained secondary cremations, many grouped in periboloi, and a wealth of metal offerings (often burnt), but the Karaeria mound has so far produced only male burials with extensive weaponry and three funerary wagons. Possible explanations for such a formal distinction (assuming the excavated portions of the tumuli to be representative) range from a *polyandrion* related to an unknown conflict to a distinct male group emphasizing its warrior status,[201] but as yet too little of the cemetery has been excavated to permit conclusions. It is, however, interesting to compare possible distinctions between the groups buried in three tumuli recently excavated at Platanos Almyrou, close to New Halos in Achaia Phthiotis, in emphasizing that the tendency to identify tumulus cemeteries with family or clan burials may conceal other distinctions in the treatment of age, gender or status.[202] Tziaphalias relates the Ag. Georgios cemetery to the settlement at Palaiochoria which may be Ephyra, a dependent of Krannon, but similarities with the organization of the Girlena cemetery (which, as suggested, may be part of the same extensive complex) imply a strong local tradition, even though the conspicuous display of wealth at Ag. Georgios lacks earlier parallels.

If the burial record of the Krannon area shows long-term distinctions in grave forms (although not artefact types), and thus at least different expressions of social organization from those at Larisa, the situation is compounded if we move beyond the plain proper into the foothills of Mt. Ossa. Here there are radical differences yet again in the Protogeometric tholos tomb at Chasambali, and the Protogeometric cist tombs and Protogeometric and Geometric tholoi at Marmariani (only 20 km from Larisa and again located over a Mycenaean settlement, as is the Protogeometric to Middle Geometric settlement at Bunar Bashi, a site identified with Gyrton by Helly).[203] To what extent and in what ways were such sites independent or interdependent for all or part of our period? It may be tempting to use the toponyms in the *Catalogue of Ships* (*Iliad* 2.681–759), our only early account of Thessaly, as a check list for regional status (noting, for example, that while Argissa is mentioned, Larisa is not), but as will be further argued, even setting aside the difficulties of the *Catalogue*'s date and textual integrity, such comparison runs the risk of conflating different forms and perceptions of social geography. From a purely archaeological perspective, while material differences between some sites, like Krannon or Atrax, clearly imply divisions, it is harder to see how other smaller sites like the isolated Protogeometric burial at Platykambos or the tholos-like tomb at Mesorachi,[204] both as closer if not close to Larisa, relate to any particular community. There is no obvious answer to this; and it is interesting to note similar difficulties in defining the later territory of Larisa by more traditional historical means (leading Helly to suggest, on the basis of nearest neighbour analysis, that Larisa's territory was defined late and to accommodate those of her neighbours).[205] During our period, however, one can only highlight factors such as differences in mortuary evidence to argue that whatever relations existed between communities (along the spectrum from independence to hegemony) had to take into account that those communities were constituted in somehow different ways (even if we cannot trace exactly what they were). In short, the potential for complexity in the construction of local and supra-local place identities is considerable.

Pherai

The situation at Pherai, also within Pelasgiotis, contrasts markedly and appears much closer to that of the southern Greek centres discussed earlier. Indeed, many of the issues arising from the structuring of proximal residence are pertinent here too. While much evidence for early settlement comes from deep soundings in relatively restricted areas within the modern town of Velestino,[206] the sheer number and extent of (chiefly rescue) excavations provides us with a level of information close to that from better-known centres such as Argos (reinforcing yet again how inter-regional comparisons depend on the chances of excavation).[207] (Figure 2.21) While settlement at Pherai dates back probably to the end of the late Neolithic, the site appears to have emerged as the local centre in Protogeometric times when, by contrast with the preceding Mycenaean period, it was the only site in the area (the closest being that near modern Aerinos, almost half way between Pherai and Phthiotic Thebes over the foothills of Mavrovouni).[208]

Dense Early Iron Age settlement was focused on the eastern part of a long plateau below and broadly east of the twin acropoleis of Kastri and Magoula Bakali, and especially in the area of the Hypereian spring. (Figures 2.22, 2.23) There is strong evidence of continuous occupation from the Late Bronze Age in most areas, although sometimes changes in the nature of activity (at least one instance of Protogeometric child burials dug into a Mycenaean settlement level, for example), but at least until the eighth century, the settlement area seems to have been considerable reduced.[209] While Early Iron Age settlement focused on the plateau, remains are sufficiently scattered to suggest an arrangement of dispersed households (individual or clusters) reminiscent of those at Corinth and Argos. Cult was established at the shrine of Enodia and/or Zeus by the latter part of the eighth century at the latest (as discussed in the following chapter), and the first temple here dates to the sixth. Traces of Early Iron Age architecture have been found undisturbed on at least two plots, and substantial Submycenaean–Protogeometric retaining walls were built to contain the slope and protect contemporary settlement north-northwest of Hypereia. Mostly, however, settlement evidence consists of sherds in more or less chronologically distinct levels. An expansion of activity in the eighth century is clear, but unfortunately, the damage caused to Archaic remains by later structures combined with our relatively poor understanding of the local Archaic pottery sequence makes it hard to assess the exact pattern of development thereafter.[210] The first fortification around Kastraki hill dates to the late Archaic or early Classical period, but while it is clear that settlement expanded considerably in Classical times (east, north-east and south-east of Magoula Bakali), public building remained rare. Apart from the sixth-century first temple, the earliest candidate for a public building is a fifth-century round structure of unknown function located south-east of Kastraki and perhaps in the agora area.[211]

There are three main Protogeometric and Geometric cemeteries at Pherai, in the area of the later temple of Zeus/Enodia, on the site of a Mycenaean cemetery on public land in the centre of Velestino, and (during the Late Protogeometric period) at Alepotrypes south-west of the acropoleis. None seems to have contained many graves, although none is completely excavated, and scattered burials have been found in a number of other places, including Kastraki where there may have been a further cemetery. It seems likely that these cemetery locations relate to different residential and/or kin groups, but these are at present impossible to define. Most graves were cists containing single inhumations with no clear evidence of grouping (unless Petros

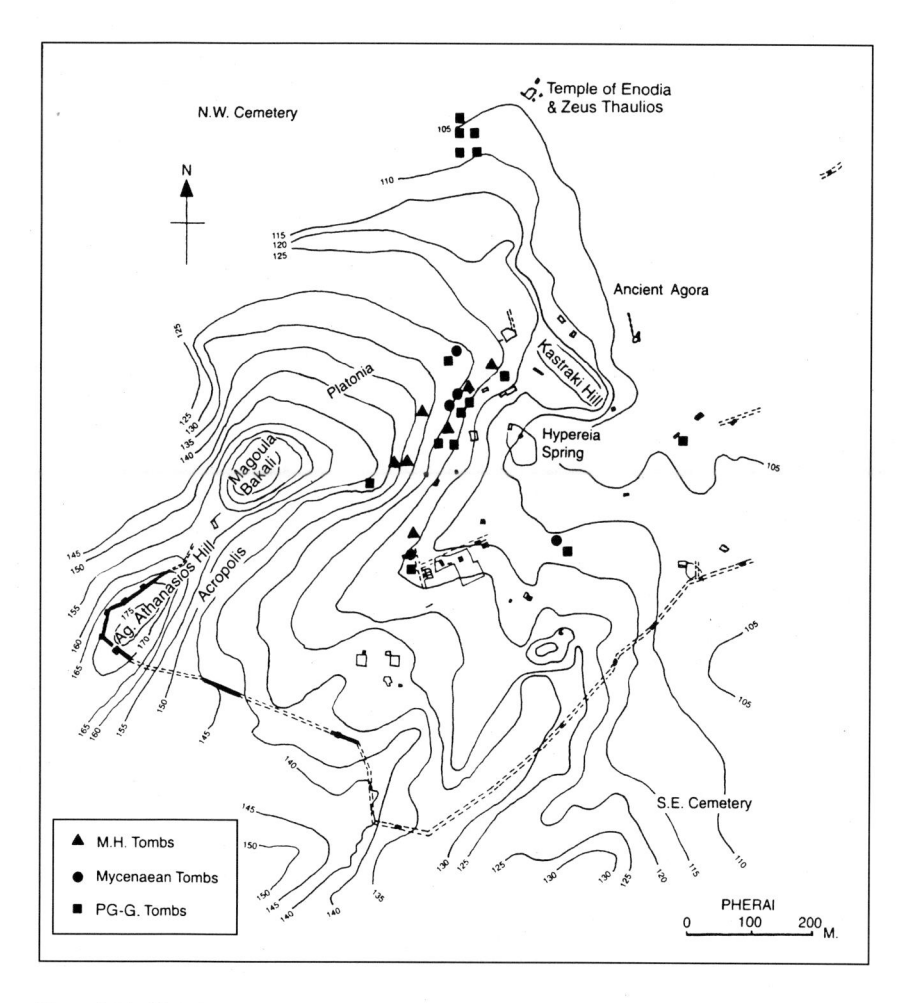

Figure 2.21 Pherai.

Kalligas' hypothesis that Protogeometric tumuli in the temple cemetery were destroyed by later construction is correct).[212] There is, however, evidence to suggest that in both the Protogeometric and Geometric periods, distinctions were drawn in tomb form, wealth of offerings and occasionally also in rite. While most of the cist burials within the modern town are disturbed, with the exception of a few child graves there is no suggestion that they were ever particularly rich.[213] However, a Protogeometric–Geometric tholos tomb on the Boura plot in central Velestino is exceptional for its longevity, use of cremation as well as inhumation, and investment in a form of structure which has hitherto been found only outside the main settlement.[214] Other Protogeometric tholoi (so far six in number), together with a Submycenaean–Protogeometric pyre pit, have been found just over 2 km from Magoula Bakali north-east of the village of Chloe. Published tholoi from this site contained multiple inhumations of both sexes covering the entire age range, with rich (especially metal) offerings.[215] At present, it is impossible to determine the basis on which certain groups, presumably families, received burial in this older and more costly tomb type, and indeed, whether the custom of placing the richest graves beside main roads outside the settlement may have been practised more or less continuously from Mycenaean times. Certainly from the late Archaic or Classical period onwards, the principal, and wealthiest, cemeteries of Pherai lay alongside the major radial roads; the north cemetery by the road to Larisa includes a burial mound at Thymarakia containing seventeen well-preserved Classical and Hellenistic tombs,[216] the south-east cemetery was beside the road to Phthiotic

Figure 2.22 Modern Velestino looking north-east from the Ag. Athanasios acropolis (photo: author).

Figure 2.23 Pherai: temple of Zeus/Enodia looking south-west towards Magoula Bakali (photo: author).

Thebes, and further cemeteries lay by the roads to Pharsalos and, north-east of Pherai, to Pagasai.

While the clustering of settlement at Pherai is surely a matter of its strategic situation on a major junction of communications, this is reflected in other aspects of the material record only to a limited extent. Pherai was the first, and later the main, centre of the cult of Enodia. Bronze votives from the earliest shrine to Enodia and/or Zeus Thaulios indicate considerable investment (see pp. 136–8), and while the majority of finds are Thessalian and may well have been locally produced, stylistic and iconographical influences (plus some imports) come from both north and south. Indeed, one of earliest depictions of the Corinthian helmet appears on a possibly Corinthian Late Geometric bronze warrior figurine.[217] But these connections are most clearly shown in small-scale metalwork, reflecting local priorities in sanctuary investment, and at least until the arrival of Attic black figure, pottery imports are few and generally Macedonian rather than southern.[218]

Dimini, Sesklo and Volos

If the cases of Pherai and Larisa reflect the different circumstances of clustered settlement in a strategic and continuously important centre, as opposed to the process by which one community defined itself among what seem to have been peer settlements across a broader plain, a third set of circumstances is illustrated by the principal Magnesian sites around the head of the Pagasitic gulf. (Figures 1.4, 2.24) Here a significant overall shift in the distribution of large-scale activity between the Late Bronze and Early Iron Ages raises the question of long-term settlement dynamics, of the ebb and flow of connections between settlements on or near a major waterway. Furthermore, there is a lingering problem of reconciling the archaeological record with the literary traditions surrounding early Iolkos, and the archaeological picture has yet to be fully resolved with the toponyms known from literary sources.[219]

To begin with the post-Bronze Age evidence, during the Protogeometric period Volos-Palia was undoubtedly the largest site in the area, with substantial settlement and extensive local cemeteries (discussed pp. 100–1 below). On present evidence this is the only site to show continuity of occupation from the Mycenaean period, since the Protogeometric tholos at Sesklo is somewhat later (although only part of a large cemetery here has been excavated),[220] and the provenance of Protogeometric pottery said to come from Pefkakia is insecure.[221] During the Geometric period, the picture at Volos and Sesklo is substantially unchanged,[222] but it is interesting to note the spread of settlement both inland to Petra[223] and along the west coast of the Pelion peninsula, with tholos tombs at Melies and Argalasti,[224] followed by an Archaic shrine at Korope.[225] It is also worth noting the proximity, by sea at least, of the Protogeometric and Geometric settlements of Achaia Phthiotis, namely Neos Anchialos (Pyrasos),[226] Mikrothivai (Phthiotic Thebes),[227] Megali Velanidia,[228] and especially Halos.[229] In short, settlement along the western coast of the Gulf in particular was dense, quite evenly spaced, and mutually accessible, thus raising questions of localized patterns of settlement movement which seem to reflect long-term perceptions of group territory and social borders.

The question of the Late Bronze Age–Early Iron Age transition in Thessaly, and especially the long-term impact of Late Mycenaean settlement upon the subsequent Early Iron Age order, deserves a monograph in its own right. Since a systematic review is beyond the scope of this book, I will focus on just this one case where the integration of Late Bronze Age data is essential to understanding longer-term regional dynamics. Indeed, while almost all of Thessaly fell more or less within the Mycenaean sphere (as defined by the presence of at least some aspects of Mycenaean material culture), in this area the strength of contacts and cultural affinities with the southern palatial world was much greater. As Bryan Feuer has emphasized, there are real differences in the material record of the coastal areas, the interior plains (where, for example, pottery influences and imports are Late rather than Early Mycenaean), and the mountains which remained the most distantly connected of all.[230]

The three major Late Mycenaean centres excavated differ greatly in preservation and form.[231] For over a century, attention has focused on the identification of the legendary centre of Iolkos, and it was this that led Christos Tsountas to excavate at Volos-Palia, a project resumed by Dimitrios Theocharis in 1956–61 and subsequently pursued via numerous, chiefly rescue, excavations conducted by Volos Ephoreia. Clearly, a substantial Mycenaean settlement has been revealed (although little has been left

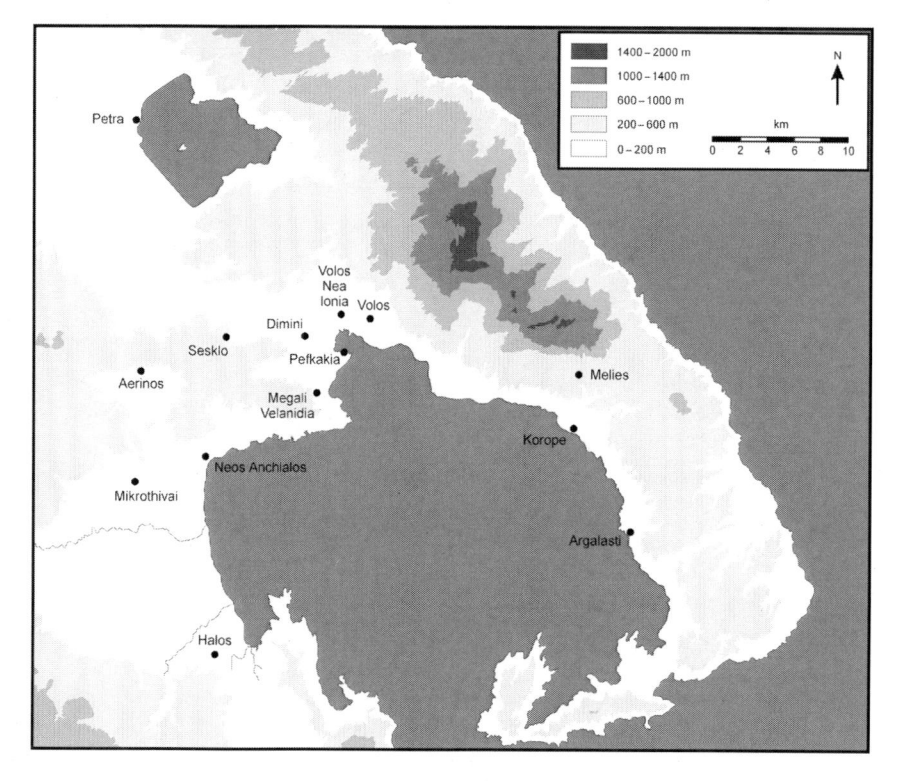

Figure 2.24 Principal sites around the head of the Pagasitic gulf (C.L. Hayward).

exposed), but doubt surrounds its identification as a palatial centre destroyed in the same way as those in the south. Theocharis partially excavated two successive large structures (the later LHIIIB) which he identified as a palace, yet no further remains have been discovered even in adjoining plots, and it is uncertain whether the published plan represents a single building; indeed, the twelfth-century fire destruction which he identified in certain sections seems to have been more localised than he claimed.[232] Furthermore, as Malakasioti emphasizes, the overall peak of settlement at Palia, as revealed both stratigraphically and in the cemeteries, is post-Mycenaean.

The picture at Dimini, 4.5 km west of Volos appears rather different, even allowing for the circumstances of excavation on a site largely unburdened by modern settlement and with shallow soil cover rather than the sections up to 6 m deep needed to reach the Late Bronze Age at Palia. Here the extensive Mycenaean settlement which surrounded the long-established acropolis (Figure 2.25) is characterized by large, well-built houses and a major paved road; it includes a shrine, pottery and metalworking workshops, and two 'royal' tholos tombs dating to LHIIIA2 and LHIIIB (Figure 2.26). The peak of activity during the fourteenth and thirteenth centuries occurred earlier than at Palia, and the site was clearly in decline through the twelfth century (when it apparently suffered earthquake damage). The latest pottery is LHIIIC Early and there is no evidence of reoccupation on the same site.[233] It should, however, be noted that the Early Iron Age burials found outside Sesklo extend in the direction of nearby Dimini, and not only have these barely been explored, but the location of the associated settlement is unknown. One cannot therefore exclude this area from the later picture, though as yet we know little about it.

The final site, Pefkakia, which lies on a small promontory south-west of Volos, also dates back to the Neolithic period. (Figure 2.27) Evidence of Mycenaean settlement is much less well preserved than at Dimini, since in many areas severe damage has been caused by overlying Hellenistic construction. Nonetheless, both tombs and architectural traces suggest an extensive settlement, perhaps only slightly smaller than that at Dimini, although evidence has been lost through long-term coastline change. There was at least one large building with a courtyard, but its nature and function are unclear. The maritime location and trading connections are reflected in a range of ceramic imports from north and south, plus two ostraka with what may be a Linear B numeral and a Cypro-Minoan character respectively.[234] Ceramic evidence suggests that settlement peaked during the second half of the fifteenth century, and was in substantial decline by the end of the third quarter of the thirteenth and gradually abandoned thereafter (certainly by LHIIIC Early, again noting earthquake damage). Here too, there is no evidence of resettlement for several centuries at least. Pefkakia's heyday was thus rather earlier than that of Dimini, but later than the peak of *prehistoric* settlement at Palia, raising the question of whether this reflects real interconnections and population movement or mere coincidence.

The relationship between these three large sites is as interesting as it is problematic. As Adrymi Sismani emphasizes, Dimini is not just any Mycenaean settlement, nor is there any reason to assume that it was a second-order site to Volos-Palia.[235] There is no direct evidence for a formal relationship, and no reason automatically to infer the existence in this region of the kind of hierarchy characteristic of southern Greek palatial systems. The chief difficulty appears to be the relative proximity of the sites, but this is a 'problem' which plainly recurred at least from the eighth century onwards, when there developed a network of what we then regard (perhaps with hindsight from the later Archaic and Classical polis standpoint) as peer communities. In considering the settlement organization of the eastern Thessalian plain, Halstead has argued for a notably lesser size hierarchy in comparison with the southern mainland (and one which emerges from a very different long-term settlement history). Direct comparison with Messenia, which has a small number of large sites and a preponderance of middle-order and small sites, shows a very different size distribution profile, with almost 50 per cent of eastern Thessalian

Figure 2.25 The acropolis of Dimini (photo: author).

Late Bronze Age sites larger than the mean of 2.2 ha and more or less randomly distributed across the region.[236] As Halstead points out, this would tend to suggest a low-level political organization, and while the coastal plains around Volos and Almyros are one of the few places in which an intensive Mycenaean-type economy would have been viable, and which also had unparalleled access to maritime trade,[237] there is no evidence to suggest that they approached the form of economic development evident in the south. I dwell on this point simply because the question of local hierarchy and the nature of connections and/or interdependence between communities, combined with the pattern of settlement growth and abandonment outlined, has a direct impact on the way in which we conceptualize settlement change across the Late Bronze Age–Early Iron Age transition. The kind of catastrophic explanation which follows from emphasis on the 'destruction' of the Palia 'palace' fits less well with the data, patchy as they are, than a rather more drawn-out episode of change within longer-term cycles.

Returning to the issue of the location of Iolkos, a combination of the archaeological record, current understanding of coastline change and topographical hints in ancient sources has led to a general consensus that the correct identification is more likely to be with Dimini than with Volos-Palia.[238] But since Volos-Palia is the only site to have been continuously occupied through LHIIIC into the Early Iron Age and far beyond (and to have produced Submycenaean pottery otherwise rare in Thessaly),[239] it is

Figure 2.26 Mycenaean tholos beside the acropolis of Dimini (photo: author).

Figure 2.27 Pefkakia promontory: looking north towards Volos (photo: author).

necessary to argue that the inhabitants of Dimini settled here and brought the place name with them. Early Iron Age settlement at Palia was particularly dense and extensive in comparison with the preceding and subsequent periods (indeed, traces of LHIIIB and LHIIIC are surprisingly slight, and in places Protogeometric levels are cut by Hellenistic). Debris of four building phases of the eleventh–eighth centuries formed a stratum 2–3 m thick immediately over Mycenaean levels, and Protogeometric pits reached down to the foundations of the Palia 'palace'. The most common form of dwelling (or sometimes workshop) was a one-roomed structure with foundations of unworked stone, a clay floor, a timbered roof and, sometimes, food storage areas. More elaborate structures existed too, and two probable mason's marks on a foundation block have given rise to much discussion about possible links with Linear B or the later Greek alphabet.[240] Whereas children were buried within the settlement, a large adult cemetery lay to the north-west of the settlement (in the area of Nea Ionia).[241] Most graves were single inhumations in slab cists, but there are now three instances of multiple burial in tholos tombs continuing the Mycenaean tradition represented by the Kapakli 1 tholos: that at Paspalia can now be dated to Protogeometric, and there are two further tombs at Kapakli, Kapakli 2 (found at the same time as Kapakli 1) and the more recently discovered Odos Kolokotroni Tomb 6. The last, a pseudo-tholos constructed during the Protogeometric period, was reused in Classical times, but its rich contents seem to have been left undisturbed.[242] Plainly, the tradition of elite family or group burial in tholoi evident at both Dimini and Palia during the Late Bronze Age continued unbroken at Palia as also as Sesklo, and it is interesting to note its continuing popularity at the new Geometric sites along the coast of the Pelion peninsula.

The chronological relationship between settlement expansion at Palia and abandonment at Dimini and Pefkakia clearly points to settlement relocation.

Given our poor understanding of the Early Iron Age remains around Sesklo, however, it would be wise to avoid simple arguments for synoikism, and indeed, the gradual nature of the decline and abandonment of Dimini and Pefkakia point to a longer-term process, noting also that the single-site focus on Palia was itself of no great duration. Strong elements of continuity, for example in the form of elite burials, suggest a cycle of population movement within a particular ambit – probably not an uncommon situation in mainland Greece, but one that has not received much attention. Overall, however, there is still far to go in investigating the long-term dynamics of settlement in this area and bridging the divide which still separates the analysis of 'prehistoric' and 'historical' situations.

Thessalian geography and the *Catalogue of Ships*

These three Thessalian case studies highlight the different kinds of story told by the settlement history revealed in the archaeological record and the social identities implied by the tribal divisions of Thessaly, as well as the toponyms associated with the leaders listed in the *Catalogue of Ships*. The settlement histories of each of our cases are radically different, yet Pherai and Larisa both belonged to Pelasgiotis, and while contingents from Pherai and Iolkos were both led by Eumelos (*Iliad* 2.711–15), historically they lay within Pelasgiotis and Magnesia respectively (the latter perioikic). One might attempt to construct an evolutionary sequence by treating the *Catalogue* as by definition the older description, finding the best-fitting period in the material record, and then using this as a historical stage in the formation of the polis network.[243] Yet setting aside the risks of handling the constantly changing archaeological record in this way, the *Catalogue* represents a genre of social-geographical mapping that should be considered in its own right, and there is no reason to assume that the perceptions which it embodies will automatically coincide with what may be inferred from physical orderings on the ground.[244]

The *Catalogue of Ships* as presented in *Iliad* 2 represents the earliest extant attempt to lay out the social geography of most of the Greek world – in Kirk's words a kind of Achaian 'national epic'.[245] While the only secure benchmark for its date rests on the formalization of our *Iliad*, for present purposes it is largely immaterial whether one places this in the eighth or seventh century, accepting that the final text represents an amalgam of information of different periods.[246] Willcock among others has drawn attention to linguistic hints that the *Catalogue* was not created for its present place in the *Iliad* but was emended to fit (he suggests an origin among Boiotian catalogue poetry).[247] Even so, there is unlikely to have been any substantial delay involved, as its narrative place in *Iliad* 2 is clearly established and there is a fundamental linguistic similarity throughout.[248] Overall,

I concur with recent commentators in believing that the *Catalogue* in general describes an Early Iron Age/early Archaic, rather than a Bronze Age, state of affairs (accepting that different dates better fit different sections).[249] But while attempts have been made to use the archaeological record to date individual areas more precisely,[250] no consistent picture emerges, and some regions (such as the Corinthia)[251] remain problematic whichever date one chooses. The *Catalogue* is clearly an uneven text, but perhaps reflecting its ultimate origin, discussion of central Greece is both fuller and more prominent than that of other regions.

The Thessalian contingents are described as follows:

Leader	Reference	Toponyms
Achilles	*Iliad* 2.681–94	Halos, Alope, Trachis, Phthia
Protesilas [Podarces]	*Iliad* 2.695–710	Phyake, Pyrasos, Iton, Antron, Pteleos.
Eumelos	*Iliad* 2.711–15	Pherai, Boibe, Iolkos, Glaphyrai
Philoctetes [Medon]	*Iliad* 2.716–28	Methone, Thaumakia Meliboia, Olizon
Podaleirius & Machaon	*Iliad* 2.928–33	Trikka, Ithome, Oichalia
Eurypylos	*Iliad* 2.734–7	Ormenion, 'Hypereia fountain', Asterion
Polypoites & Leonteus	*Iliad* 2.738–47	Argissa, Gyrton, Orthe, Elone, Oloosson
Goneus	*Iliad* 2.748–55	Kyphos, Dodone
Prothoos	*Iliad* 2.756–9	–

A brief review of the toponyms mentioned shows that almost all have produced evidence of Geometric and in many cases Protogeometric occupation.[252] But this is only part of the story. Omissions are often highlighted, whether referring to an entire people like the Thessalians of Thessaliotis,[253] or the absence of specific, apparently major sites, as for example Arne-Kierion or Larisa, both of which existed during the Early Iron Age.[254] Attempts to explain specific cases have been made since antiquity. Much of Strabo's account of Thessaly (Strabo 9.5) consists of a critical discussion of the Homeric *Catalogue* in relation to the later settlement history of the region. His explanation for the omission of Larisa, as that of other sites on the plain, is that they were either not yet settled or were slight on account of the floods which occasionally occurred there (9.5.20). Among modern commentators, Corvisier has suggested that Larisa's proximity to Argissa Magoula (Gremnos), which is mentioned, worked to her detriment.[255]

Challenges to this site identification do not invalidate the basic argument. Whatever the case, the focus on the presence or absence of specific settlement names draws attention from the way in which Homer uses toponyms in relation to ethnics. Ethnics are included in three of the nine contingents listed, but in a different way each time. The contingent of Prothoos is simply described as the Magnetes, with a very general location of residence ('about Penieus and Pelion') and no further toponyms. Goneus' contingent is led from a specific site (Kyphos), but consists of two ethnic groups, the Enienes and the Peraiboi, again located generally 'about wintry Dodona' and 'in the ploughland about lovely Titaressos'. Finally, and in contrast, that of Achilles has a more complex structure in which specific settlement names are combined with the regions Phthia and Hellas, and the ethnics of the groups concerned are given as Myrmidons, Hellenes and Achaians.[256] As Strabo's detailed discussion highlights, in many cases the tribal boundaries of the later Thessalian tetrads are transcended by the Homeric divisions (see for instance Strabo 9.5.6–7 on Phthia), but as he rightly points out (9.5.4), Homer 'intimates a fact which is common to, and true of, all countries, that whole regions and their several parts undergo changes in proportion to the power of those who hold sway' (transl. Jones). In short, the treatment of Thessaly in the *Catalogue* frames in a highly abbreviated fashion[257] what was probably a dynamic situation in terms of interlocking tiers of political affiliation and identity, and thus reveals a mentality of social geography which at least for our purposes transcends discussion (let alone the 'accuracy') of specific details.

For those primarily concerned with the role and development of cities in Thessaly, this reading of the *Catalogue*, and especially its acceptance as pertaining to the Early Iron Age,[258] creates a problematic relationship with the later polis world. Thanks to a combination of epigraphical and literary analysis, field survey and work on artefacts such as funerary stelai, the historical geography of a number of Thessalian cities and their territories is relatively well understood, at least from Classical times onwards.[259] As Bruno Helly points out, the establishment of such a city network would seem to imply a real change in Thessalian political geography, a phenomenon which he regards as beginning only in the late eighth or seventh century (in step with developments in southern Greece).[260] The development of Thessalian poleis and the politicization of the Thessalian ethnos were thus simultaneous and interacting processes, i.e. poleis created new communities which were at once ethnic, territorial and political, and this could involve long-term demographic instability.[261] One cannot exclude from the sixth-century equation the interaction of place community and social 'leaders and followers' geography, even though it may be more grounded in the city per se than the Homeric picture would imply (taking as a guide Helly's comparative nearest neighbour analyses of the *Catalogue* settlements and those of later Archaic and Classical times, accepting that this is but one approach to the issue of territory).[262] Indeed, there are comparable hints in other sources on early Thessalian military campaigns (p. 203),[263] and even more strikingly, in the offer of Magnesian Iolkos to Hippias (Herodotos 5.94.1) which reveals the political disposability of physical communities. In other words, Homer offers us a view into a set of probably dynamic relationships that are not readily traced archaeologically and are easy to overlook. According priority to polis formation as a catalyst for political change of all kinds is largely an act of hindsight, and the sheer variability of the settlement trajectories and constructs of social geography which can be traced during our period should make us wary of relying on simple models of group closure at polis and ethnos level.

Conclusion

The questions raised and cases considered in this chapter combine to suggest that the implicit or explicit view that 'urbanism' reflects dynamic sociopolitical development is at best a half truth. The expansion of settlement sites, often creating or intensifying links between proximal residential areas, presented new problems, the solutions to which had the potential to enhance the place community as an entity with which groups could identify, and the settlement itself as the physical location within which that identity could be expressed. Furthermore, expansion created new needs of supply and thus the potential for economic, and especially producer, interests to come in time to see the settlement as a prime arena of activity. Not until the latter part of our period is there significant and widespread evidence for monumental construction linked specifically to big sites. Before that there is much stronger evidence for sanctuaries as the main contexts of public investment (public in the sense of publicly visible as well as representing dominant group interests), and the role of religion in the expression and underpinning of political authority remained important throughout our period. Consideration of phenomena such as coinage and written law illustrates the extent to which the construction and acceptance of group identity and political authority demanded that those concerned look beyond the confines of the major settlements within which much of their practical business may have been conducted.

Sites and monuments are always attractive fixed points around which to construct arguments. Yet if we are to understand the role of big sites in shaping place identity and avoid the inherent biases in reading political structures from archaeological data towards 'stable' and 'visible' features like long-term site occupation, it is necessary to compare the kind of issues and observations raised here with other potential arenas of individual or communal expression – the mobility of goods and peoples, for example, and especially the ideologically charged contexts of sanctuaries and cemeteries. This is not a matter of urban versus rural issues, of city politics versus rural subsistence. Quite apart from the questionable validity of any such distinction, much flowed from the same overarching constructs of social power, and the ways in which modes of expression interlocked or conflicted is fundamental to understanding how nested identities were constructed and expressed in any particular case.

3

COMMUNITIES OF CULT

One of the most striking qualitative and quantitative transformations in the mainland archaeological record of the twelfth to eighth centuries concerns sanctuaries. Shrines dating back to the transitional period between LHIIIC and Early Protogeometric have now been identified at the Amyklaion in Lakonia, Kalapodi in Phokis, the Polis Cave on Ithaka, Olympia, Mende-Poseidi in Chalkidike, and Isthmia in the Corinthia – in a wide scatter of regions whose political development varied greatly.[1] By contrast with Crete, where there is ample evidence of physical continuity from the Late Bronze Age at open-air sites (such as Kato Symi) and those within settlements (as Kavousi),[2] as well as the continued use of such Bronze Age imagery as the goddess with the upraised arms,[3] there is as yet no mainland Early Iron Age sanctuary which definitely predates LHIIIB2,[4] and LHIIIC/Submycenaean seems a real phase of transition. Even the sanctuary at Kalapodi, of central importance to the Archaic and Classical Phokian ethnos, dates back no further than the transition between LHIIIB2 and LHIIIC Early. It should, however, be stressed that the discontinuity lies primarily in physical location and to significant, if varying, extents in the material expression of religious belief (especially the nature of votives). The continuity or otherwise of whatever social power resided in priesthoods or the provision of resources, or of aspects of ritual practice itself, are separate issues.[5] Certainly, the richness and diversity of the material record, particularly in areas like Elis, Arkadia and Phokis which are awkward for models centred on perceptions of the polis as an autonomous city state, requires discussion of the values, power structures, material practices and physical contexts inherited, acted upon, developed or rejected through the centuries before the late eighth and seventh centuries. Clearly, therefore, if we are to avoid perpetuating untested assumptions about the nature of contemporary society, later religious practice cannot be used as a filter through which to view evidence from the preceding centuries.[6]

Whereas by the early 1980s the eighth century had come to be regarded as a period of renaissance, when material evidence of cult either reappeared or was qualitatively and quantitatively transformed after centuries of darkness, and the resulting spatial formalization of shrines seen as an aspect of polis formation,[7] it is nowadays clear that in many regions this is merely an interesting episode within a much longer history of cult activity. This is not to imply crude continualism,[8] merely recognition that certain aspects of sanctuary conduct (however they were organized in each individual case) had been important for centuries, and that the systems which had evolved to administer them were those which had to cope with such new needs as arose from the eighth century onwards. To put this last point more positively, inherited structures of this kind provided those most prominently involved with the greatest opportunity to exploit whatever opportunities for material and social aggrandizement arose with the expansion of the cult system and especially with that of the sacral economy. In this respect (as in many others, as will be argued), cult organizations represent important social and economic structures which, not least due to their often longer and more varied histories, did not always coincide with those of particular place communities and territories, even though their functions and interests overlapped. Indeed, whereas, as was argued in the previous chapter, we lack evidence to characterize big settlement sites as economic centres in the period $c.1200$–800, sanctuaries throughout the Greek world were major centres of consumption, production and supply beyond the strictly sacral.

A cynic might argue that the emphasis that has come to be placed on the eighth century reflects a fortuitous conjunction of retrojected trust in literary evidence and projected trust in archaeology. Nonetheless, there is a prevailing acceptance of the eighth and seventh centuries as a watershed, with an increase in the numbers of rural and 'urban' shrines and in the quantity and variety of votives, and the appearance of recognizable temple architecture setting the stage for the emergence of polis religion, with at least the tacit implication that development thereafter followed a more familiar course. It is certainly true that at least in the southern and much of the central Greek mainland,[9] secure evidence for purpose-built cult structures (setting aside the case for locating cult in so-called 'rulers' houses')[10] does not as yet predate the eighth century. Eighth-century mainland evidence is, however, increasingly plentiful and geographically widespread, ranging from Tegea, Asine and Ano Mazaraki in the Peloponnese, to Kalapodi in Phokis.[11] The coincidence and extent of this phenomenon raises a range of important questions. On one level, the spread of the idea of such building can be attributed to inter-regional emulation. Yet variation in the physical appearance of early religious buildings, their relationship to settlements, and their possible role within established cult practice suggest that such emulation is likely to have operated on a relatively superficial level, and that the creation of a more uniform conception of a built shrine is rather a phenomenon of the later seventh and sixth centuries.

Many of these issues will be addressed in the course of this chapter, but it is worth stressing from the outset that, as with pre-eighth-century cult sites, a large proportion of our evidence for temple building at both new and established shrines is found in 'ethnos' territory. If such a spread of evidence makes more traditional polis-centred approaches to eighth- and seventh-century religious developments unduly one-dimensional, it also demands reappraisal of the long-argued view that cult centres in ethne served as regional meeting places before the development of city centres, with the ethnos thus primarily a religious league with a shared sanctuary and its festival as a national meeting.[12] From the late fifth or fourth century onwards, certain ethnos shrines did host major regional gatherings; hence Polybios' (5.7–8) description of Thermon as the acropolis of all Aetolia, an ideal location for a sanctuary which hosted regional gatherings for cult, politics and trade. But the process by which federal organizations drew upon and manipulated earlier cult orderings in developing such shrine functions is a complex issue (which will be considered in detail in this chapter in the case of Phokis).

I have argued elsewhere that the geographical extent of, and social and political interests represented within, the constituencies of most long-lived sanctuaries located within both ethne and poleis as traditionally conceived (Kalapodi, the Amyklaion and Olympia, for example) varied significantly over time.[13] Convincing cases of shrines as regional meeting places for a stable constituency (let alone territory) over long periods of time (and certainly continuing beyond the eighth century) are very rare. Ironically, perhaps the best such case, Isthmia in the Corinthia, is located within a polis, albeit hardly a typical one. (Figure 3.1) As we have seen, the available evidence suggests that both the territory and the settlement structure of Corinth were unusually stable throughout the Early Iron Age, and the Isthmian votive record shows early and consistent gender and status marking, as well as the representation of long-lived forms of economic interest.[14] Isthmia's central location in Corinthian territory is evident in relation to regional settlement immediately before the shrine's establishment (i.e. in LHIIIC) and during the eighth and seventh centuries (the next occasion when there is substantial evidence from areas outside the city centre), while there are hints in what may be post-tyrannical tribal divisions that the Isthmus continued to be perceived as a 'hinge' area.[15] Indeed, the sustained double focus of the settlement centre at Corinth and the shrine at the Isthmus is one of the most prominent features of early Corinthian social geography, modified (but not overturned) only from the second half of the eighth century when a wider network of rural and urban shrines was established (notably that on Temple Hill at Corinth, see also p. 57).[16]

Even so, the characterization of Isthmia as a regional meeting place should be nuanced. There is clear evidence of change in the nature of wealth investment (especially in comparison with burial offerings), most strikingly during the first half of the eighth century,[17] and the proliferation of shrines during the eighth–sixth centuries was accompanied by closer definition of the role of each one, and thus of the nature of investment there.[18] Furthermore, in view of Isthmia's roadside location, the role of outsider investment even

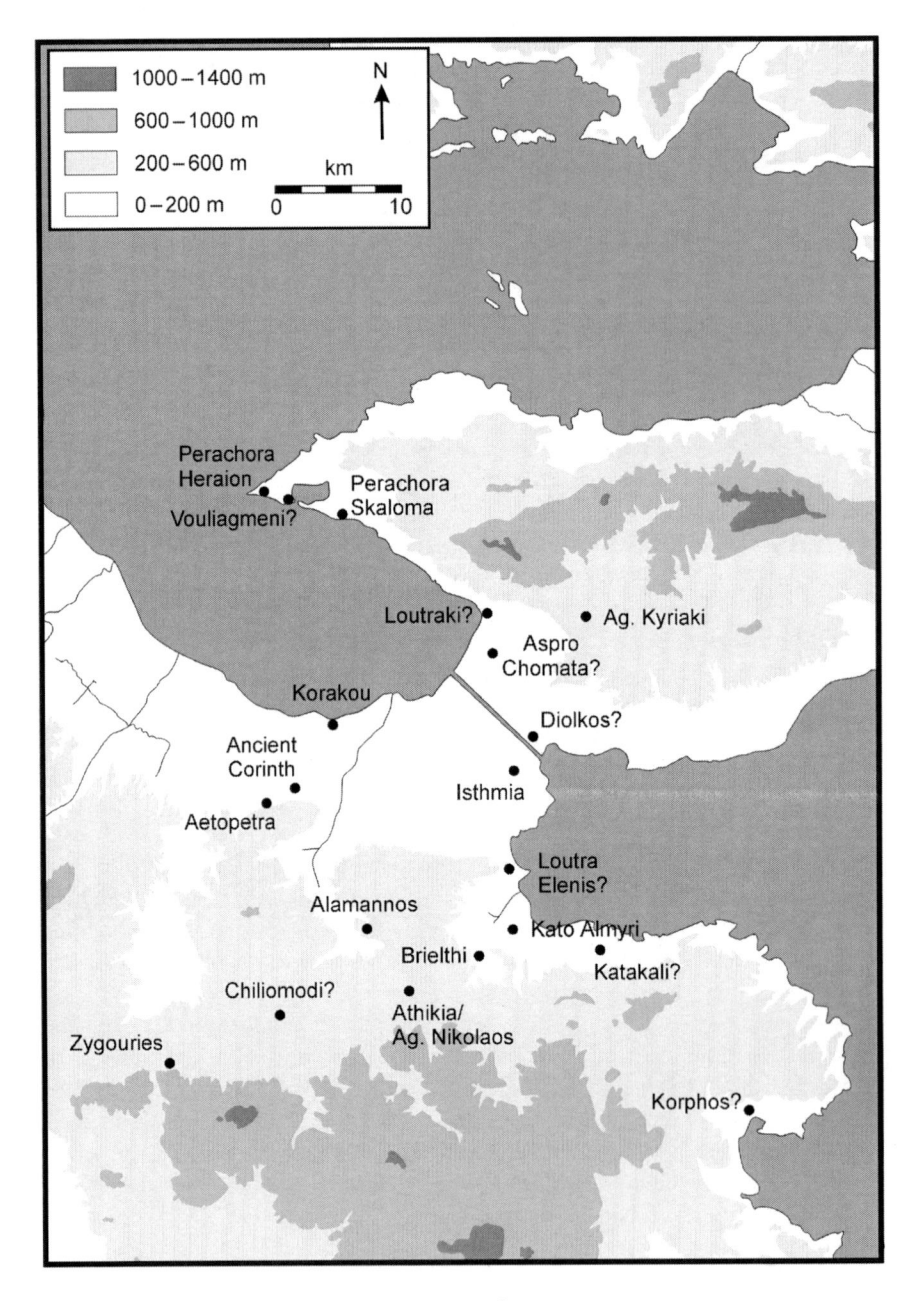

Figure 3.1 The Corinthia in LHIIIC (C.L. Hayward).

before the foundation of the Isthmian games is potentially significant, if difficult to determine from the available evidence. While some have seen Isthmia as a socially open site,[19] there is a strong case for suggesting that much of the non-Corinthian portion of the extant Early Iron Age record had passed through Corinthian hands. A foreign sanctuary is an almost unparalleled context for certain types of Attic import (boot figurines and a Late Geometric closed vessel with a prothesis scene for example, Figures 3.2a and b), and so whereas Isthmia would be the logical choice for anyone operating within the local system of material values (noting that pre-Classical Corinthian wells and graves have yet to yield a single figurine), it may be hard

Figure 3.2a Boot figurines: Morgan 1999a, F38 (left, Corinthian), F36 (bottom right, Attic), F37 (top right, Attic) (University of Chicago Excavations at Isthmia: photo: Ioannidou and Bartzioti).

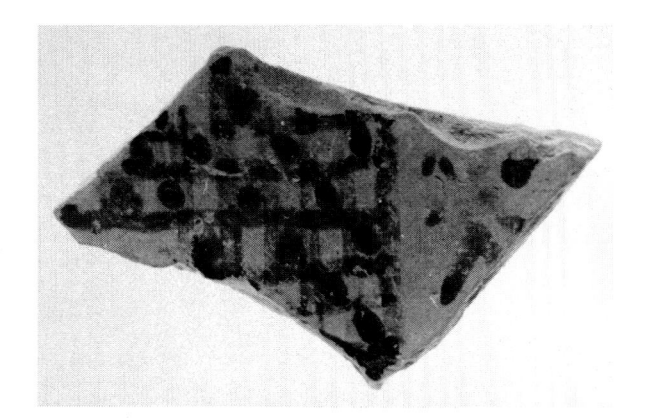

Figure 3.2b Attic closed vessel shoulder sherd with part of prothesis scene: Morgan 1999a, cat. 370 (University of Chicago Excavations at Isthmia: photo: Ioannidou and Bartzioti).

COMMUNITIES OF CULT

to envisage anyone but a Corinthian choosing such a place.[20] Indeed, arguments for wider participation at this early date rest largely on more mundane categories of drinking vessel, principally those made in terra rossa clays which, while similar to Attic to the naked eye, also resemble those local to the Corinthia. Given the present limitations in our knowledge of the eastern Corinthia and the Megarid, and also in the analytical data currently available, it is very hard to source this fabric and thus to discriminate between a minimal (solely Corinthian) and maximal (central Athenian) import.[21] It should, however be emphasized that particular kinds of conspicuous display, and especially the dedication of monumental metalwork, came to be focused at this prominent location; in the case of tripods (Figures 3.3a and b), this occurred at around the same time as they first appeared on Temple Hill and (in the case of imported Corinthian tripods) at foreign shrines such as the Argive Heraion and Olympia.[22] This latter point is of particular significance as Corinth is exceptional for its frugality with metal wealth, with metal items unusually rare in both graves and domestic contexts.[23] Overall, therefore, far from being a paradigm for the long-term development of state religion, Isthmia is in many respects exceptional. Indeed, the only other similarly long-

Figure 3.3a Isthmia: bronze tripod, c.750 (Morgan 1999a, M14) (University of Chicago Excavations at Isthmia: photo: Ioannidou and Bartzioti).

Figure 3.3b Isthmia: bronze tripod attachment, second half eighth century (Morgan 1999a, M18) (University of Chicago Excavations at Isthmia: photo: Ioannidou and Bartzioti).

lived shrine within the territory of a polis as traditionally conceived, the Amyklaion, had a much more complex history by virtue of its location within a synoikized, and subsequently conquest, state.[24]

Clearly, there is much to be learned about the operation of cult communities as complex entities which both reinforced and transcended other political boundaries and interests. In terms of demarcation of territory, for example, a polis-centred emphasis on centre and boundaries is simplistic, and indeed, many ethne made sophisticated use of shrine locations to mark routes and boundaries through and within the palimpsest of 'territories' that defined the various forms of activity undertaken by groups within them.[25] The conception outlined in the introduction to this book of poleis and ethne as nested tiers of identity rather than mutually exclusive state forms thus demands analysis of the multiple and complex roles of cult in terms of definition of territory, group history, social interests and power relations.[26] Since the history of most ethne is littered with synoikisms, dioikisms, the politicization of tribal or urban identities, and domination and subordination within regions and in relation to neighbours, one might expect to find this complex of shifting personal and communal statuses paralleled by shifts in group representation at an ideological level. It is clear that by the end of the Archaic period, shrines were used to knit together communities on a variety of different levels (territory, history, communication between different communities with different histories, material practices and traditions). The manner in which this was achieved varied greatly. In some cases, sanctuaries with very different traditions and constituencies in different parts of regions came to be linked together in the charter myths of newly created or politicized ethne, while maintaining all or part of their specific local roles. In others, a cult long established in one part of a region developed a panregional character. In other instances, sanctuaries helped to articulate economic relations via the exchange of goods and services, the marking of territory or the symbolism inherent in particular votive practices. These functions were not mutually exclusive, and there is to some extent evidence of all or most of them at all of the shrines discussed in this chapter, as is well illustrated in the case of Phokis, to which we will now turn.

The cult systems of Phokis

As highlighted in the introductory chapter, by the end of the Archaic period the territory of the Phokian ethnos incorporated the topographically distinct regions of the northern uplands, the southern coastal plains, and the central mountain zone around Parnassos. (Figure 1.5) As Jeremy McInerney has shown,[27] the creation of a single Phokian myth-historical identity involved the reconciliation of a complex of epichoric myths reflecting individual communities' claims to distinct origins and descent over and above their common Phokian ethnicity. A parallel process may be observed in sanctuary development, since the cult history of each of these broad geographical regions is markedly different. In the south, the principal shrine grew up within the already long-established settlement at Delphi from the late ninth or early eighth century onwards, and rapidly began to attract substantial external interest and investment (a process enhanced by the growing reputation of its oracle).[28] To extract the bare bones of the events later aggrandized into the first sacred war (see pp. 124–7 below), it seems that early in the sixth century the sanctuary and neighbouring lands (including the largest area of coastal plain) were forcibly detached from local control, and constituted into a separate polis with oversight of sanctuary affairs vested in the Delphic amphictyony.[29] By contrast, in the north the principal shrine, near the modern village of Kalapodi, was a rural site close to the historical border of Phokis and Lokris. Its much earlier foundation date raises the question of changes in the geographical extent and social composition of its constituency, as well as the long-term salience of that border. In Classical times the shrine was controlled by the neighbouring city of Hyampolis, and was ideally placed to monitor and benefit from communications down towards the plain of Phokis, where most cities congregated.[30] Cult evidence from central Phokis is very slight before the latter part of the Archaic period, which begs the question of the extent to which its development followed upon reassertion of post-Thessalian political unity. As has been emphasized, the later Archaic Phokian ethnos as a political entity was to a great extent forged by conflict. The expulsion of the Thessalians lay at the heart of its charter myth, and as McInerney has recently stressed, the loss of plain land around Delphi, combined with the expanding demands of the sanctuary, had a substantial impact on the long-term economic development of the region as a whole.[31] We will therefore review the different histories of the northern and southern Phokian sanctuaries before considering the manner in which old and new shrines alike were integrated within the overarching religious system of the new *koinon*.

To begin in the north of the region, detailed consideration of the pre-eighth-century archaeological record of the sanctuary at Kalapodi (Figures 3.4, 3.5) and surrounding sites well illustrates the shrine's changing constituency.[32] The image of Kalapodi as a regional meeting place during the Early Iron Age, emphasized by Pierre Ellinger and François de Polignac, is in large part an echo of its later role.[33] Not only does it sit ill with the LHIIIC record (and that of subsequent centuries), but there is no real material evidence either for Phokian regional unity at this stage or for the existence of any strong border between self-conscious northern Phokian and East Lokrian social groups. I have argued elsewhere that at the time of its institution in LHIIIB2/LHIIIC, the shrine served to articulate relations between communities within a fairly narrow geographical radius.[34] (Figure 3.6) During LHIIIB, the surrounding area had been densely inhabited, with numerous chamber tombs around the Exarchos valley and close to Kalapodi, and settlement traces at Smixi and nearby on the Hyampolis acropolis, for

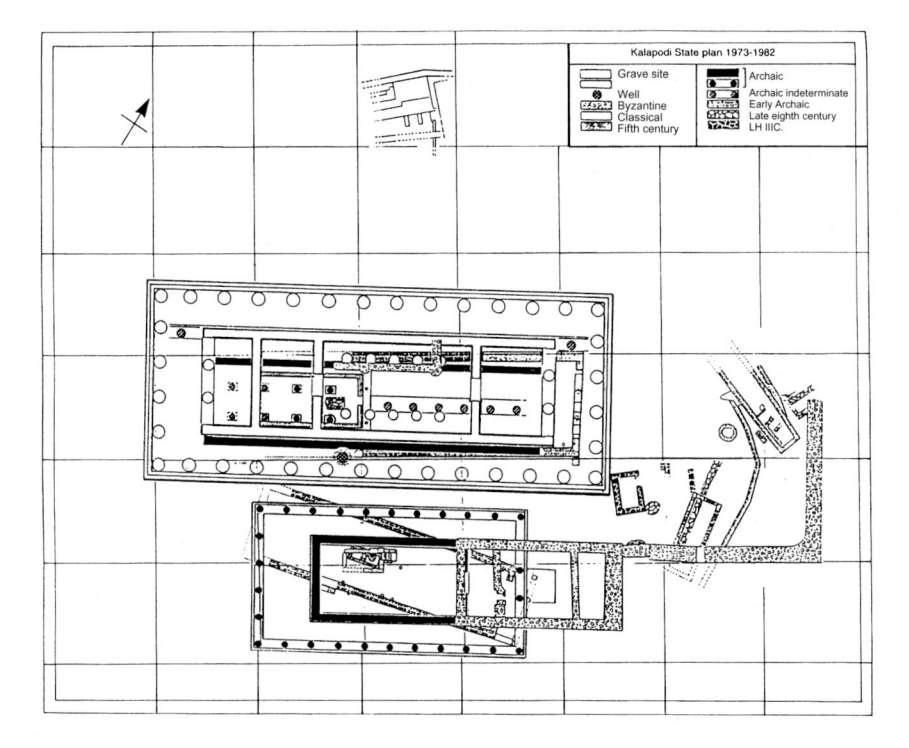

Figure 3.4 Kalapodi (Prof. R.C.S. Felsch). The following two amendments should be noted (R. Felsch pers. comm.): the terrace wall east of the temple and the building in front of it are late sixth century and not early Archaic in date; the well inside the Classical temple colonnade is not Byzantine but Classical or perhaps earlier.

example.[35] During LHIIIC, sites are fewer (although the reduction is less marked than in many southern regions), but almost all are extensive chamber tomb cemeteries which continued in use at least from LHIIIB, often into the Protogeometric period and sometimes beyond (as for example, at Elateia, Figure 1.9).[36] Of these, Amphikleia, Modi and Elateia (and perhaps also Zeli, as Fanouria Dakoronia has speculated) lie along a main route of communication on the edge of the plain immediately west of Kalapodi. Further south lies Vrysi-Sykia near Exarchos, and to the east, in Lokris, are Golemi, Agnandi, and the port at Pyrgos, which was probably the *skala* of ancient Kynos (an important production centre for LHIIIC pictorial pottery, and perhaps the source of that found at Kalapodi).[37] The likely shrine constituency thus spans the later Phokian–Lokrian border.

In the earliest years of the sanctuary, cult activity focused on dining – a means of social bonding as well as symbolizing the fruits of the land – with evidence for the sacrifice and consumption of meat and a wide range of grain types (perhaps as a *panspermion*).[38] Sacrificial victims also included a striking

Figure 3.5 Kalapodi: sanctuary looking south to Mt. Chlomos (photo: author).

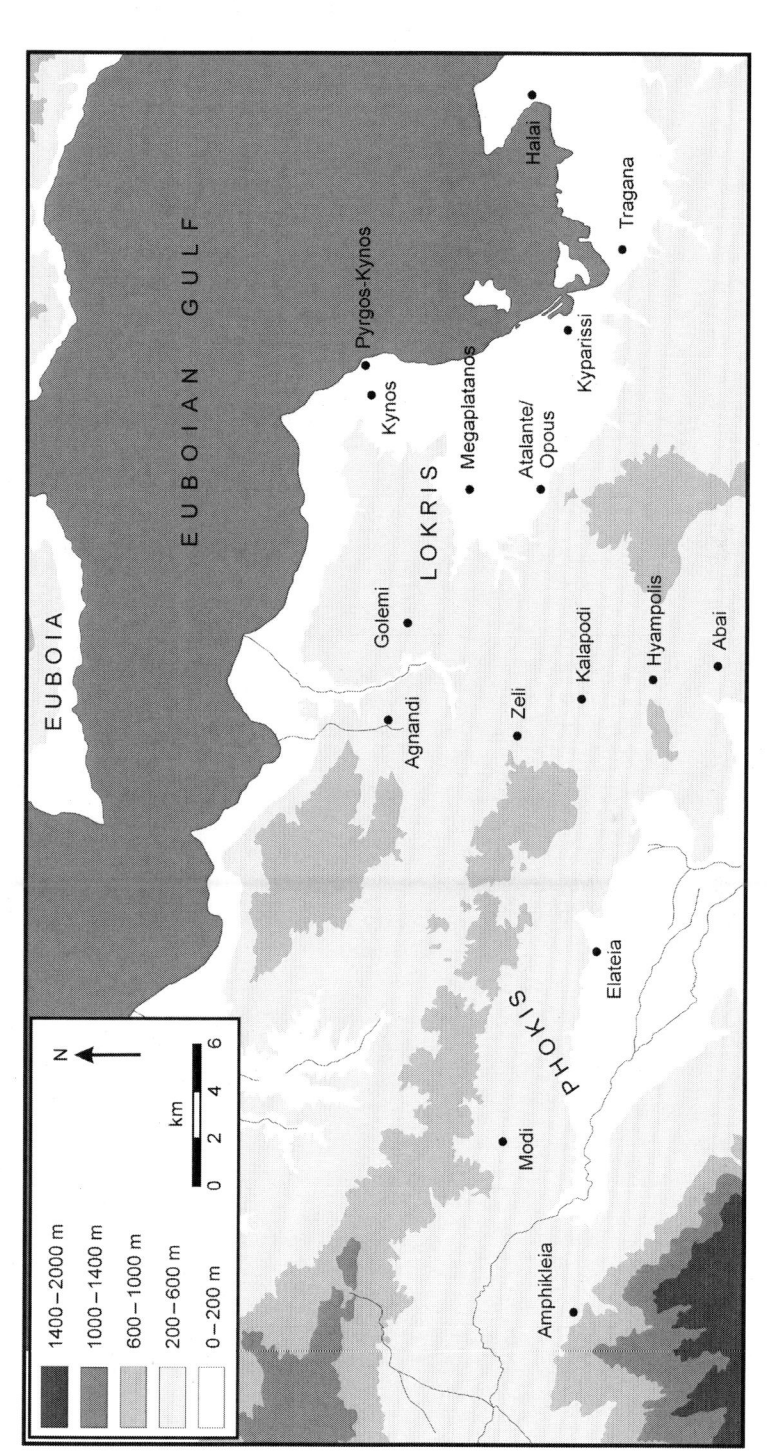

Figure 3.6 The environs of Kalapodi (C.L. Hayward).

proportion of wild animals (notably deer and tortoise)[39] appropriate to Artemis and perhaps evocative of hunting.[40] Finds of spinning and weaving equipment reinforce Artemis' patronage of handicrafts and her role for women.[41] In comparison with finds from the later ninth and eighth centuries, early metal offerings are relatively few (although they are more common at Kalapodi than at contemporary sanctuaries elsewhere),[42] and metalwork appears to have been more plentiful (both in volume and range of types) in local graves. Nonetheless the presence of small metal votives closely similar to those found in graves does suggest a basic similarity in attitudes to the disposition of wealth.[43] As is to be expected, fine pottery forms are biased towards open shapes rather than the closed forms current in graves, but stylistically, the shrine finewares belong within a local tradition with close parallels at, for example, Elateia.[44] Detailed analysis of material values and social representation in ritual as compared with other forms of ideological display (notably grave contexts) must await more extensive excavation especially of cemeteries. Yet perhaps the most striking feature of the record as it stands is the scale and wealth of activity right from the beginning; the projected area of the first shrine, some c.400 sq m, well illustrates the fact that LHIIIC-PG was a peak period in this area, rather than the trough so well documented in much of southern Greece.[45]

From c.950, there was a marked change both in the physical development of the shrine and probably also its likely constituency. (Figure 3.4) Present evidence (limited as it is) suggests a decline (or at least a change in location) in the neighbouring big cemeteries: later graves have been found at or near some sites (Modi, Agnandi and Amphikleia, for example),[46] but, perhaps through chance of excavation, only Elateia shows continuous activity into the early Classical period, and even here the geographical focus has shifted.[47] By contrast, the Lokrian coast, on and around the plain of Atalante, became an important focus of activity. Cemeteries with a proportion of rich graves appear from Protogeometric times onwards at, for example, Tragana (where Geometric pyres have oriental and Egyptian imports), Atalante and Veryki Megaplatanou.[48] The majority of Lokrian acropoleis which continued to be occupied into Archaic and Classical times (or were first settled then) are also located in this area – for example, Megaplatanos (perhaps ancient Kalliaro), Kastri (ancient Larymna), Kyparissi, and also Halai which is perhaps the best known of later foundations.[49] As the imports in the Tragana cemetery suggest, connections with Euboia are likely to have been an important factor,[50] and it is likely that many of the imports from Kalapodi discussed below came via this route. In short, the previous cohesion of settlement in the vicinity of Kalapodi seems to have loosened, and circumstances favouring a territorial border between continuing mountain settlements in northern Phokis and coastally oriented Lokrian settlement began to emerge more strongly.[51] While the shrine may have had dominant interests on one side of a newly effective boundary, the way in which that was crossed by goods or people is a further question. Both the pottery and metalwork assemblages at Kalapodi show long-distance connections which may either indicate the continuing presence of worshippers from other areas, Lokris in particular, or may reflect the connections of local communities, in the light of Kalapodi's proximity to an important route of communication.

To consider material changes at the shrine in greater detail, large-scale construction at Kalapodi began with the terraced extension of the temenos *c*.950. This was followed during the eighth century by the construction of a hearth altar which was to become an important focus for future building, by the first cult structure(s), and early in the seventh century by two small mudbrick temples, one (Temple B) to the south by the previous cult centre, and the other (Temple A) on virgin soil further north.[52] Such investment in facilities highlights both provision for increased numbers of participants and investment by those with a dominant interest in shrine affairs. Dining continued to play an important role, and the composition of the ceramic assemblage remained similar even if the styles of the Thessalo-Euboian ambit were now dominant, with Euboian imports and influences (notably pendant semi-circle skyphoi) probably reflecting the Lokrian connections discussed above, and followed only later in the eighth century by Cycladic and Corinthian imports.[53] The bone assemblage, however, is now altogether smaller (even though the ratio between wild and domestic species did not alter significantly) and the plant and seed record is also reduced.[54] Yet perhaps the greatest change occurs in the votive record, with a steady increase in the number and variety of metal dedications. Jewellery (pins and fibulae) shows stylistic connections with central Greece and the Peloponnese, and bronze figurines feature bird pendants and quadrupeds (horses, deer and lions), subjects appropriate to Artemis, a high percentage of which are Corinthian, Thessalian or central Greek in style. Most striking is the popularity of larger items such as arms and armour (of types paralleled in graves), tripods and *phalara* especially from the last quarter of the eighth century.[55] If, therefore, the bone record implies a diminution of hunt symbolism in favour of husbandry, the presence of armour, also in graves, highlights masculine roles. From the second half of the century there is direct evidence of bronzeworking at the sanctuary, and as Rainer Felsch has suggested, this may not have been confined to votives but may have included the production of functional items, particularly weapons. A model of itinerant craftsmanship has been widely considered in relation to votive production, but this evidence from Kalapodi (as also from Philia in Thessaly, discussed below) points to sanctuary-related workshops as being (at least by the eighth century) embedded within wider regional economic structures, with visitors either taking advantage of the visits of metalworkers to obtain functional goods, or the shrine housing a more permanent facility.[56] We will return to the wider issues raised by this observation later in this chapter, while the question of whether weapons production or maintenance might relate to a specific form of activity conducted at certain sanctuaries, namely the recruitment of mercenaries or followers, should also be borne in mind (see Chapter 4).[57] Here I merely note, following from the discussion of the previous chapter, the potential economic implications of shrines supporting services at least complementary to those which one might expect to find within or near settlements.

Consideration of the southern coastal area, in the lower Pleistos valley and around the bay of Antikyra to the east, reveals substantial points of contrast in the material record, historical development, and likely local role of cult. (Figure 3.7)[58] The area was in many ways a crossroads between the

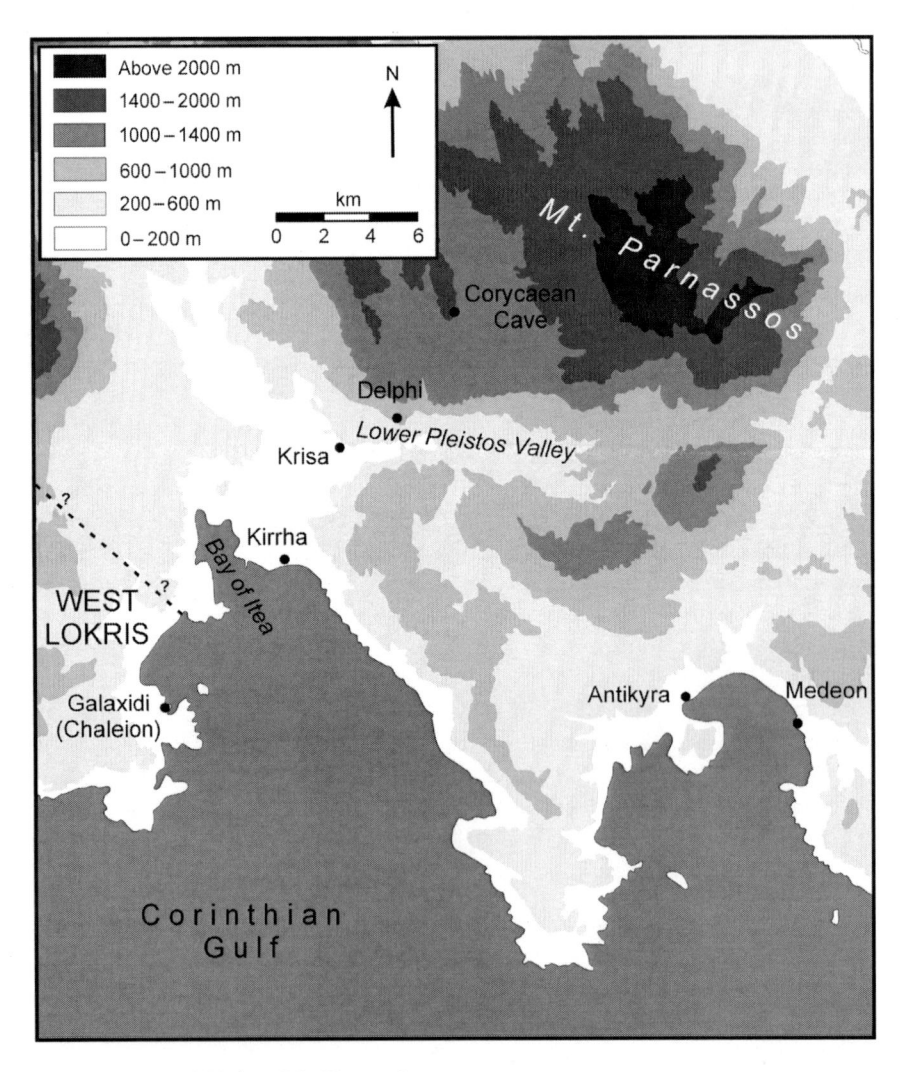

Figure 3.7 Coastal Phokis (C.L. Hayward).

Peloponnese and northern Greece, yet while there was prosperous settlement at Delphi and Medeon throughout the Early Iron Age, there is as yet no secure evidence of any post-Bronze Age shrine until the late ninth or eighth century. In considering the development of settlement from LHIIIB into LHIIIC, Sylvie Müller highlights the growing importance of Delphi which remained prosperous throughout LHIIIC (perhaps in part, as she notes, as a refuge since the ancient settlement had no clear and direct line of sight to the coast). As she notes, the presence of large hollow-bodied wheelmade figures probably indicates an open-air shrine within the settlement operative from LHIIIA2/B at least until LHIIIC Middle, but she rightly rejects the argument for Late Bronze Age cult in the Marmaria.[59] Thereafter, at least until the appearance of bronze votives at the end of the ninth or early eighth century, surviving evidence appears to relate to settlement. Occupation is probably continuous, and bearing in mind the obvious constraints upon exploration in the later temenos, indicative of a substantial site. Secure settlement evidence dates from the mid-tenth century onwards, but twelfth- and eleventh-century sherds are well represented in the lower levels of the most recently excavated plots (especially that surrounding the Rhodian Chariot). Whether one perceives a gap in activity towards the end of the eleventh century or (more probably) settlement continuity rests largely on the absolute dates preferred for LHIIIC Late-EPG, as well as the later Lefkandi sequence.[60] It should also be noted that while there are material (principally ceramic) similarities between the assemblages at Kalapodi and Delphi, for example in the style of certain pithoi and the presence of pendent semi-circle skyphoi,[61] these appear to be outweighed by differences.

Delphi was not the only Phokian coastal settlement, but on present evidence it was the only one to have, from the eighth century onwards, a shrine that rapidly attracted international participation, fostered complex vested interests and made major economic demands upon its hinterland. This raises the issue of the shrine's potential effect upon long-term regional development. At Medeon on the bay of Antikyra, limited rescue excavation has produced evidence of more or less continuous occupation from the Early Bronze Age to Hellenistic times, although not as yet a local shrine.[62] Most Early Iron Age evidence comes from burials following various rites: in succession from the eleventh to the eighth century, single cremation, concurrent inhumation and cremation (both with few goods), and finally inurned and pit cremation. These differ markedly from the northern Phokian practice of multiple cremations in chamber tombs which eventually gave way to single burials. Alongside local handmade wares, imported pottery from the Medeon graves well illustrates the existence of northern and Euboian connections,[63] but also the dominance of coastwise links. Connections with Achaia and Ithaka are exemplified by three near-identical Protogeometric kantharoi with fringed decoration found at Medeon, Derveni and Aetos on Ithaka.[64] Those with Corinth are even more striking, reaching a peak during the eighth century but beginning as early as Late Protogeometric (an exceptionally early date for Corinthian export, paralleled by occasional finds from Mycenae and Thebes, and most strikingly, at Otranto).[65] By the second half of the eighth century, Medeon was a substantial and expanding settlement, at least as large if not larger than Delphi if the excavated remains are a reliable guide. Its subsequent marked decline from the seventh century onwards would therefore seem to demand some particular explanation. In a previous discussion,[66] I framed this in terms of intolerance of such a neighbour by the increasingly powerful vested interests developing around Delphi, but one might also consider broader questions of the (especially economic) attractions which probably increased as the sanctuary grew. If one accepts Petros Themelis' interpretation of the reuse of Mycenaean tholos 239 on the west side of the acropolis as ancestor cult,[67] it is tempting to take this as evidence of emerging local tensions as early as the eighth century. Yet as Carla Antonaccio notes,[68] caution seems advisable as it is hard to discriminate between conflicting accounts of a tomb which has yet to be fully published, and even the excavator, Claude Vatin's report, which stressed eighth-century evidence and on which Themelis' account is based, could as well be interpreted as reuse for burial. The possibility of localized movement of settlement cannot be discounted, although it is as yet impossible to evaluate as no other southern centre is as thoroughly researched as Delphi or Medeon. In the case of Antikyra, for example, only part of an extensive cemetery dating mostly from the seventh century to the Roman period was discovered during a rescue campaign in 1978.[69]

As recent excavation has highlighted, Early Iron Age and early Archaic Delphi was an extensive and rich town. (Figure 3.8) It may have been surpassed by Medeon, but it can certainly be compared favourably with neighbouring centres around the Corinthian gulf, including Corinth itself.[70] The establishment of a shrine to Apollo, probably early in the eighth century, did not seem to have had an immediate impact on the physical form of the settlement (although one might reasonably conjecture that it greatly enhanced its economic growth), and the pace and process by which housing moved out of the sanctuary area are only slowly being understood.[71] Substantial, probably domestic, structures, continued to be built late into the seventh century, and the construction of a peribolos c.575 marks the first real disruption of the associated system of terraces. The so-called Maison Rouge was built in the late seventh century and destroyed c.585–575, and buildings like the Maison Jaune, which were destroyed by at least one major fire around the middle of the eighth century, were subsequently rebuilt. The reorganization of the Apollo sanctuary following the temple fire of 548 is a likely *terminus ante quem* for the removal of private housing, but since this also damaged earlier levels, attempts to reconstruct the sanctuary plan of c.600, on the eve of the first sacred war, are fraught with difficulty.[72] The only strong candidate for a major public building at this time is the first

Figure 3.8 Delphi: Apollo sanctuary from above the Marmaria (photo: K.W. Arafat).

temple, conventionally dated to the late seventh century largely on the basis of the rooftiles supposedly associated with it.[73] However, in a recent review of early Delphic building, Anne Jacquemin has questioned the reliability of this date, since the existence of a marble sima of *c.*580–550 (which must be from this building) points at least to the re-roofing of an older temple, and perhaps to the initial date of the entire structure (which might also explain chronological discrepancies in other architectural elements attributed to it). If the only evidence for a late seventh-century temple should prove to be the rooftiles, which could belong to some other building, the whole issue of the physical formation of the early shrine would be thrown open. Unfortunately, we lack evidence with which to discriminate between the various possibilities.[74] The case becomes firmer during the first half of the sixth century with the beginning of monumental state offerings, both treasuries and freestanding monuments such as the Naxian sphinx.[75] But as Jacquemin emphasizes, it is impossible to detect any priority for amphictyonic interests in this respect, and if, as is likely, non-amphictyons were better represented, there would seem to be some separation between interest in the political and/or financial benefits of sanctuary administration, and in monumental investment.[76] Furthermore, comparison with sites like Olympia indicates that a move towards monumentality was a general sixth-century phenomenon, and the state offerings at Delphi should also be seen within this broader context.[77]

The case for an early distinction between the material connections and interests represented at Delphi and those in northern Phokis is perhaps most evident in pottery and smaller portable votives. Although central Greek bronzes are present in the sanctuary assemblage during the eighth century in particular, they are generally less prominent than at Kalapodi[78] and Peloponnesian (and especially Corinthianizing) styles are more conspicuous.[79] Indeed, the distribution of northern (including Thessalian) bronzes at Delphi is not dissimilar to that at Olympia – a salutary reminder that geographical proximity is not in itself always sufficient explanation. Most conspicuous, however, in comparison with Kalapodi are the relatively large numbers of eighth-century and later tripod dedications which may to a significant degree reflect non-Phokian or non-Thessalian votive practice (notable inscribed seventh-century pieces probably being Boiotian).[80] The range of mostly seventh-century Orientalia (scarabs, Cypro-Cretan and Cypro-Levantine bronze stands, for example) and Italian imports also implies primary connections along the Corinthian gulf; indeed, the pattern at Perachora from the end of the eighth century onwards is comparable.[81] Pre-eighth-century ceramics from the settlement at Delphi owe much to central Greek styles, but from the eighth century, the strength of the Corinthian and Peloponnesian (including Achaian) presence is striking, and this continues through the seventh and sixth centuries with the addition of Attic imports also.[82]

Sources for the first sacred war are, as is generally acknowledged, deeply problematic. Taken at face value, accounts of the war indicate a watershed in sanctuary affairs, with the defeat of Krisa by an alliance of Athens, Sikyon and Thessaly probably in the decade 600–590, followed by the passing of control of the sanctuary to an amphictyony. Patently, many elements of the story are hard to untangle: the causes of the conflict are obscure and the allies ill-assorted, although the elusiveness of the supposedly powerful city of Krisa/Kirrha may be overcome if Despoina Skorda's proposed identification of Krisa with Ag. Varvara proves correct. I would agree with J.K. Davies' conclusion that as preserved, it represents a late and probably rapid crystallization of a long-established oral tradition, and cannot be taken literally as a document of central Greek history.[83] Noel Robertson's more extreme suggestion that there was no conflict and that the received account was a moral tale created around the time of the third sacred war by the partisans of Philip of Macedon is harder to sustain in its entirety. The notion of propagandistic aggrandizement is wholly plausible, yet as Jeremy McInerney points out,[84] Isokrates' allusion (*Plataikos* [14] 33, composed *c*.371) to the sacralization of the Krisaean plain means that at least one aspect of the war story was already current in earlier times, and as Robertson himself accepts, a purely propagandist explanation requires the pre-existence of some hypothetical local tradition upon which later mythographers could work, effectively an 'ur-sacred war'.[85] We may lack detailed contemporary evidence for the organization of the new polis of Delphi, but the existence of the phratry of the Labyades, of known importance in later records, is attested in the well-known late sixth-century *cippus* inscription relating to the conduct of sacrifice at the festivals of the Dioskoureia, Megalartia and Herakleia.[86] Moreover, as early as the sixth century there seems to have been a shift in Delphic imagery: the Homeric *Hymn to Pythian Apollo*, for example, voices a strong rhetoric of separation from local interests, with Apollo personally responsible for the choice of site for his sanctuary, the building of his temple, and the capture of Cretans whom he installed as his priests, enjoining under threat their obedience.[87] While the investigation of change in the archaeological record focused on the supposed physical consequences of war and amphictyonic control, the material picture seemed equally elusive (the construction of the first peribolos being the major work that can be safely dated *c.*585–575).[88] More recently, however, it has been recognised that rather than searching for a simple divide at the start of the sixth century, it is better to think in terms of the cumulative effects consequent upon the expansion of all forms of cult activity, including growing international interests, and to assess the shrine in the context of the southern Phokian environment (cultivable land was needed, but so also, and especially, access to pasture for both sacrificial animals and local herds) and local settlement. At issue, therefore, is the extent to which Delphi was transformed, for a variety of reasons, beyond the reach of local Phokian interests. With the benefit of hindsight, could Delphi ever have played a fully integrated part in a Phokian cult landscape in the sixth century in the same way that, for example, Olympia operated as an Elean shrine?

Accepting the basic point that early in the sixth century the sanctuary and the Krisaean plain were removed from Phokian control, explanations have tended to focus on the sanctuary per se, postulating a growing conflict of interest between sanctuary participants and local populations.[89] There is still much to commend this view, but it is important to recognize the complexity of the matter and the danger of being seduced by later amphictyonic rhetoric of Krisaean impiety and the kind of 'outsider' imagery exemplified by the Homeric *Hymn to Pythian Apollo*.[90] A different but complementary perspective, outlined by Jeremy McInerney, takes a broader view of regional circumstances. Noting the low number of Archaic Phokian settlement sites compared with the expansion evident during the eighth century (perhaps not so much a decline as a failure to continue expansion in the manner evident in neighbouring regions such as Boiotia), he suggests that settlement levels and location reflected continued emphasis upon stock rearing not merely for local needs, but to satisfy the exceptional demands of the ritual economy of Delphi.[91] As he points out, one of the few points on which the sources for the first sacred war agree is that it focused on control of the plain of Krisa, a vital economic resource close to the sanctuary. The issue of resource pressure resulting from eighth-century settlement expansion has already been raised in discussion of Medeon and Antikyra, but in the immediate area of Delphi, it is also worth noting that settlement in the area of modern Galaxidi (ancient Chaleion) on the west side of the bay of Itea, seems on present evidence to have been re-established late in the eighth century. (Figure 3.9) While this site was within easy reach of Delphi and shows similar links with the south coast of the Corinthian gulf, it lies within the territory of Ozolian Lokris, and although we lack direct evidence for the rationale behind, and date of, the positioning of this border, one might reasonably suggest that the assertion of ethnic rights in this key area was a response to some perceived external pressure.[92] Overall, however, the handing over of all sanctuary affairs of any importance to an amphictyony, and the creation of a Delphic polis with limited powers, left the Phokians as victims twice over – political outsiders, yet outsiders upon whom considerable economic demands continued to be made despite the loss of a large and important area of territory. Against this background, the chance of a temple fire in 548 might be seen as the nail in the Phokian coffin in that it physically cleared the way for sanctuary expansion[93] and at the same time gave rich opportunities for states and factions to attempt to purchase influence by aiding the process of rebuilding (as Herodotos 5.62–3 notes in the case of the Athenian Alkmaeonids).

The development of cult sites within the immediate ambit of Delphi may be considered in this light. The proposed seventh-century date for the peribolos at Ag. Varvara is clearly of great interest especially if the site is to be identified with Krisa (although excavation to date has been limited). Its location, on the likely route from the coast to Delphi, is surely significant: free access along the most favourable route must have been of ever greater importance, especially when one considers the extent of sixth-century construction at Delphi using imported Corinthian stone.[94] The sixth-century shrine at Kirrha has already been mentioned, noting that on present evidence

Figure 3.9 The bay of Itea: looking towards the Chrysaean plain and Delphi from the headland due north of Galaxidi (Chaleion) (photo: author).

its establishment postdates the separation of Delphi and the Krisaean plain from Phokis. The second major Archaic shrine, that to Pan and the Nymphs in the Corycaean Cave, was probably established towards the end of the seventh century.[95] The relationship of the Corycaean Cave to Delphi is of some interest. It lies north-east of Delphi at an altitude of 1,160 m on the slopes of Parnassos, close to the route north around Parnassos via Arakhova, and looking down on to a substantial upland plain. (Figures 3.10, 3.11) The cave would not be obvious unless one had business in the area (according to Herodotos 8.36, the Delphians concealed their property in it when they took to the mountains before the Persian advance in 480), and those most likely to have known such an upland milieu were shepherds exploiting summer pasture (for which the area is used nowadays) and perhaps seasonally resident in the area. A mere five small bronze offerings probably date between the late eighth century and the end of the seventh, a time when such items were hugely popular at Delphi,[96] and it is therefore likely that the establishment of cult should coincide with the beginning of the pottery sequence in the latter part of the seventh century (i.e. Corinthian Transitional), especially as this also coincided with the mass dedication of Archaic Corinthian molded figurines (of which some 50,000 survive) as well as small personal items like rings and bracelets.[97]

Bearing in mind the development of Delphi at this period, it is interesting to review the interests represented in the votive record. The cave's location

Figure 3.10 The Corycaean Cave (photo: C.L. Hayward).

Figure 3.11 Upland plain: looking south-east from the Corycaean Cave (photo: C.L. Hayward).

makes it likely that a significant part of the record represents shepherds' or herders' offerings to Pan and the nymphs, and given the extraordinary economic circumstances of the Delphi area, there is no reason to assume that such people would be poor (indeed it is interesting to note similar arguments surrounding the shrine of Pan at Berekla in Arkadia, discussed below at p. 161). Rites of passage have also been suggested, noting especially the number of inscribed knuckle bones as used in children's and adolescents' games.[98] Personal items such as rings and bracelets may be seen in this light too, although they would also be suitable offerings to the nymphs (and even more specific to the cult are fragments of auloi).[99] The shrine therefore seems to have been an extension of the main sanctuary at Delphi in a variety of ways, as much related to economics and the daily life of local citizens as to cult, although cult connections were clearly in place by the end of our period. In the second half of the sixth century, the Homeric *Hymn to Hermes* (550–65) mentions divination conducted by three sisters, the Thriai, who lived 'under a ridge of Parnassos'. And by the mid-fifth century, the intimate association between the cults of Apollo, Athena Pronaia, and Pan and the nymphs is explicit in the prologue to Aeschylus' *Eumenides* (1–29), where the Pythia addresses in turn Apollo and the divinities who preceded him, Pallas Pronaia, the nymphs of the Corycaean Cave (although here associated with Bromius, i.e. Dionysos, rather than Pan), the springs of Pleistos, Poseidon and finally Zeus.[100] The importance accorded to the Cave is well illustrated by the level of investment implied by the long sequence of sculptural dedications which, while most plentiful in the later fourth and third centuries, began with a Daedalic head of *c*.625 and the bust of a limestone *peplophoros* of the first half of the sixth century.[101]

Before moving to compare shrine development in northern Phokis during the Archaic period, it is worth pausing briefly to consider one further issue. I have so far stressed that the eighth- and seventh-century sanctuary at Delphi lay within a sizeable settlement whose principal connections were with the wider ambit of the Corinthian gulf; indeed, relations with Achaia must have remained close since, according to Herodotos (8.36), the Delphians sent their women and children to Achaia to escape the Persian advance while their menfolk took to the mountains. In the concluding chapter I will return to the question of the role of such localized maritime communication in binding together ostensibly very different political communities. Here I note that attempts to provide historical depth for the balance of power within the later Delphic amphictyony have focused on the putative role of a supposedly earlier Pylaean amphictyony which met in Thessaly. This approach downplays, or even negates, the distinctive southern-oriented connections of pre-sacred war southern Phokis, yet is of long-term historical interest given the role of Thessaly as an occupying power during the Archaic period. The Pylaean amphictyony clearly existed close to the relevant time. Herodotos (7.200), writing in the present tense, reported that it met at a sanctuary of Demeter at Anthela near Thermopylae, but gives no further information about its date, composition or antiquity, nor does he connect it explicitly with the Delphic amphictyony.[102] Indeed, evidence for Delphi's participation in any pre-sacred war league comes from much later, myth-oriented sources.[103] It is of course possible to create hypothetical scenarios, as, for example, Jacquemin's suggestion, citing Hermes' threat to plunder the riches of Delphi in the Homeric *Hymn to Hermes* (178–81), that the shrine joined the amphictyony for protection (a need apparently not felt by other equally rich sanctuaries). She then argues that the inclusion of the rich poliad shrine of a major city would have caused difficulties within the league which could most easily be resolved by granting the shrine ethnos status independent of Phokis, and that this would be a likely source of tension within the region.[104]

However plausible, this is quite untestable. There is indeed archaeological evidence to suggest that some eighth- and early seventh-century shrines served as gathering points, as Anastasia Gadolou has argued for the Kynouria for example, but to assume that these were embryonic versions of later amphictyonies (or that all later amphictyonies had such an embryonic existence) is unwarranted.[105] Furthermore, using the later composition of the amphictyony to argue for a major early Thessalian role is methodologically unsound. The idea that Delphi joined an early Pylaean amphictyony which then moved to the sanctuary after the first sacred war in part rests on a perception of amphictyonic primitivism, and in part on geographical echoes in the titles of officers of the Delphic amphictyony and its later movement between Anthela and Delphi. Anthela is also, as Parke and Wormell point out, geographically close to the real centre of the historical amphictyony, a point which would help to reinforce Thessalian claims to control. As Parke and Wormell note, there are three conflicting candidates for the role of mythical founder: Amphictyon son of Deucalion, whilst politically neutral, has the advantage of primeval ancestry, but both Akrisos son of Argos (linked to Thessaly), and Pylades the Phokian carry clear regional claims. But we have no chronological control over any of aspect of league conduct or 'history'. Parke and Wormells' view that they are real and primitive is possible,[106] but the sources are late, and the case for a propagandist construction (or substantial aggrandizement) based upon Thessaly's 'historical' role beginning in the sixth century seems more plausible, since this was a time of vulnerability when defeat by the Phokians may have left her needing to reinforce her authority within the Delphic amphictyony. The only incontrovertible 'fact' is that the earliest evidence for amphictyonic responsibility for the upkeep of Delphi is Herodotos' (2.180) account of the rebuilding of the temple of Apollo after the fire of 548. The wider importance of this should not, however, be underestimated, not least because the authorities would have had to decide whom to approach for help and on what basis (as a city, an ethnos or a family, for example).

Direct evidence for Thessalian presence at Delphi is, if anything, more problematic. The lack of evidence for regular consultation of the oracle is typical of central Greece as a whole, and almost certainly says more about the nature of political authority in this area than about interest in Delphi, but it has nonetheless given rise to doubts over the reality of Thessalian power at the shrine. While there may be other grounds for such doubt, citing the oracle in this context is misleading since the extent to which Thessalian *basileis*, at least during our period, would need such legitimation of their decisions is highly debatable.[107] A rare instance of apparent Delphic involvement in Thessalian politics concerns not the Apolline oracle, but the involvement of a lot oracle in the selection of Aleuas the Red as *basileus*.[108] Whether one regards the Aleuas reported by Plutarch as the quasi-mythical ancestor of the eupatrids of Larisa and/or as the late sixth-century reformer is almost immaterial;[109] the utility of such an exceptional figure as a *genarchos* or national reformer specially selected by a god is plain. Indeed, the story contains several *topoi* from colonial foundation legends, namely surprise (Aleuas' name was inserted into the selection by his uncle against his father's wishes), Aleuas' apparent unsuitability (since he had been haughty and violent in his youth), and his questioning of the verdict, which had to be repeated. Adorning local history with Delphic advice was common practice in many regions of Greece especially from the fifth century onwards, but the weakness of the oracle's place within Thessalian politico-religious consciousness is a significant point of difference.

Materially, although the presence of eighth- and seventh-century Thessalian pottery and small bronzes has been noted, monumental dedications of any period are strikingly rare, especially given the strength of Thessaly's military tradition (Pausanias, for example, mentions just one dedication by the city of Pharsalos, of unknown date).[110] The main exception, the Daochos monument of around 330, belongs within the same historicizing milieu as the Phokian monuments which will be considered presently.[111] Pausanias does note (10.16.8) that the first (albeit small) statue to be offered at Delphi was the gift of Echekratidas of Larisa, and here he explicitly reports local tradition even though it is doubtful whether he actually saw the piece. Yet this fits well within the scope of *protos heuretes* stories, and it is interesting to note how often Thessaly features in such tales concerning different aspects of Delphic tradition. The legendary first temple (Pausanias 10.5.9–13)[112] was built of laurel branches from Tempe, for example, and Tempe was also the place of Apollo's purification after killing the dragon and the source of the laurel with which he crowned himself (an event celebrated in the boy's *theoria*, which involved the gathering of the laurel used to make Pythian victors' crowns). Sources for the *theoria* in particular probably begin with Ephoros, but it is possible, as Christiane Sourvinou Inwood has argued, that its origins are Archaic.[113] Why Thessaly should have come to hold such a place is a complex and ultimately unresolvable issue, but it is possible to speculate. Accounts of the first sacred war put Thessaly firmly in the forefront of the allied powers, with Eurylochos (probably an Aleuad) in command of the Thessalian contingent.[114] Real or not, Thessaly's role in the war formed part of a living tradition which helped to justify her self-perceived later status. More recently, it has been regarded as central to the hegemonical view of sixth-century Thessalian history, a strategic move in the process of control of Boiotia and Phokis (the latter granting valuable access to the Corinthian gulf).[115] Yet if the battle of Keressos in 571 really was the immediate precursor of Thessaly's defeat at the hands of the Phokians, and if the first sacred war (whatever it may have been) is to be placed in the first decade or so of the sixth century (followed swiftly by the establishment, or reorganization of the Pythian games), then Thessaly would have had a mere decade or so to exploit her role in the defeat of Krisa/Kirrha to enhance her position within central Greece (and it is possible to read her prominent place in the Homeric *Hymn to Pythian Apollo* in such a light). Thereafter, her role in Delphic tradition may reflect an attempt to maintain or enhance her status within the amphictyony (emphasizing the political nature of her continuing interest in the sanctuary), as well as the later aggrandizement of regional myth-history.[116] It also serves as an index of Delphi's detachment from Phokis.

To return to northern Phokis during the seventh and early sixth centuries, as noted earlier, two new temples (A and B) at Kalapodi replaced the earlier structures in a probably Phokian initiated building programme during the first half of the seventh century. (Figure 3.4) The northern and larger of these was a mud-brick building with a rush roof and an interior hearth-altar superimposed on that of its Geometric predecessor, and the smaller southern temple, built in the same technique (with alternating black and yellow brick courses), also had a hearth altar and incorporated the Mycenaean and Geometric cult centre under a raised area. Both opened onto the area where ash debris, presumably from the altars, was deposited. There was a new outside altar, and terracing provided a larger assembly area to the east.[117] This was a substantial aggrandizement, but it should not be taken to imply any form of religious proto-league for which there is no other evidence.[118] An equally striking feature of this phase, however, is the poverty of votives (pottery shapes remain the same, for example, but are largely local Subgeometric with few imports), together with the appearance of isolation which the site presents.[119] The contrast with the wealth of the second half of the eighth century is indeed notable, and Ellinger's tentative suggestion that this may relate to Thessalian occupation is plausible. Yet a decline in dedication around this time is not unusual, and the poverty of Corinthian ceramic imports (a major element in the change in the ceramic assemblage) relates to wider changes in the distribution of Corinthian pottery. Equally, following extensive fire destruction at the very start of the sixth century, the apparent delay in rebuilding until the second quarter of the century is hardly exceptional (that at Isthmia after the first temple fire, $c.470$–450, was at least as long).[120]

Perhaps the major factor in Phokian ethnogenesis was the region's response and resistance to Thessalian occupation. From later Archaic times onwards, Kalapodi's pan-Phokian status was expressed via its place in what has been aptly dubbed the Phokian National Saga – the often savage events surrounding the ending of the Thessalian occupation.[121] The area of Hyampolis played a key role in these events: near here, for example, the Thessalians were defeated at the hands of the Phokians, who on the advice of their seer, Tellias of Elis, employed the stratagem of burying hydriae as traps for the Thessalian cavalry. Equally, the final Phokian victory, won at Kleonai near Hyampolis, was marked by the celebration at Kalapodi of the Elaphebolia, the greatest festival of all Phokis.[122] The date of the liberation of Phokis remains controversial, but consensus, in so far as it exists, places it around the time of the battle of Keressos in $c.571$. Archaeologically, evidence of Phokian domination of the Kalapodi shrine by the time of the Phokian league is clear; league issues dominate the coin assemblage, for example, in striking contrast to the absence of Lokrian coins.[123] From this time onwards, Kalapodi's place in Phokian history and national identity is clear, and there followed considerable new investment at the shrine – the terrace was further enlarged and two peripteral, mud-brick temples were constructed with tiled roofs and wooden columns. Pottery imports (mainly Corinthian and Attic) reappeared, but metal votives changed markedly in nature, with weapons, body armour and solid bronze rings now reflecting military concerns and storable metal wealth.[124] Indeed, in its building and votive record, Kalapodi far outstrips the Phokikon, the physical centre and communal hearth of the Phokians created soon after liberation, probably as a complement to the definition of frontiers however belated (the earliest shrine evidence here being fifth century).[125] Ellinger goes further in arguing that the use of the name of the ethnos hero, Phokos, by the Phokians as rallying cry in their battles against the Thessalians presupposes his central role in the national myth-charter, although here the late date of the sources should be acknowledged.[126] The renewed celebration of the Elaphebolia at the sanctuary of Artemis at Hyampolis (Kalapodi), combined with the physical redevelopment of the shrine, gave a new national victory festival a lavish new context, and the fact that, according to Pausanias and Herodotos (8.27), half (i.e. some 2,000) of the captured Thessalian shields were dedicated at the oracular shrine of Apollo at Abai (which has yet to be located) and half at Delphi[127] reflects an interesting ambiguity, with Delphi serving as both a national memory and an international arena.[128]

Ideology apart, it should be noted that evidence for Phokian dedication and oracular consultation at Delphi is very slight, a picture comparable with most of central Greece as we have seen. The only city offering mentioned by Pausanias (10.18.7) is late, a bronze lion given by the Elateians in gratitude for the city's survival of Cassander's siege. The earliest candidate for a pan-Phokian offering is the dedication of the captured Thessalian shields noted above, which were reportedly grouped around a tripod in front of the temple. Pausanias (10.1.10) says that the Phokian thank-offering at Delphi for the defeat of the Thessalians was a statue-group of Apollo, the seer Tellias, the Phokian generals and their national heroes, which was the work of the Argive Aristomedon (of whom we know no more).[129] It may be significant that this reference appears in the context of an excursus into Phokian history, outside Pausanias' main description of the sanctuary (where there is no mention of it, even though two of the three Phokian monuments listed there are explicitly linked to the same sequence of events). There is no independent evidence with which to date this group, and while Ioakimidou has recently argued for an early date (c.490–480) for this and one further Phokian group on historical grounds, its form and the quasi-historical theme fit into broader sculptural trends of the late fourth century onwards, and thus in turn with what is known of the other Phokian monuments at Delphi.[130] These all relate to conflict with Thessaly, are certainly late in date (late fourth or third century, following the third sacred war of 360–346), and as Ellinger suggests, are best seen in the context of a reassertion of Phokian identity after the re-establishment of the Phokian league. Pausanias mentions an Apollo, Athena and Artemis erected from the 'spoils of the Thessalians' (10.13.4, with no date), a bronze group marking the defeat of the Thessalian cavalry in battle (10.13.6, alluding to the events of the Saga), and a Herakles and Apollo struggling over the tripod flanked by Leto, Artemis and Athena, commemorating the battle in which the Phokians were led by Tellias (10.13.7).[131] Furthermore, an inscription dating to the archonship of Kleon (343–3) mentions two statues of the Phokian generals Onomarchos and Philomelos plus other mounted figures (presumably generals).[132] As these references suggest, not only were Phokian monumental offerings few in number, but the majority can be tied to the commemoration, during or perhaps after the third sacred war, of what was by then a quasi-mythical period in Phokian history.

Setting aside the dominant northern and southern cult systems, what of the central area? Were there different, more localized levels of cult activity? If so, they were of lesser antiquity. Protogeometric and Early Geometric sites of any kind are few and widely spread, with at present only Anthochori in the centre of the region.[133] (Figure 1.5) By the late eighth century, however, a chain of sites ran down to the south coast, and the basis of the Archaic city structure was in place.[134] Links between north and south are also reflected in grave goods, for example at Amphikleia and Polydroso.[135] This settlement structure was consolidated through the Archaic period, and was reflected by the sixth century at the latest in the location of a network of shrines which were very different in their physical appearance and were dedicated to a range of divinities, notably those at Elateia (Athena Kranaia, where, after Late Bronze Age occupation, the first votives are eighth-century and show points of comparison with Kalapodi),[136] and Erochos/Polydroso (Demeter, established in the sixth century with finds dating mostly to the sixth and fifth centuries, although some, mainly pins and fibulae, which should date to the late eighth or seventh).[137] At Exarchos a shrine to an unknown deity may have sixth-century origins: Yorke's excavations at the end of the nineteenth century did not reveal many votives, but he refers to bronze phialai and repoussé sheets as probably pre-Persian.[138] Taking these sites together, and allowing for the very limited archaeological research undertaken in comparison with that at Kalapodi and Delphi, it seems on present evidence that these are late foundations, following upon the establishment of the settlement chain linking north and south. Our knowledge is too slight to establish the true foundation date of most of them and to interpret the usually few later eighth- or seventh-century votives present in most cases, but clearly there is at least an escalation of activity during the sixth century which is likely to reflect a post-Thessalian consolidation. It is, however, clear that they echo the evolution of the regional settlement structure. Bearing in mind the strong case for herding as a primary subsistence activity (not least to fulfil the demands of the sacral economy of Delphi), one might argue that the articulation of north–south communications reflected in these shrines and their associated communities was at least as important to herding as to any other subsistence strategy, but there is as yet no evidence for the specific use of cult to articulate landscape in a way directly related to such subsistence interests.

The spread of cults

The case of Phokis well illustrates how localized cult organizations, themselves dynamic entities, can be drawn together within wider regional systems and thus come to operate in an ever more complex fashion as arenas for the expression of different forms of group identity. It also highlights a point, to which we will return, namely that by the Archaic period at the latest, sanctuaries, even more than big residential sites, were prime movers for a wide variety of economic activities, and that it is hard to maintain a meaningful distinction between sacral and secular economies. Before exploring this claim, however, we should explore one further assumption, namely that those cults which came to play a dominant regional role within Classical and Hellenistic ethne had inherited that role from the earliest times. *Prima facie* it is easy to reject this view as simplistic, not least for want of any convincing supporting case. But it is interesting to consider the way in which initially localized cults attached to strong and successful communities came to be replicated or adapted to local circumstances across a wider geographical area. In the case of Phokis, we have seen distinct and parallel local traditions maintained and exploited within the overarching system of the new post-occupation ethnos structure. In Thessaly, by contrast, while there is important Early Iron Age evidence from two major shrines, that of Enodia/Zeus Thaulios at Pherai and that of Athena Itonia at Philia, the way in which Enodia came to be adopted as a pan-Thessalian deity raises a number of distinct social and political issues (Figure 3.12).

Enodia is a perhaps the most distinctive and best known of the deities worshipped in Thessaly, spreading, from the late fifth and fourth centuries onwards, into surrounding regions, Macedon in particular. Associated with the underworld and also roads (a logical connection given the common roadside location of Thessalian cemeteries), Enodia was in later times syncretized with Hekate and also Artemis.[139] The earliest and later the main centre of the cult was Pherai, a town strategically located on major routes of communication and one which, with its extensive cemeteries and settlement traces, bears comparison with contemporary southern centres such as Argos (see pp. 61–4). The first shrine probably dedicated to Enodia and/or Zeus Thaulios (and in fact the first shrine of any kind here) lies immediately to the north of a large Protogeometric and Geometric cemetery not far from the main road to Larisa, perhaps a tumulus cemetery as it is possible that a mound was demolished for the construction of the first temple in the late sixth century. The full extent and chronology of this cemetery is unknown as the only excavation conducted here was primarily concerned with the second, Hellenistic, temple, and thus investigated only those parts of the cemetery contingent upon it.[140] While there is no direct evidence for the deity worshipped during this early period, there is also nothing to indicate a later change in cult and so at least as strong a case for Enodia as Zeus Thaulios.

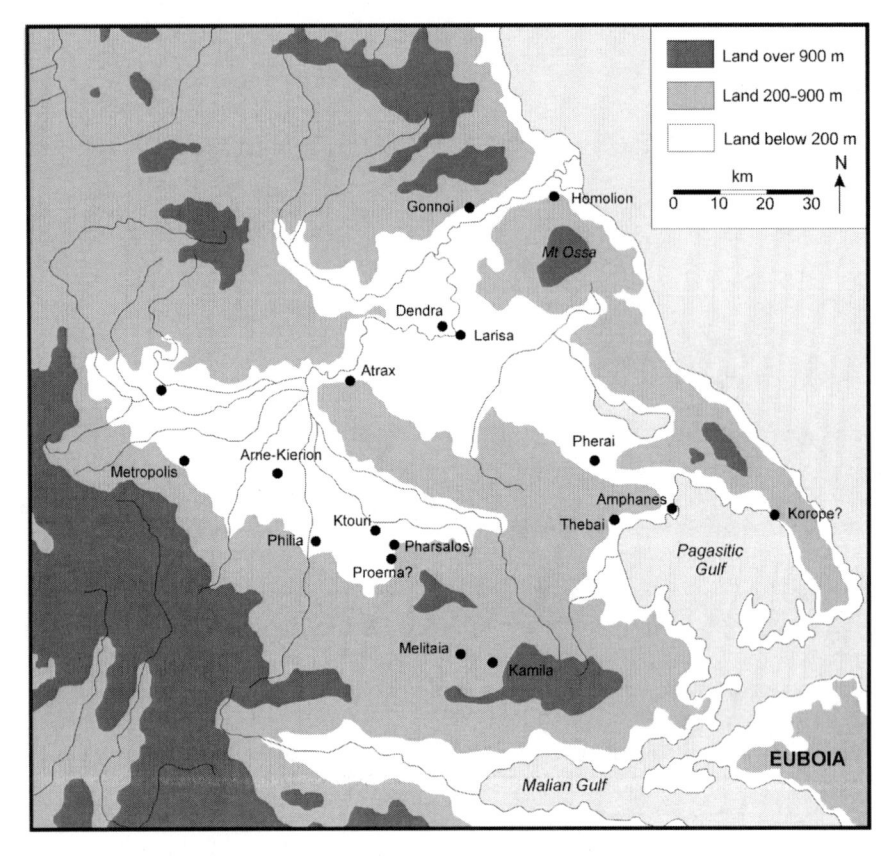

Figure 3.12 Principal sanctuaries in Thessaly (C.L. Hayward).

The institution of cult to a deity treated as comparable to an Olympian within the area of a Protogeometric and Geometric cemetery is exceptional outside the realms of hero or ancestor cult.[141] (Figure 3.13) Yet it is highly appropriate for Enodia with her underworld connections, and is later paralleled at, for example, the shrine in the west cemetery at Pherai, where the co-deity may be Demeter or Zeus (this is only partially excavated, but on present evidence the cult is Classical whereas the cemetery has Protogeometric tombs).[142]

The foundation date of the first Enodia/Zeus shrine at Pherai is a matter of some controversy. Until the construction of the sixth-century temple, worship almost certainly took place in the open air,[143] and votives consisted mainly of small bronze and iron objects (jewellery of all kinds but mainly fibulae, bird and animal figurines) with the addition of (mainly female) terracottas from the seventh century onwards.[144] Given the long life of the shrine, it is not surprising that the earliest material was found not *in situ*,

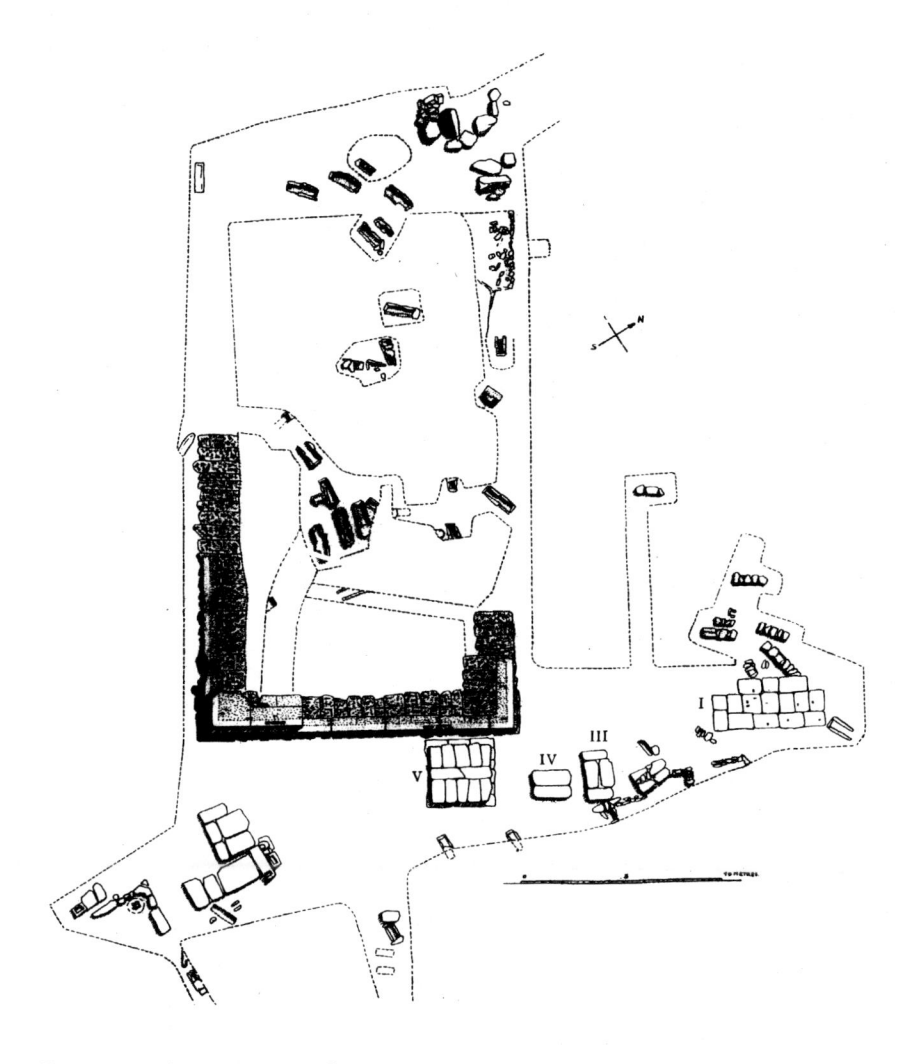

Figure 3.13 Pherai: sanctuary of Enodia /Zeus Thaulios (Béquignon 1937a).

but redeposited in two pits dug west and south of the temple probably during cleaning operations surrounding the construction of the two temples.[145] Inevitably, over the centuries material from various shrines and graves in and around Pherai has passed into a number of private collections, and the exact provenance of such material is rarely traceable. Nonetheless, Imma Kilian-Dirlmeier has identified a total of 3,739 items as reasonably securely linked to the early Enodia/Zeus shrine, suggesting a substantial volume of activity, and while these are mostly Late Geometric and seventh-century in date, there are also a few Submycenaean finds. This is not an uncommon situation at Greek sanctuaries, and as Klaus Kilian (among others) has pointed out, rather than arguing for a Submycenaean foundation (for which we have no further evidence), it is more likely that pieces displaced perhaps from local tombs were dedicated later in the eighth or seventh century. Continuous burial and settlement in the town offered ample scope for the disturbance of earlier contexts (witnessed by the inclusion of a Mycenaean pot in a Geometric tomb), and given the extent of Protogeometric burial activity in particular, the paucity of pre-eighth-century votives at the shrine is a powerful argument against any early institution of cult.[146] Conversely, it seems unlikely that the eighth- and seventh-century bronzes were stripped from graves and deposited at a still later date, given the comparative scarcity and nature of later Archaic material – indeed, items like a griffin *protome* would be unlikely funerary offerings in this region.[147] While we cannot be sure of the time lapse between the cessation of burial and the institution of cult, current evidence suggests that it may have been as little as fifty years (i.e. within the ancestral memory of the living community), and this could be closed further by renewed excavation in the cemetery or revision of the shrine chronology.[148]

In this light, it is tempting to associate the popularity of fibulae (which form almost half of the extant votive record)[149] with their ritual use to fix funerary clothing in Thessalian graves. Fibulae are generally preferred to pins throughout Thessaly, and their popularity at the Enodia shrine suggests that mortuary imagery may have been relevant to the cult. Comparison with grave goods from the contemporary Pherai cemeteries (which feature similar types of small bronzes along with pots) reinforces symbolic links between the two contexts and thus the character of Enodia. Unfortunately, the shortage of comparative sanctuary evidence makes it impossible to test this proposition.[150] The other major Thessalian eighth-century sanctuary, at Philia, has produced barely a third as many pieces over the same period, but only a very small area has been excavated (see p. 141 below). If the level of investment indicated by the Pherai cemeteries is representative, it seems that it was the shrine that attracted the greater wealth.[151] It is, though, important to stress that the picture is incomplete, and that the discovery of rich Protogeometric (and in one case, Protogeometric-Geometric) tholoi containing multiple burials (in one case of thirteen individuals) within the town and north-east of modern Chloe may either reflect a pre-sanctuary pattern of investment, or that the habit of burying the wealthiest citizens beside roads leading out of town (and in a different tomb type) had earlier origins than the late Archaic beginning currently supposed (see pp. 93–5). There is, however, more than just funerary imagery in the shrine record: as Pavlos Chrysostomou has emphasized, the animal figurines feature a range of species (dogs, horses, perhaps also bulls and snakes – and indeed, the fragmentary Archaic sculptural record includes a bull head) which include those sacred to Enodia as to other underworld deities, notably Hekate.[152] One should not overstress the chthonic aspects of the cult, but there is clearly an element present that is not well represented at other Olympian shrines. Other items probably reflect the gender and status interests of their dedicators, and in later times, the shrine's civic role is well illustrated by bronze inscriptions recording matters such as proxeny decrees.[153]

In view of the wealth and early date of the Pherai shrine and the later regional role of Enodia, it is perhaps inevitable that a pan-Thessalian or even international importance has been assigned to the cult from its inception. Arguments based on the likely origins of votives (usually assessed on style) are perhaps the most vulnerable to criticism.[154] As Imma Kilian-Dirlmeier's analysis of the origin of eighth- and seventh-century metal votives shows, only some 2 per cent are non-Thessalian in style, and of these half are Macedonian or Balkan, with the rest ranging widely from Italy to Egypt.[155] Whereas the contrast with, for example, Olympia could hardly be more marked, the situation at Pherai is hardly untypical of the city shrines (like Perachora) included in her analysis. However, in attempting to determine whether foreign votives were brought by visitors or acquired and dedicated by Pheraians, the question of volume is sometimes adduced, on the grounds that the richer the shrine, the less likely it is to be the product of one community. It is indeed very likely that there are other deposits of votives still to be found, and that the large volume of evidence currently known will turn out to be a fragment of the whole. Yet the shrine lay within a substantial settlement by contemporary standards, and one located on the hinge of a major road network – it served, and was maintained by, a substantial local population with territorial ambitions and ready access to overland and maritime trade. Furthermore, assessing the proportion of a community's wealth dedicated in different contexts is an impossible task, not least for being open to anachronistic value judgements. I suggest that the Pherai votive record, considered in the wider context of the contemporary Greek mainland, does not appear particularly unusual.

In terms of the cult itself, considered in its eighth- and seventh-century context it is less internationalism than the peculiar circumstances of a cult closely linked at least in its earliest manifestation to death and the underworld that is immediately striking. Indeed, so unusual is it when compared to shrines in other parts of Thessaly (considered presently) that it does not seem surprising to find no secure material evidence for the worship of Enodia outside Pherai until the fifth century. At Pharsalos, a late Archaic–early Classical temple dedicated to Zeus Thaulios was constructed in the area of an Early Iron Age cemetery, but while the hypothesis that this was shared with Enodia is attractive, it is unproven and the votive record is not comparable.[156] The earliest secure evidence comes from Larisa and Melitaia (Othrys). At Larisa, an inscribed base of a bronze statue dedicated to Enodia Astike, found by the south bank of the Peneios in the north-east part of the ancient city, dates to the third quarter of the fifth century.[157] At Melitaia, the first phase of the shrine, clearly identified by a dedicatory inscription and with an *oikos*-like cult building, dates to the second half of the fifth century.[158] Enodia's link with cemeteries and roads was not consistently emphasized. At Pharsalos and Atrax her hypothetical presence rests in large part of the similarity of shrine circumstances to those at Pherai.[159] The Melitaia shrine, however, lies close to the city walls but not within a cemetery, and while the original location of the Larisa inscription cannot be demonstrated (since ancient masonry was moved over a wide area for the construction of the modern town), the text implies that Enodia was treated as an ordinary Olympian and given the distinctive epithet of a civic tutelary deity.

Thereafter, the cult seems to have spread rapidly within Thessaly and surrounding regions, notably southern Macedon.[160] Thus, for example, a funerary epigram, variously dated to the late fifth or early fourth century and found in the area of the Classical cemetery of Pella, describes the Corinthian Timarete as *propolos* of a deity who is most probably to be read as Enodia.[161] It seems likely that the kind of nationalistic, primeval imagery evident in, for example, Polyaenus *Strategemata* 8.43 (published *c*.162 AD) who describes Enodia as the national deity at the time of the Ionian migration, was a propagandist creation dating back no earlier than this period of expansion.[162] To a great extent, the expanding political power of Pherai must have lain behind the spread of the cult; the decision to associate with such a distinctive deity must imply a deliberate sharing of values, and it may be significant that Enodia of all deities was associated with settlement centres rather than rural locations (a point reinforced by her epithet Astike in Larisa). At Pherai, after an initial vogue for bronze votives, the pattern of dedication shifted during the sixth century to favour terracottas, and the Classical image of the torch-bearing Enodia emerged. This change in votive practice certainly fits within wider trends across Greece, but the appearance of a fixed divine image also accords with Pavlos Chrysostomou's view of Enodia as a deity syncretized within the panhellenic pantheon of which she did not initially form a part.[163] While her fundamental character did not change with syncretism, her image and the material conduct of her cult were constructed in more widely familiar terms. Also interesting is the physical shift in the main shrine at Pherai from the open-air placing of offerings within a cemetery, perhaps around a burial tumulus, which followed upon the construction of the first, Doric temple, a civic monument tied into wider Greek canons, and one which reiterated the shrine's association with the established Greek pantheon.[164]

In considering the reasons for the establishment of such a cult place at Pherai during the eighth century, I have suggested that the most likely explanation for such distinctive and lavish investment lies in some perceived advantage in reinforcing local identity at a time when settlement expansion may have been raising difficult and complex questions of territory and community structure.[165] If so, it is interesting to note that only Arne

(Philia) far to the west, and perhaps also Phthiotic Thebes,[166] elected to establish (or expand) local shrines at this stage, and while there are similarities in the types of votive offered, local differences are even more marked. The shrine of Athena Itonia at Philia remained an open air site at least until the third century.[167] The debris of offerings, sacrifice and dining contained within layers of ash and fat-laden earth include pottery, two-handled bronze cups which presumably served as high-status dining equipment, a range of metal votives similar to that at Pherai (jewellery, including elaborately decorated plate fibulae, and figurines including birds and deer) but also vase pendants, double axes, lead shields, cymbals or *phalera*, as well as terracotta figurines and bone and ivory reliefs. There is extensive evidence of bronze and iron working and the dedication of iron objects, including *obeloi*, spears and swords.[168] Even allowing for the different dates and scales of excavation, votives suggest the symbolic representation of a wider range of social interests than can be traced at Pherai, as well as the production of both votive and everyday items (especially weapons), echoing the observations about metalworking raised earlier in connection with Kalapodi.[169] Evidence for sacrifice and dining and the sustained wealth of small votives through the Archaic period are further features which differ from the extant record of Pherai.[170] As a panhellenic deity and common poliad protectress, it is unsurprising to find Athena later worshipped elsewhere in Thessaly – at Pherai, for example, a marble Promachos-type statue has been found on the acropolis and Athena also appears on the Altar of the Six Goddesses.[171] But Athena Itonia has very distinctive characteristics; it is sometimes asserted (on minimal evidence) that she originated as an underworld deity, but she certainly had a warlike persona, and bearing in mind the hoplite Apollo from Metropolis discussed below at p. 142, it is interesting to note that the limited cult evidence available from western Thessaly shows such military interests.[172] What is striking about the Philia sanctuary is its distinctive cult history compared with that of Pherai. Together with the pattern of Archaic temple building, this suggests that the spread of the Enodia cult, which may have been a result of localized (and sometimes factional) politics, was interwoven with and around older cult preferences.

It is worth emphasizing that such changes as occurred during the Archaic period occurred within a fundamentally stable settlement structure. Marked expansion at individual sites (Pherai included), and changes in regional structures, are phenomena of the fourth century, belonging within the well-documented framework of later Thessalian politics. It is thus interesting to find that at least on present evidence, temple building was not common in eighth–sixth century Thessaly. A Late Geometric rectangular structure at Kamila Marmari (near Neochoraki) has been tentatively identified as a temple of Athena Itonia; the first temple of Athena at Gonnoi probably dates to the second half of the seventh century; that at Dendra may be mid-sixth; the first phase of the temple (of Apollo?) at Amphanes is loosely dated to the

Archaic period, and that at Pharsalos was noted above at p. 139. Most strikingly, the mid-sixth-century temple at ancient Metropolis had a monumental bronze cult statue of Apollo in full hoplite armour, very likely alluding to the god's role as protector of mercenaries, a role of some interest in Thessaly (as will be discussed in the next chapter).[173] There is no obvious connection between the act of temple building and any particular cult, and it seems that it had more to do with communal investment and identity expression than particular religious concerns. The identity of three further structures at probable cult sites is less clear; at Proerna, a building of the late sixth or early fifth century may be a stoa, Archaic terracotta revetments from Korope have been published by Papahatzis as belonging to a temple, and a further questionable structure (a temple or stoa) at Ktouri was partially dug by Béquignon. Elsewhere, however, open or natural sites were preferred; thus in the territory of Pharsalos, votives in the cave shrine of Pan and the Nymphs at Koukouvaia and the shrine of Demeter at Ambelia may date back to the late sixth century.[174]

Much of the available data on pre-Classical Thessalian sanctuaries comes from partially published and often very old excavations, and it would be unwise to rest complex interpretations upon it. Nonetheless, it is clear that by the end of the Archaic period, archaeologically attested sanctuaries, if not plentiful, are widespread (only the historical territory of Hestiaiotis currently lacks evidence), show some potentially significant spatial patterning (being especially numerous in the area of the Pagasitic Gulf, for example), and display both inter- and intra-regional variation (here the three very different shrines around Pharsalos would seem to indicate a more complex local cult organization by the end of the Archaic period at least). Equally, the earliest reasonably secure evidence for a cult building comes from Gonnoi in Perrhaibia; and although the influence of southern Greece, notably Attica, on Classical and later Thessalian monumental architecture has been well documented,[175] if the original inspiration for a monumental temple came from further south, or from Euboia, then it is interesting to note that its first manifestation is in the north of the region, and this in turn must make a north Aegean, and perhaps ultimately an Ionian, connection most likely.[176]

Temple buildings

Discussion of Thessalian temples raises the fundamental question of the origins and function of early temple buildings. For most southern and (perhaps to a lesser extent) central mainland communities, these structures are perhaps the major innovation of the eighth–sixth centuries, although it is worth noting that the gradually widening geographical spread of evidence for rather earlier purpose-built cult structures elsewhere is beginning to make this part of the mainland seem distinctive. Admittedly, evidence from regions like the Chalkidike or the Cyclades[177] is at present limited to just one or two sites, but these are regions which have until recently suffered from a mixture of lack of investigation and/or publication, and the need to reevaluate data from very old excavations. At Thermon, Megara A and B may have been *heroa* or a central residence/cult places,[178] but at Mende-Poseidi in the Chalkidike, the extraurban shrine relating to the settlement on the Vigla acropolis acquired a long apsidal mud-brick structure (Building Στ) in the tenth century, built around an ash altar which had been established in Late Mycenaean or Submycenaean times (it is unclear whether this was roofed).[179]

In assessing the likely motivation for temple building, a wide range of functions has been proposed. The housing of specific, religiously sanctioned social institutions, for example, has been most strongly advocated on Crete, as in the case of the *andreion* proposed at Afrati (where Didier Viviers restores the so-called temple as an armour-lined hall)[180] or Prinias, where our earliest sculptural ensemble includes a frieze whose iconography has been linked to favoured male pursuits and perhaps initiation.[181] Alternatively, the temple has been seen as the descendant of the ruler's house, either in the form of a quasi-bouleuterion (as perhaps Pallantion discussed below) or as the *oikos* of the god.[182] In the latter case, it is clear that at certain sanctuaries in later times gods could hold property as landowners (the sacred herd at Lousoi is an obvious example),[183] authorize decisions about the conduct of their own affairs, receive for approval the decisions of their communities of followers (as the sixth-century Elean treaty inscriptions from Olympia discussed in the previous chapter, p. 80), and could themselves be personified (the quasi-human treatment of cult statues in shrines like the Samian Heraion is a case in point).[184] But the relative chronology of the creation of the *oikos* model seems more problematic. The case for an essentially eighth-century progression from ruler's house to temple, with the logical power-flow of the god assuming part of the previous ruler's role among the newly enfranchised political community[185] and thus the *oikos* as something embedded in the conception of divine presence, rests on particular interpretations of a very few relatively well-preserved archaeological cases. The most often cited, Nichoria, did not of course last beyond the eighth century, and a potentially more persuasive case may be advanced for Aetos on Ithaka, where reappraisal of data from excavations in the 1930s radically alters our understanding of the building sequence.[186] Elsewhere, the fragmentary state of the archaeological record frequently requires much inference, and so while the overall line of argument could be right, it is often hard to demonstrate, and in any case it is only part of the story. There is at least as convincing a case for reversing the process, with sanctuaries increasingly adopting the form of an idealized and perhaps archaizing *oikos* rather later in Archaic times, perhaps reflecting the way in which sacral economic expansion had been managed,[187] as well as offering a comprehensible and acceptable means of expressing the role of the divine to reinforce ideal values and smooth over potential areas of conflict within individual communities.

Moreover, at least on the mainland (by contrast with Ionia), there is no real evidence to suggest that temples were developed to house divine imagery. There are rare cases of earlier large-scale, probably divine or priestly figures on open sites (the LHIIIC life-size image from the Amyklaion is perhaps the best example),[188] but until we know more about the placing of larger terracottas, like the eighth-century Amyklaion figures or the sixth-century Mantineia-Ptolis *peplophoroi*,[189] within sacred areas and in relation to altars and to other categories of votive, it would be premature to make assumptions about what they represent. Discussion of the origins of religious sculpture often focuses on cult statues and the later literary tradition of *xoana*,[190] but one should not forget the much wider range of imagery in the extant record of Early Iron Age sanctuaries. Indeed, it is likely that earlier approaches to the use of both figurative and non-figurative imagery in graves and sanctuaries must have underpinned certain of the innovations in the use of monumental sculpture in the Archaic period. At the vast majority of sanctuaries (and certainly those of the mainland) the relevant spatial relationships have been lost, and the material record may itself be very fragmentary. A rare case where progress has been made is Ephesos, where study of the distribution of votives, and especially the unparalleled collection of large amber and ivory figures, in the area of the eighth- and seventh-century Artemision offers important insights into the way in which the area around the *peripteros*, which housed the divine image, was 'peopled'.[191] It can, however, be argued that temple buildings gave greater scope for the use of costly and/or fragile materials like gold and ivory especially during the second half of the sixth century, and thus promoted, rather than responded to, the development of freestanding cult imagery.[192] A final possibility for the function of the temple is as an art-offering in its own right – the so-called western 'baroque' of the first Heraion at Mon Repos, or Kalydon, are cases in point.[193] It is tempting to relate these various interpretations of function to different regional patterns of development. Yet, as will be illustrated in the case of Arkadia, they can be sharply juxtaposed within quite small areas in a way that raises questions about the roles played by the cult systems within which they belonged, and also about the rise through the later Archaic and Classical periods of a wider consensus concerning the proper external appearance of a temple (sometimes, as for example in the case of Bassai, to the point where the form of construction runs counter to the more logical way of building with local stones, Figures 3.14, 3.15).[194]

Material evidence (in the form of their contents) for the function of early temple buildings is rare. It is therefore worth pausing to consider evidence from the Corinthia, where the later of the early to mid-seventh-century pair of temples, that at Isthmia, has produced a well-preserved record from the area within the first temple cella (Figure 3.16). In doing so, it is important

Figure 3.14 Bassai: limestone outcrop close to the Classical temple, showing bedding planes (photo: C.L. Hayward).

Figure 3.15 Bassai: architectural use of local limestone (photo: C.L. Hayward).

Figure 3.16 Isthmia: temple of Poseidon during the 1989 University of Chicago Excavation season (Archaic temple postholes seen at right) (photo: author).

not to lose sight of the fact that both these buildings are votives in their own right, and however they may compare with the lost buildings represented by the few eighth-century *spolia* from Corinth, the elaboration of their painted decoration (especially in the case of Isthmia) marks them out.[195] Indeed, the principle of dedicating built space may already have been symbolized in the votive architectural models from Perachora, although their chronology in relation to Corinthian temple building is once again a matter of debate.[196] Yet this still leaves the question of the buildings' practical function(s). There is little direct evidence to be gleaned from Corinth, as extant remains consist of debris from the sixth-century temple fire much of which was used in the construction of a roadway on the north side of Temple Hill. This is certainly sufficient to reconstruct the form of the building, even if its precise location is unknown, but we have no evidence for the full range or position of its contents.[197]

Isthmia, however, offers a rare opportunity to look in detail at the physical evidence of the building's contents, as opposed to the kind of literary evidence upon which we are usually forced to rely.[198] Following the fire of *c*.470–450, collapsed structural remains were removed and used mainly for landscaping, and we must assume that any other recyclable materials were also taken. But this left a thick layer of debris which remained exposed down to the later fifth century when it was spread out to support the floor of the

Classical temple constructed on the same site. The surviving parts of this layer (Figure 3.17) have produced over 500 items dating from the early seventh to the later fifth century, with a heavy concentration in the second half of the sixth, a period of particular wealth, and spatial variation in their distribution suggests that different kinds of item were stored in different parts of the temple. The nature of the objects suggests that the building was used principally for the storage of valuables and consumables – and plentiful metal fittings may suggest that at least some were kept in chests or on shelves. Within the cella were many amphorae (presumably for oil as well as wine, since the burning pattern on some shows that oil had penetrated into their fabric), and also the majority of the plain juglets from the site (perhaps measures or single portions, Figure 3.18), and a few bronze vessels including imitations of this ceramic shape. This kind of evidence suggests that the existence of the temple facilitated the longer cycle of provision and storage throughout the year which may have become essential as the festival expanded. Elsewhere, aryballoi (in much more complete condition than those outside in the temenos) are perhaps to be counted as stored equipment rather than straightforward offerings. Valuables, which are separately concentrated, consist of small items of jewellery, gems and scarabs, and also coins probably accumulated over time, if not as offerings then perhaps as revenues paid to the sanctuary and stored in the temple. (Figure 3.19) Some tools (for example, fishing equipment) may have been personal dedications, but others, along with raw materials like gold and silver leaf and the red ochre used to

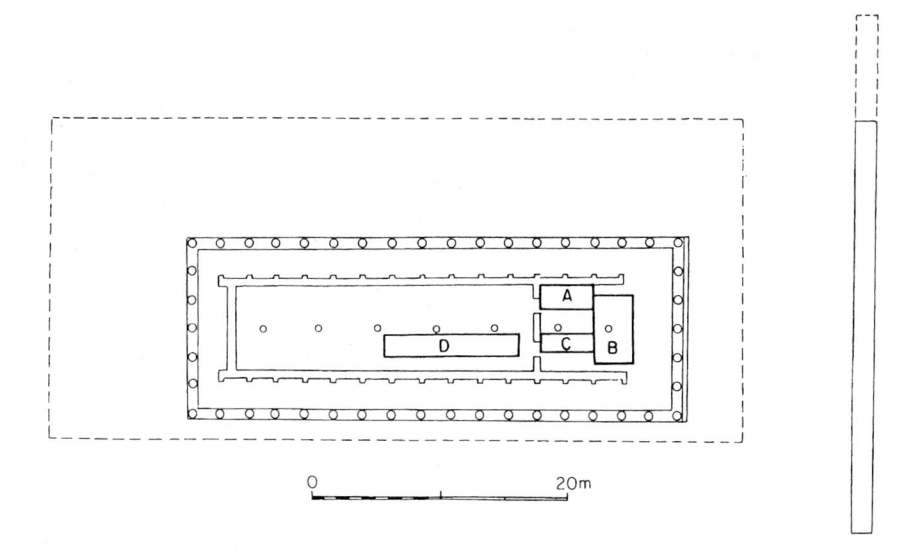

Figure 3.17 Isthmia: Archaic temple of Poseidon showing area of excavated deposits (reproduced by courtesy of E.R. Gebhard, plan by Pieter Collett).

Figure 3.18 Isthmia: temple of Poseidon, plainware juglet (photo: K.W. Arafat).

Figure 3.19 Isthmia: temple of Poseidon, sealstone IM 581 (University of Chicago Excavations at Isthmia: photo: Michiel Bootsman).

apply them, were probably part of a craft store perhaps used to repair dedications (reflecting the practicalities of maintaining increasingly lavish sanctuary furniture). Among the clearly votive items, some, like tripods, arms and armour, which also occur outside in the temenos, may have been brought in from display as space became tight, but others are concentrated inside and in the case of chariots (mainly wheels) may have been victor dedications hung up in the temple. There are, of course, many parallels for the storage of historically significant items within temples, as also for temples as strongrooms (as noted, p. 79, two mid-fifth-century bronze inscriptions at Tegea record cash deposits held in the temple for one Xouthias son of Philachaios, a foreigner and perhaps a Spartan or Achaian). Yet it is striking how much of the Isthmia material relates to practical shrine activities: for example, most heavy metal castings had been deliberately broken up, and the temple may have been a secure store for sacred scrap awaiting reuse.[199] By contrast, there is little to suggest ritual within the temple or regular access by worshippers – no hearth, statue base or image, no bench or space for seating – and cheaper votives like figurines are largely found outside. In many ways, the first temple at Isthmia looks like a very elaborate storeroom, a facility which enabled better management as needs for festival provision grew, and also answered new needs to safeguard revenue, manage the flow of votives on display and maintain the appearance of costly items.

The economic roles of sanctuary authorities

At all of the very earliest mainland shrines – Isthmia, Olympia, the Amyklaion, Kalapodi and Mende Poseidi – the archaeological record shows clear emphasis on dining and the consumption of the resources of the land (real and/or symbolized in figurines). All have produced a pottery assemblage focused on dining (Olympia now included), as well as bone and in some cases seed debris, and figurines among which bull imagery features strongly – and rarely much else.[200] Given the geographical spread of these shrines, it is of course predictable that there are differences in their records which are understandable in their very different local contexts. At Olympia, for example, the shrine started as a local institution at the heart of a small network of settlement around the valley. It was founded in the power vacuum created by the collapse of the palace system to the south, yet, as the evidence of two exceptionally large and elaborately decorated kantharoi from the Pelopion shows, it perhaps adapted some aspects of Late Bronze Age ritual (a link enhanced by the latest reading of some of the bones from Blegen's excavations at the palace at Pylos as evidence for burnt sacrifice in the palace).[201]

It would clearly be unwise to overemphasize early similarities between shrines, which in many respects diminish over time. But it is worth emphasizing that right from the start, sanctuaries were consumption centres with subsistence resources at the core, and while the sacrifice and the common meal have often been perceived as a means of closing and defining a social group, the practicalities of creating and sustaining a sacral economy are of greater long-term significance. How supplies, including sacrificial animals, were obtained (perhaps via liturgies of some form), and how incidental benefits such as hides or bones were subsequently distributed (or even sold on), perhaps for the manufacture of items such as jewellery or tools (as in the much later, Hellenistic, case of the Lousoi sanctuary workshops),[202] raise important, if presently unanswerable, questions about the nature and extent of 'sacral' as opposed to 'secular' authority (if indeed there is any meaningful difference), and the way in which social and economic power was exercised in the practicalities of organization as well as the enactment of ritual. The question of the distribution of secondary products, of which we have as yet rather patchy direct evidence (for example, the well-known inscription from Tegea of *c*.400 concerning the *hiera probata*, including the sale of *kopros*),[203] is a fruitful area for continuing archaeological research.[204] There is ample documentation of sanctuaries as contexts for consumption, as also of shrine workshops (especially for metalworking) which sometimes produced more than just votives (notably weapons at Philia),[205] yet shrines were also producers with complex links into a range of everyday craft activities beyond the purely sacral.

To illustrate the way in which such established links may underpin the expansions and innovations of the seventh and sixth centuries, we should pause to consider the comparatively well-documented case of Corinth. Following the first big expansion in the number and variety of shrines across the region from around 750 onwards, early Archaic Corinth ran one of the largest sacral economies of any single mainland polis, and shrine numbers increased steadily through the sixth century.[206] Yet with the exception of Perachora,[207] the votive record remained relatively modest until the sixth century. The most striking feature is the level of consumption of the fruits of the land which continued to grow through the Archaic and Classical periods, as evidence from the shrine of Demeter and Kore at Corinth attests (and even at Perachora, the first major building programme undertaken from the late seventh century onwards featured a *hestiatorion*).[208] This fits well with the priorities of eighth-century Corinthian export: while Corinthian contacts with the west in particular have tended to be reconstructed on the basis of fine pottery, this says little much about direct Corinthian involvement, especially as a significant proportion of what is found especially on Ithaka and around the bay of Naples is not in fact Corinthian.[209] More significant are the eighth-century amphorae from the Salento and Syracuse which are clearly Corinthian and place Corinth together with regions like Lesbos in the forefront of production of recognizable containers to suit the shippers of her produce.[210] Considering the longer span of her history, Corinth is exceptional for the extent to which she favoured imported and indigenous food, drink and small luxuries over more lavish display.[211] Indeed, given the extent of her cult activity, it is striking that with the principal exception of the late seventh- and early sixth-century *Frauenfest* (heavily biased in its distribution to two shrines closely associated with women, that of Demeter and Kore on Acrocorinth and the Perachora Heraion, the latter probably the context for initiation rites), Corinthian vase painting has next to no religious iconography.[212] Such trends beg the question of the construction and function of the two earliest shrine buildings, on Temple Hill and at Isthmia, which, while not the very earliest on the mainland, are early enough to imply conscious innovation rather than simple peer pressure. Given that existing cult celebrations relied heavily on the preparation and consumption of meat and drink, one might assume the existence of well-established supply systems to mobilize resources at the right time. It has already been argued that the Isthmia temple facilitated this process, and is therefore interesting to consider the related issue of the extent to which the organization of temple construction drew on the pre-existing connections of such systems.

The supply of building material is a logical starting point. The oolitic limestone of the walls (Figure 3.20) and the clay used for the rooftiles of both buildings (Figure 3.21) are Corinthian and can be quite closely provenanced. Chris Hayward's study of Corinthian quarry locations (Figures 2.8, 2.9), and his demonstration that oolite can be closely provenanced within each individual centre of Corinthian quarry activity, raise interesting questions of the social mechanisms underlying supply (a major gift, perhaps,

COMMUNITIES OF CULT

Figure 3.20 Isthmia: oolitic limestone block from the Archaic temple of Poseidon (photo: C.L. Hayward).

Figure 3.21 Isthmia: rooftiles from the Archaic temple of Poseidon (photo: author).

or individual liturgies either involving personal gifts or the role of a middleman supplier enabling others to fulfil their obligations).[213] Admittedly, we have almost no direct evidence for Corinthian landholding and resource control before Roman times, but the assumption that individuals controlled resources on their own land would avoid the need for overarching 'state' control, which may be hard to envisage this early (especially as the buildings' likely dates seem to flank the establishment of the tyranny). The rooftiles are a slightly more difficult matter. The manufacturing process of the Isthmia tiles has been replicated using clay from the area of Solomos, and the similarity of this clay with those used from the late seventh century onwards for a distinct range of artefacts such as tiles and architectural terracottas would suggest that this was also a possible source in antiquity.[214] By the eighth century there is evidence for the careful selection of clay mixtures for specific forms of ceramic production (amphorae, burnished plainwares and different forms of fineware). The absence of early production sites makes it difficult to reconstruct the chain of extraction and manufacture (although it seems likely that large and heavy items such as tiles were made close to the buildings for which they were destined). But we can only guess at whether clay beds were effectively private property and thus the supply of raw material (as opposed to the labour involved in manufacture) was a potential form of liturgy, or whether there was more open access to a basic resource.[215]

Further organizational issues arise from comparison of the practicalities of oolite extraction and rooftile manufacture. Experimental firing of the Isthmia tiles indicated that the first temple roof could have taken up to two years to complete, allowing for seasonal variation in drying times, year-round firing, but not for 'agricultural breaks'.[216] An optimal construction schedule would thus have tile manufacture set in train immediately, at the same time as the stone was quarried (assuming that this was done to commission), noting that seasonal constraints also affect quarrying, not only in the availability of manpower, but also in the passability of quarry tracks in winter.[217] These two sets of production needs therefore dovetail, but in order to exploit this fact and make optimum use of labour, management is required in the same way as supplying a festival. Some of these needs may not have been entirely new, since there are a very few stone architectural members (partially worked blocks and a column base spoiled by fire and discarded) in contexts of the second half of the eighth century by the Sacred Spring in central Corinth, although no evidence for the type or location of the buildings for which they were destined.[218] But it is likely that the scale of operations involved in constructing two monumental temples in swift succession presented major new challenges. Overall, however, it is not hard to see the managerial issues involved as complements to, or extensions of, the existing organization involved in sanctuary conduct.[219]

That sanctuaries were important movers of commodities and people, and that by the second half of the eighth century at the latest there is widespread evidence that they hosted metalworking (in certain cases for the production of more than merely votive material) are amply attested. Discussion so far has emphasized the embeddedness of cult economics within wider organization. This reflects not merely the fact that subsistence strategies had to provide increasing quantities of sacrificial animals, food and drink for festivals (and in exceptional cases, such as Delphi, we have seen that this could have a significant impact on fundamental issues such as landholding and the very nature of subsistence activities perhaps on a regional level), but also the cycle by which resources and commodities flowed in and out of what might be narrowly defined as the purely sacral economy.[220] In other words, sanctuaries were focuses for a wide range of economic activities by virtue of the scale on which they operated, but they were not closed systems nor did they hold a monopoly of any kind of production.[221] Indeed, the potential for open circulation is highlighted by the very frequency with which sanctuaries attempted to assert the rights of the deity or cult personnel to the fruits of ritual activity, be they by-products like hides and dung, or forms of dedication (notably weapons) which would be attractive personal possessions.[222]

It is, however, important to note that such arguments for the deep embeddedness of early sacral economies, and for the lack of rigid (or even clear) boundaries between sacral and 'secular' activity do not represent a universally accepted view. The case for a significant degree of sanctuary autonomy in organizing both production and the import of raw materials and finished goods has been made with reference to metalworking by both Ingrid Strøm (particularly noting the case of the Argive Heraion) and Tamsey Andrews (based on Olympia). Strøm's argument rests on the difference both in the volume of imports at sanctuaries as opposed to settlements (begging questions of circulation and preservation) and the stylistic origins of imported, especially orientalizing, metalwork found in the specific case of the Argive Heraion in comparison with Argos, which leads her to suggest that these offerings were not made by Argives.[223] While her suggestion that bronzeworking ateliers were attached to sanctuaries seems uncontroversial, the assumption of exclusivity, and in this case the specific denial of Argive offerings of monumental metalwork at the Heraion, have both been subject to criticism.[224]

Andrews' case is rather different in that she focuses on the exceptional volume of metal dedication at Early Iron Age and seventh-century Olympia (she estimates that some 9,000–10,000 items have been recovered, presumably a fraction of the total offered).[225] Arguing that the majority of items were locally manufactured by both local and itinerant craftsmen, she suggests that the supply of metals to those who worked on site was likely to have been controlled by the sanctuary authorities. While the extent of *in situ* casting, especially of certain artefact types such as tripods, is less clear than she allows, there is plainly a major issue of supply here, especially as the least controversial case concerns figurines, which are among the earliest and consistently the most numerous offerings.[226] It is highly likely that sanctuary authorities were closely involved in the organization of recycling of casting debris and older votives. In later times, such metal remained the property of the deity and was often used for the manufacture of further votives, as attested epigraphically and archaeologically, as has been shown in the case of Isthmia.[227] At an exceptionally metal-rich shrine like Olympia, this probably took place in earlier times also – indeed, it has been suggested that there was so much metal in circulation here during the ninth and eighth centuries that it was even unnecessary to collect and melt down all the available miscastings and scrap.[228] And over and above the need for raw materials, display space may have been an issue. The growing number and monumentality of tripods in particular, considered in the context of what was, at least until the diversion of the Kladeos in the seventh century, the relatively confined area of the Altis, highlights the problem of the manner and scale of exhibition of monumental offerings.[229] How were earlier dedications treated as time passed? At what point were they regarded as too numerous or socially insignificant, and thus disposable? As argued in the case of Isthmia, it is likely that by the seventh century at the very latest any reasonably long-established shrine would face growing problems in managing space, maintaining the condition of certain offerings and recycling others.

To some extent, therefore, differences between the cases argued by Strøm and Andrews and that presented here may be a matter of focus, since I have concentrated on subsistence products, whereas the question of metal recycling is as much an issue of management as procurement. Beyond this, however, the absence of analytical data leaves us with no direct evidence for the sources of metal used or for patterns of procurement. Andrews' identification of central Italy and the Balkans as the sources of supply used at Olympia rests on their geographical proximity and the external connections revealed in the votive record (which rarely date back to the earliest years of the shrine). She thus assumes that sources of supply will be directly reflected in the votive record, whereas supply may be complex and indirect, and other motivations for dedication should be considered.[230] Perhaps the most fundamental problem in arguing for the economic autonomy of sanctuaries arises from trying to separate religious and secular interests in Early Iron Age and Archaic Greece, especially given the intimate relationship between religious power (notably in priesthoods) and social status. Even in the case of metalworking, while sanctuaries clearly were important centres of production, the fact that there is extensive literary and archaeological evidence for workshops elsewhere would seem to argue against long-distance procurement focused on just one context (especially in regions like the Argolid or the Corinthia where several shrines were operative),[231] while localized redistribution returns us to the problem of the multiple social roles and connections of community leaders. In short, predicating the reconstruction of economic organization upon the mechanics of large-scale dedication of metal votives seems not only slanted but tenuous, since this was a comparatively short-lived phenomenon and more localised than is often assumed.

Arkadia

The case of eastern Arkadia well illustrates many of the issues of social representation and identity raised so far. Arkadian shrines remained sharply differentiated through our period, and fulfilled a variety of public purposes: by contrast with Phokis, they were not incorporated within an overarching regional system, and unlike Thessaly, no single cult achieved 'national' status. The shrine of Athena Alea at Tegea (Figure 1.18) is perhaps the best-known early Arkadian cult site – indeed it is almost the only Tegean site of any kind yet known before the later seventh century, when isolated capitals must come from some form of public building in the settlement.[232] Evidence from this sanctuary has given rise to much discussion of the range of public roles it played, from metalworking to banking and guaranteeing commodity movement.[233] Here, however, we will concentrate on the various shrines of Pallantion and Asea, south-east of Tegea, which have recently been the subjects of extensive reappraisal and renewed excavation, and which differ markedly from Tegea in their physical form.[234] While Madeleine Jost has made a strong case for Arkadian sanctuaries as territorial markers,[235] with the implication of mutual awareness of temple design and dedication, and the spread of such architectural traits as capital proportions documented by Eric Østby supports this,[236] it is clear that such shared traits overlay more profound local differences. It is also important to emphasize that territoriality in Arkadia is a particularly complex issue. As noted (and see also Chapter 4), Arkadian poleis shared installations such as drainage systems and upland roads that required maintenance, and the region's topographical diversity combined with the nature of subsistence crops surely demanded regular exchange and also access to different types of land.[237] All this may have meant that borders were, if not less clear, at least more complex palimpsests of different kinds of division than are commonly found elsewhere.

Pallantion was one of the smallest Arkadian poleis, little more than an acropolis and a small extension of the Tegean plain (Figure 3.22). It shared with Tegea the maintenance of the Lake Takka drainage, but while clearly within the Tegean ambit, it was sufficiently politically independent to be acceptable as a place of exile from Tegea (as it was, according to tradition, for Stesichoros around 560–550).[238] The collection of four temples on the acropolis is at present unique in Arkadia, and the ambition of such a building programme undertaken by this tiny community is self-evident. Clusters of temples within sanctuaries are perhaps best known in Magna Graecia, where explanations have included patronage by different families, ethnic or interest groups.[239] But the fact that the four buildings at Pallantion

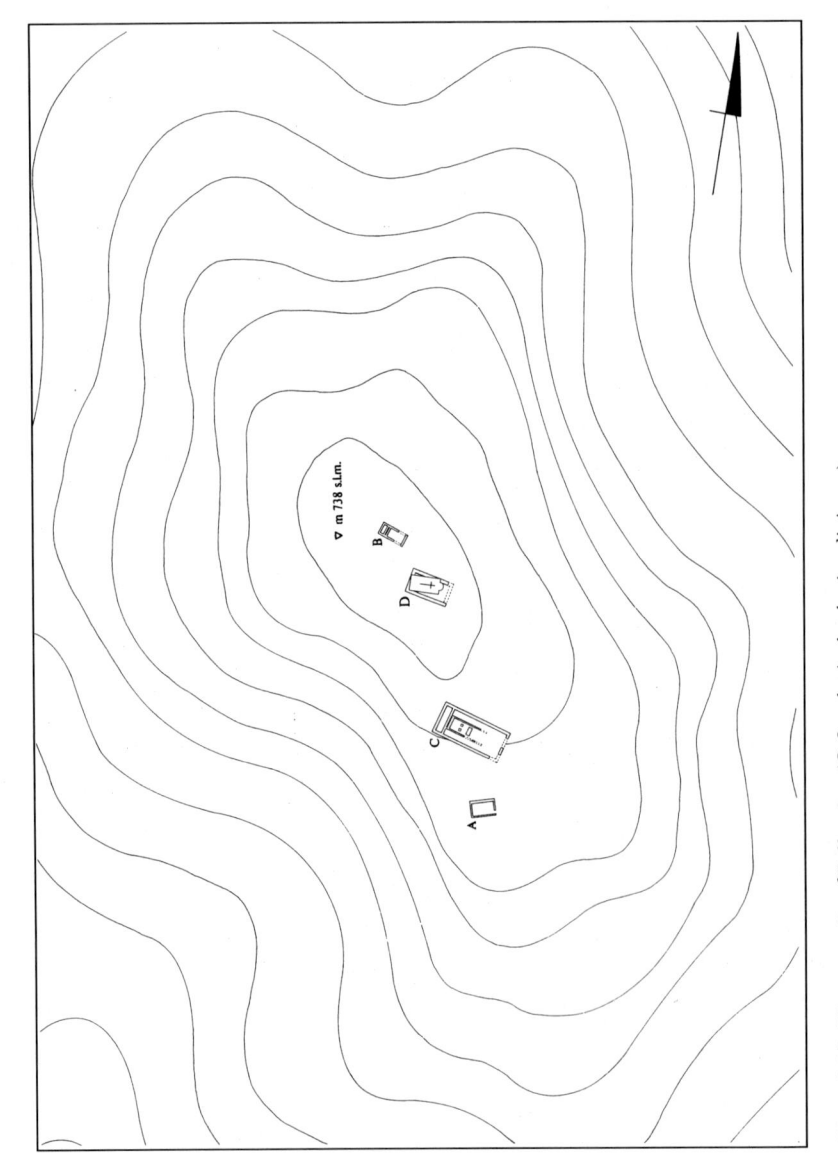

Figure 3.22 The acropolis of Pallantion (© Scuola Archeologica di Atene).

continued to operate together, and were maintained and modified over several centuries, raises interesting questions of their respective functions.

Temple A, the earliest, sits on a small terrace on the southeast slope of the acropolis.[240] (Figure 3.23) It was a relatively plain structure, probably of mud brick on a rubble socle, with an undivided cella and an eccentrically placed entrance in the south-east corner. Its original internal hearth was later replaced by a marble altar, probably when the building was remodelled in Classical times to support a tiled roof. Votives apart, the hearth/altar and an aniconic 'herm' suggest cult, but the large capacity of the undivided cella and the hearth may imply meetings of some form, and since Temple A continued in use alongside the later temples, these functions must have complemented whatever occurred elsewhere. Eric Østby compares it to the Archaic *hestiatorion* at Perachora, and in the absence of internal evidence, this comparison offers the best clue to a date around the end of the seventh century. Temple B, on top of the hill, was a technically similar, if slightly smaller building with an eastern entrance offset markedly to the north.[241] Here, however, the internal cella arrangement is more complex; a cross-wall separates an adyton set at a lower level which contained a bench or table invisible from the cella, and was perhaps therefore designed to accommodate specific ritual objects. Since this arrangement has no Arkadian parallels it must reflect some particular ritual need. No altar or votive deposit has yet been located (although a small room nearby probably served to store votives). A date for Temple B somewhere in the first half of the sixth century is likely. By contrast, Temples C and D are rather different in form. Temple C (Figure 3.24),[242] set between A and B on the south slope, originated as a long, narrow cella with a cult statue base inside, as well as bases which probably belong to an interior colonnade; the result is an almost tripartite cella with an adyton at the rear, akin to the arrangement at Bassai. At the very start of the fifth century an external colonnade was begun but probably not completed. Temple D appears similar in proportion down to the addition of an external colonnade, but is poorly preserved under the hilltop chapel of Ag. Ioannis.[243] No altars have been found related to either of these temples, but this may be due to erosion or shortage of space. In short, we have here a building complex created within a very short period, using common architectural techniques exploiting the properties of local stone and minimizing the need for transport of materials, with no sign of elaborate decoration and no architectural sculpture (or much imagery of any kind).[244] This is not simply a case of a small state aiming to impress by the scale of the project, but is perhaps the most spectacular mainland example of the provision of enclosed space for complementary cult functions as reflected in building plan. The rationale for it must lie in the particular nature of local cult practice, although the investment may answer a perceived need to assert local identity in relation to neighbouring Tegea and Asea.

Asea could not appear more different. In addition to evidence from the acropolis, the development of five rural sanctuaries reveals a progressive

Figure 3.23 Pallantion Temple A (photo: author).

Figure 3.24 Pallantion Temple C (photo: author).

concern from the late seventh century onwards with marking boundaries (beginning with that shared with Pallantion), which coincides with an expansion of rural settlement.[245] To consider these in turn, on the north side of the acropolis (Figure 3.25), looking out over the line of the roads inland, a small votive deposit dates back securely to Late Archaic times and perhaps earlier. No architecture has yet been found on the surface, and very little of the extensive acropolis area has been dug.[246] The most elaborate architectural evidence at present comes from Vigla by the border with Pallantion, where there are two Archaic temples, the earlier, dated *c*.630–620 and represented by rooftiles and acroterion fragments, probably lying beneath the later. However, the associated altar deposit survives and also a fragmentary limestone *anakalypsis* relief, similar to that from Mycenae and in fact the earliest piece of relief sculpture yet known in Arkadia.[247] Without the relevant wall blocks it is impossible to tell whether this was a metope, although if the present absence of early stone construction debris is representative, it is more likely to have been a freestanding votive. The later temple, of the second half of the sixth century, is one of the most elaborate yet found in Arkadia: it is Doric, peripteral, with both elevation and roof in Doliana marble, elaborate floral acroteria, and a sculpted pediment featuring a lion similar to a near-contemporary figure from Sparta.[248] Clearly, Aseans were swift to adopt ideas from their neighbours, and the wealth of the sanctuary may reflect its border position and proximity to a main road. Nonetheless, at least two more shrines have produced monumental seated

Figure 3.25 Asea acropolis: looking on to the line of the main route north (photo: author).

female statues – the well-known Ἁγεμο- probably from a shrine of Meter near the Han of Frankovrysi, and a second similar one found in 1986 by the Tripolis-Kalamata road near Kato Asea.[249] Doliana marble was also used for the late Archaic second temple on an elevation north of the acropolis at Ag. Ilias Kantrevas (Figure 3.26) – this is a much older shrine, with a votive sequence which predates the temple by over two centuries and is the subject of continuing research.[250] The extent of use of Doliana marble in the region is striking, and its transport to such a height has provoked comment on the sheer extent of investment in materials by a relatively small polis.[251] It certainly implies much labour, but especially in the circumstances of Arkadia where, as suggested, there are likely to have been regular and complex economic interchanges between neighbours, it seems perfectly possible that accumulated lesser obligations could have been called in together at key movements to provide very substantial help indeed, and we should not therefore treat stone movement in isolation.

As these two cases highlight, Arkadian communities' perceptions of the role and form of temples differed markedly – an observation which fits the strong role proposed for Arkadian place communities and further explored in Chapter 4. While one might argue for a shared need to assert identity via building, the form taken depended on a range of factors from cult needs to the nature of connections with Arkadian and non-Arkadian neighbours. Archaic Arkadia was certainly not the enclosed heart of the Peloponnese depicted by later authors, but rather a disparate collection of small poleis who looked outwards to Argos, Lakonia (as shown, for example, by the Lakonian comparandum for the Vigla pediment), Elis and Arkadia, as much

Figure 3.26 Ag. Ilias Kantrevas (photo: C.L. Hayward).

as to each other.[252] Indeed, this fragmentation was actively fostered by the Spartans at least from the sixth century to 371. In other parts of Arkadia different aspects of material culture seem even more revealing of local concerns. For example, interpretations of the mid-sixth- to mid-fifth-century bronze shepherd figures from the shrine of Pan at Berekla and also from Lykosoura vary from symbols created for a rustic clientele to depictions of an elite rite of passage, although Madeleine Jost has rightly stressed that since herding was likely to have been a very profitable activity in this landscape, the shepherds who may have dedicated these images are unlikely to have been poor peasants.[253] Yet just to reinforce the extent of local variability, the contemporary votive deposit from the acropolis of Alipheira to the north is especially rich in Lakonianizing metalwork (for instance, cauldrons, lead coronae). (Figure 3.27) The extant temple is early fifth century in date (here too with a Doliana marble roof), but antefix and acrogeison fragments of around 550 imply an earlier structure somewhere nearby.[254] Overall, it is not hard to account for this variability. Arkadia, as is often emphasized, was essentially a human rather than a geographical construct, and there is no real evidence that Arkadian ethnic identity was politically salient much before the end of the sixth century – even then, its emergence was complex and slow (unlike that of Phokis), and being an Arkas was only one form of identity among several possible alternatives.[255] By the end of the Archaic period, Arkadian sanctuaries were coming to represent these same multiple levels – articulating internal and external political and economic relations, representing local history, and slowly, having added pan-Arkadian myths. The chronology of the large number of hero shrines mentioned by Pausanias

Figure 3.27 Alipheira: Classical temple (photo: C.L. Hayward).

in particular is one of the greatest outstanding puzzles, although we have at present no grounds to date them early, and it seems more likely that they developed through Classical and Hellenistic times as part of the wider process of creating an inclusive mythology for the otherwise rather fragile Arkadian ethnos.[256]

Conclusion

This chapter has focused on the way in which sanctuaries articulated group identity within the changing social and political geography of communities and regions. In the case of Phokis, very distinctive local trajectories were united within the overarching structure of the new *koinon*, thus acquiring an additional tier of political salience. In Thessaly, we have seen how a distinctive cult originating in, and strongly identified with, a powerful and influential community spread widely from late Archaic times onwards. Finally, Arkadia maintained strong, locally distinctive cult traditions, with shrines serving a variety of local functions, but with comparatively little evidence of any wider ethnic cult interests evident during our period. Indeed, it is tempting to suggest that the primary route to wider Arkadian syntheses was via the local myth-historical traditions expressed in local hero cults, the date of which is uncertain but probably later than the kind of evidence we have been considering.

Emphasis has also been placed on the economic aspects of early cult activity, stressing that from the earliest times cult celebrations offered particularly rich opportunities for social and material gain as well as requiring investment in resources and management. But in addition to these concerns we should also bear in mind other forms of status expression (according to gender or age for example) evident both in the nature of votives offered, and from Archaic times onwards, more explicitly in sculpture and other inscribed offerings. The Genelaos Group from the Samian Heraion is a striking example of a family dedication,[257] and one might also note a fragmentary *boustrophedon* inscription of the second half of the sixth century which originally accompanied an unidentified kouros offered at the Ptoon, and records the dedication of a fine statue by men described as *hetairoi* (some form of formal or informal association such as that between a chief and his followers, or perhaps just a group of friends).[258] Equally suggestive (and obscure) is a reference in an inscription of *c.*610–550 on a bronze mesomphalos phiale dedicated to Hermes Karykeios during the archonship of Phloax, to a group of Thebans described as 'chosen'.[259] In short, by the end of the eighth century at the latest, most cult communities embodied a complex palimpsest of different social, and in many cases also geographical, interests. Considering how changing political circumstances were reflected (or legitimated) in cult activity and in the relationship between shrines therefore begs the question of how such complex cult communities realigned or adapted themselves. The potential for disjunction as this process continued may help to explain how and why shrines were such important contexts for the expression and maintenance of those relationships often useful to, but extending beyond, the bounds of the contemporary political order (*xenia* in relation to the later Archaic and Classical polis is a case in point). In turn, this raises the question of what constitutes territory, and it is to this that we should now turn.

4

TERRITORY, POWER AND THE ANCESTORS

The idea that a defined territory was integral to the polis has been deep-rooted ever since Aristotle (*Politics* 7.4–7.5.2) described suitable territory and definition of the citizen-body as the twin priorities of the city-state.[1] Control of land plainly has a political dimension beyond that of subsistence, but it is a further step to treat state territory as a bounded entity capable of being mapped and read in the terms of Cartesian cartography, echoing the preoccupations of modern nation states.[2]

Of course not every Greek community had one specific, unique and immutable territory throughout its history. Instances of urban relocation in Archaic and Classical times show that wholesale movement was an acceptable solution to outside pressures: the movement of Homeric Scheria in response to harassment from the Cyclopes (*Odyssey* 6.2–10) is arguably the earliest literary attestation.[3] But the rarity of this kind of movement (as of good evidence for early physical synoikism), and the fact that it required some overwhelming external threat,[4] should not be taken to imply that once ancestral migrations ended (whenever, or if ever, one dates them), mainland Greeks somehow settled down. A variety of Early Iron Age and early Archaic settlement movements of various kinds reflect considerable dynamism, even though I concur with Nancy Demand in rejecting them as evidence of synoikism.[5] As the Thessalian cases presented in Chapter 2 show, big sites with long settlement histories could change role in relation to neighbouring settlements, or interconnect with other similar sites in a particular area in long cycles of demographic and economic change. In short, if ethnic groups are characterized by the manner in which they lived, migrated and settled together, the concept of place identity raises the question of how it was constituted. What kind of 'home range' is required by different activities, how do these relate to the kinds of identification with big sites discussed in Chapter 2, and how do the various strands add up to the political territory of a polis or an ethnos? Place identity, as a palimpsest of interests, has the potential to operate on different levels, with greater or lesser political salience in different situations.

The definition of state territory in the archaeological record tends to rest (more often implicitly than explicitly) on two interconnected lines of argument. Together these form the framework within which we have come to understand the political geography of the early Greek mainland, yet each raises issues pertinent to our conception of political territory and the territorial manifestation of the tiered identities with which we are concerned. The first involves inevitably subjective assessment of the physical extent of a given archaeological 'culture' (to use the term in its most neutral sense, see pp. 17–18, 229). Here we should distinguish between artefact distributions per se (be they pottery styles, tomb forms or epichoric alphabets) and the geographical extent of the behaviour patterns within which they were deployed. The latter, while highlighting numerous phenomena for explanation, is not in itself particularly problematic (indeed, it underpins many of the arguments presented in this chapter). It is generally accepted that a community shared norms of conduct covering a range of activities from burial to the preparation and consumption of food. Individuals followed these (according to personal status) with varying degrees of competence and/or willingness, the collectivity used them to construct and/or react to social deviance,[6] and an individual or group could exploit them to highlight a distinctive identity (sometimes in ethnic terms).[7] This does not mean that 'reading the rules' in the material record is straightforward, not least because of the complex of mediating factors including the standpoint of the modern observer.[8] Using the spread of such norms of behaviour to define the geographical boundaries of a community is thus a highly subjective exercise, as was shown by the Thessalian burial evidence discussed in Chapter 2. But this should not detract from the basic significance of behavioural differences as indicators of group closure.

Less often discussed, and in some ways more problematic, is the significance of the geographical extent of the artefact style pools on which individual communities drew. The primary unit of analysis of most artefact styles (scripts included) has long been the region rather than the individual community, yet these 'regions' vary greatly in nature.[9] Nicolas Coldstream's 1968 *Greek Geometric Pottery* is subtitled 'a survey of ten local styles and their chronology', and he rightly stresses the importance of these distinctions after the relative uniformity of the Late Mycenaean period.[10] Nonetheless, the level at which they operate ranges from coincidence with a single polis (for example, Corinth, and, by the late eighth century, Sparta), to well-defined regions containing a small group of poleis (the Argolid) and extensive areas as Thessaly and western Greece. In the case of mid-scale regions like the Argolid, variation in preferred motifs and details of syntax may imply deliberate differentiation at polis level (something also evident in the burial record),[11] yet this is slight when compared to the strength of similarity across the region (and it is difficult to attribute individual vessels to particular poleis on style alone).[12] In extensive regions, often termed stylistic *koinai*, overarching similarities conceal at least partially localized differences in some (but not always all) shapes and decorative schemes. In pre-eighth-century Thessaly, for example, one can distinguish between the rather old-fashioned handmade wares with slight decoration well attested in the Gremnos area, lingering Mycenaean influences around Trikka, the Macedonian and Epirote connections strongest in the north and north-west,[13] and connections between East Thessaly, Euboia and the north Cyclades shown in the Thessalo-Cycladic style (and especially Thessalian Subprotogeometric), followed (especially after 850) by an increase in Attic influences.[14] Yet these distinctions are not clear cut, nor do they pertain to any individual community. In other words, while there was variation in the style pools upon which individual groups of craftsmen drew, their geographical extent was always greater than the individual polis. Similar arguments can be made for local scripts.[15] Achaian script, for example, while a recognizable entity, was, to judge from the scanty homeland evidence, a bricolage of traits culled from around the Corinthian gulf which probably just predates colonisation, but was still at a formative stage when it began to be used by the Achaian colonists in Magna Graecia – from which time the colonial and mainland versions began to diverge.[16]

Such patterns in the data owe much to modern classificatory schemes: they lack explanatory power and any political interpretations put upon them must be independently justified. Nonetheless, the few explicit discussions of the phenomenon have focused on the political dimension. Observing that the sharper distinctions between regional ceramic styles which appear through the eighth century coincide with improved communications, Coldstream argues that they reflect self-conscious differentiation linked to the rise of autonomous city states with a pride in their own traditions.[17] But state-political explanations of this kind do not address the question of scale, and it is notable that regional ceramic styles grew fewer and were often less sharply differentiated during the Archaic period when numerous city states were clearly present across Greece.[18] Equally, Coldstream's suggestion that elaborate decorative styles were a feature of poleis rather than ethne is perhaps a little misleading.[19] Some polis styles, like those of the Argolid, were shared across a region (as Coldstream points out), others, like that of Corinth, have a very small figurative repertoire,[20] yet some communities within ethne produced distinctive figure decoration (for instance, the Pharai valley in Achaia).[21] Whatever the repertoire, the generation of complex imagery is a distinct phenomenon to be understood within its immediate social context rather than as a broader characteristic of a regional style. In a rare attempt to explain style pools at region level, Anthony Snodgrass has suggested that, along with the Homeric use of ethnic plurals, they reflect broad social affiliations across a wide political territory. At first sight this may seem an attractive entrée into higher-level affiliations, but we cannot move directly from classificatory observations of style to political interpretations without identifying the processes that generated each distribution.[22] We will return in the concluding chapter to the role of spheres of interaction (especially around waterways like the Corinthian gulf) in bringing together different groups and helping to shape self- and outsider perceptions (a kind of median level of alteriority). Here I merely suggest that in focusing directly on politics, there is a risk of neglecting the socio-economic underpinning of different kinds of production and resource mobilization. Rather than assessing distributions of finished products from a consumer perspective, we should consider how exchange circles operated as complex interconnections of skills, specialization in particular kinds of vessel, access to raw materials and facilities like kilns, mobility of craftsmen, the location of markets and the mechanisms of exchange of finished products.[23] From this perspective, the question of the location of production sites for commodities like pottery, where considerable freedom of choice was possible, is, as emphasized in Chapter 2, of some significance.

If archaeological cultures cannot serve as indicators of political territory, predictive assessments based on site location are hardly self-explanatory, and taken out of historical context can be deeply misleading.[24] For example, application of nearest neighbour analysis predicated on an average territorial radius of 10 km, and thus an area of *c.*100–200 sq km, fits the city network of Thessaly as evident by the end of our period. Applying the same approach to the principal sites listed in the *Catalogue of Ships* (recognizing the irretrievable selectivity in the construction of such a geography) in some cases doubles this territory.[25] But what is the appropriate comparison for these data? At one extreme one could cite the existence of physically large southern polis territories (*c.*600 sq km for Argos for example, or 2,600 in the case of Athens) to argue for radically different conceptions of territory in north and south, or even distinct processes of urbanization. At the other, one could take these same regions and point in the case of Argos to the existence during the Early Iron Age and Archaic period of peer centres like Tiryns[26] and Mycenae,[27] some 12 km apart around and just beyond the Argive plain, or in Attica to the absorption of old centres like Eleusis, and the existence of what were to become deme centres of a similiar order of magnitude.[28] Neither comparison admits the territorial consequences of the longer-term trajectories of co-operation, conflict, independence or subordination that variously characterized these regions.

For our purposes, it seems less important to learn how much territory was controlled by a central place than to understand how the various activities of communities in very different environments were conducted across the landscape, and to assess the impact of, for example, activities like cult or warfare which both created and maintained particular group loyalties and identities and could be enacted over a territory wider than that of the individual polis. It would clearly be simplistic to assume that the 'filling up' of the landscape from the eighth century onwards (which affected most regions of Greece regardless of their political ordering) resulted in a one-dimensional kind of partitioning. Naturally, no study of the creation of political identity (let alone ethnicity) would diminish the role of boundaries, which are vital to group closure and the articulation of insider and outsider perceptions of particular communities.[29] The issue is rather the levels on which they operated, the circumstances under which they gained or lost political salience, and the resulting scope for the informal, and subsequently sometimes formal, creation of different tiers of political relationship across the landscape.

Ethne in the landscape

Such general characterizations of early ethne as have been made by historians such as Ehrenberg or Daverio Rocchi have tended to rely on the supposedly close relationship between topography, demography and socio-economic development. Since the fragmented terrain of the Greek mainland is seen as instrumental in the creation of small, self-contained poleis,[30] ethne, as their negative images, must be large-scale units both in terms of their populations and the area over which they were scattered.[31] Daverio Rocchi goes further in underlining economic differentiation from the polis,[32] taking a broadly Thucydidean view of ethne as reliant on pastoralism (in the loosest sense), piracy and raiding for their subsistence, imperatives which are seen as imposing a mode of life characterized by scattered settlement (*kata komas*) with no stimulus to create stable institutions or administrative systems.

None of these hypotheses can be sustained.[33] Not only are they are belied by the settlement structures discussed in Chapter 2, but the ecological reductionism implied in this linkage between political superstructure and economic base is deeply flawed. That mixed agriculture was practised on the plains of eastern Thessaly and eastern Arkadia is beyond doubt, as evidence from Late Bronze Age Dimini, Early Iron Age Iolkos and Early Iron Age-Archaic Tegea attests.[34] And when in later sources (notably Xenophon's *Anabasis*) we learn of the origins of Arkadian mercenaries, a high proportion come from the rich plains of the east – further highlighting the folly of simplistic characterization of particular economic activities.[35] Specialized pastoralism[36] can be argued only in a few cases (and then on the basis of indirect evidence), notably the uplands of central Phokis and (especially western) Arkadia, and in none should it be seen as a route to poverty or isolation. In Phokis, as McInerney points out,[37] the growing, and in time unusually large, sacral economy of Delphi (with its constant demand for sacrificial animals) probably sustained upland pastoralism throughout the Archaic period and beyond. In Arkadia, as noted in the previous chapter, the bronze shepherd figurines dedicated to Pan at Berekla have given rise to considerable debate about the status and wealth of their donors.[38] Furthermore, if one accepts that here, as perhaps elsewhere in Arkadia, transhumance would have been necessary to avoid the expense of overwintering at least the larger flocks at high altitudes, then physical geography decreed that even though the distances involved might be quite small, one would have to cross polis boundaries within and beyond Arkadia, presumably by prior agreement.[39] Such co-operation was hardly unusual in the Greek world given that most subsistence strategies involved a balance between agrarian activities and animal breeding, the latter demanding a degree of movement which could not always be confined within polis territory.[40] That access to land beyond that used for cultivation was an important issue is reflected in the later literary and epigraphical record not simply of agreements, but also of disputes over boundaries or marginal land in a number of regions.[41] In Magna Graecia too, Whitehouse and Wilkins have suggested that the definition and development of the Metapontine *chora*, combined with long-term trends in the distribution of Greek goods in the native hinterland, reflects a deliberate decision to limit direct control to agricultural land, with needs for pasture and secondary animal products satisfied via negotiation and exchange with native neighbours.[42] In short, the Arkadian situation may be complex, but the kinds of relationships and co-operation involved are not exceptional in the wider Greek context.

While the rich and diverse resources of Arkadia as a whole do not readily fit models conditioned by the perceived importance of the Mediterranean triad, this is no reason to treat this, or any other mountain region, as by definition poor or disadvantaged.[43] Instead, the complexity of exploitation, exchange, mobility and specialization that came to characterize the Arkadian economy raises difficult and largely unanswerable questions about the nature of authority exercised in any particular context, the extent of territory involved, and the evolution of different levels of tie between communities and regions.[44] Dependence on co-operation and exchange, even on a very local level, could serve as a powerful cultural integrator, whether for the access to land and markets needed for pastoralism or for the maintenance of shared facilities like sink holes.[45] This is not to imply uniformity or Utopian harmonization, merely constant decision-making about issues of mutual importance which had the potential to generate conflict as much as compromise or co-operation.[46] Arkadia was not alone in this respect. Flood prevention on the Thessalian plain required the maintenance of embankments and a clear channel between Lake Karla (Boibe) and the Nessonis marshlands north of Larisa. In later centuries (according to Strabo 9.5.19) the Larisans, whose arable land was in immediate danger, controlled the Nessonis by means of embankments, but the antiquity of this arrangement is unclear as is the distribution of wider responsibility for protection during our period.[47] In Arkadia, however, effective control of drainage necessitated co-operation, given the marginal locations of many springs and sink-holes. Thucydides (5.65.4) reports that this was long a source of conflict between Tegea and Mantineia, most famously (if unsuccessfully) exploited by invading Spartan forces in 418.[48] The extent of the problem is reflected in the specific and long-term association of Herakles with waterworks, strikingly evident in the Peloponnese but present more widely across Greece.[49] Maintenance of roads also carried shared obligations, not simply to ensure passage across what were sometimes the only viable routes, but in the case of cart roads, to keep tracks and beds clear, and perhaps also to provide watchmen to ensure the safe operation of single tracks in mountain zones with restricted visibility and steep gradients. While direct dating evidence is lacking, on circumstantial grounds Pikoulas dates the creation of a formal Arkadian road system to the period between the late seventh and mid-sixth centuries, coincident with Spartan expansionism.[50]

Individually, these relationships of co-operation, exchange and obligation might be very localized and/or specific. Together, however, they could form a complex network across which might flow anything from skilled labour to raw materials from distant sources (like metals, which were worked during the Geometric period at Tegea)[51] or building stone (for example the Doliana marble which travelled long distances overland, as highlighted in the case of Ag. Ilias Kantrevas). As Nicholas Purcell has stressed,[52] complex systems of this kind, within which both people and goods circulated, and transactions related imports to local products, relied less on environmentally given diversity and more on acceptance of economic, social and political differences – on agreement to differ in a mutually helpful way. It is thus easy to envisage the advantages of enhancing or even creating differences, and over time producing genuinely different 'ecologies' in the broadest sense of the term.

In short, one can readily understand how the bodies of spatial knowledge which underpinned different activities did not merely overlap, but helped to structure each other. Together they defined and redefined the limits of essential group territory (and the physical place and mobility of individuals of different age, status and gender within it), as against that accessible on a shared basis or via concessions from others.[53] Such 'maps', a form of orally transmitted knowledge open to constant revision and reappraisal, might emphasize the experience of particular kinds of movement. They might make reference to travel for other purposes, or to natural and man-made landmarks[54] like shrines (such as that to Hermes at ancient Klimax, on the road between Mantineia and the Argolid),[55] tombs or other monuments (as the early Classical hoplite relief from the plain of Tegea), or the residences of particular individuals or groups. The point of closure would also be defined, where a traveller would stop or alter his behaviour or expectations. This might be expressed in terms of the alien group beyond, and here, as we will see, group ethnics probably played an important role. Like all constructs of memory, this is unrecoverable, but circumstantial confirmation may be sought in the location of monuments such as shrines, the later record of treaties, and especially in the expression of spatial relationships in early literature. As Christian Jacob among others has emphasized, whatever one's view of their moral or philosophical purpose (or the reality of the experiences embodied in them), Odysseus' journeys in the *Odyssey* are described in the same terms of directional movement linking a sequence of experiences of physical geography, peoples and places. To an extent the same is true of the *Catalogue of Ships*, although as a muster roll it inevitably presents a sequence of peoples and homelands.[56] Conversely, as Jacob further notes, the making of physical maps, beginning with that of Anaximander of Miletos, must be seen in the philosophical context of Ionian cosmology rather than the practical, oral construction of spatial knowledge – a contrast highlighted by Agathemeros's (1.1–2) emphatic use of *grapsai* to describe Anaximander's achievement.[57]

These approaches to spatial experience are also relevant to actions involving mobility across community boundaries, from the many pervasive and interconnected movements implied by marriage, craft mobility, *xenia*,[58] trade and warfare, to travel to festivals (undertaken with varying regularity according to individuals' wealth and status), and long-distance voyaging and colonization. All required what might be deemed specialist knowledge, i.e. that accessed less regularly and/or by specific kinds of individual, and since all involved movement through 'foreign' territory, information about the location and character of different peoples as well as points of social contact. In Chapter 2, we noted the way in which the *Catalogue of Ships* described groups by place of residence or ethnic plus area, and the regularity of ethnic plurals has led McInerney to cite the *Catalogue* as evidence for strong regional ethnic consciousness.[59] This is possible, although such a muster roll is as likely to reflect outsider perceptions as insider claims. Indeed, it is in dealing with outsiders that identities were likely to have been simplified to such terms as were comprehensible and sufficient to articulate the degree of difference and/or similarity relevant in context. Activities like the military service represented in the *Catalogue*, which regularly took individuals or groups outside home territory, were thus likely to have played an important role in shaping perceptions of identity.

We will return to these issues presently. First, however, we should address further issues concerning the construction and role of territory from a primarily insider viewpoint.

Community of territory?

In one rather different sense, the notion of territory as political space has played a central role in discussion of early ethne. Linked with the notion of the ethnos as essentially unurbanized during our period is the *topos* of synoikism so widely used in later sources (notably by Strabo, see for example 8.3.2 on the Peloponnese).[60] This assigns a distinctive role to the territory where ethnic ties were recognized as the primordial political space across which were scattered those groups later to unite into a state. While this may seem particularly relevant to ethne, a diverse range of ancient texts, from Aristotle's hierarchy of *oikos*, *kome* and polis (*Politics* 1.1.7–8) to Thucydides' account of the synoikism of Athens under Theseus (2.15.1–2), have been assembled as evidence for the role of synoikism in the rise of the polis.[61] For ancient commentators from Thucydides onwards, synoikism was a useful bridge between the heroic past and the largely polis-centred contemporary world. This is not to imply that the concept did not exist in earlier thought, merely that its role in modern scholarship, and thus its importance as a force for change, is largely predicated on this later role. By Strabo's time there had been examples of true physical synoikism within historical memory, Megalopolis being an obvious mainland case (8.8.1). More pertinently, however, Strabo's desire to present settlements in historical context and to convey the meaning of place forced him to engage critically with past world views, and when discussing Homer in particular (a source of very great interest to him) to find mechanisms to deal with the all too obvious chasm between the deep past and the present.[62] The geographical range and time depth involved in such a universal geography demanded selectivity. As a result, Strabo highlighted what he regarded as defining points in city history, and especially moments of foundation or transformation (including decline and demise) across the centuries – acts of *ktisis*, *oikisis*, *synoikisis*, *dioikisis* and even complete abandonment. In other words, his approach produced (or perhaps formalized) a framework of vocabulary rooted in the contemporary world of the city, yet applied universally.

In describing synoikism as a *topos*, I do not mean to detract from its conceptual force in later historical and geographical writing. I merely stress that as a supposed model for early Greek settlement history it has been poorly defined and over-used. As Nancy Demand's review of both archaeological evidence and past scholarship shows, on the Greek mainland it is hard to find a convincing example of early physical or political synoikism in the polis world as traditionally conceived.[63] One is left implicitly or explicitly to attach such meaning to judgements about political unity made on the basis of observations of residence patterns and assumptions about their implications (as discussed in Chapter 2). In the case of Argos, for example, Robin Hägg argues for political unity on the Protogeometric-Geometric transition whereas Marcel Pièrart places it around the beginning of the eighth century. Yet the value of drawing such lines across data of this kind seems questionable.[64]

Survey results also cast doubt upon the relevance of physical synoikism. Drawing upon data from the Boiotia survey, Bintliff and Snodgrass have identified a widespread pattern of an Early Iron Age base of usually one dominant site (either a single nucleus or multiple but proximate nuclei), with major expansion occurring simultaneously in the countryside and at the big site, usually from the sixth century onwards.[65] Within this general trend, they formulate two models of expansion. Model A (exemplified at

Haliartos and Askra) has a single, compact Early Iron Age centre (often located within a Mycenaean settlement) growing gradually through the Archaic period, a relatively early move to the countryside, yet a quite modest climax overall. Model B (exemplified by Thespiai) has a larger, more dispersed big site with expansion occurring later and on a greater scale (producing substantial rural installations during the Classical period). Both models feature a very limited Early Iron Age and early Archaic record, and as Bintliff and Snodgrass remark, evidence for eighth-century expansion in Boiotia is slight in comparison with regions further south (although many southern cases rest on burial evidence which is relatively scarce here – and compare the Arkadian situation discussed below). But these basic trajectories are widely paralleled on the mainland across the traditional ethnos/polis divide. Perhaps the key point is that maximal rural settlement usually coincides with the maximum expansion of the polis centre, and however one interprets this in terms of population growth (depending on residence patterns in each individual case),[66] there is no absolute move from country to town.

Nonetheless, synoikism remains prominent in historical discussions of the few regions where settlement centres have been seen as late developments. Arkadia is a good example, especially as the richness of the Early Iron Age and Archaic sanctuary record implies the existence of local inhabitants to form cult communities. The apparent near-absence of settlement evidence has been taken to imply that this population was scattered in small villages, and considerable discussion has surrounded the process by which these villages were agglomerated (largely couched in the political vocabulary used by Pausanias in recounting Arkadian synoikisms, especially that of Megalopolis [8.27]).[67] Mauro Moggi, for example, while recognizing the existence of early Arkadian poleis, proposes that they were settled *kata komas* as some kind of low-level *koinon* which left no significant archaeological trace. He locates the origins of this system in the eighth century, with the development of a series of human aggregations and territories which retained a certain autonomy yet shared a common identity. This situation remained relatively unchanged for a long period (in contrast with, for example, the development of Attica or the Corinthia), and when polis centres did emerge, it was within existing systems of rural settlement characterized by a strong centripetal tendency.[68]

Moggi's model directly conflicts with the strong association identified by the Copenhagen Polis Centre between the polis as a physical centre and as a political community. As discussed in Chapter 2, this association cuts across the geographical divide between poleis and ethne as traditionally conceived, and if Moggi is correct, Arkadia would be a rare exception. His case is, however, abstract and lacks supporting evidence. That is not to say that evidence of any kind is lacking, even though what exists highlights the extent of our difficulty in reconstructing an indicative picture of any part of the region, especially during the Early Iron Age. As emphasized in Chapter 1, few settlement sites of any period have been excavated and Early Iron Age pottery shows up badly in surface scatters. That this is an Early Iron Age rather than an Archaic problem is clear from the ample representation of later seventh- and sixth-century pottery in surface collections, and the record of excavated sites (mainly sanctuaries), combined with occasional Geometric surface finds and also graves, confirms it as primarily a problem of visibility.[69] The Arkadian Geometric burial record is similarly problematic, although dating is not helped by the fact that graves in southern Arkadia seem to follow Lakonian fashion in containing only small bronzes (attractive to tomb robbers). As yet, no large cemeteries have been located – a situation analogous to that in Sparta (although here too, the principal approaches to the city have not been systematically investigated).[70] Under such circumstances, any material traces are potentially important, and very small quantities of pottery have indeed been found at a significant number of findspots other than sanctuaries. (Figure 1.18) These include finds made on or close to the acropoleis of Mantineia, Orchomenos, Asea, Oresthasion, Teuthis, Gortys, as well as in southern Tegea, and it is interesting to see that the evidence is so widely scattered, given the bias of research towards the east. The lack of finds outside sanctuaries in south-central Arkadia surely reflects limited exploration, and only in the Megalopolis area can one point to a genuine shortage (although not a total absence) of Geometric findspots in a well-surveyed area, noting with Pikoulas that this is surprising given the extent and stability of settlement from the Archaic period (principally the sixth century) onwards.[71] In short, we have sufficient information to reject Moggi's hypothesis as a global model for Arkadian development, yet not enough to propose any archaeologically grounded alternative.

The rather different approach taken by Madeleine Jost in her discussion of Classical and Hellenistic Arkadia is of greater value in clearing the way for a better understanding of the relationship between the Early Iron Age/Archaic and later records.[72] A useful first step is taken in her review of the political vocabulary used by Pausanias (in common with most later Hellenistic and Roman sources on the region), and especially the distinctions between polis, *kome* and *chorion*. Jost notes the wide application of *chorion* to all manner of places (such as tombs, shrines, woods), yet no instance of it describing a village in the usual sense. *Kome* is rather the term used for a community with some form of juridical autonomy, not formally distinguished from the polis and at times apparently overlapping with it. As she emphasizes, this terminology does not fit the earlier historical and archaeological records as we know them, and its application may oversimplify a complex situation. Bearing in mind Pausanias' focus on the synoikism of Megalopolis and its later effects, there is a real danger of applying *kome* and polis in senses which are not directly transferable to our period. Looking back through what is most likely a distorting lens can only be a source of confusion.[73]

Setting aside Pausanias' approach to political terminology allows us to consider long-term trends in the material record which, accepting problems of retrieval and variation in the extent and nature of exploration, do not differ greatly from those observed in Boiotia and elsewhere. If we compare the Early Iron Age and Archaic picture down to *c*.500–480 with that of the Classical period,[74] it is clear that there is continuity at the very least from the sixth century, and usually much earlier, at most polis centres, and that the local variation in settlement structure evident in the early period is carried through into the later record. Subdividing the region archaeologically is a highly subjective exercise, but certain distinctions can be drawn. Contrast, for example, the eastern poleis, as Tegea and Mantineia,[75] with the distinct ethnos of the Azanes in the north, which is best understood in connection with inland Achaia (as discussed below at pp. 176–87). The roots of these distinctions lie partly in topography, but the salience and nature of external borders is also important. Where neighbours were expansionist and potentially hostile, notoriously Sparta in relation to Tegea (although the effects were felt right along the south-eastern border, as the case of Asea has highlighted), cohesion and sometimes elaborate material display, notably at sanctuaries, occurred early. By contrast, the Elean border became salient only relatively late (as shown by the treaties discussed in Chapter 2), but thereafter was disputed over many decades.[76]

Such was the framework within, or in parallel to which localized identities developed, be they explicitly tribal/ethnic or other forms of close association. It is hard to see Arkadian poleis, or their antecedents as place communities, as significantly later to emerge, even though the relationship was probably variable across Arkadia.[77] In the *Catalogue of Ships* (*Iliad* 2.603–14), Arkadian geography is constructed entirely in terms of settlement names, with the exception of the land of the Parrhasians which is nonetheless presented as a place rather than in terms of the ethnic alone. Herodotos too favours the formula 'toponym + *arkadon*' ('of the Arkadians'; see, for example, 4.161 on Mantineia). Yet there remains a strong scholarly consensus in favour of a fifth-century date for the synoikism of a number of primarily eastern poleis, including Tegea and Mantineia, even though in both cases the only source explicitly to mention the first synoikism is Strabo, and in the case of Mantineia as Stephen and Hilary Hodkinson conclude, neither this nor the subsequent dioikism is likely to have had much impact on the social and political conduct of the community.[78] In Mantineia, the key element seems to be a relocation of the central place from the old Ptolis acropolis.[79] (Figure 2.16) But since, as Jost among others has noted,[80] most rural sites in the Mantinike (shrines included) date from the late Archaic period, the chronological discrepancy with what might be better termed urban relocation may have been quite slight, and it hardly seems a crucial stage in the creation of the political community. Here, as in the Boiotian models discussed earlier, change at the centre had no negative impact on the countryside,[81] and while there were specific local needs for maintenance of facilities like drainage, the distances involved were generally too small (5–7 km) to have had a significant impact on settlement. In short, while the Arkadian data are fragmentary and require careful evaluation, and while the extent of intra-regional variation defies simple models of polis formation, there are strong hints that the overall trends do not differ greatly from those evident elsewhere (Boiotia or Achaia, for example).[82] Arkadia may be problematic, but it is not the exception that proves the rule.

Marginal areas and routes of communication

As discussion so far has suggested, place community, constructed as much through big sites as territories, was an important feature of all regional systems where excavation strategies have been likely to reveal it, or where early evidence is reasonably visible in survey.[83] This invites us to push back community of place in this dual sense as *the* strong feature in all regional systems, regardless of the strength of other ethnic or wider regional affiliations. Yet in considering the nature of the political role of territory, it is worth pursuing further the question of whether there are genuine cases without real centres, and whether these were effectively backwaters. The answer to the first question is a qualified yes. The Early Iron Age Sperchios valley in Thessaly[84] for example, or the pre-sixth-century Pharai valley in Achaia have yet to produce evidence of settlement centres. However, such areas tend to occupy particular kinds of environment, and at least in the case of the Pharai valley, dispersed settlement proved fragile and relatively short-lived. Moreover, settlement structure alone does not make an area a backwater: the complexities and wider connections of the archaeological record of the Pharai valley, and its location on an important route of communication and bordering Arkadian Azania, argue against this.

The *meros* of Pharees is one of the three listed by Herodotos (1.145) whose names take the form of ethnic plurals. (Figure 1.11) The other two are neighbouring Tritaies to the southwest, and Patrees, which, according to Pausanias (7.18.2–7) and Strabo (8.3.2), had a long history of synoikism and dioikism (hard as this is to trace in the pre-Classical archaeological record).[85] From a very slight Protogeometric base, settlement in the later *chora* of Patras expanded greatly during the eighth century (notably to the west of the modern city),[86] and included some substantial sites (Drepanon, for example, which is identified by Petropoulos with ancient Boline).[87] Such a record is fundamentally different from that of the Pharai valley, highlighting the fact that Herodotos' use of the ethnic plural does not imply any archaeologically evident shared settlement or organizational characteristics. The settlement structures of these areas are generally less stable in the long term than those of the north-coast cities, but not in any uniform way.[88] Yet as noted, the term *meros* implies a part of a whole, and it is interesting to find such different trajectories described in equal and parallel terms.

Herodotos gives no hint that the Achaian *mesogeia* had ever been less than a full part of that geographical entity whose inhabitants shared a common sense of Achaian identity. That the *mesogeia* is not included in the Achaian listings in the *Catalogue of Ships* (*Iliad* 2.573–7) may simply reflect its location. After all, the inclusion of landlocked but militarily skilled Arkadians, who knew nothing of seafaring and had their ships supplied by Agamemnon, was cause for comment (*Iliad* 2.611–14). This cannot, however, explain the omission of Patras, and it is important to stress that the inclusion of Hyperesia, Goneoussa, Pellene, Aigion and Helike within Agamemnon's command (a broad fief that also included Corinth and Sikyon) is among the most problematic aspects of the *Catalogue*. I have argued elsewhere that this cannot imply regular political control, yet major discrepancies with both the Bronze and Iron Age archaeological records (especially of Corinth) are more striking here than in most other regions described, and doubts must remain about this particular section of the text.[89] While the coastal *mere* may have been more closely bound into networks of interaction around the Corinthian gulf (as will be discussed in the concluding chapter), there is no reason to assume that they alone were involved in enterprises such as colonization, especially given the late date and problematic nature of the Achaian colonial oikist traditions (see below, p. 199). Nor were inland regions 'backward' in relation to overall regional development. While differences in coastal zone development owe much to engagement in maritime interaction, so connections with northern Arkadia (Azania) in particular were influential upon the *mesogeia*. (Figure 4.1)

The Pharai valley was intensively settled during the Mycenaean period, with nucleated settlements at Katarraktis and Stavros Chalandritsas, and extensive chamber tomb cemeteries continuing into LHIIIC Late.[90] There followed what on present evidence appears to be a gap until late in the Protogeometric period (possibly until the early eighth century), when a grave at Lopesi[91] marked the start of a sequence of burials that continued until c.690. The gap may be fortuitous since the area has not been systematically investigated and many tumuli remain to be explored, yet it is interesting to note a comparable shortage of evidence revealed by intensive survey in the coastal area of Patras, as well as in the Peiros basin and the western plain (focusing on the territory of Dyme).[92] The eighth-century record from the Pharai valley consists almost exclusively of scattered burial sites, with settlement evidence represented by sherds within a mainly Archaic and Classical scatter surrounding a badly disturbed structure excavated at Ag. Giorgios, and by an illegal excavation at Ai-Lias south-east of Chalandritsa.[93] The sample is clearly problematic: early excavations are poorly documented, most tombs are disturbed, the longevity of some grave types makes them hard to date in the absence of offerings,[94] and the full

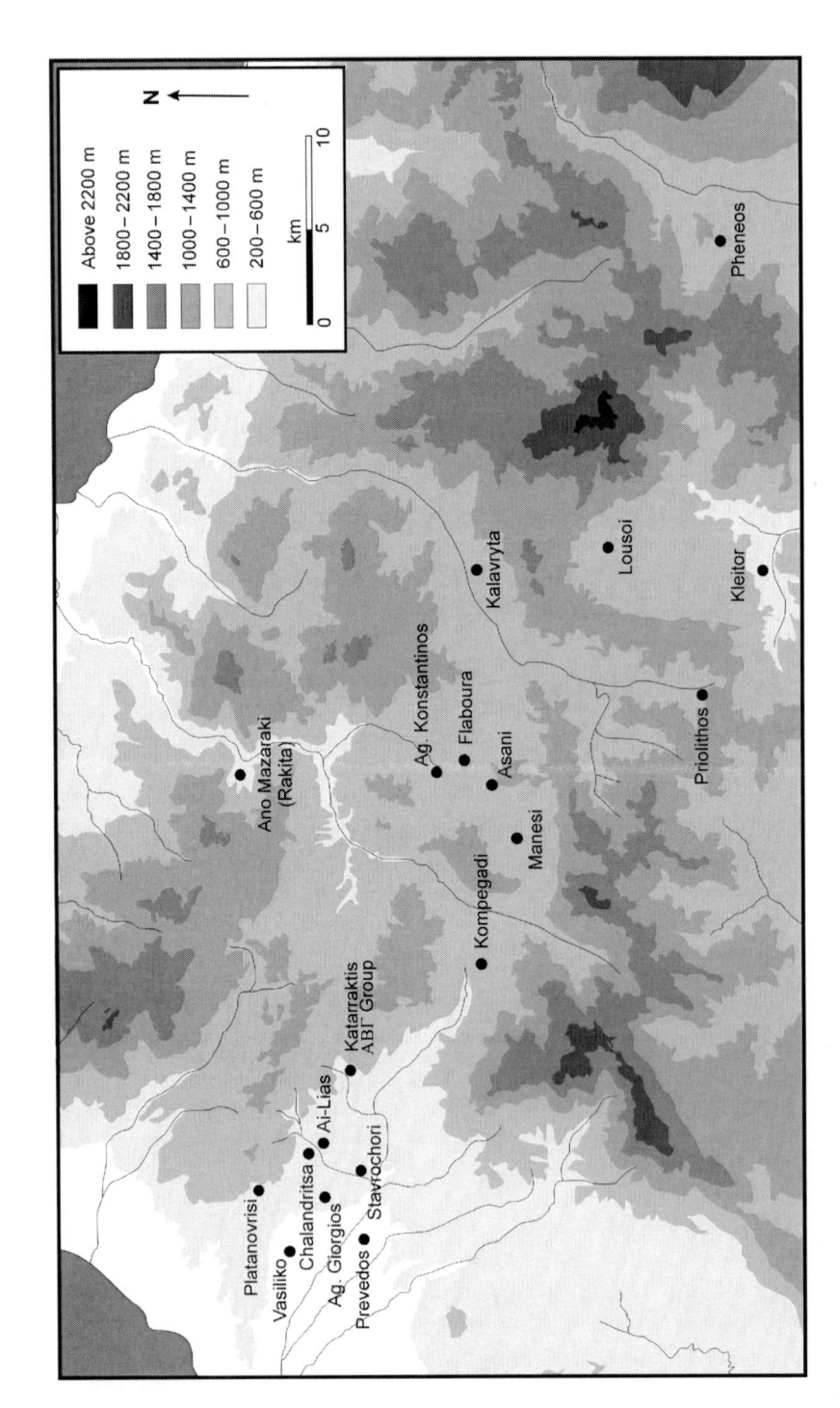

Figure 4.1 Pharees and northern Azania (C.L. Hayward).

extent of cemeteries is unknown (in several cases, as Chalandritsa and Troumbe, burials close to those excavated were merely noted).[95] Negative conclusions are therefore impossible, but even the evidence we have reveals the existence of different grave forms, grouping strategies and offerings across a small area. This diversity contrasts with evidence from the only other Achaian site with a significant burial record, Aigion, where adults were normally inhumed in pithoi and children in cists.[96]

Inhumation was also the rite practised in the Pharai valley, and Late Geometric pithos burials are attested, at, for example, Fteri and Starochori-Koufales Pyrgaki.[97] But cist graves are more common in the extant record, either set in close proximity with no surviving tumulus (as the Α, Β, Γ Group by the 28 km marker on the road from Patras to Kalavryta, or Platanovrisi-Kamini which contains a double burial),[98] or covered with a tumulus. This could be a simple mound over the grave (as at Fteri),[99] but in at least two cases, at Troumbe and Skoros,[100] hybrid-style built tombs, which are more elaborate than simple cists and seem to echo the tholoi and chamber tombs that formed the heart of prehistoric mounds, are found within quite substantial tumuli. At Troumbe, two of a group of three such mounds have been investigated, one with Mycenaean goods and the other (the only one systematically excavated) Late Geometric, and there are more unexplored examples in the area.[101] The most elaborate tumulus so far investigated, outside Lalikosta on the plain of Pharai, contained in its upper levels two cists and two pithoi, and at the base a more elaborate built tomb with incurving chamber tomb-like walls. There are no finds to date this group, although the conjunction of tomb types has been taken to indicate a Geometric date.[102]

Of these tumuli, the Late Geometric burial at Troumbe was tentatively singled out by Nicolas Coldstream as a possible instance of tomb cult. Noting a Mycenaean animal figurine among the finds, he suggested that the tomb might be a plundered Mycenaean 'tholos' which received offerings in the late eighth century. Papadimitriou has recently restated the architectural case for a Mycenaean construction date, with internal partitions (founded some 0.20–0.30 m higher) added probably in the Geometric period, although as he notes, the associated finds have not been fully studied or published, and precise dating is impossible. The case for Geometric cult has not been generally accepted (Antonaccio, for example, sees this as a straightforward case of tomb reuse), although it has been restated, somewhat uncritically, by Maria Deoudi, who dates the tomb structure to LHIIIC with no further explanation. Bearing in mind the similarity of the offerings to those from other eighth-century burials in this area, and the parallel case of Skoros (and perhaps Lalikosta), there seems to be no good reason to doubt that this was an eighth-century burial, whatever the date of the tomb structure.[103] And as Ioannis Moschos highlights in a recent review of Achaian tumuli,[104] the Pharai tumuli belong within a long-established (if poorly understood) tradition which dates back to the Middle Helladic and continues through the Late Bronze Age.[105]

The similarity shown by these putative 'Geometric' cases extends beyond the notion of the mound to the unusual hybrid form of the central built grave. By contrast with, for example, Thessaly, the absence of Protogeometric tumuli is striking. Late Mycenaean and eighth-century burials are found in close proximity at all of the sites considered, but overall there are too many lacunae to rest much on this fact. Nonetheless, by the latter part of the eighth century some elements of the local population subscribed to the old style of burial (whether as part of a living tradition or a recreation of the past however undertaken) whereas others did not. It is tempting to go further and, bearing in mind the military character of elite male burials in LHIIIC,[106] to cite offerings such as the spearhead at Troumbe,[107] the early to mid-seventh-century panoply from Ag. Konstantinos in Arkadian Azania (close to modern Kalavryta),[108] and the late Naue III sword and iron knife from a burial at Kato Mavriki in the territory of Aigion,[109] as the latter stages of a long-standing tradition. But a fragmentary record of metal offerings from robbed graves cannot sustain much interpretation. Two related points should, however, be emphasized. The first is that these funerary gifts were contemporary with votive offerings of weapons at the shrine of Artemis Aontia at Ano Mazaraki made from the second half of the eighth century onwards.[110] This shrine was closely linked to Aigion and lay on an important road south through the Meganeitas valley, from which one could continue east via modern Kalavryta towards Lousoi, or branch off west towards Patras via Pharai.[111] The importance of these interconnections will be explored presently. Here I merely highlight the different ways in which weapons were deposited in ritual contexts in physically related areas over a short time, bearing in mind that subsequent changes in practice may reflect attitudes to resource consumption as much as military ethos.[112]

The Archaic period in the Pharai valley is little known, although there are hints of major change in the limited extant record (which dates mostly to the sixth rather than the seventh century). No new Archaic graves have been located at the established sites, and if this is not a matter of chance, cemeteries must have moved. The only Archaic burials so far discovered are reuses of earlier tombs (the Late Geometric slab-cist B of the A, B, Γ Group, accompanied by Corinthian conventionalizing pottery, and a Mycenaean chamber tomb at Ag. Basileios, Chalandritsa).[113] One can only pose the question of whether these burials might reflect an ideological claim on the past at a time of change. Considering the latest, Archaic and Classical, tholoi to be built in Thessaly (near Pharsalos and Krannon), Maria Stamatopoulou has raised the interesting possibility that they represent deliberate archaising on the part of the Echekratides and Skopads in order to evoke their glorious past.[114] Reusing old tombs is not the same as continuing an old building tradition, however, and the Pharai burials may just represent opportunistic exploitation of convenient structures which differ greatly in date and appearance. Other Archaic evidence has been found at the Ag. Giorgios settlement, and black glaze sherds from Ai-Lias near Chalandritsa, while less securely datable, may also begin this early (see p. 177 above). Evidence also begins to appear in the area of the Classical city of Pharai to the west: at Vasiliko, a late Archaic public building of some kind is indicated by a sima, stone bases, and rooftiles,[115] and a votive deposit has been found c.250 m to the north at Prevedos (ancient Pharai).[116] These finds represent kinds of activity absent from the previous record, and it seems that by the sixth century at the latest, the integration of settlement, with a cult place and public building, reflected an organizational structure which remained relatively stable through the Classical period, but which was accompanied by the loss of the complex material symbolism of the earlier record (discussed below).[117] It may have seemed to commentators from Herodotos onwards that this particular *meros* had always been as they saw it, and could thus contribute little to accounts of the developmental traits (notably synoikism) regarded implicitly or explicitly as characteristic of Achaian cities – but this perception conceals profound change in earlier years.[118]

The connections both facilitated and to some extent imposed by routes of communication linking the Pharai valley with Azania and the southern territory of Aigion raise the important issue of the role of this network, combined with factors like access to the seasonal pasture crucial in such uplands, in promoting both material and social interaction and the definition of social boundaries, usually expressed via the selection and manipulation of specific traits from a more widely shared pool. These boundaries were not constant (either in political salience or, very often, physical location), and their material expression thus varied in chronology, intensity and manner, reflecting contemporary perceptions of positive image and the articulation of difference.[119] Indeed, reviewing our study areas, with the exception of Phokis (where particular pressures followed the end of the Thessalian occupation and the separation of Delphi),[120] the strong expression of borders in the material record is a very patchy phenomenon, with the complex of Achaian *mere* and Azania being one of the earliest and most distinctive examples.

It is therefore worth pausing to explore the commonalities and distinctions expressed in this area, considering not only the eighth-century record but also changes through the Archaic period. A much-discussed example offers a convenient starting point. (Figure 4.2) The appearance in three graves in the Pharai valley of single Late Geometric figured vessels (a lion hunting a deer on a prochous from Troumbe, fish on a skyphos from grave A of the Α, Β, Γ Group, and birds on a round-mouthed oinochoe from Fteri) is striking and, especially in the case of the lion and fish, unparalleled in Achaia (although a single horse has been found at Ano Mazaraki).[121] In previous studies I have focused on the rewriting of imported ideas to create

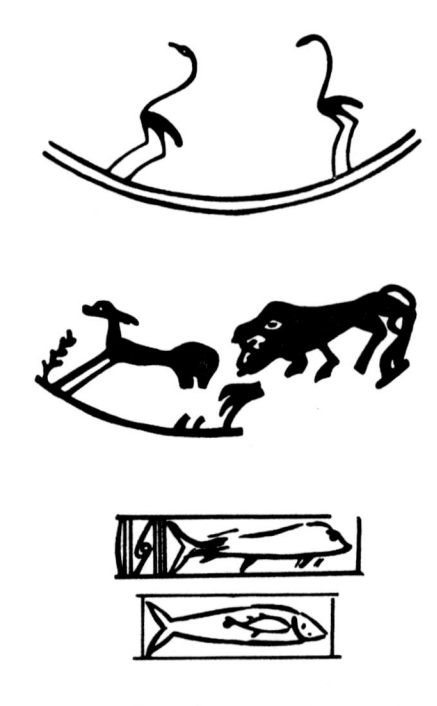

Figure 4.2 Achaian Late Geometric figure decoration (drawing: author, after *PAE* 1952 and 1956).

assertive style markers as an aspect of the definition of identities within and between burying groups.[122] A Darwinian approach may be helpful here, emphasizing as it does the intimate relationship between need, immediate circumstances, other patterns of choice, and the pool from which selections can be made.[123] Assessment of the specific meaning of these images should therefore be set against evaluation of the place of the Pharai pottery in its Achaian context. Discussions of their origins, while acknowledging local innovation, have tended to focus around Corinthian and Protoattic models probably mediated through styles such as Ithakan and also western Corinthianizing (Cumaean in particular).[124] Bearing in mind that non-figurative motifs, decorative syntax and the shapes represented in the Pharai assemblage in general show connections with Ano Mazaraki and thence Aigion and the wider gulf ambit, the structure of the style pool and the transmission route do not seem problematic.[125] The ceramic repertoire does not, however, overlap completely with that of Aigion and Ano Mazaraki: the impressed ware found primarily at Aigion, neighbouring Trapeza and Ano Mazaraki, and exported north to Delphi and south to Lousoi, has yet to be found, and the coastal and central Peloponnesian imports present at Ano Mazaraki in particular did not move further west.[126] Above all, the particular connections implied by the circulation both of vessels and style traits form but one aspect of the articulation of similarity and difference between adjacent Achaian and Azanian communities, and should be considered together with the parallel phenomena of sanctuary development at Ano Mazaraki and Lousoi, and the very different burial records of the Pharai valley and the Manesi plain in north-western Azania.

The establishment of a sanctuary, especially with a monumental temple like that at Ano Mazaraki, clearly involves great and lasting investment. By mainland standards, the early development of Ano Mazaraki is spectacular. The temple constructed at the end of the eighth or early in the seventh century was a hecatompedon, double apsidal in appearance thanks to an apsidal prostoa, with a wooden colonnade on stone bases and initially a thatched roof, replaced (probably during the sixth century) by tiles. The bedding of the east wall in a Middle–Late Geometric votive deposit (one of two on site) confirms the existence of cult at least from the mid-eighth century.[127] The early votive record is rich: in addition to miniature as well as standard pottery shapes, it includes a range of bronze figurines, jewellery and a miniature tripod,[128] and a notable collection of (mostly iron) offensive weapons, including a large group of Cypriot type-four arrowheads which could have arrived directly or via Crete (where they are also well represented).[129] A close connection with Aigion is shown not only by the ceramic record, but also by the presence of imports like scarabs, not as yet found elsewhere in eastern Achaia, which reflect the importance of Aigion's harbour.[130] While it would be anachronistic to characterize this sanctuary simply as a boundary marker, its location must reflect a perceived need for a strong presence close to a border zone and beside an important road. Indeed, the bleakness of the site is reflected in the cult epithet Aontia ('windy Artemis').[131] The long-term nature of this interest is shown by the continuous sequence of dedications into the fourth century AD, even though there is as yet no evidence for rebuilding after the destruction of the temple by an earthquake (probably that of 373).[132] By contrast with Lousoi (at least from the fifth century onwards),[133] there is no sign of settlement immediately surrounding the shrine, but survey of the wider region has revealed a few small sites (the closest being c.1.5 km to the south) suggesting perhaps pastoral exploitation of the area.[134] At present the evidence for local settlement is late (mostly Roman), but exploration is at an early stage and the dedication of Late Geometric granary models implies the commemoration of some early landed interest.[135]

The material record at Lousoi is rather different, yet the chronology of the sanctuary's establishment, towards the end of the eighth century and perhaps just later than Ano Mazaraki, is interesting. (Figures 1.20, 1.21) Attention has focused on the remoteness of the site in its mountain location,[136] but while it lies at an elevation of some 1,200 feet, its situation (on a low hill just above a plain crossed by a major road) is hardly inaccessible, and it is best considered in the context of the border zone.[137] The early votive record features pottery showing connections with the central Peloponnese as well as Achaia,[138] and most strikingly, a rich collection of small bronzes (especially animal figurines depicting many species). Stylistic analysis of these bronzes (and, slightly later, terracottas) shows some overlap with dedications at Arkadian shrines such as Tegea or Asea further south, but the preponderance of local traits has led to the hypothesis of a local production with clear links to Olympia.[139] There is as yet no evidence for monumental architecture before the sixth century, coincident with the appearance of a cult statue rapidly imitated by distinctive figurine types.[140] The monumental development of the sanctuary was thus substantially later than that of Ano Mazaraki, but this fits with the little we know of overall trends in Azanian polis development. Nonetheless, there is an interesting symmetry in the creation of these two sanctuaries which may have later echoes too. As noted in Chapter 2, an early fifth-century inscription apparently records a treaty between Lousoi and an Achaian neighbour. This is problematic both in terms of provenance and content, but it can hardly be coincidental that soon afterwards, Bacchylides (11.113–17) claimed that Artemis of Lousoi accompanied the Achaian colonists to Metapontion. And while Metapontion had a variety of founder traditions and one can hardly base political arguments on just one, it is interesting that the claim was made at all, especially at a time when cross-border relations of some kind were being formalized, and the sanctuary at Lousoi was undergoing a phase of monumentalization.[141]

Outside Lousoi, the early archaeological record of Azania is as slight as that of the Pharai valley, but shows interesting points of comparison and contrast. (Figure 4.3) Few of the principal Azanian settlements (Kleitor, Paion, Lousoi, Pheneos, Psophis and perhaps also Kynaitha)[142] have been substantially investigated and even fewer have yielded Geometric or early Archaic material. Most finds, especially inscriptions and monumental buildings, date to the sixth century or later.[143] However, at Drosato Vrisariou Lakes surface evidence, probably of settlement, dates from the eighth century onwards,[144] and there is a cluster of late eighth- and early seventh-century burials (Figure 4.3) around the plains of Manesi and Kalavryta (at Kompegadi, Manesi, Asani, Ag. Konstantinos and Flaboura),[145] the area of Azania closest to the Pharai valley. These burials stand out from the general Arkadian record both in number and for the inclusion of pottery, although the fashion for single burials (often in pithoi) fits the wider pattern. The Manesi area, like the Pharai valley, has produced at least one Late Mycenaean burial tumulus,[146] but the tradition was not continued or revived here, and the three robbed cist graves that may date to our period appear to have been simple constructions with no evidence of tumuli.[147] The pottery shows a continuation of the mixed southern Peloponnesian and Achaian coastal influences evident from the time of the earliest Early Iron Age burial yet

Figure 4.3 Northern Azania: the area of Manesi (photo: author).

found, at Priolithos south of Kalavryta, where an Argive-style conical oinochoe is the only stylistically Middle Geometric vessel yet discovered in Azania or Achaia.[148] Finds from the Manesi area show close similarities with the local styles of Ano Mazaraki, as well as imitating Lakonian and East Greek traits and, as Coldstream has recently argued, Phoenician metalwork too.[149] As the Ag. Konstantinos panoply burial illustrates, the occasional grave could be rich, but there is no real evidence for the differentiation, aggregation or discontinuity evident further west, and the area continued to produce similar single burials (especially in pithoi) into Classical times.[150] In other words, significant aspects of shared material culture, especially pottery styles, must be offset against differences in the form and long-term development of the burial record.

In broad terms, it is easy to understand the attraction of a distinctive Azanian identity with a ready point of oppositional definition provided by Achaian neighbours. Indeed, it may have been the experience of at least the northernmost of these Azanian communities in relating to these neighbours, as much as commonly cited factors like their distinctive upland environment, that distinguished them from the rest of Arkadia. However, as Heine Nielsen and Roy rightly stress,[151] there is no evidence that Azania ever formed the basis of a political identity, and a range of sources points instead to the role of individual poleis from an early date.[152] These include the toponyms mentioned in the *Catalogue of Ships* (such as Pheneos: *Iliad* 2.605), city dedications at Olympia (as the mid-sixth-century offering of spoils by the Psophians, *SEG* 24.299), and the fact that only cities, and not the

Azanian ethnos, struck coinage (see p. 83 above). Nonetheless, during the sixth century, as is clear from Herodotos' mention (6.127) of one Laphanes, an 'Azanian from Paion' among the suitors of Agariste daughter of Kleisthenes of Sikyon, Azania was a concept with which elite individuals chose to identify, perhaps in the same way as Arkadia, since the individual immediately before Laphanes on Herodotos' list, Amaintos of Trapezous, is called Arkas. Whether Azan and Arkas were alternative or complementary (nested) ethnicities is impossible to tell, but clearly they were distinguishable.

Over time, changes such as the settlement reorganization noted in neighbouring Pharees, the reinforcement of Azanian poleis as the dominant mode of political organization, shifting (and perhaps more closely defined) city territories,[153] and the gradual consolidation of Arkadia itself as an ethnic entity could all have contributed to the loss of political salience and thus the 'disappearance' of the ethnos. The outlines can be sketched, even though the details are lacking. The *ekleipsis* of ethne is well attested by later authors, Strabo in particular, for whom it is an important tool to explain the differences between the modern and ancient worlds.[154] Clearly some of Strabo's more general comments, as that on the decline and depopulation of Arkadia (8.8.1–2), are more philosophical than strictly historical, and find echoes in, for example, Pausanias' discussion of the fate of Megalopolis (8.33). Nonetheless, it is plain that an ethnos could disappear as a political entity even though those who formerly identified with it continued to inhabit the same area. In the case of Azania, this may have happened too early for later commentators to note the details, but they do describe the Azanes as among the most ancient peoples of Arkadia (for example Strabo 8.8.1). Certainly, there is nothing in the post-Archaic record to suggest that the Azanes maintained a distinctive identity,[155] and when the name appears in later times, it is rather in the context of constructed pan-Arkadian collective memory (as, for example, on a victory group dedicated at Delphi in 370–369: Pausanias 10.9.5). Hejnic's analysis of the Arkadian historical tradition as presented in Pausanias Book 8 adds further support for the idea that Azania may have experienced a distinct process of assimilation with Arkadia, in the form of the varied fates of Azanian city myths and histories. Although the historical traditions of some Azanian cities, like Kleitor, were fully integrated into that of Arkadia as a whole, a significant number of the cities who stood outside it, in terms of absence from the Arkadian king lists and maintenance of local historical and religious traditions, were Azanian (Pheneos being a case in point).[156] In short, the case of Azania, considered in relation to its Achaian neighbours, highlights the point that if ethne could effectively disappear from all but historical consciousness, or deliberately formalize subordinate roles within wider state structures, then they could also be created or politicized as circumstances and needs arose.[157]

This discussion began by evaluating the political development (or lack of it) of an area of scattered settlement in the Achaian *mesogeia*. The apparent absence of a central site until the sixth century (if it is not an archaeological aberration) cannot be taken as evidence of backwardness. The Pharai valley, together with its neighbours, was the scene of complex internal and external interaction, of interrelated and shifting strategies of settlement and material expression reflecting exploitation of the connections offered by the existence of a major road system. This case highlights the general issues of how and when borders become salient, how this was expressed, on what level similarities and differences were articulated using shared aspects of material culture, and the impact of these interactions upon long-term development in individual regions. A further question to which we should now turn concerns attitudes to the past, often seen as one of the major points of distinction between poleis and ethne.

The territory of our ancestors?

Collective myth-history is one of the most commonly cited indicators of the existence of an ethnic group, as indeed of almost any form of socially closed community. It is a tenet that recognition of putative shared descent is not only central to ethnic consciousness but serves as a fundamental means of social closure.[158] This is not confined to large-scale ethne: place communities at polis level were often constructed in such terms, and tiered identities can be expressed though mythological interconnections (as in the cases of the Phokian and Arkadian epichoric myth-histories already noted). Claims to group cohesion in a particular place were thus articulated through a shared past in which political communities at all levels were engaged.

Archaic Greek myths of origin are characterized both by genealogies, which give time depth and a means of describing and accommodating changing relationships with others, and by accounts of the migrations experienced by the group collectively in reaching its present home. In discussing the relationship between ethne and their territories, attention long focused on this migratory aspect, as if, to quote Jonathan Hall, it describes 'a hazy and refracted recollection of genuine population movements that occurred at the end of the Bronze Age', leaving myths as the 'passive trace elements of groups whose "objective" existence is deemed to stand independently of these same myths'.[159] In part, mythological emphasis on the shared journey is a response to the methodological problem of explaining origins. Unless a group claimed autochthony it had somehow to arrive in place.[160] And, as emphasized in the introductory chapter, while autochthony was balanced by the Athenians with Ionian connections of varying degrees[161] and the Arkadians were also credited with it (Herodotos 8.73), its effectiveness was limited in a Mediterranean articulated via interconnection rather than exclusivity.[162]

Nonetheless, there were real practicalities to be explained and discussed. Greeks were always on the move. What we rationalize, often using ancient terms (if sometimes, as in the case of synoikism, in an inappropriate way), reflects the usual fission, fusion, changes of political distance, emigration and immigration characteristic of most societies through history, and readily conceptualized in the established language of kinship and/or conflict.[163] It is therefore predictable to find the shifting parameters of identity reflected in myth (as we will see presently in the case of Achaian colonization). It is, however, important to distinguish this kind of mobility, which was a constant of Greek existence over the centuries, from the migrations described in the sagas with which communities shaped their identity and made myths of common origin located in the deep past.[164] The two phenomena are distinct, but inevitably they share common expression in the language of kinship and consanguinity which can make them easy to confuse. The notion that ethne were born of the great tribal migrations of the post-Mycenaean era does a deep disservice not only to our understanding of how and why Greeks conceptualized their own group identities in terms of the past, but also to our contemporary archaeological reconstructions of these regions. It is hard to see how it can be acceptable to consider the Late Bronze Age/Early Iron Age transition in Thessaly in terms of the Thessalian migration and expulsion of the Boiotians to Boiotia (Thucydides 1.12),[165] while the archaeology of the Dorians has been discarded as a flawed modern construct.[166] A cynic might suggest that the difference lies in the perceived role of tribalism, but in fact the language and structures used to conceptualize origins in relation to present circumstances form a conceptual unity which cuts across supposed political boundaries within and between old Greece and the colonial world.[167]

That the mythological and genealogical aspects of Greek identity expression receive only limited treatment in this book is no comment on their importance. They have been expertly discussed elsewhere,[168] and I prefer to approach the same underlying problems from a different angle. Nonetheless, attitudes to, and the construction of, shared myth-history can sometimes be traced in the archaeological record. To give but one example, there are hints of the performative aspects of specific local rituals in the dedication of equipment like the masks from the sanctuary of Artemis Orthia in Sparta,[169] and in iconography such as that of a Late Geometric bronze dance group of four males wearing horse masks from the sanctuary of Poseidon Hippios at Petrovouni in the *chora* of Methydrion in central Arkadia.[170] But the aspect of the archaeological record which has received perhaps the greatest attention concerns attitudes to the dead, either in the form of named heroes or the generic dead claimed as 'ancestors', whose graves gave the authority of antiquity to the association of peoples and places.

With the exception of Herakles, cults of named heroes in the early record are relatively rare, and none are attested in our areas.[171] There are of course important later hero shrines such as that of the Archegetes of the Phokian ethnos (Pausanias 10.4.10), although what were long considered to be its

TERRITORY, POWER AND THE ANCESTORS

physical remains have now been identified as an early (fifth-century) federal meeting place. In this case, the creation of a cult to a national hero represents a distinct kind of activity constructed at a higher level than that of the local heroes of epichoric myth, yet in terms which allowed individual communities to set it in relation to their own myth-histories.[172] In Arkadia too, the worship of local heroes played an important role in expressing the relationship between individual city and collective Arkadian mythology. Pausanias mentions a number of such shrines, often in the form of tombs such as that of Penelope outside Mantineia (8.12.5–6),[173] but as has been emphasized, most have yet to be located, let alone excavated, and we lack chronological controls. As noted, however, there is no reason to assume that any were early (especially given the general chronological trend across Greece), and it might well be argued that they represent a powerful physical articulation of local in relation to regional identity that implies a stronger sense of Arkadia as an entity than is traceable much before the Classical period.[174] Yet such heroes are not the dead of immediate or 'ancestral' memory, but belong within group genealogies deliberately located in the remote past. The situation is very different when it comes to the parallel phenomenon of worship at specific tombs or cemeteries, where links with ancestors can be more or less direct. This in turn raises the question of the extent to which the dead were allowed to become (in Appadurai's terms) a debatable aspect of the past in our regions,[175] how this was expressed and on what level of social identity.

One trait which has been claimed to distinguish the worlds of the polis and the ethnos as traditionally conceived is the geographical spread during our period of cult at Bronze Age tombs or within contemporary or near-contemporary Early Iron Age cemeteries.[176] It is certainly true that few cases have been claimed in ethne and most are tenuous.[177] In Arkadia, putative instances of tomb cult at Analypsis and Palaiochoria probably represent intrusion and re-use respectively,[178] and there are, as noted, more convincing interpretations of the Troumbe 'tholos' in Achaia. But there is at least one clear instance of Geometric dedication in a Bronze Age tomb some 3 km from Metropolis in western Thessaly,[179] and in Phokis, Medeon tholos 239 was noted in the previous chapter.

Explanations of the phenomenon as a whole have focused around the idea of 'heroized' ancestors as guarantors of access to critical resources, although the specific issues involved and the way in which cult was used have been keenly debated and clearly varied from region to region. Bearing in mind the heavy concentration of evidence in Attica, the Argolid and Messenia, discussions have tended to centre on the emergence of the polis in the first two cases, and in Messenia on the effects of Spartan conquest and the post-liberation reconfiguration of the landscape in the fourth and early third centuries.[180] Land has been perceived as the critical resource, with changing perceptions of ownership and access underpinning its status as the only medium of wealth. It is in this context that Anthony Snodgrass has highlighted the implications of what he identifies as a widespread switch from pastoralism to arable.[181] Here, however, I agree with Lin Foxhall that, quite apart from doubts about specific interpretations of faunal remains as indicative of pastoralism, the diverse range of positive evidence for agrarian activities throughout the Early Iron Age in 'poleis' and 'ethne' alike makes a post-palatial decline into pastoralism unlikely, even though a major shift in scale probably occurred in most areas.[182] The case must therefore rest on the impact of settlement expansion – but this is hardly peculiar to the traditional polis world.

Two particular explanations have been cited for the supposed lack of evidence in ethne. The first relates to burial customs. Tomb cult requires that the tombs in question appear sufficiently alien or exotic to be convincing indicia of a past age, and this is hard to achieve in regions where Mycenean-style practices of (usually collective) interment in chamber or tholos tombs were maintained (as in Thessaly, Achaia and Phokis, notably at Elateia).[183] Nonetheless, the Metropolis tomb (the first such find in a region which has been little investigated) shows that at least one Thessalian tholos was so used. Furthermore, while this may explain the poor representation of a particular material manifestation of worship, it does not preclude the involvement of tombs in other expressions of similar concerns. As has already been suggested in the case of Achaia, where the maintenance of older traditions formed only part of the contemporary record, its selection is unlikely to have been innocent. The second line of explanation, Snodgrass' suggestion that tomb cult would not be useful in regions (such as Thessaly) without a free peasantry,[184] has rightly been criticized both on the grounds there is evidence for unfree labour in areas with prominent tomb cult (like the Argolid: Herodotos 6.83), and also because it is unclear that the peasantry were responsible for these cults, and so their freedom or lack of it may be irrelevant.[185] While we will not dwell on this argument, it is, however, worth digressing briefly to consider the *penestai* of Thessaly, since they form a potentially complex if poorly understood case of identity construction which sits ill with Snodgrass' model.

Penestai

Early evidence for the status and role of *penestai* is lacking, and we are obliged to work from often much later sources. Nonetheless, and despite their disagreements, there are revealing points of overlap in ancient authors' approaches to the problem. Most do not attempt any direct description of the *penestai* themselves, but consider them in relation to other subjugated groups.[186] The particular tendency to conflate *penestai* with helots is, as Ducat emphasizes, not only misleading but has also been exaggerated by modern commentators.[187] Aristotle (*Politics* 2.6.2) is one of the few ancient sources to make a clear and unequivocal association between the two in describing how the *penestai* repeatedly rose against their masters in the same way as the helots. Others present a more complex picture. Plato (*Laws* 776c-d), for example, mentions them in discussion of the ethics of slave owning, and ranks 'the ethnos of the *penestai* with regard to the Thessalians' (a rather neutral formulation) at the opposite end of the spectrum from helotage. A similarly graded comparison is made by Pollux (3.83) with respect to the helots and the Cretan *klarotai*. Overall, there is a strong impression of indeterminacy: *penestai* are clearly dependent labourers, but while not as subjugated as some, the extent of their subjection is not specified. A particularly interesting comparison is made by Dionysus of Halikarnassus (2.9.2) who, in describing how Romulus improved upon the systems of the Greek cities when setting up the Roman client system, brackets the *penestai* and the Athenian *thetes* as groups of free men who were not treated as such by their patrons. A client relationship is also implied by a scholiast to Aristophanes *Wasps* 1271, undertaken as a deliberate choice to end hunger. The fundamentally economic nature of such dependency is equally plain in our earlier sources: Theocritos (*Idylls* 16.34–5) lists the many *penestai* who earned their monthly food in the households of Antiochos and Aleuas as as much part of the wealth of those rulers as their sheep or cattle, and while his Homeric, archaizing tone is plain,[188] a similar sense of *penestai* as people who could become a personal resource is present in Demosthenes' mention (13.23; 23.199) of the mounted *penestai* supplied by Meno of Pharsalos to fight beside the Athenians at Amphipolis.[189] Plainly, *penestai* could be armed when expedient and could do well from it,[190] and we should probably see Xenophon's reference (2.3.36) to Critias and Prometheus' arming of *penestai* against their masters as a development of such attitudes and practices rather than as indicative of a simmering helot-style state of revolt.[191]

If the (perhaps voluntary) dependency of the *penestai* does reflect a kind of middle ground among the various systems evident across Greece, this would allow their status to be depicted in different lights, reflecting subordination or economic security according to advantage or context. As noted, Plato called them an ethnos, and plainly they were a group that could construct a distinct identity for themselves, or have one constructed for them. This is evident in the clearly articulated difference from their Thessalian masters, a common theme in accounts of their origins and history.[192] Hence the notion of an Illyrian origin, and the even more pervasive idea that the *penestai* were ethnic Boiotians who, rather than leaving to settle in Boiotia when the Thessalians entered Thessaly, stayed (as *menestai*) and submitted voluntarily in exchange for guarantees of personal security and protection from sale outside their patron's land.[193] The Boiotian pedigree embodies a complex balance of negative and positive factors in relating the two group identities. Thessalians and *penestai* are clearly differentiated by ethnicity, but whereas the Thessalians had the power to control, their claim on the land was via conquest, and the *penestai* had the advantage of a longer history *in situ*, and could partly offset their weaker social position by the fact that it was negotiated and chosen rather than enforced. This well illustrates how a group that wanted to reverse a negative social identity could do so by a combination of assimilation (cultural and/or psychological) to the dominant group, positive redefinition of negative characteristics, and creation of new dimensions of comparison to by-pass those by which it was formerly disadvantaged.[194]

Burial and the past in Thessaly

Thessaly presents complex evidence for the use of the past in the mortuary record. It is a tenet that ethnic status is ascribed rather than acquired. Birth into a group is in theory therefore very important, although that should not imply a fixed identity for life as changes in group boundaries may occur, and there may also be regular cross-border movement, of women for example if the group is exogamous.[195] It may be more accurate to say that ethnic status is justified by reference to descent rather than strictly determined by it. Nonetheless, Carla Antonaccio has suggested that the shortage of evidence for ancestor cult in ethnos regions is surprising if kinship and descent really did play an important role in social structuring.[196] Setting aside the contradictory evidence of the Metropolis burial which was discovered after the publication of her book, her conclusion rests on two main assumptions which should be challenged. First, since ethne are characterized by tiered political identities, there is no reason to assume that the factors governing the presence or absence of tomb cult in a particular geographical area are to be located in the ethnic register, or that such ethnicity had sufficient political salience to be marked in this way during our period. Second, we have no grounds for inferring a general correlation between this particular form of cult and the value placed on kinship and descent (or for expecting a principle always to be expressed strongly whether or not it was under stress).[197] Instead, there are numerous hints in the Thessalian burial record to suggest that the role of descent was marked in several different ways.

It is generally accepted that the ritual which constitutes a funeral and leaves the material regularities which we read as 'burial customs' rests on a community's shared values and views on matters such as who was entitled to formal burial, in what manner according to gender, age or status, and what elements of social persona would be stressed in the associated symbolism.[198] Burial thus represents a kind of group closure, but one that is by no means straightforward to read, since assumptions of unity across ethnos territory, or the idea that large collective burials of different forms (tholoi and tumuli) were family tombs, are simplistic and often speculative.[199] In Thessaly, the selection of traditional tomb types such as tholoi, the use of tumuli to associate differently constituted groups within a single cemetery, and the presence of funerary cult associated with some mounds, implies that tradition, ancestry and the physical commemoration of certain associations were actively deployed in the definition of individual or group persona. (Figure 4.4) Large-scale excavation of what are often very extensive cemeteries will be necessary if we are to gain any real understanding of the extent and nature of synchronic and diachronic variation, and the full range of groups represented in death. Nonetheless, present evidence at least shows the existence of certain important phenomena.

A good example of intra-cemetery variation in the composition and treatment of burying groups may be found at Platanos Almyrou close to New Halos. Survey indicates an extensive cemetery, with at least thirty-seven tumuli visible in this immediate area alone (and indications of similar numbers elsewhere), although much damage has already been caused by ploughing.[200] Close by is the collection of ten tumuli noted by Wace and Thompson early last century, of which only the early to mid-eighth-century tumulus A, a separate group of ten Protogeometric cist graves, and one

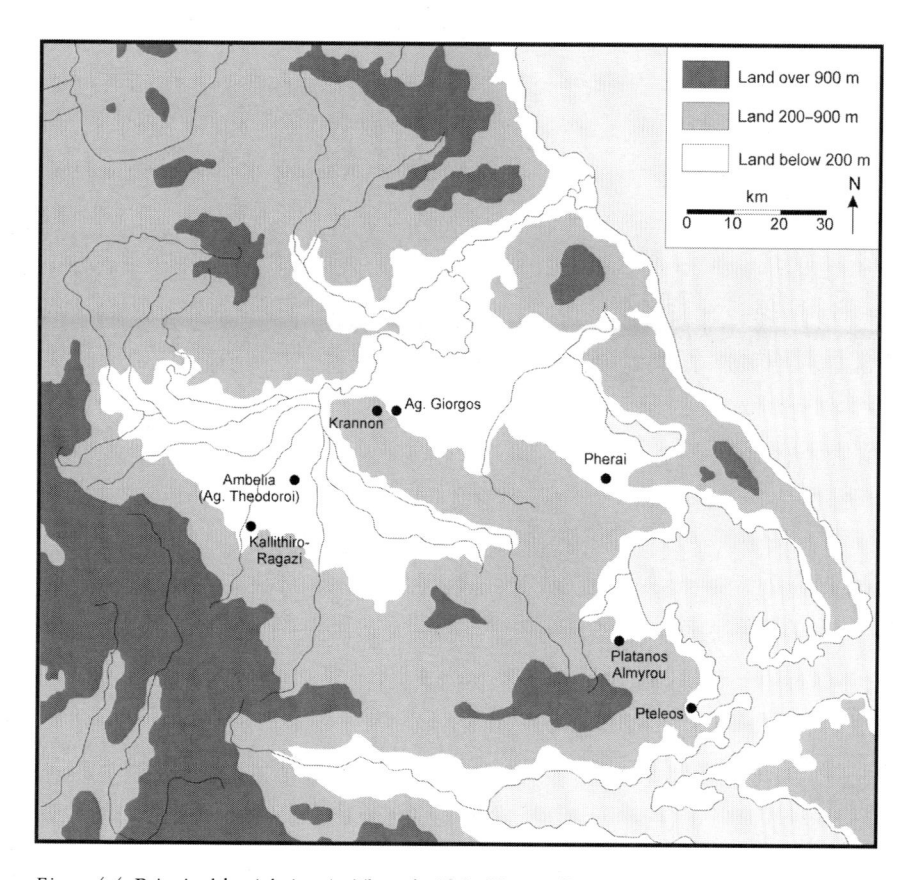

Figure 4.4 Principal burial sites in Thessaly (C.L. Hayward).

round enclosure, all but one of which contained child burials, were excavated. The tumulus contained primary adult cremations with small cairns heaped over each pyre and gender-distinctive goods (such as weapons and jewellery). The change of rite from Protogeometric to Geometric times has been emphasized (noting, however the earlier preponderance of children), but in fact the primary nature of the cremations as well as the earlier adult inhumations are points of contrast with other parts of the same cemetery.[201] More recently, three tumuli of the Platanos cemetery have been excavated; in all the standard rite for adults was secondary cremation, with individual pyres preserved close to the cist graves which contained the gathered remains, and consistent gender distinctions marked with weapons and jewellery.[202] In two cases, A and B, the cist graves were arranged around a central tholos tomb, and in Γ, five tholoi were scattered through the mound, perhaps indicating distinct foci within the overall structure. A greater point of distinction, however, is the age range represented. Tumulus A (of the ninth to late seventh or early sixth century) contained only adults, whereas Tumulus B (of the same date) had two adult pot cremations in addition to the cists, and twenty-five child inhumations segregated around the perimeter of the tumulus but with the same range of goods as the adults. In Tumulus Γ (Protogeometric to Archaic), child inhumations were again ranged around the edge, but are relatively late in date and contained only a little pottery. Most strikingly, Tumulus Γ contained evidence of funerary cult in the form of fourteen stone bench-like constructions on the outer boundaries, set between the cists and child graves especially in the south-west and south-east.[203] In several other parts of the Greek world (including Mycenae, Asine, Naxos and Troy), funerary dining areas are attested, usually in the form of round or occasionally square paved structures.[204] The nature of the cult at Planatos is not yet clear (only a preliminary notice has been published), but the structures look like more elaborate forms of offering table. Tumulus Γ is the only such case yet discovered, although only a very small proportion of the cemetery has been investigated and there may well prove to be others. Overall, therefore, burying groups which shared basic gender values and attitudes to the disposition of goods in graves seem to have differed in their treatment of children, the use of primary or secondary cremation, and the presence of single or multiple tholoi. The marking of tumuli would presumably indicate to the living population which group was which, but funerary or ancestor cult added a further, very public dimension to this.

An even more striking case is that of Ag. Giorgos near Krannon, where, as noted in Chapter 2, there is a strong contrast between the gender balance represented in the excavated portion of the tumulus at Xirorema and the burial of only heavily armed males at Karaeria.[205] I have suggested elsewhere that the Karaeria population might be a status-interest group rather than war dead in a *polyandrion*, and in this light it is interesting to note the similar perception of the heroic male indicated by the weapons dedications at the Pyra Herakleous at Oiti in Malis.[206] Thessaly is not alone in this respect: considering the seventh-century monumental tumuli in the Athenian Kerameikos, Sanne Houby-Nielsen has argued for a greater emphasis on more gender-based constructs, setting men in the context of socio-political organizations such as sympotic and priestly groups rather than the family per se. As she notes, for Homer, the *sema* is a mound heaped over individuals or friends, and he does not mention family tombs. Nonetheless, the fact that the dead are celebrated by public values is also a comment on the family, since while *eugenia* is inherited, *arete* is a matter of public conduct.[207] Observations of this kind invite comparison between mortuary associations and the whole range of potential groupings (by age, gender, professional or political association) represented in, for example, sanctuary dedications and festivals (and, as the epigraphical record occasionally reveals, within cities).[208] Here too, we face the question of how such a physically and socially monumentalized landscape reflected and helped to shape the perceptions of the living population.

It is sometimes claimed that larger 'looser' ethne continued with more old-fashioned ceremonial systems as if this observation is simple or unproblematic.[209] Yet the choice of tomb type, especially in a region like Thessaly where there were a number of possibilities, seems unlikely to have been innocent. Building a new monument (let alone reusing an old one) is always a comment on a pre-existing world. The decision to reuse or continue to build tholoi is a good example, as the evidence varies greatly across the region. In some instances reuse can be relatively limited, as perhaps with the three Late Bronze Age to Protogeometric burials found in tholos II at Pteleos (although this tomb was robbed probably in Roman times).[210] But much longer-lived tholoi include the Protogeometric construction with a monumental covering mound at Ambelia (Ag. Theodoroi), west of Ancient Kierion, which continued in use from Protogeometric times at least to the end of the eighth or the very early seventh century,[211] and represents a continuation of a local building tradition (to judge by the proximity of Mycenaean tholoi).[212] Further south-west, however, a single pithos burial containing handmade Geometric-influenced pottery is the earliest grave at modern Kallithiro-Ragazi, illustrating the point that alternatives were always available.[213] The decision to build or reuse an existing tholos (especially over such a long period of time) must involve at least an element of reflection on the past. And at sites like Pherai, where tholoi were relatively rare and conspicuous in the context of contemporary custom, they suggest reference to the past as an important means of articulating difference. Overall, the body of evidence is small and often poorly preserved, but it does indicate, albeit in general terms, that ancestry was in some way incorporated into expressions of status and/or group identity in the mortuary record.

Beyond the boundaries

By the end of our period, it is clear that all of our study areas had come to be perceived as territorial entities which could be subdivided with varying degrees of strength or salience, but which had an overall meaning to those who subscribed in whatever way to the regional ethnic. This is not a comment on the political salience of that ethnic – indeed, only in post-liberation Phokis is there is reasonable case for a politicized ethnos structure as a formal tier of government. But in the case of Arkadia, Apollo's famous 'grant' of Tegea to those Spartans who sought via the Delphic oracle 'all of the Arkadian territory' (Herodotos 1.66–8) well illustrates the conception of an ethnic territory overlying place communities. And in Thessaly too, there is an overarching perception of an entity, whether one believes, with Helly, that the Aleuad reforms of the second half of the sixth century sustained a territorially based levy for a regional army,[214] or with Link that they were at best a feudal readjustment primarily at local level.[215] Central to this particular debate is the unanswerable question of the extent to which Aleuas could have acted outside Larisa, not least since while a prominent figure (and thus, as any oikist or tyrant, liable to attract credit for land and law reforms, not to mention Delphic sanction for his rule),[216] he is not the only Archaic Thessalian ruler so praised.[217] Similar debates surround the interpretation of the elder Skopas' fixing of the level of tribute payable by *penestai* as reported by Xenophon (*Hellenika* 6.1.9). Helly, for example, sees this as a means of establishing the place of non-citizens within the military order, but one might also view it as a systematisation (whether local or pan-Thessalian) of economic ties with individual aristocrats.[218] Overall, Pindar's praise of aristocratic rule (*Pythian* 10.69–72) makes it hard to imagine that much of importance lay beyond their control – and there was plainly a Thessaly to be invoked, feared by outsiders, fought for, and defended.

Achaia is perhaps the most complicated case, and one which leads us directly into the issues of the impact of mobility which will occupy the remainder of this chapter. As noted, there is no good evidence for the existence of any regional political organization, let alone a league, before the very end of the fifth century.[219] 'Achaios' appears as an ethnic designation in a number of fifth-century contexts, ranging from Herodotos' description (8.73.1) of the seven ethne inhabiting the Peloponnese, to the inscription on a statue base erected in 460 for the victorious athlete Oibotas (Pausanias 7.17.7) whose *patris* is given as Paleia. But these two examples highlight the peculiar complexity of this identity, since not only could it straightforwardly designate the inhabitants of Peloponnesian Achaia and those of her western colonies (two identities which progressively diverged though the Archaic period), but as an epic ethnic, it also had the power to link those so identified with the heroic world of the great tribal ethnicities. This ambiguity was particularly finely exploited in the west as Jonathan Hall has shown,[220] but mainland Achaians also drew on it (albeit marginally later on present evidence), for example in establishing their migratory ancestry (Herodotos 8.73) and in an offering made ἐν κοινῷ at Olympia in the mid-fifth century of a bronze statue group by Onatas representing the Achaian chiefs casting lots to determine who should face Hector (Pausanias 5.25.8–10).[221] In the latter case, the clear regional sense of the ethnic is reinforced by the imagery, although this is not evidence for a formal federation at this stage. Clearly, therefore, while the colonial and epic usages are not of primary concern here, care is required in teasing out the various strands of meaning.

Oibotas' dedication is also interesting as an illustration of the way in which regional ethnics were used, often alongside more local designations, when individuals wished to specify their geographical origins to an outside audience, a practice which recurs in many areas. As a further example, one might cite Echembrotos' description of himself as 'Arkas' on a tripod which he dedicated to Herakles at Thebes in celebration of a victory in the Pythian games (Pausanias 10.7.6).[222] By the fifth century at the latest, there was therefore an external perception of Arkadia as an ethnos with a territory, to which the Arkadians themselves subscribed when dedicating in a panhellenic context. However, its internal political force when set against the various localized settlement patterns and trajectories of community development is a matter of debate.

It remains therefore to review the circumstances under which the movement of individuals or groups across territorial boundaries fostered the use by themselves and by others of simple overarching descriptions like group ethnics. It must be emphasized that not all forms of boundary-crossing are liable to produce this effect. Regular movements between geographically or socially close communities (for example surrounding commodity exchange) could promote the kind of close familiarity that sees complexities of identity as either positive or at worst neutral factors. By contrast, exchanges of group members which require those involved to change or modify their identity (exogamous marriage, for example) can, as has been argued, serve to strengthen by repetition group identity in all its complexities. The kind of ethnic labels with which we are concerned are more likely to be emphasized under circumstances where an individual retained his original identity but needed to explain it to a socially distant or alien group, or where s/he selected one particular level of that identity as the basis for creating something genuinely new. Colonization and warfare were the two main forms of movement which produced this effect during our period.[223] Achaia and Lokris certainly colonized and if Achaia's later reputation is any guide, she probably joined Arkadia and Thessaly as a provider of military manpower.

Economic return (combined with a temporary or permanent removal of manpower) was certainly a major factor in both cases, being either immediate (in terms of booty or traded goods) or long term (in the sense of the definition and development of opportunities). Demographic issues are more complex. The use of burial evidence for population size is of course a much debated issue. While it is clear that the pre-eighth-century record of most parts of Greece is now much larger than that cited by Snodgrass, and that his direct connection between burial numbers and population levels must be mediated via changing social perceptions of formal burial, taking mortuary and settlement evidence together, the basic notion of a population rise beginning in the eighth century in most regions of Greece remains broadly valid.[224] Its effects almost certainly depended on locally variable factors such as ecology, and ability or willingness to adapt or change altogether economic strategies and socio-political structures. These are unlikely to have been wholly new experiences, and may have underpinned the group fissions and fusions evident in the Early Iron Age record of most regions, but they probably occurred on a greater scale than previously experienced. They certainly had major implications for place communities (including those later firmly attested as poleis) within ethne, and it is easy to understand how radical changes in the material record, such as the shift in settlement scale and the nature of identity display evident in the Pharai valley, could result from even quite small demographic shifts. This in turn raises the question of the extent to which communities which identified with the same ethnos but had different developmental histories, adopted common solutions when faced with similar problems (thereby potentially strengthening their sense of shared identity).[225] This is one possible model for Achaian colonization, since as we will see, the sources tying oikists and settlers to particular parts of the region are late, few and fragile.

To begin with colonization, Achaian settlement on the Ionian coast of Italy is the most securely attested case of ethnos colonization, and raises a range of important questions about the nature of early colonial enterprises and their place within established maritime activity. But Achaia was not the only ethnos to colonize: Lokrian settlement at Epizephyrian Lokri and Naupaktos is also attested, although as discussed in the introductory chapter, the sources are vague about the precise origins of those involved. In one further instance, that of Elis, three colonies in the territory of the Cassopaians in south-west Epirus are mentioned by the fourth-century writers Pseudo-Demosthenes (7.32) and Theopompos (*FrGHist* 115, F206, cited by Harpocration *s.v.* Elateia), neither of whom give even an approximate foundation date. This tenuous evidence, which lacks archaeological support, has nonetheless been used to reconstruct an elaborate scenario of colonial rivalry between the Eleans and Corinth in north-west Greece from the Late Geometric or early Archaic period onwards, to the extent of seeing opposition to foreign presence as a factor in Epirote ethnogenesis.[226] There is, however, a simpler explanation which eliminates colonization. As David Asheri points out, a sub-ethnos of the Cassopaians, the Elaians, inhabited the area supposedly settled by Eleans; their harbour was called Elaia (Ps.-Skylax 30) and the area as a whole Elaiatis (Thucydides 1.46.4). Asheri therefore suggests that the three 'colonies' were Elaian towns, and that Pseudo-Demosthenes switched the name to convey the impression that Philip II had transgressed the rights of the Peloponnesian Eleans, a comparable action to his attack on the Corinthian cities of Ambrakia and Leukas (Demosthenes 9.34). If we therefore set Elis aside, we are left with Achaia as the only instance of ethnos colonization with a large and reasonably secure body of evidence, although as I will suggest, there are certain important points of comparison with the circumstances of Lokris.

Achaians were among the earliest Greeks to settle in the west. (Figure 4.5) In recent years a number of studies, including those by Jonathan Hall and myself,[227] have reviewed and analysed the foundation traditions in detail. I therefore simply note that while connections with Peloponnesian Achaia are clear, specific oikist traditions linked to particular Achaian sites tend to be more fragile and to appear late. Is of Helike (for Sybaris), Myskellos of Rhypes (for Kroton), and most tenuous of all, Typhon of Aigion (for Kaulonia, probably a daughter colony of Kroton) are all tied to coastal settlements either of contemporary or ancient importance to the writers (Strabo, Pausanias and Ephoros) who provide our information. In the case of Rhypes, the question of the site's location in relation to Aigion remains problematic, although renewed excavation on the site long claimed as the acropolis, Trapeza hill, has now revealed evidence from the late eighth century onwards, including a later Archaic temple, and architectural evidence of a substantial Classical city. A Hellenistic date for synoikism with Aigion seems likely (especially with the discovery of late Hellenistic/Roman rooftiles with the stamp of Aigion) although this is yet to be resolved.[228] By Roman times, however, Rhypes would likely have been seen as a former centre of importance which was now part of what had been the finest harbour along the Gulf before the development of Patras. It may not be fortuitous that the three sites singled out are the major Greek cult centre, a major port and a city closely associated with it, and one cannot therefore dismiss the suggestion that the 'essential' element of oikist tradition[229] was grafted on at a later date. That being said, it is wholly plausible that the coastal *mere* should have been at the heart of a maritime enterprise: what we cannot preclude, given the lack of evidence, is the involvement of the *mesogeia* also.

At first sight, it may seem puzzling that Achaian colonization in the west predated more local expansion. The Dyme region was certainly not empty during the Early Iron Age, but both intensive survey and excavation (notably in the ancient city centre) show it to have been comparatively lightly settled before the sixth century at the earliest, even allowing for the usual under-representation of material of our period.[230] Yet the fact that internal and external colonization were not mutually exclusive not only casts doubt on

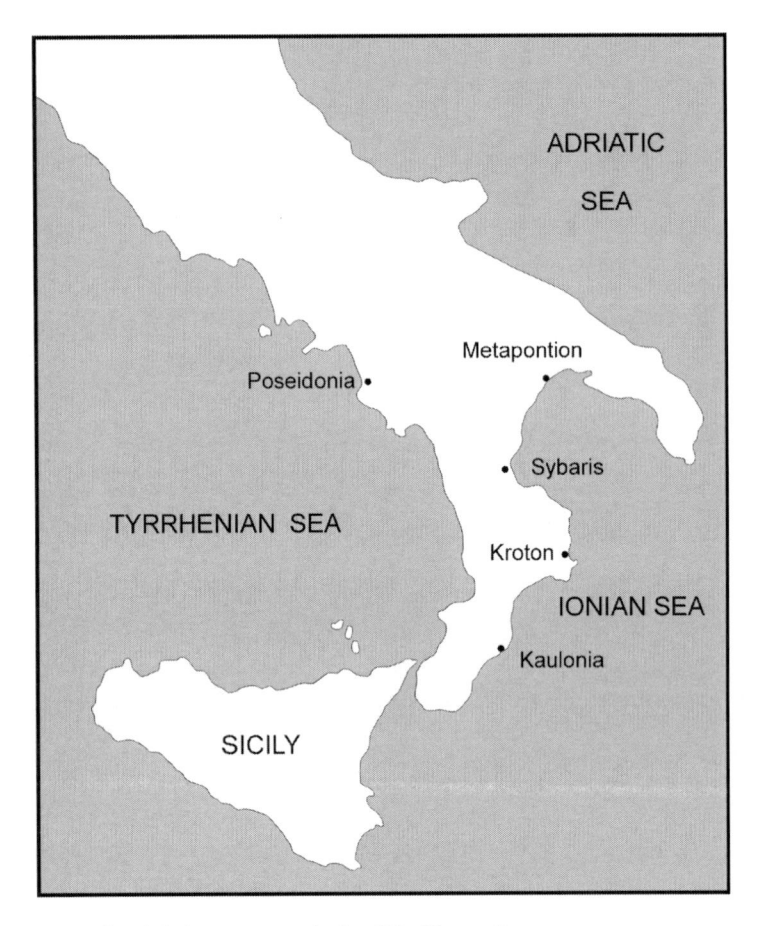

Figure 4.5 Achaian western colonies (C.L. Hayward).

the validity of any such distinction, but raises the more fundamental issue of how we are to understand and categorize the spectrum of strategies of land acquisition and settlement evident in the early Greek world. Was 'overseas' territory (be it in Italy in the case of both Achaia and Lokris, or the Gulf coast in the case of Lokrian Naupaktos) necessarily more alien than somewhere like Dyme within the later political territory of Achaia? Indeed, there is a risk of hindsight in treating the political incorporation of Dyme as an important factor at this early stage. As will be further argued in the concluding chapter, during the eighth century Achaia played a full part in a complex network of interactions and interconnections across and along the Corinthian gulf and (via Ithaka in particular) out to Italy, and it is thus unlikely that those who settled in the west were heading into *terra incognita*. In this respect the situation of East Lokris seems similar, since coastal

Lokrian cities like Kynos show close material connections with the Lefkandi sequence from Protogeometric times.[231] The Middle-Late Geometric cemetery at Tragana also contains imports from surrounding areas, Euboia included, and Euboia may have been the immediate source of the two bronze phialai found in tomb Π-9, one of which bears a Hittite inscription (noting also a further omphalos phiale in a grave at Anavra).[232] Both Achaian and East Lokrian communities were therefore closely engaged with neighbouring poleis within maritime networks.

Colonization by a group recognized primarily via a regional ethnic rather than a *politikon* is an uncomfortable proposition only for those wedded to the quasi-Thucydidean view of colonization as a neat transfer from polis to polis.[233] If one accepts that most expeditions were not exclusive undertakings, then it is easy to see the choice of the Achaian *ethnikon* as the point of reference for the construction of communal identity (undoubtedly enhanced by its epic connotations) as just one end of a spectrum. At the other, one might put the numerous Black Sea colonies who claimed Milesian origins sooner or later in their history: Pliny the Elder's tally of ninety (*NH* 5.122) is surely an exaggeration but perhaps not a great one. Here a combination of factors seems likely.[234] As Alan Greaves points out, the loss of a disproportionate amount of the finest agricultural land to the Persians probably created exceptional population pressures, certain Milesian colonies clearly included non-Milesians (Parians, Erythraeans and Klazomenians for example), some (like Apollonia on the Rhyndacus) claimed Milesian identity much later, and it is possible (if unproveable) that some claims of identity stemmed simply from the oikist or from Didymaean sanction.

Given this wide spectrum of possibilities, factors such as the geographical and ethnic diversity of those involved in an act of colonization, or the existence of a dominant organizing partner, are likely to have had a considerable influence on the terms in which group identity was constructed. So too did the subsequent history of the colony, especially in relation to neighbours of different ethnic backgrounds, as the rivalry between the Achaian colonies and Dorian Taras highlights.[235] The idea that eighth-century colonization either indicates the pre-existence of the polis in mainland Greece or that it was a formative influence on its development has been much discussed, but is open to criticism in many respects.[236] In the case of Achaia, while polis status in the political sense defined by the Copenhagen criteria is a phenomenon of the fifth century at the earliest (and thus rather later than, for example, Arkadia), it is clear that major coastal settlements such as those at Aigion and Aigeira existed by the eighth century, and that at least some of those who settled in Italy would have had as much practical experience of 'city' life as the inhabitants of contemporary Corinth. Nonetheless, those colonists chose to constitute themselves in the overarching register of the regional ethnic — and it is important to stress that this was positive choice and not a limit of experience. In doing so, they almost certainly enhanced the political salience of the *ethnikon* outside Achaia, but there is no evidence to suggest either that it had real domestic political salience at this time or that its use in the colonial world had an immediate impact on homeland development. Achaia, as we have seen, contained a variety of differently structured local systems with little real archaeological evidence of convergence before the sixth century at the earliest – a general sense of 'Achaianness' may have existed earlier, but the *politicization* of Achaian identity and the creation of a formal federation followed upon the first signs of actively claimed polis status from the fifth century onwards. By contrast, the sixth century was a major phase of expansion in the colonies. The pace of change in Achaia and her colonies was thus very different, and rather than creating a hybrid notion of 'Achaian', the logical conclusion, as suggested, is to see Achaian ethnicity as a phenomenon with distinct strands serving separate needs.

Turning to warfare, studies of early Greek military activity have tended to focus either on armies themselves, in terms of social composition, equipment, tactics and their wider implications for state political development, or (at least more recently) on the notion of warrior status as a means of defining elite masculinity (a subject on which we have touched in discussion of the Karaeria tumulus). Here too, it is not my intention to revisit well-trodden ground, nor to restate the case for a lack of fundamental difference in attitudes to the ceremonial disposal of equipment (at least south of Macedon) and the basic organization and conduct of warfare between poleis and ethne as traditionally conceived.[237] Likewise, I emphasize in passing the various ways in which conflict was an important factor in ethnogenesis (either in the form of 'real' wars within historical memory or as an element of communal myth-history located in the deep past). In Phokis, as we have seen, identity was forged around the collective struggle to end the Thessalian occupation, but the violent loss of the plain around Delphi was also of long-term significance. Wars of conquest, such as those by which Sparta reduced first Lakonia and then Messenia, shaped states, and migration sagas, such as those recounting the arrival of the Thessalians in Thessaly, often deal in dispossession of varying forms. Overall, the centrality of violence highlighted by Carol Dougherty in discussion of early colonial legends has much wider resonances.[238]

All of these topics would fill monographs in their own right. I shall merely comment on two interconnected aspects of human mobility related to warfare which have potential consequences for the way in which groups were perceived by themselves and others. As is clear from the record of ethnics used to describe the ten thousand who fought with Cyrus,[239] external classifications of individuals like Arkadians or Achaians, whose identities balanced *politikon* and *ethnikon*, tended to favour the *ethnikon* as the simplest common denominator, and may thus have been an important channel by which the value of the *ethnikon* became internalized. As background to these considerations, it is important to stress that while the condition of war as a constant for Greek states of all kinds is plain from a number of sources (Plato *Laws* 625e–626e in particular), it is a major (and unsustainable) further step to the idea, derived from modern nation-state politics, that order maintenance was a specialization and a prerogative of the state.[240] Certainly, issues of conflict such as control of territory and boundary maintenance were of wider group significance (or could readily be presented as such).[241] And it might be claimed that in focusing on the mobility of manpower and the forces behind it, I am effectively describing Archaic state politics, since, as Lin Foxhall aptly puts it, 'the poleis of Archaic Greece were little more than a stand off between the members of the elite who ran them'.[242] But this would be true only in part. The causes of conflict and the choice of leaders to undertake the fight (perhaps in the name of the collectivity although with an eye to personal *kudos*, as Frank Frost emphasizes in the case of pre-Kleisthenic Athens)[243] are usually rooted in the power politics of individual communities, and can serve to differentiate them from neighbours. Yet the practicalities of manpower and equipment supply frequently relied on cross-border connections articulated by aristocratic wealth and *xenia*.

The first aspect is precisely this *xenia* which may have articulated much 'friendly assistance' between regions during our period (including major alliances, if we accept Watrous' reading of the frieze of the Siphnian Treasury).[244] There are numerous hints of the role of *xenia* in the admittedly fragmentary and problematic sources for early conflicts involving Thessalians. Thus, for example, Chalkis requested the assistance of Kleomachos of Pharsalos and his cavalry during the Lelantine war (Plutarch *Moralia* 760e–761b), *basileus* Kineas (probably of Gonnoi) aided the Peisistratids against Sparta in 512 (Herodotos 5.63.3), and the Thessalian contingent in the first sacred war was led by the (Aleuad?) Eurylochos (according to a scholiast to Pindar *Pyth*. 10.5; Strabo 9.42.1; Hippokrates *Ep*. 36.17). Herodotos' remark (5.63.3) that Kineas' expedition went κοινῇ γνώμῃ may seem unusual in what is otherwise a straightforward account of assistance to a *xenos*, but the exact meaning of the phrase is unclear. Even if it does imply unusually wide consultation rather than just a popular move, it is an unwarranted further step to reconstruct pan-Thessalian debate (let alone a formal decision-making structure) on this basis. Such networks of alliances had the potential to be long-lived,[245] and the basic notion that a named leader, on his own initiative or answering a request, would assemble followers to assist friends and neighbours, whether or not he did so in the name of the community as a collectivity, seems to describe a number of occasions across the Greek world (as, for example, Frost's analysis of Athens suggests).

The second aspect concerns military service outside the community – what is often termed mercenary service, although this should not be taken to imply personal hire for payment as standard during our period.[246] In later times, Arkadian mercenaries were especially renowned, and formed a prominent part of Cyrus' force.[247] But there is a hint of their role as early as the *Catalogue of Ships* where, as noted in Chapter 2, their military prowess led Agamemnon to supply a wholly unseafaring people with ships as part of his contingent (*Iliad* 2.611–14).[248] And the tradition was maintained: Ephoros (*FrGH* 70 F54) places the origins of instruction in *hoplomachia* in mid-sixth-century Mantineia. The earliest specific mention of Arkadians as mercenaries is Herodotos' account (8.26) of deserters who approached Xerxes after Thermopylae (a battle in which large Arkadian contingents had fought: Herodotos 7.202). Ostensibly their motive was to relieve poverty, although the rhetoric of disapproval is strong here, and emphasis is later placed on how well those Tegeans who fought at Plataea did from the spoils (Herodotos 9.70). Arkadians are mentioned as fighting in earlier foreign conflicts, but there is no direct evidence that they were mercenaries. According to Pausanias (8.39.4–5; 8.41.1), for example, one hundred hand-picked men, sent by Oresthasion to aid the Phigaleians in their attempt to liberate the city from Sparta during the second Messenian war, were killed and buried in the agora of Phigaleia. This carries with it the historiographical difficulties typical of most accounts of this war, and it is perfectly plausible that the Oresthasians were allies of rebels rather than paid mercenaries. More convincing evidence for a specific military interest by those unwilling to dedicate personal equipment is the miniature votive arms and armour found in the greatest quantities at the sanctuary of Apollo at Bassai and in lesser numbers across Arkadia.[249]

As a form of seasonal labour, military service had the twin advantages of removing costly dependants from the household and bringing in booty.[250] In the case of Arkadia, Callmer saw it as a response forced by a fifth-century population increase,[251] but not only does this fail to explain the earlier dedications and hints in the historical record, but there is no reason to doubt that it was a positive choice. As noted earlier, the involvement of some of the richest agricultural areas in Arkadia, and especially the eastern plains, is a powerful argument against military service as a counsel of despair for impoverished mountain dwellers. There is no sound evidence linking Arkadians with any colonial movement, and it may be that this seasonal strategy was in some ways an alternative, and perhaps more attractive solution to similar underlying problems. Pausanias (5.27.1–7) saw at Olympia the lavish dedications offered from his gains by the Mainalian Phormis, who fought in Sicily for Gelon and Hieron, and made similarly wealthy offerings at Delphi too. Not all can have done so well, but the attractions must have been plain.

As these two issues highlight, focusing on the state as the driving force in early warfare – on fighting for the group under the leadership of an aristocrat as a means of reinforcing (or on reformist models reshaping) social cohesion – is only part of the story. The actual forces involved were rarely closed social groups, and the processes by which they were constructed highlight the importance of wider social and economic interconnections. These in turn regularly demanded definition (or at least restatement) of personal identity within this supra-community milieu. As I noted in the opening paragraph of the introduction, patriotism was not a virtue stressed in the public context of elite funerary epigrams, whatever was expressed in the privacy of the symposium.

This has brought us full circle, and in the concluding chapter we will consider some of the implications of the issues discussed, and the question of wider regional levels of social interconnection and integration.

5

BEYOND THE POLIS

Political communities and political identities

> The geography of the present day is but a thin layer that even at this moment is becoming history.
> Darby 1953, 6

Discussion so far has taken us literally and metaphorically beyond the polis world as traditionally conceived. Whatever one thinks a polis actually was in any given situation, it is patently unsustainable to use ancient (especially Aristotelian) analyses which treat it as the *telos* of Greek state formation to set standards against which ethne are defined by default. If, as Mogens Hansen has argued,[1] the polis for Aristotle was the 'atom of political society', it must be capable of forming part of larger structures, and the existence of communities right across the 'ethnos' world which were explicitly termed poleis by their own members or by contemporary outsiders, in some cases (like Arkadia) as early as the Archaic period, raises the question of how they operated in such contexts. As emphasized in the introductory chapter, reconstruction of the early social and political history of Greek ethne thus demands consideration of the ways in which groups closed and opened, and the resulting definition of insiders and outsiders on different levels and in different contexts.

One important question which has emerged on several occasions is the relative chronology of the emergence of poleis and ethne as politically salient entities. Not least thanks to the fragmentary nature of early written sources, interpretations have tended to reflect either preconceptions about the 'primitive' place of ethne in Greek state formation (as the early Archaic unification of Thessaly proposed by Corvisier), or the more concrete evidence of formal political institutions (Hatzopoulos, for example, emphasizes the role of the assembly as *the* unifying institution in both Macedonia and Thessaly).[2] The former favours early dates, whereas the latter, if more solidly grounded, inevitably pushes dates down as it rests on the end products of political processes. Direct evidence for the participation of ethne *qua* ethne in wider Archaic political institutions is both rare and problematic. In the case of the Delphic amphictyony, for example, the later prominence of Thessaly, the tradition of her role in the first sacred war and her geographical proximity to the sanctuary, combine to suggest that Thessalians as a group are likely to have been involved somehow from an early date. But this must remain conjectural since (as noted in Chapter 3) neither the foundation date nor the composition of the early amphictyony are known, and the fact that later records list amphictyonic states by ethnos as a matter of course makes it dangerous to retroject. The decisions taken about who were interested parties and on what basis they were to be admitted (as a place community, ethnos or other group) would indeed have been important benchmarks in assessing the political geography of central Greece and the Peloponnese, but we have no means of reconstructing them.[3]

A potentially more fruitful area of enquiry concerns the construction and use of names, considering when and how city and regional ethnics came to be deployed to describe the kinds of political identity claimed by individuals or groups. We have already stressed the difference between the simple, descriptive use of ethnic plurals (which may imply a general sense of ethnic consciousness but are not reliable political indicators), and regional ethnics as self-consciously politicized statements of identity. While clear in theory, certain instances are complicated to classify, perhaps due to the nature of the sources concerned or the way in which they embody different kinds of outsider or insider perceptions. This is well illustrated by the presentation of the Thessalian contingents in the *Catalogue of Ships* as discussed in Chapter 2, where the manner of description hints at a variety of territorial and social relationships which do not correspond closely to the equally varied settlement systems archaeologically visible across the region. The combination of the *Catalogue* and the archaeological record may well imply the existence of differently organized complexes of (probably tiered) relationships in different parts of Thessaly, but the literary genre and narrative purpose of the *Catalogue* make it hard to discriminate between politically salient identity and (probably external) classificatory judgement.

In Chapter 2, late Archaic and early Classical coin issues and legal inscriptions were considered as evidence for the political register in which certain kinds of problem and solution were perceived to lie. By this stage, it is clear that certain political decisions (as, for example, that behind the Arkadikon coin issue) addressed issues on a wider level than that of the individual city. This is not in itself reliable evidence for the existence of formal supra-communal decision-making structures, but it highlights the existence of the kind of needs and perceptions which contributed to their creation. In addressing the related question of the registers in which individuals perceived their own political identities (or were described by others), the epigraphical record (a contemporary document, created in a context of social action and with directly readable meaning) is the most attractive source of evidence. However, our regions are fairly typical in having as yet produced rather small collections of often fragmentary inscriptions which tend to raise more questions than they answer. A case in point is the list of names cut by different hands during the second half of the sixth century on the blocks of an Archaic treasury at Delphi (an 'international' site which would seem an obvious forum for the advertisement of social and political identities). The interpretation of these names as donors or masons, local or foreign, is a matter of conjecture, and in many cases the full form of the name is lost.[4]

Overall, it is worth emphasizing that while inscriptions offer important clues to the circumstances under which different kinds of affiliation were expressed, there is insufficient evidence to support general conclusions, let alone to trace chronological development in the deployment of polis and regional-ethnic identity. It is not surprising to find both in use by the sixth century and the effective start of any meaningful epigraphical record in most of our regions (Achaia excepted), since this was relatively late in the process of political convergence and consolidation. By this stage, it is possible to trace the emergence of some degree of shared regional consciousness in, for example the cult systems of Arkadia or Phokis, or the formation of Elean boundaries, even though in most cases the process of territorial acquisition and definition was to continue for many years. Even in Achaia, where the lack of direct evidence for polis status before the fifth century[5] may at least in part reflect a shortage of inscriptions combined with a lack of interest on the part of early Classical historians, the kind of archaeological problems discussed in Chapters 2 and 4 highlight the much longer, parallel processes of local and regional consolidation evident from the material record.

The epigraphical records of our regions (as of the mainland in general) clearly shows that in the majority of instances where writing was used primarily for communication between local community members (funerary inscriptions, for example, or dedications at local sanctuaries), the simple personal name plus perhaps the patronymic was sufficient. This is evident in sixth-century funerary inscriptions from Thessaly and Phokis (for example, at the Phokikon and Abai), and in the case of dedications, one might cite offerings from Halai in Lokris.[6] Indeed, it is interesting to note the lack of evidence in our regions for the consolidation of family names into place identities (as in the case of the Eupuridai and Kuantidai in Athens, see p. 6). Exceptions involving the use of regional ethnics are most commonly associated with votives at prominent foreign sanctuaries, where the origins of the dedicator may have been expressed in the simplest terms for foreign consumption, and in the case of Achaia, using an ethnic with powerful epic connotations. The dedications of Echembrotos and Oibotas mentioned in the previous chapter (pp. 196–7) are such cases, and it is worth stressing our dependence on Pausanias in particular for the text and date of many of these inscriptions. Rarely, the regional ethnic appears on memorials to the achievements, in life or death, of those resident abroad. Echembrotos' dedication may in fact reflect both circumstances, since as Thomas Heine Nielsen has noted, the fact that the dedication, which celebrates a Pythian victory, was made in Thebes may imply that he was resident there.[7]

Ethnics may also be expressed in personal names derived from the ties of *xenia*. Peisistratos' choice of the name Thessalos for his son (Thucydides 1.20.2, 6.55.1) reflects a focus on the regional level of identity (via the eponymous hero) presumably shared by those with whom he had close ties, and it is tempting to suggest that the same could be true of Ptoiodoros of Corinth, whose son Thessalos won the Olympic diaulos in 504 (Pindar *Ol.* 13.35). Such names could also relate to the city or geographical area of one's *xenos* (as Kimon's son, Lakedaimonios: Thucydides 1.45.2), or his personal name.[8] In general, formal interstate connections during the Archaic period were most often expressed via conspicuous display reflecting shared elite values. The treasuries at Delphi are a good illustration, and if Watrous' reading of the political implications of the frieze of the Siphnian Treasury is correct, enmity too could be depicted in terms of the interstate family-based alliances that characterized *xenia*.[9] Perceived in this light, it is interesting to find regional ethnics included in the range of name forms from which a *xenos* might select, and the whole subject of *xenos* names deserves greater attention than it has hitherto received.

With the exception of colonial situations (as, for example, the mention of an individual named 'Arkadian' in an inscription from Selinus which may date back to the sixth century),[10] the use of regional ethnics or names derived from them in Archaic inscriptions rarely goes beyond the few, usually external, situations so far described. This may seem surprising given the mobility of, for example, traders or craftsmen, and to some extent it may be that the rarity of such named individuals in the early literary or epigraphical record is a product of the nature and purpose of that record.

That the principal exceptions are stoneworkers is perhaps predictable, given the prestige of the resource, the link between craftsman and stone type, the specific locations from which marbles in particular were extracted, and the nature of the works created. Of the repertoire of Archaic signatures, a significant proportion reflects the movement of craftsmen from the most prestigious stone producing areas (the signature of Euthykartides of Naxos at Delos during the second half of the sixth century is a case in point).[11] As a result, ethne are largely excluded: Doliana marble is the only prestigious resource in our regions, and its early use was largely confined to Arkadia. Other signatures may demonstrate the origins of a craftsman who produced a dedication to be made at a foreign sanctuary by his own community (as perhaps the '-medes' who signed the controversial 'Kleobis and Biton' group at Delphi as 'Argeios').[12] Many simply advertise the work of an individual abroad (as, for example, Archermos, son of Mikkiades of Chios, who signed works at Delos and on the Athenian acropolis during the second half of the sixth century) – common practice from Classical times onwards.[13] Even so, extant or reported signatures (let alone well-preserved ones) are hardly common, and many craftsmen working abroad did not advertise their origins in any lasting manner: such is the case in the relatively well-documented sixth-century ateliers of Endoios, Philergos and Aristokles in Athens.[14] Here too, whatever statements of political identity were needed must have been made orally.

A more revealing source for our purposes is vase inscriptions. The existence of individuals with foreign ethnic names (like Mys or Lydos) among Archaic and Classical vase painters working in Athens is well known, and is usually taken to reflect their migrant (and probably slave) origins. Indeed, one Lydos (probably not the well-known painter) signed explicitly as a '*doulos*'.[15] Names in the Athenian record point to strong connections with the East Greek world, Sicily and Magna Graecia. Archaic Corinth, however, has produced evidence not only for these regions (with names including Phryx and Taras), but also for neighbouring regions on the Greek mainland. A pinax dedicated at Penteskouphia lists one 'Lokris' (presumably the potter and perhaps the dedicator) as well as a partially preserved compound name ending in '- phoke' which probably alludes to Phokis. The fact that the Corinthian record also includes some very local names, including an 'Argeos' (an immediate neighbour) and even one 'Qorinthios' on his home territory, suggests that it was common practice among a mixed group of craftsmen to name by origin, and in this context, it is interesting to find a Lokrian and a Phokian using their regional ethnic.[16] Unfortunately, the comparative internal record for Phokis and Lokris is small during this period, so the fact that there is as yet no evidence of such names means little. From the fourth and third centuries onwards, when the record of almost all regions is substantial, names derived from both city and regional ethnics were common throughout, but clearly it would be dangerous to retroject and the question must remain open.[17] Whatever the case, the Corinthian evidence is surely the tip of the iceberg, and much explanation of origins, whether expressed as nicknames or added ethnics, must have been oral. Indeed, in many graffiti and dipinti, including those from Kommos discussed in the introduction (pp. 3–4), attribution of foreigners to region rests on the script used and not on the nature of their names.

In one important way, the observation that regional ethnics were used in early inscriptions for specific explanatory purposes, aimed primarily at outsiders (or at least a mixed audience), may inform approaches to the material record. In the introductory chapter, I stressed the oral context within which early inscriptions in particular must be understood, with written information as a particular, rather than a general, form of communication. The content of oral claims of personal or group political status is of course impossible to recover, and their very existence is a matter of conjecture. Nonetheless, the archaeological record can highlight the kind of circumstances under which such oral explanations might have been advantageous, or where individuals might have found themselves characterized by the various 'others' with whom they came into contact. In other words, we can demonstrate the existence of a potential problem, even if we cannot tell how it was solved.

From an archaeological perspective, this has the advantage of moving beyond the purely classificatory focus of much past work, and especially the concentration on ethnic indicia which has rightly been rejected in recent scholarship.[18] It also allows us to develop the predictive potential of the material record. If, as Siân Jones puts it, the construction of ethnicity is a product of the intersection of the *habitus* (in Bourdieu's term) and specific social conditions,[19] we can focus on such intersections as circumstances liable to give rise to ethnic expression, and consider whatever literary, historical and material evidence is available for the resulting response in each particular case. This is a long-term agenda for the periods and regions we have considered, especially since, as this book has highlighted, our understanding of the *habitus* in many parts of the Greek mainland remains limited. But given this potential, it would be unfortunate if a hardly radical critique of outmoded concepts of archaeological culture and ethnicity were to lead to pessimism about, or downright rejection of, the contribution of the material record. Jonathan Hall's claim that archaeological evidence cannot *identify* ethnic groups in the past is obviously true to the extent that it cannot actually name them.[20] Yet as discussion of the Achaian *mesogeia* and northern Arkadia has shown, it can certainly identify situations where group identity was asserted and offer a wholly different range of insights into the practical nature of that assertion — and the visual rhetoric used in, for example, the coinage issued by ethne and poleis alike should not be underestimated. Equally, Hall's conclusion that working from archaeological evidence alone offers little prospect of success in finding ethnic groups,[21] quite apart from problematizing the study of group identity in prehistory, begs the question of the nature and register of different kinds of ethnic claim, as Greek ethnicities themselves came to be tiered identities articulated through different channels of communication. Setting aside the complications which can result when our main or only literary source for an ethnic group is an outsider summary (as, for example, Thucydides 6.1–5 on Sicily),[22] more or less contemporary 'insider' and 'outsider' literary, epigraphical and material sources can contribute differently to the communication of various forms of ethnic claim (bearing in mind the lost aspect of oral context). I fully agree with Hall that ethnicity at the level of the great 'tribal' identities (such as Dorian, Ioniana or Achaian) was *primarily* a myth-historical construct. But the more localized ethnicities considered in this book are a somewhat different matter since, as I have argued, they developed around, and helped to articulate, shared concerns, needs, and practical interactions on a different level from that of the individual big site, and at various points gained (and lost) political salience, sometimes to the extent of later becoming formal levels of government. So while it is hard to see how one could now formulate an intellectually credible research strategy to find Dorians in the archaeological record of the Peloponnese, the same cannot be said of, for example, the Azanes of northern Arkadia. In short, debate about what can or cannot be achieved on the basis of material as opposed to written sources seems not only one-dimensional (and irrelevant at least for the Archaic period, when we are rarely completely without either), but also to miss the point. We should rather assess the nature of each claim and the modes of communication used to convey it, and then trace the contribution of each kind of source individually and in combination (to allow for the different preservational and historiographical factors involved), accepting the potential for dissonance between them.

Through the previous chapters we have sought to identify and explore the registers in which different forms of activity were conducted – the kinds of groups to which individuals might belong, their organization and the activities associated with them, how they overlapped or interacted, and how they might have served to articulate aspects of an individual's social persona. While it was not a primary aim to trace back particular phenomena like the role of city life, the problem of time depth (i.e. the extent to which we can retroject meanings and associations evident in the later Archaic record) has been a recurrent issue. It is certainly true that some kinds of association – big settlements, for example, or cult communities in some regions – are more readily traceable in the material record than others, and are present from a very early date. However, the danger of emphasizing what is most visible has been stressed on a number of occasions. While, for example, the evidence presented in Chapter 2 reinforces the fact that place identities centred on specific sites are likely to have been an important factor from early in the Early Iron Age in most of our regions, thus refuting the idea that poleis were late developments within 'primordial' ethne, we cannot conclude that the polis was *the* fundamental form of organization. Indeed, in using the term 'polis' here, I simply reflect the fact that at least by Archaic times, Greeks themselves used it for a place community with a settlement centre, with no specific implications for the mode of political organization. Given both the existence of the word in Linear B and the fact that we have no means of tracing the origin of the association between polis status in the political sense and a central settlement, as identified by the Copenhagen Polis Centre, it seems largely immaterial to debate whether it should be used during the Early Iron Age. The key point is to avoid retrojecting our expectations of later poleis on to early big sites, and here I share the concerns voiced by Lin Foxhall about the risks of hindsight in assuming that the roots of democracy lay in the eighth century, and reading from that a general view of early poleis.[23] Hence, in part, my attempts to establish what the archaeological record can tell us about the activities which occurred within big sites, to what extent they overlapped with associations focused on cult or different forms of subsistence activity, for example, and what problems and pressures were likely to have been specific to big sites.

One outstanding issue, which continues the discussion in Chapter 4 in moving beyond the internal concerns of individual ethne, is the impact of communication routes, especially those surrounding major waterways like the Corinthian gulf, in focusing interaction between regions across the old polis–ethnos divide. In tracing how ethnic identities came to be formulated and adopted, the role of insider and outsider perceptions is often emphasized. Just as identities are formulated by contrast with others, so outsider classifications can be internalized as part of this process. But who were these outsiders in the cases with which we are concerned?[24] What I have previously described as a 'median level of alteriority' focuses upon the role of relations with the various other groups with whom individuals came into more or less regular contact depending on the activity involved, and with whom they might have much in common. It is this level of relationship which we will now explore in considering connections between the communities surrounding the Corinthian gulf (here used as a shorthand designation for the gulfs of Corinth and Patras, comprising the areas from the Isthmus to the Ionian islands).

Regional interconnections: the case of the Corinthian gulf

In the previous chapter, we considered the impact upon the expression of ethnic identity of moving beyond community boundaries, focusing upon occasions when the need to find a common denominator or when a comparatively high degree of social distance might have promoted the use of simplified descriptions, and thus perhaps a preference for the regional over the city ethnic. This is not to imply that the distinction between 'home' and 'abroad' is a simple dichotomy, or that it embodies the totality of interaction between internal and external perceptions.[25] There were clearly degrees of familiarity with 'others' resting on the frequency, nature and physical location of contact, and these sometimes produced dense interconnections between communities structured with varying degrees of complexity (simple poleis, dependent poleis, poleis within ethne which might themselves be dependent, for instance).

How these communities thought about each other and in what context raises interesting questions about the importance of such interactions for the manner in which identity was regularly expressed. When, for example, was it important or relevant to describe someone as from Aigion or Delphi, as opposed to being Achaian or Phokian (perhaps in the straightforward geographical sense of living on a particular stretch of coast)? Some such descriptions could flow from everyday interactions and come to be internalized by those so described, but there may also have been a more formal concern to establish points of convergence or difference on a group level. The effects, in terms of the level at which political salience was most enhanced, might also vary from strengthening the identity of particular sub-regions or individual poleis to promoting a sense of wider regional identity. This is easy to conceptualize but almost impossible to document in detail: while archaeology reveals something of the pattern and date of interconnections, any explicit identity statements have either been lost from the written record or were confined to oral communication. Nonetheless, the potential importance of this kind of network should not be underestimated, especially as it may also have had a significant impact on more practical matters like the spread of the navigational and 'ethnographical' knowledge necessary for colonization and trade, and on the circulation of staples and prestige goods. This is especially true for regions like northern Phokis and East Lokris, which were linked more or less directly with both the Corinthian gulf and the straits of Euboia (hence, for example, the eastern metalwork in eighth-century graves at Tragana and Anavra in East Lokris, which probably arrived via Euboia).[26]

The Corinthian gulf as an entity has received little attention from ancient geographers or, until relatively recently,[27] modern scholars, although Classical historians in particular offer numerous clues to its strategic importance both as a channel of communication and, from the Peloponnesian war onwards, as a (literal and metaphorical) battle ground between the conflicting interests which surrounded it.[28] Hence, for example, Thucydides' account (5.52.2) of Alcibiades' attempt to persuade the citizens of Patras to extend their long walls to the sea, a system to be augmented by his own construction of a fort at Rhion (which was forcibly opposed by Corinth, Sikyon 'and all those to whom the fortification of Rhion would have been a menace'). Both Strabo and Pausanias preferred to focus on Greek states, poleis and/or ethne, as entities, but Pausanias' choice of land routes for his travels had more far-reaching consequences in that most eighteenth- and nineteenth-century antiquarians followed in his footsteps.[29] The exception was Ludwig Salvator, whose decision to sail from west to east in 1874 was taken on the express grounds of the importance of the seaway in antiquity: his descriptions of landscape and navigation, and his maritime perspective on ancient settlement, remain valuable.[30]

Similar concerns with states as entities, plus the privileging of poleis (as unitary city-states) over ethne, have also coloured approaches to the area in modern scholarship. Attention has long focused on Corinth, as a territorial unity with ports on both the Saronic and Corinthian gulfs (and from the sixth century, a transhipment facility in the Diolkos), and as an early colonial power, with extensive trading interests in Italy from the first half of the eighth century inferred largely from the spread of fine pottery.[31] What appears on present evidence to be a significant, if not the greatest, proportion of Corinthian Middle Geometric II exports was directed far to the west. In

Epirus, Corinthian imports at Arta and Vitsa are well known,[32] and particularly striking are the oinochoai and cups in the drinking sets used by the Messapian elite of Otranto in the Salento (noting the presence here of a very few sherds dating as early as Late Protogeometric or Early Geometric).[33] While it is possible that these finewares could have been obtained indirectly from a more local source (perhaps Ithaka),[34] the presence at Otranto of the rare Corinthian amphorae discussed in Chapter 3 (p. 122) may rather suggest direct trade in wine and the equipment for its consumption.[35] Corinthian Middle Geometric II imports are also found at Veii and the area of the bay of Naples (at Pontecagnano), but they are very rare, and since (at least in the latter case) they were accompanied by Ithakan pottery,[36] they may have arrived indirectly. As Bruno d'Agostino and Andreas Soteriou have demonstrated,[37] the real increase in the volume and distribution of Corinthian imports in the Ionian islands (Ithaka and Kephallenia) and the area of the bay of Naples took place through the second half of the eighth century, when they were accompanied by (and sometimes hard to distinguish from) other Peloponnesian and Ithakan local products. The participants in, and interests represented by, the activities which produced these distributions are not, therefore, easy to disentangle.

Within the more immediate gulf area, with the notable exception of exports to Medeon from the Late Protogeometric onwards,[38] evidence for Corinthian engagement also begins in the eighth century, and until well into the seventh appears to have been highly selective.[39] The majority of finds come from Delphi, Aegira, Aigion and Ano Mazaraki. On present evidence, imports to Delphi are slightly earlier than those in Achaia, but this may reflect poor preservation and/or lack of excavation of the Achaian coastal cities. We cannot yet establish how widespread imports were in Achaia and whether their circulation reflects separate contacts or entry into local networks, although the latter may be more likely given the manufacture of local copies which can be hard to distinguish.[40]

Turning to Corinth itself, while there otherwise seems to have been strikingly little interest in importing finished goods (or at least those likely to be archaeologically visible),[41] the most obvious product of engagement with the wider gulf milieu is the sanctuary at Perachora. Attention has tended to focus on the balance of eastern and western imports in the eighth- and seventh-century votive record,[42] but it is also worth emphasizing the location of the shrine and the nature of the rites celebrated. (Figure 5.1) While the harbour may be small and not easy of access,[43] the headland is a strategically useful shelter for ships to ride at anchor, as well as a prominent landmark for navigation. It is also, in Horden and Purcell's words, in an 'interface' zone, on the end of land and open to the sea, as well as lying poised between the Corinthia (of which it formed part) and the territory of Boiotia and Phokis to the north.[44] These traits may have been reflected in the decision to site here certain cult activities, as identified by Menadier,

Figure 5.1 Perachora (photo: author).

notably the oracle which must have been operational at least by the sixth century if the hypothesis that it was housed within the Archaic temple by the harbour is correct. Menadier also locates female, and perhaps male, rites of passage at the Heraion, tied to the myth of the death and burial of Medea's children, and as noted in Chapter 3, the sanctuary, along with that of Demeter and Kore, is a rare recipient of the so-called *Frauenfest* iconography.[45]

Overall, therefore, early Corinthian activity in the gulf area appears to have been targeted, and to reflect specific interests. It certainly complemented, and may have developed, pre-existing links formed by other communities, some of which also expanded markedly especially during the second half of the century (as will be shown in the case of Achaia), but it is only one part of a wider picture. Studying the gulf area as a system of interconnections demands that the surrounding ethne and their poleis be given full and equal weight, something that, at least in the case of Achaia, has only recently become possible thanks to new excavation and ongoing reappraisal of older finds.[46] What follows is only a brief sketch highlighting key issues – the topic merits a monograph in its own right, but full treatment must await the publication of renewed (and often continuing) archaeological research especially in Aetolia, Elis and western Achaia.[47] It is already clear, however, that the idea of a Geometric western *koine* identified on ceramic grounds[48] is an over simplification of the complex variety of interconnections which took very different shape between LHIIIC, Protogeometric, and the eighth century (especially following the resumption of western links and the first colonial settlements).

In the case of the Corinthian gulf, perhaps more than any other Greek waterway, it would be wrong to focus on settlement interconnections without considering the sea as an active, and at times very treacherous, force in its own right. The gulf is tidal, with a current of up to two knots highly susceptible to the alternating sea and land breezes off the surrounding mountains and valleys. This current is stronger in the narrows than by the coast, and the surface waters are choppy more often than not.[49] These conditions could be put to good use by those who understood them – as for example the Athenian commander Phormio in defeating the Peloponnesian fleet (Thucydides 2.83–4)[50] – but they are liable to change swiftly and require careful observation. Given the shortage of good anchorages, the mountainous nature of much of the north coast, and the uplands and river deltas which punctuate the south, it is doubtful whether coastal routes were commonly used for anything but very local transport. And if most shipping did tend to run with the currents in the narrows, then the rare good landings and accessible harbours (notably Aigion), and the rather more common sheltered locations (usually behind headlands, like Perachora) where ships could ride at anchor during squalls, would have been of long-term importance, irrespective of the social and political factors underlying changes in regional settlement and trade.[51]

From a maritime perspective, coastal zones are potentially distinct areas whether or not they formed part of wider state territory. Indeed, as Jamie Morton has recently emphasized, the names of a significant number of gulf landmarks suggest a maritime perspective: Cape Drepanon in Achaia, for example, reflects its shape as seen from the sea.[52] Delphi is an extreme illustration of the effects of maritime connections both on the development of a coastal zone and on its the integration within the wider region of which it formed part. For most of our period, this relatively large Early Iron Age town with its surrounding plain was (with Medeon) a major focus of southern Phokian settlement. It lay at the end of land routes running west and south from Euboia and southern Thessaly (indeed Lemos included it within the Euboian *koine* of the eleventh to the ninth centuries),[53] and had links across the gulf to Corinth and Achaia (as discussed in Chapter 3).[54] While Medeon initially enjoyed closer links with Corinth, by the mid-eighth century at the latest, the range of pottery imported to Delphi was closer to that of Corinth itself than the more limited selection shipped west (human figure decoration included).[55] There is no strong reason to doubt that Delphi would have shared in such wider sense of Phokian identity as was current before the sixth century (whatever its strength, let alone political salience). But from the eighth century onwards, the Apollo sanctuary become a factor, beginning the process of intervention which culminated, from the 580s onwards, in the polis of Delphi being formally created as a closely defined geographical entity, at least notionally politically independent but formally circumscribed by the outside interests focused on the shrine. Maritime access, for people, goods and building materials, was a critical factor in sustaining both a panhellenic sanctuary and the polis of Delphi as an entity, and was thus one contributor (along with the loss of crucial plain land and the demands of the growing sacral economy) to the economic skew exerted by the coastal zone on the development of the remainder of Phokis. As highlighted in Chapter 3, the long-term effects on the interior also reflect this shift from the coast as an outlet and point of communication to the coast as a voracious, almost parasitic, consumer.

Finally, it is important to emphasize that in terms of human geography, the Corinthian gulf ends not at the west coasts of Achaia and Aetolia, but at Ithaka and Kephallenia. These islands served as nodes of interaction linking the Peloponnese and Aetolo-Akarnania, the Tyrrhenian zone, the Salento and, with Achaian colonization, the Ionian coast too. Ithaka was not merely a strategically placed landfall with good harbours at Piso Aetos and Polis bay (Figure 5.2),[56] although the reference to a '*xenos* and faithful companion', as restored in a long inscription on a conical oinochoe from Aetos, more than hints at the hospitality of the community.[57] It was an independent maritime force in its own right, since, as has been a constant since antiquity, the comparative shortage of farmland leaves a sector of the population to be supported by other means (chiefly trade and the supply of labour overseas).

Figure 5.2 Polis bay (photo: author).

As both archaeological remains from settlements and shrines like those at Aetos, Polis bay and Polis Cave,[58] and the modern historical record show, the result could be considerable material wealth as well as complex long-distance connections. When Henry Holland visited Ithaka in 1812–13, he reported that the island had 7,000–8,000 inhabitants yet could only produce grain for around a quarter of the year's consumption, with the balance coming from the carrying trade in, for example, currants and Ithakan oil and wine, across the Mediterranean and the Black Sea. Such was the dependence on shipping that seven years previously, William Gell reported a huge demand for sailors and ship hands, with high pay and other rewards attracting workers to Ithaka from Italy following the collapse of the Kingdom of Naples, but a decline in arable and pasture, and low land values.[59]

Ithaka's external connections during our period are closely reflected in the pottery and small finds from the sanctuary and settlement at Aetos in particular, as well as Ithakan exports as they are now coming to be recognised. Perhaps the weakest of these external connections runs north along the chain of islands to Corfu. In precolonial times, as noted above, a very little Ithakan pottery can be recognized within a much larger body of Corinthian at Otranto, but otherwise there is a clear material distinction between north and south and relatively little sign of interchange.[60] Direct Ithakan connections with Italy are oriented towards the bay of Naples, where imports at Pithekoussai, for example, include a figured kantharos of the third quarter of the eighth century in San Montano tomb 949 (by the same hand as that of the so-called 'house model' Aetos 600), as well as the common monochrome kantharoi. At Aetos, imports like lyre player seals, which are particularly common at Pithekoussai, and the eclectic range of Italian, Phoenician and Cypriot-influenced imagery used by local vase-painters, further attest to the connection.[61] This combination of evidence (and especially the chariot scenes on the San Montano kantharos, which suggest an Italian patron given Homer's characterization of the Ithakan landscape as not fit for driving horses; *Odyssey* 4.607–8; 13.242), lends support to the suggestion that Ithakans themselves were actively engaged in this trade.[62]

Ithakan exports also moved east, thus entering, as we will see, Corinthian and Achaian networks of interaction. Imports at Perachora and Vitsa include vessels bearing the distinctive potters' marks of the Kandyliotis Group from Aetos,[63] and in the case of Vitsa, these links form part of a group of west Peloponnesian ceramic imports and stylistic influences which, together with many Corinthian imports, highlight the importance of trade routes north from the gulf (especially the land route via Arta).[64] On a lesser scale, Ithakan imports and influences have been identified among the Volimedia group in Messenia, indicating what may prove to be a wider pattern of links with the far west of the Peloponnese,[65] and at Aetos itself, ceramic imports include Achaian[66] and probably Elean vessels,[67] as well as the generic styles of the western Peloponnese.[68]

Ithakan evidence is patently important, and renewed research on Kephallenia is further enriching the picture.[69] But clearly, Ithakan activities should be set within the wider context of differing patterns of interaction around the gulf. Further east, changes in our understanding of Achaian activity suggest a different, if intersecting, range of contacts which varied in strength and direction over time. Indeed, it is worth stressing that gulf interconnections offered a series of options. In the case of Achaia, there is a marked contrast between the LHIIIC emphasis on the west of the region, more limited Protogeometric settlement focused along the north coast, and the eighth-century interconnections between the coast and the *mesogeia* which enhanced the role of the relatively few good routes to the coast.

During LHIIIC, western Achaia in particular had a number of extensive and wealthy chamber tomb cemeteries, including those at Klauss, Krini, Kallithea, Lousika, Kanghadi and Portes. Such cemeteries are also found on the north coast (for example that at Nikoleika near Aigion), but on present evidence, the largest and richest were focused in the west, especially around the entrance to the gulf of Patras. Funerary offerings indicate that LHIIIC was a period of considerable wealth, and the continuity of cemetery locations and grave types implies an established population, with no clear evidence of any post-palatial influx. To this phase, for example, belong a series of rich weapons burials by which elite male status was clearly demarcated.[70] Achaian-style pottery (if not actual Achaian products), notably stirrup jars and amphorae, is found widely. Examples occur further east, for example in the Argolid, in the Corinthia at Korakou, at Delphi, Medeon and Elateia, and on the Aetolian coast to the north. Most, however, went west, to Ithaka and Kephallenia, and possibly to the Adriatic (Piskovë, Barç and Sovjan),[71] and were a strikingly strong influence on the locally produced LHIIIC at Punta Meliso (Santa Maria di Leuca) on the southern tip of the Salento.[72] The case for a Late Mycenaean *koine* linking the west Peloponnese and the Ionian islands has long been made,[73] but as we can now identify more precisely what is Achaian, it is possible, as Penelope Mountjoy has emphasized, to highlight the role of western Achaia as a bridge to the Adriatic.[74] These connections are quite different from those surrounding later colonization, and as yet no Achaian or Achaian-style vessels have been found in the relevant part of the Ionian coast.[75]

Achaian links with Italy were lost during the Protogeometric period, and connections with the Ionian islands were slight until the early eighth century, just predating Corinthian imports at Aetos. Settlement was focused further east, in the north coastal zone, and throughout this period there were particularly close links with the Aetolian coast, articulated around the narrowest point of the gulf (the modern Rhion–Antirrion crossing).[76] (Figure 5.3) The major north coast settlements were located on plateaux of varying height, with access to cultivable plain or uplands (Figure 1.12) as well as to the sea. And while communication between these sites is possible

Figure 5.3 Rhion–Andirrion crossing: from the north (photo: author).

by land, passage was impeded (especially in winter) by often substantial rivers. Under these circumstances, local communication by boat along the coast may well have been a more attractive option. From the second half of the eighth century onwards, at all centres where significant archaeological research has been undertaken, there is evidence of expansion and a wider range of contacts represented primarily in pottery assemblages (noting especially Corinthian, and to a lesser extent Lakonian and Argive, imports), but also small items like the scarabs and Boiotian fibulae in graves at Aigion.[77] Indeed, reflecting the importance of her harbour, Aigion and her shrine at Ano Mazaraki have produced a particularly rich record of relatively local and more exotic imports. In addition to the connections noted in Chapter 4 (p. 183), metal votives at Ano Mazaraki include, for example, imports from north-western Greece and a quantity of Cypriote type-two arrowheads (perhaps shipped via Crete where they were particularly popular).[78] A similar picture of contacts around and along the gulf is presented by the early Achaian alphabet which, as Jeffery highlights, is a fusion of traits from surrounding areas, including Corinth, Sikyon, Phokis and Elis. Its distribution, reaching the southern Ionian islands (Aetos) by *c.*700 and present in the Achaian colonies, reinforces both Achaian colonization and the importance of sea routes via Ithaka and Kephallenia.[79] In the colonies too, in addition to the alphabet, material influences from the homeland included the kantharos forms popular in Achaia as most of the western Peloponnese, which were produced locally (and perhaps imported) at Sibaris (including Francavilla Marittima) from the very end of the eighth century or the beginning of the seventh.[80]

As this brief review highlights, the Corinthian gulf played a crucial role in linking coastal zones and, as the end point of a number of major land routes, also inland areas, into wider markets and networks of communication. It thus had a major impact on the development of surrounding regions, and was an important factor in creating and sustaining various forms of contact between very differently organized communities. The gulf could work as one large-scale system, but (especially if one takes into account the Ionian islands) it could also be subdivided in different ways over time and according to regional interests, and it is worth stressing that the long term shifts evident between LHIIIC and the end of the eighth century owe much to the interests of Achaia and Corinth.

Envoi

In the introductory chapter, I emphasized that tracing the political development of mainland Greek ethne requires a more nuanced understanding of how and when social boundaries at different levels came to be drawn, who and what crossed them, how and to what effect, and the circumstances under which various levels of (especially ethnic) cohesion became salient. The long-term aim must be to document the palimpsest of individual and group identities expressed in a variety of ways, including the acquisition and disposition of material goods, the creation of visual and oral group images (including collective myth-history) and the deployment of names, and to assess their relative weighting in different places, periods and contexts and from different perspectives. This may seem reminiscent of Marcus Bank's critique of scholarship on ethnicity as 'a collection of rather simplistic and obvious statements about boundaries, otherness, goals and achievements, being and identity, descent and classification, that has been construed as much by the anthropologist as by the subject'.[81] On the latter count at least I plead not guilty, as it is the Greeks' own descriptions of, and modes of thought about, their societies that give us the tiered end products to which they accorded greater or lesser salience according to time, place and context. Patently there is a process here which needs to be traced and described, even if it sometimes requires modern terminology to do so. On the former count, I accept that, in a more positive spirit of archaeological revisionism than Banks implies, the balance of discussion frequently tips towards the *habitus* aspect of Jones' formulation.[82] But this simply reflects the need to re-evaluate past, and often rather simplistic, interpretations of the regions discussed in the light of large bodies of new or neglected material. Without a more sophisticated grasp of the *habitus* we cannot hope to understand the kinds of power flow that promoted and sustained strategies of ethnicity

This amounts to a huge and far-reaching agenda, and a book like this can only be a first small step. I make no apology for not offering a coherent alternative history of central Greece and the Peloponnese at this stage, but I have endeavoured to show how this could eventually be achieved as ideas are further developed and the material record expands. Certain areas of discussion have been heavily stressed – economics, for example, emphasizing the way in which social power derives from a range of activities, including sacrifice, dedication and public building, which have major implications for the control and supply of key resources. Others have been omitted or merely touched upon for a variety of reasons. In part, the complex interconnections and multiple viewpoints inherent in the construction of identity lead in endless directions, and every modern commentator will approach the problem differently. Chiefly, however, we lack data with which to approach certain issues, sites or areas, either through limitations of research or because important and often ongoing projects await final publication. A word of caution should perhaps be added here concerning the number of preliminary reports cited, as these serve to highlight not just the volume of material under study and awaiting publication, but the fact that our understanding of many regions is changing very quickly. To those who criticize the empirical approach sometimes adopted, I would reiterate the need not merely to trace the implications of a particular approach to the archaeological record, but also to draw new or understudied data into syntheses such as this, and to evaluate their position within the archaeological history of a region (in terms both of deposition and retrieval).

One topic which has not been explicitly treated, although it has implications for several of the questions raised, is attitudes to imports (orientalia in particular, both objects themselves and travelling craftsmen). Comparison between East Lokris and Euboia might be revealing, for example, as would investigation of perceptions of luxury in Archaic Thessaly. A further area which merits more detailed examination is that of gender. Relatively little work has been done to trace female activities or evaluate expressions of femininity in the archaeological (as opposed to art historical) record during the Early Iron Age and Archaic period, largely for want of evidence with which to tackle issues like the engendering of labour and domestic and social space (although a longer-term perspective would enhance work on the Classical and Hellenistic periods too).[83] Attention has recently been drawn to constructs of masculinity, not least due to renewed interest in material and textual evidence for warfare (as touched upon in Chapters 2 and 4), and, as Hans van Wees has argued, changing relationships between male and female in key areas of ritual behaviour too.[84] In the case of warfare, there is clear potential for very different insider and outsider perspectives on, for example, the socio-political significance of the bearing of arms (as was clear from the discussion of Thucydides 1.5.2–6.2 in the introductory chapter). When is this primitive barbarism, when legitimate self-defence in the absence of government, and when just men being (high status) men?[85]

This also raises the more general question of long-term transformations in the expression of status, especially spanning periods of major socio-political chance. The Late Bronze Age/Early Iron Age transition is such a case – in some areas this is a period of transition to a post-palatial order, allowing for the LHIIIC *floruit* of what Klaus Kilian termed late Mycenaean city life,[86] yet in large parts of central Greece in particular, it was a stable period of considerable wealth which simply does not fit our current periodization. In western Achaia, for example, where the material record changes dramatically between LHIIIC and PG, there is a strong link during LHIIIC between burial with arms and elite male status, and as Eder argues, the selectivity of these burials implies a distinctive social persona over and above the military prowess of the particular individual concerned.[87] What happened to this connection? Why were only some forms of Submycenaean and Early Protogeometric ritualized expression constructed in some areas using recognizable elements from their Late Mycenaean precursors (as, for example, the early cult deposits at Olympia in comparison with evidence from Pylos)?[88] In discussing Late Bronze Age Pylos,[89] John Bennet has recently emphasized the scope for rethinking 'Mycenaean' material culture in terms of the way in which palatial elites constituted themselves in relation to their peers and to the internal structure of their kingdoms (in the case of Pylos, a territorially expanding entity and one which, to judge from the link between toponyms and personal names in the Linear B record, may have been ethnically diverse). There is clearly much to be done alone these lines, and a more nuanced view of the meanings attached to certain aspects of 'Mycenaean' elite culture would aid our understanding of their role in subsequent cultural choices.

Given the geographical focus of this book on the central Greek mainland, there has been an inevitable concentration on certain kinds of political society and on more or less archaeologically visible long-term processes. Most comparanda have reflected this mainland Greek perspective. Yet many of the issues raised have wider relevance. A very different, but equally promising area for analysis would be the Cyclades and neighbouring islands, with their distinctive and often fragile economic and demographic structures, export and import of populations via colonization and internal movement within and between islands, shared institutions (such as the sanctuary of Delian Apollo), and somewhat erratic and unpredictable polis formation.[90] Often regarded as being characterized by transitory occupation and cult activity, the rapidly expanding settlement and sanctuary record rather shows a complex balance between long-term stability and short-term movement. Compare, for example, long-lived sanctuaries such as that at Hypsile on Andros (from the second half of the eighth to the fourth century)[91] with the many rich but transitory shrines inside and outside settlements, including eighth-century Zagora and Archaic Aprovatou on Andros.[92] How were the social structures which we infer from the layout of many short-lived sites sustained or transformed beyond the life of those sites? To what extent did the polis-focused political identities which dominate the record from Archaic times onwards reflect the range of affiliations experienced by those who subscribed to them?

Such a plethora of questions and viewpoints, both ancient and modern, might raise doubts about whether we can do more than highlight ways of looking at the entities and processes involved in the study of early Greek ethne and, in general terms, delineate the shapes of the regional organizations that emerged. This may be so, but even recognition of the sheer complexity of early ethne, and the intimate connection between polis and ethnos development, are major steps forward, and the continuing pace of archaeological study and discovery will surely guarantee that debate and discussion continue for many years to come.

NOTES

1 Introduction

1 Herman 1987, 156–61; Robertson 1997.
2 Phokis: Head 1911, 338; Williams 1972, 5–12; McInerney 1999, 178–9. Achaia: Head 1911, 412; Kroll 1996, 52 note 14 (with previous bibliography) redefends the attribution to Aigai rather than Aigion. City coinage is no more a *sine qua non* of polis status (Martin 1995) than the existence of wider regional coin issues (as the Arkadikon coinage: Heine Nielsen 1996b) necessarily implies formal leagues. Many poleis did not coin (let alone in the Archaic period) or shared common, federal coinage: Martin 1995. I merely differentiate the political level at which value is guaranteed, in turn raising the question of differing motivation behind the instigation of coinage (further discussed in Ch. 2).
3 See e.g.: Archibald 2000; Morgan 1991 and 2001c; McInerney 1999, 3–35; Bommeljé et al. 1987, 15 (S. Bommeljé).
4 Oropos: Mazarakis Ainian 1996 and 1998. Kyme: Sapouna-Sakellaraki 1998.
5 Praisos: Whitley 1998. Kavousi: Haggis 1996.
6 Isthmia and Olympia: Morgan 1999a (see 379–82 on Olympia; see also Eder 2001a and 2001b; Morgan forthcoming a). Agora: Papadopoulos 1996a.
7 For reviews, see Morgan and Hall 1996; Greco forthcoming; Morgan 1999b, as generally *CPCActs* 6.
8 Lokris: Dakoronia 1990, 1992b and 1993a and b; Onasoglou 1981; cf. Fossey 1990a, 105–12. Kozani (Voion): Karamitrou-Mentesidi 1999, 142–56.
9 S. Morris 1992 remains the fullest evaluation of the impact of eastern connections, a widely debated theme to which she has frequently returned; see also papers in Kopcke and Tokumaru 1992. On western connections, especially the nature of colonialism and the impact of Greek settlers and indigenous communities upon each other, see reviews presented by Antonaccio 2001; Morgan 2001c; Albanese Procelli 1996.
10 See, for example, Cartledge 1993.
11 Jeffery 1990 provides a fundamental geographical overview; Johnston 1996 (fig. 1); Wachter 1989.
12 Hall 1997, xiii; Cartledge 1995. As Thomas Heine Nielsen points out to me (pers. comm.), the mainland perspective is of some importance here, as awareness of 'Greekness' surely played a different, and perhaps more important, role in the colonial world (noting, for example, the *Hellenion* of Naukratis).

13 Morgan 1998a and 2001b; *contra* Waterhouse 1996.
14 Kourou 1990–1; Popham 1994, 12–26; Popham and Lemos 1995; Antonaccio 1995b.
15 For an eclectic selection from the extensive bibliography on this issue, see: Popham 1994, 26–33; Boardman 1990; Sherratt and Sherratt 1992; Sørensen 1997; Coldstream 1989; Graham 1986; Crielaard 1999. Pithekoussai, see most recently: Ridgway 1994; Coldstream 1994; Docter and Niemeyer 1994; Boardman 1994. On Euboians in Macedonia, see Snodgrass 1994; Papadopoulos 1996b.
16 Csapo et al. 2000, cats 11 (Euboian, dedicatory?), 17 (probably Attic rather than Euboian or Cycladic, owner's mark), 19 (probably Boiotian, cf. Thessaly, Phokis or less likely Euboia, owner's mark), 27 (probably Lokrian, Phokian or northern Boiotian, owner's mark). See Csapo 1991 and 1993 for an overview.
17 Appadurai 1986. Case studies in the Greek world have rarely focused on early data: see Polignac 1992 for imports in EIA/Archaic shrines.
18 Among extensive literature, see most recently Hoffman 1997; papers in Karageorghis 1994; papers in Karageorghis and Stampolidis 1998; Swinton 1996.
19 Hoffman 1997, conclusion; Kourou 2000 takes a more positive view.
20 Purcell 1990.
21 Morgan n.d.; Pfaff 1999, 114. A possible exception is a collection of eighth/seventh-century gold repoussée bands now in Berlin which are reported to come from the Corinthia: Furtwangler 1884. On analogous conservatism in Classical times, see Pemberton 1999.
22 Davies 1997 encapsulates many of the key questions.
23 Hansen 1997d offers a succinct account of the programme.
24 See, for example, concerns raised by Rhodes (1995, 91–2) about the degree of precision with which Greeks used their own political terminology, and the reply of Hansen (1996, 18–20).
25 As Snodgrass 1980, 44, concludes.
26 Ruschenbusch 1978; Gehrke 1986; Gawantka 1985 offers a thorough critique; Kinzl 1988.
27 Sakellariou 1989 for a systematic review.
28 As in the work of Victor Ehrenberg (see, for example, Ehrenberg 1969, xi-xii; for a review of responses see Sakellariou 1989, 49–52).
29 Hansen 1996.
30 Heine Nielsen 1996a, 117–32; Heine Nielsen 2002, 161–3, 199–200, 212–14.
31 Hansen 1995a.
32 Hansen 1997c.
33 Shipley 1997; Hall 2000; Roy 1997; Perlman 1996.
34 Morgan and Hall 1996; Heine Nielsen 1996a, 132–41; Heine Nielsen 1996c; Hansen 1995b.
35 Athens is an exception, but, as Hall 2000 points out, Sparta probably not.
36 Ehrenberg 1969, 25. Sakellariou 1989 offers the most comprehensive review of scholarship; see also Daverio Rocchi 1993, Pt. I Ch. 1.
37 For instance, Giovannini 1971, 71–93; Runciman 1990; Larsen 1966, 22–31; Larsen 1968, 3–8, 11 (albeit more concerned with the internal circumstances of ethne in the context of early federalism).

38 The term and its pedigree is discussed most fully by Gschnitzer 1955; see also Gschnitzer 1960, 11–28.
39 Thus, for example, Wade-Gery 1924, 60 refers to 'the recognition of the fact that Thessaly was no longer an ethnos but a collection of poleis'. Effenterre 1985b, 157–67 is a partial exception.
40 Gschnitzer 1971, 1.
41 Gschnitzer 1971. For a critical view of literary sources, but accepting Homeric poleis: Raaflaub 1993, 46–59.
42 Sakellariou 1989, 333, echoing Aristotle's view of the *kome* as the link between *oikos* and polis (*Politics* 3.5.14–15).
43 Raaflaub 1993, 77–8, note 167; Roussel 1976, 3–13. See also Funke 1993.
44 Hall 1997, Ch. 3; a similar point is made by Daverio Rocchi 1993, 107–12.
45 Evolutionary perceptions surrounding the *Stammstadt* also sit ill with a diverse variety of general developmental models, such as Donlan 1985 and 1989; Welwei 1983, Pt. II; Welwei 1988; Welwei 1992, Pt. II. In the case of Arkadia, Heine Nielsen 1999, 60 argues that attempts to politicize ethnic identity (chiefly in opposition to Sparta) were never wholly successful.
46 See Funke 1997, 169–72 (noting the existence of substantial settlement centres, and poleis, in Aetolia) with appended comment by M.H. Hansen (173–4).
47 Larsen 1968, 6.
48 Müller 1878, 102–77. Thessaly: Rose fragt. 497, 498; *FrGHist* IIIb, 602, Kommentar, 677–81. Achaia and Pellene: Cicero (*Ad Att.* II, 2) mentions that both were written by Dikaiarchos, a pupil of Aristotle. Larsen 1945, 74 and note 55. On Archaic historiography and local traditions, see Lasserre 1976.
49 For analogous reflections on the use of Rhianos's *Messeniaka* in later accounts of the first messenian war: Pearson 1962.
50 Hansen 1999.
51 Huxley 1980; Barker 1946, introduction; for an overview of Aristotle's aims and methods, see Johnston 1988.
52 Coldstream 1984a and 1984b.
53 Sakellariou 1989, 297–8; Snodgrass 1980, 42–7. A rare exception is Tritsch's definition (1929, 1) of ethne as peoples rather than states, although this rested on his belief that the presence of cities was the principal criterion of statehood, and their absence signified a 'stateless society'.
54 Snodgrass 1980, and subsequently 1991 and 1993. Cf. Whitley 1991a, 39–45.
55 Morris 1987, 6–7.
56 McInerney 1999, 4. Morris 2000, Pts 3 and 4, while acknowledging difference, offers an Athenocentric analysis in largely conventional terms.
57 For a summary critique, see McInerney 2001, 51–63,
58 Hall 1997, 34–5; Smith 1986, 21. Searches for 'ethnos' and its cognates in *TLG* widen the range of uses along lines that may be predicted from *LSJ* without revealing distinctive new traits. The term 'ethnos' could indeed play a important role in describing human societies, but as Jones 1996 and Hall 1997, 35–6 highlight in discussing the Herodotean and Thucydidean distinction between ethnos and *genos*, it is as the less precise term for a group of whatever character may be relevant in a particular context.
59 Citing the Epirote confederation, Giovannini 1971, 14–20 suggests that confederacies were not termed ethne because of their ethnic origins, but because

they could not be poleis. By contrast, Sakellariou 1989, 163 note 1 uses 'ethnos' for states identified with an ethnos or tribe, and '*koinon*' for a confederacy; the ethnos' acquisition of the meaning of confederacy arose from the coincidence of numerous confederacies with ethne, hence ethnos/nation=*koinon* of poleis or communities within it. Yet this underrates the dynamism of ethne; in both Achaia and Arkadia, for example, the *politicization* of ethnic identity postdated the development of local communities, including poleis, but apparently predated formal leagues: Morgan and Hall 1996; Heine Nielsen 1996a. The fact that the term ethnos does not imply any particular form of political organization is also emphasized by Bakhuizen 1989.

60 My views thus fall between those of Giovannini 1971, 14–16 and Walbank 1985, 21–6, since in rejecting the constructions put upon the term in modern (but not ancient) usage, I do not argue against it being invested with meaning in the specific contexts within which it was used in antiquity. That the term ethnos is revealing of early Greek classificatory mentality seems clear; my concern is with the results in individual cases.

61 McInerney 1999, see 10–22 for a critical view of approaches to the ethnos in the context of analysis of Phokis. Arkadia: *CPCActs* 6.

62 Notably Hall 1997; Morgan 1991 and 2001c (noting the relevance of the volume as a whole); McInerney 1999, 25–35. For a general theoretical review and discussion of archaeological implications, see Jones 1997. Among earlier literature, see, for example, Horowitz 1975: Chapman et al. 1989; Mullings 1994.

63 Patterson 1975, 308; cf. Barth 1970. For critique: Smith 1986, 9–10.

64 Patterson 1975. For a review of approaches, see Hall 1997, Ch. 2; on criteria, Isaacs 1975. The definition and meaning of archaeological 'cultures' have been extensively discussed, especially with regard to the equation of '*Kultur*' and '*Volk*' (chiefly in the works of Kossina and subsequently Childe), Nazi exploitation of this, and the ensuing reaction which produced a reversion to more neutral ideas of 'culture' replacing 'peoples or races': Shennan 1978; Shennan 1989, 5–14; Veit 1989; Childe 1929, v-vi, equates the term 'people' with culture, and uses 'race' where skeletal remains of specific physical types are present; Trigger 1980, 40–53; Trigger 1989, Ch. 5; McNairn 1980, 46–73; Hodder 1978, 3–24; see Hall 1997, 1–2, 168–71 for a review, and most recently Brather 2000 for discussion of its impact on the archaeology of Medieval Europe. Even those who accept that archaeological cultures need not have direct ethnic connotations may still treat them as representations of groups; Clarke 1978, 363–408. In the present context, I treat 'culture' as that level of classification which to the modern observer represents the point of maximum concidence of the distributions of various artefact types and styles, and thus as an artificial 'average' boundary surrounding the material debris of the palimpsest of activities undertaken by a group. The group is defined not by the 'culture' but by the various behaviours represented within it. Analysis of those behaviours, for instance by context or artefact type or style, will reveal both subdivisions within the whole and areas of activity that transcend the boundary, yet on a general level the culture can still be a useful heuristic tool.

65 Smith 1986, see especially 22–32; cf. Snodgrass 1980.

66 Shipley 1997, 203–4.

67 Morgan 1999a, 369–72, for analogous points with regard to ritual behaviour, drawing chiefly on the work of Pascal Boyer (Boyer 1990 and 1993); Morgan 2001c, 76–7, 81–4. Amnesia: Anderson 1991, 204; Pretzler 1999, 96–9, well illustrates how the local Tegean historical traditions reported by Pausanians deliberated excluded major post-Archaic events (especially those surrounding the Persian wars) where Tegeans co-operated closely with Sparta.
68 For a review, see Silverman 1990, 124–43. Shanks and Tilley 1987, Ch. 3; Handler 1994.
69 Cohen 1985, 11–12.
70 Sakellariou 1989, 46–7 for a review.
71 Here, for example, I differ from the more uniform models presented by e.g. Donlan 1989.
72 Gellner 1987, Ch. 2; Gellner 1983, 1–2; Anderson 1991; Kellas 1991, 4–5, 72–85, 98–105; Oommen 1994. By contrast, Smith 1986, Ch. 7, in tracing long-term development from ethnic groups to nations, accepts that the progression is not inevitable and that the historical context of each case must be considered. Hobsbawm 1992.
73 In the latest of a series of important discussions of Arkadian tribes (Roy 1996, 107 note 1), James Roy emphasizes that the translation is far from ideal and dissociates his discussion from any wider implications of the term tribe.
74 See most recently Heine Nielsen 1996a, 132–41, with bibliography.
75 As Heine Nielsen 2002, 266–9, 272–8 also concludes in the case of the Arkadian tribes. It is for this reason that I have avoided Anthony Smith's distinction (1986, 84) between ethnic identity, sub-ethnic identity and more localized loyalties, even though at first sight it may seem to correspond quite closely to the kind of nested and parallel identities current in the early Greek world. Weber 1978, 393–5, distinguished the tribe from the ethnic group on the basis that the tribe was the creation of a polity, a distinction which prejudges the issues which we are here investigating.
76 For such issues in Arkadia, compare Heine Nielsen 1996a, 132–41 with Roy 1972b, Roy 1996 and Jost 1986.
77 Maine 1861, Ch. V; MacFarlane 1991. On the intellectual context, see Burrow 1991; Kumar 1991. Maine was not concerned with a theory of progress per se, nor was he greatly influenced by Darwin; his comparative evolutionism, emphasizing increased rationality as a sign of progress, reveals a strong intellectualist bias: Burrow 1966, 142–53; Collini et al. 1983, ch. VII, noting especially 212–13.
78 For critique, see Crone 1986, 56–68; full statement, Sahlins 1968, 1–13; Service 1975.
79 Snodgrass 1980, 25–8; cf. Crone 1986, 52–5.
80 Donlan 1985.
81 Crone 1986, note 110.
82 Exemplified by Ehrenberg 1969, 9–14; on Athens, Hignett 1952, Chs 4–6. For a review of the problem of subdivisions within poleis, see Davies 1996b.
83 For reviews of approaches, see Sanderson 1990, Chs 2, 7 and 8; Crone 1986, 56–68; Hall 1997, 14–16. Dunnell 1980; Shanks and Tilley 1987, Ch. 6; *contra* Lewis 1968.
84 Roussel 1976; Bourriot 1976; cf. Donlan 1985; Davies 1996b. The observation

that *phylai* were a polis creation (often attributed to founders, reformers or lawgivers) absent in ethne was long since made by Max Weber (1924, 95–7). Effenterre 1985a, 299–300, and Nagy 1987, both reassert the anteriority of *phylai* to the polis, *contra* Roussel and Bourriot, although neither seeks to restore those social-evolutionary aspects of earlier conceptions which are of particular concern to the present argument. Gehrke 2000 offers a thorough and stimulating review of the historiography of approaches to the problem.

85 Roussel 1976, 3–4; Finley 1985a, 90–3; Gehrke 2000; see also Vlachos 1974, 256 note 41, 289. Humphreys 1978c, 195–6 expresses uncertainty about the relationship between tribes as subdivisions of a city-state and the peoples, ethne, who formed the loosely organized, (supposedly) non-urban federations of northern Greece (stating that we do not know how the latter were structured).

86 Fox 1967, 16–24; Humphreys 1978a, 17–18.

87 Grote 1854, esp. Ch. ix.

88 Sanderson 1990, Ch. 2; Roussel 1976, 9–22; Kuper 1982 and 1991 (NB 107); see note 77 above. Both Morgan and Maine's other major critic, J.F. MacLennan (in his 1865 *Primitive Marriage*) argued for matrilineal rather than patrilineal descent as a feature of early tribal systems; Maine subsequently restated his case in his 1883 *Dissertations on Early Law and Custom*. An earlier statement of the place of early tribal organization in social evolution has received less attention: in the 1857–8 manuscript of his *Grundrisse*, Karl Marx distinguished tribes constituted by kinship from those based on locality, and argued that the latter generally postdated and displaced the former (Marx 1857–8, 76).

89 Helm 1968 contains a range of relevant papers; Leach 1989.

90 Sahlins 1968; Crone 1986 for summary and bibliography.

91 This is the basis of the contrast between control of time and control of space in the ordering of Greek states drawn by Morgan 1991, 148–9.

92 Hall 1997, 10.

93 Crone 1986, 48–50.

94 Sahlins 1968, 5–13, 96–113.

95 Roussel 1976, 18–19; Shils 1991.

96 S. Morris 1992, Ch. 5, citing especially Wells 1980; Wells 1984 (for critique see Arafat and Morgan 1994; Champion 1987).

97 Champion and Champion 1986; on limitations of data, see Harke 1982. On kinship and tribal structures: Kristansen 1998; Rowlands 1998.

98 For example, Jones 1997, 29–39, 129–35; Woolf 1998, Ch. 1 presents the problem in terms of deliberate subscription to a set of cultural referents.

99 Contrast, for example, Nico Roymans' processual, functionalist assessment of northern Gaul (Roymans 1990) with Lotte Hedeager's broadly post-processual and longer-term examination of Scandinavia in relation to northern Europe (Hedeager 1992). For a critical view, see Rowlett 1989.

100 Nor does anthropology provide many more instances of general theory worked out in comparative case studies: see, for instance, Cohen and Schlegel 1968.

101 Cf. Ardener 1989; Anderson 1991, 67–82, 144–7. For more critical reviews, see Hall 1995b; Hall 1997, 2.

102 Lasserre 1976 offers a brief review of the likely earlier textual sources.

103 See, for example, Thomas 2000, introduction, who cautions against the assumption that Herodotos consistently archaizes.

104 Fletcher 1996; Morgan 1999b, 383; Morgan 2001c. For reviews: Hodder 1987 and 1991.
105 Hall 1997, 3, 59–63; see also Patterson's (1975, 312) objection to Isaacs' (1975) observation that the quintessence of ethnicity is primordiality.
106 Bradley 1990, Ch. 2; Bradley 1991 (cf. Morgan 1999a, 369–72, especially note 12); Alcock 1993, Ch. 5; Antonaccio 1994, 86–104; Spencer 1995.
107 For review and bibliography see Melas 1989.
108 Explorations of such issues using Greek data are few but growing in number: examples are Morgan and Whitelaw 1991; Morgan 1991; Hall 1995a; Spencer 1995.
109 Coldstream 1983; Morgan 1999c. Argolid: Morgan and Whitelaw 1991. Corinthia: Morgan 1999a, Ch. II.3; Morgan 1999d. Arkadia: Morgan 1999b. Attica: e.g. Whitley 1991a; Rombos 1988; Morris 1984 (although a study of Protoattic which includes the large bodies of unpublished material is much needed: for discussion and bibliography, see Morgan 1999c, 215 note 11). Metalwork: Rolley 1992a.
110 Shanks and Tilley 1987, Ch. 4; Shennan 1989, 17–22; papers in Conkey and Hastorf 1990; Carr and Neitzel 1995.
111 Literature on the interpretation of mortuary evidence in particular is now vast. For reviews, see, for example, Huntington and Metcalf 1979, introduction, Pts I and II; Chapman and Randsborg 1981, 1–24; Whitley 1991a, 23–34; I. Morris 1992.
112 Shennan 1989, 14–30; Morgan 1999b, 383; Morgan 2001c; Hall 1997, 111–31.
113 Philippson 1897, Chs I-IV; Philippson 1950; Sivignon 1975; Feuer 1983, 32–8; Garnsey et al. 1984, 30–5; Van Andel and Runnels 1995. On landscape change, Stiros and Papagiorgiou 1992 and 1994. The region's mineral resources appear limited if ill-studied: on copper in Pelasgia, see Papastamataki et al. 1994 (although as they note, it is hard to find evidence dating the exploitation of these sources before the third century).
114 Stählin 1924. For a review of earlier scholarship, see Gallis 1979.
115 Pherai: Dougleri Intzesiloglou 1994.
116 Iolkos: papers in Koliou 1994 offer valuable summaries of decades of research. Gonnoi: Helly 1973.
117 For a review of the region, see Malakasioti 1997b.
118 Helly 1979; *Praktika Theochari*; *ΘΕΣΣΑΛΙΑ*.
119 Tziaphalias and Zaouri 1999.
120 For example, Blum et al. 1992. For reviews of methodology and studies in progress, see Helly 1994; Decourt and Darmezin 1999.
121 Decourt 1990.
122 Salvatore 1994.
123 Basic (if sometimes contradictory) analyses of Thessalian constitutional history are offered by Sordi 1958 and 1992; Helly 1995.
124 Axenidos 1947, 43–8.
125 Helly 1995, introduction.
126 Axenidos 1947.
127 Helly 1995, Ch. 2.
128 Archibald 2000, 212–13.

129 For a brief summary, see Dakoronia and Tziafalias 1991.
130 Helly 1995, *passim*, *contra* the pervasive acceptance of an early federal *tageia* current since the nineteenth century, on which see, for example: Hiller von Gärtringen 1890; Momigliano 1932; Sordi 1958; Daverio Rocchi 1993, 405; Carlier 1984, 412–17.
131 A scholiast to Euripides' *Rhesus* 307 (Rose 494) refers to Aleuas' division of the polis into *kleroi*; see also Polyaenus 8.44. Despite attempts to amend the text, the use of 'polis' should be understood in the sense of the basic unit salient to the argument: Hansen 1997a. A scholiast to Pindar *Pyth.* 4.246 (Drachmann ii, p. 131) also calls Thessaly a polis, but the sense here appears poetic rather than political.
132 Archibald 2000, 215, in arguing for a higher degree of regional cohesion than in many other parts of Greece, emphasizes that it is this collective voice which is most often heard. While I accept her overall conclusion, the choice of geographical/ethnic/place reference made by any author depends on the degree of precision required by the context of that reference, and it could be argued that neither Herodotos nor Thucydides needed to be more precise for the purposes of their narratives. It is therefore interesting to note the existence of hints of localized actions: Morgan 2001a, 31–2, and see pp. 85–7.
133 Lefèvre 1998, 13, 24–6. On the *penestai*, see Ducat 1994; Corvisier 1981.
134 See, for example, Larsen 1968, 12–26.
135 Archibald 2000.
136 Philippson 1951, Chs II, III. McInerney 1999, Ch. 3; Dasios 1992, 19–23. For an early but still valuable regional study, see Schober 1925. On the topography and communication routes in the area of the Pleistos valley: Skorda 1992 and 1998–9.
137 Jalkotzy and Dakoronia 1990; Dakoronia 1993b; Jalkotzy 1999a; Paris 1892.
138 Felsch 1999.
139 See most recently, *BCH* 116 (1992) 694–8; *BCH* 117 (1993) 619–31. Mycenaean settlement: Müller 1992. Settlements listed in the *Catalogue of Ships* (*Iliad* 2.517–23) are largely in the southern part of Phokis.
140 Vatin 1969.
141 Dasios 1992; Petronotis 1973 is more useful for later periods, and Rousset 1999 offers a valuable analysis of Classical political geography. See McInerney 1999, 87–92 for a summary.
142 As proposed by, for example, Larsen 1968, 40–1 (*contra* McInerney 1998, 154–6).
143 Rousset 1999.
144 Coinage: Williams 1972, 9–17, 71–3. Phokikon: McInerney 1997 with previous bibliography (re-identifying the structure described as the Archegetes' *heroon* by French and Vanderpool 1963). Date: McInerney 1998, 179–80.
145 McInerney 1998, 173–8, although in the light of the discussion above, I differ from his assessment of the extent of Thessalian unification at this date.
146 *RE* XIII, i, *sv.* Lokris (Oldfather); Philippson 1951, Chs II, III; Dakoronia 1993a, 117–22.
147 Graham 1983, 115–16. On the problem of Lokrian ethnicity and the subdivisions of the Lokrians, see Heine Nielsen 2000.
148 *ML* 20; Effenterre and Ruzé 1994, no. 43; Graham 1983, 40–66.
149 Larsen 1968, 52–3; *contra* Heine Nielsen 2000, 109–15.

150 Fossey 1990a.
151 Coleman 1992.
152 Dakoronia 1993a; on the PG phase at Kynos, see *Delt* 50 B (1995) 338–9.
153 Stiros and Rondogianni 1985; Ganas and Buck 1998 (modelling based on Halai).
154 See Morgan and Hall 1996 for a review of literary and historical data principally concerning the eighth–sixth centuries.
155 On the physical landscape of western Achaia, see Dalongeville 2000.
156. Philippson 1959, Ch. V, c, d; Philippson 1951, Chs II, III. Petropoulos 1985 on the border with Arkadia.
157 Notable among these is Anderson 1954, albeit unsurpassed in other respects; see also Koerner 1974. For more recent reviews, see Morgan 1991; Morgan and Hall 1996.
158 See Morgan and Hall 1996 for a summary of the results of archaeological research throughout Achaia for the Early Iron Age and Archaic periods. Rizakis 1995 offers a thorough revew of the literary testimonia in relation to archaeological and topographical data.
159 Rizakis 1992; Petropoulos and Rizakis 1994; see also papers in Rizakis 2000.
160 Early evidence is summarized in Alzinger et al. 1985 and 1986; Gogos 1986; see also Bammer forthcoming.
161 Vordos forthcoming; *Delt* 50 B (1995) 238–9. On the identification of Rhypes, see the summary discussion of the 6th Ephoreia/KERA-EIE regional survey: *Delt* 50 B (1995) 231–2.
162 Papakosta 1991.
163 *PAE* 1929, 86–91; *PAE* 1930, 81–8; *PAE* 1952, 400–12; *PAE* 1956, 193–201; Morgan and Hall 1996, 189–93, 231, noting the discovery of an Archaic votive deposit from a shrine at Prevedos: *Delt* 44 B (1989) 133.
164 Strabo 8.7.4; Skylax 42; Polybios 2.41; Pausanias 7.6.1; 7.18.7; 7.22.1; 7.22.6.
165 Morgan and Hall 1996, 168–9, 217 note 25. Helly 1997 has recently sought to extend to the Achaian *mere* the constitutional-military purpose which he assigns to the Thessalian divisions from their inception (Helly 1995, noting that Hellanikos of Lesbos, *FrGHist* 4, fr.52, terms the Thessalian tetrads *moirai*, see 56, 150–1). He thus defines a real mathematical division of a citizen body, with ninety-one demes in existence by Herodotos' time (demes which he argues need not have physical centres visible in the archaeological record). It is hard to see how Helly's case can be evaluated given the lack of Achaian evidence, although it begs the question of the early date of acceptance of a uniform scheme (if not overarching authority) within such a diverse region. Comparison between the archaeological record (see Morgan and Hall 1996) and the *meros* names and locations does not show any great misfit, and Herodotos' use of these names could therefore reflect rationalizations of localized settlement systems readily translatable to the structure of explanation required by his discussion of Ionia. By contrast with Thessaly, however, the fact that Achaia as a regional entity was largely uninvolved in the military affairs of the wider Greek world (including the Persian wars) makes it hard to understand the military relevance of such divisions (mercenary service more likely being organized on a personal basis). In short, the constitutional reconstruction advanced by Helly does not follow automatically from the (uncontroversial) mathematical meaning of *meros* as a division.
166 Morgan 1999b, 383–5.

167 Rizakis 1998, 20–1.
168 Morgan and Hall 1996, 186–9; for a systematic review of excavation and survey data from the area, see Rizakis 1992; Lakaki-Marchetti 2000.
169 Rizakis 1991a, 53; see also Walbank 1972, xi.
170 Morgan and Hall 1996, 164–5, 193–9. Walbank 2000, 22–7 reiterates the case (of which Hall and I remain critical) for a pre-fourth-century league based on substantially later discussions (chiefly Polybios and Livy) of the role of the sanctuary of Zeus Homarios, although it is unclear how early he wishes this to begin (on the issue of early religious leagues, see Ch. 3 here below). Parker 1998, 31–2 is more cautious in suggesting that by the fifth century the cult of Zeus Homarios might have come to be seen as a symbol of Achaian identity, and in so far as it does not carry formal political implications, this seems plausible, if inevitably less securely attested than one would wish. Cf. Larsen 1968, 80–9, 216.
171 Larsen 1968, 83. Morgan and Hall 1996, 199–214. On Peloponnesian and western Achaian identity in the colonial and immediate post-colonial period, see Morgan forthcoming b; Hall forthcoming.
172 Economic constraints and opportunities: Roy 1999 (see 324 on rainfall and drainage). Drainage: Knauss 1988 and 1990; Knauss et al. 1986. Roads: Pikoulas 1999.
173 *CPCActs* 6 is the most comprehensive and recent review
174 Asea: Forsén et al. 1996; Forsén et al. 1999. Tegea: Østby et al. 1994; Ødegard pers. comm. Pheneos: Tausend 1999.
175 Exemplified by Pikoulas 1988.
176 See Morgan 1999b for a review of Early Iron Age and Archaic evidence with bibliography (graves are listed in note 32).
177 Voyatzis 1999; see also Jost 1985 for comparison of literary and archaeological evidence.
178 Heine Nielsen 1999.
179 Heine Nielsen 1999, 47–51; Morgan 1999b, 383–5.
180 Williams 1965; Heine Nielsen 1996b; Psoma 1999.
181 Jacob 1980–1.
182 Roy 1972a and b; Heine Nielsen 1996a.
183 Heine Nielsen and Roy 1998; Petropoulos 1985.

2 Big sites and place identities

1 Hansen 1996, 7–8.
2 Reviewed by Hansen 1997b.
3 Snodgrass 1991; Snodgrass 1980, 28–33; Vink 1997. Colonial planning: Fischer-Hansen 1996; see also Malkin 1994 on its potential impact in the homeland, and contrast Tréziny 1997, emphasizing variation in plot size at Megara Hyblaea perhaps dating from the eighth century. On possible motives for divisions, Morgan 1999e, 106, 127–8 with bibliography.
4 Morris 1991 is an exception in arguing that an eighth-century acceleration in the development of political institutions was accompanied by relatively minor developments in settlement nucleation which do not amount to urbanization.
5 Camp 2000, 48–9. Crete: Hayden 1988; Nowicki 1992 and 2000. Islands:

Marangou 1988. Old Smyrna: Nicholls 1958–9. Walls and polis status: Snodgrass 1980, 32; Snodgrass 1986; Ducrey 1995.
6 Snodgrass 1980, 28–33.
7 Among others, suggested by, Ehrenberg 1969, 19–20, 23–4; Daverio Rocchi 1993, 113–14; Sakellariou 1989, 135, 136. See also Dakaris 1987, who distinguishes the city as part of the city-state as constituted during eighth and seventh centuries in southern Greece (a fortified agglomeration of local importance with a territory, which served as the political and administrative centre of the state), from fifth–fourth century northern cities, citing the particular case of Epirus. Yet such new cities were not confined to the north (see e.g. Megalopolis), nor is the corollary of the older unurbanized ethnos valid. See likewise Corvisier 1993, who stresses regional differences between Epirus, Thessaly and Macedonia.
8 Pherai: Dougleri Intzesiloglou 1990, 78–9, figs 1, 2. Aigion: Papakosta 1991; Petropoulos forthcoming. Argos: Touchais and Divari-Valakou 1998; Barakari-Gleni and Pariente 1998. Megara: Travlos 1988, 258–81: Morgan 1999a, 478–9; *Delt* 49 B (1994) 55. As Archibald (2000) highlights, the comparison does not stop at the borders of Macedon.
9 Ehrenberg 1969, 23.
10 Morgan and Hall forthcoming list sixteen sites within categories A (certain poleis), B (probable poleis) and C (possibly poleis); the status of a further nine Archaic and/or Classical settlements is unknown.
11 Smith 1986, 22–31.
12 See Ch. 1 note 168.
13 Roy 1997 and 2000; Minon 1994. See for example: Effenterre and Ruzé 1994, 21, *c*.500–475 (*IvO* 11: concession of civic and territorial privileges between the damos of Khaladrioi and Deucalion), 51, *c*.475–450 (*IvO* 10, fifty-year accord between the Anaitioi and Metapoioi), 52, *c*.500 (*IvO* 9; Roy and Schofield 1999, fifty-year accord between the Eleans and Euaians?), 56, pre-450 (*IvO* 16) procedures for dealing with rebellious Skillountians.
14 On defining a city, see Drews 1981; for review, Effenterre 1990 (analogous reflections on the prehistoric record are offered by Konsola and Polychronopoulou in the same volume): Childe 1950.
15 Fustel de Coulanges 1864, III.iii, iv. See also Momigliano 1970; Humphreys 1978b.
16 Sakellariou 1989, 424–28. On archaeology, Morgan and Coulton 1997.
17 Morgan and Coulton 1997 for a review with bibliography. On surface evidence, Bintliff n.d. and pers. comm. makes a case similar to that argued for prehistoric periods by Bintliff et al. 1999 (with subsequent debate in *JMA* 13 [2000] 100–23), stressing that the traditional picture of substantially depopulated Early Iron Age landscapes probably reflects archaeological failure to recognize and surmount this problem.
18 See for example Finley 1981; Cornell and Lomas 1995, introduction; Nippel 1987–9; Bruhns 1987–9; Murray 1990; Hansen 1997b.
19 Morgan and Coulton 1997, 87–91, 120–9, with specific reference to Childe 1950 (still the most systematic formulation and evaluation of criteria for the archaeological definition of urban entities, although hardly unique; see for example Trigger 1972; Wheatley 1972).

20 See Wheatley 1972 for a review of concepts of urbanism.
21 Morgan 2000.
22 Tritsch 1929 argues that a state must have a city, an ethnos being simply a '*Volk*'; Gschnitzer 1955.
23 E.g. Malkin 1994. *Contra*: Danner 1997; Antonaccio 1997 on 'Hellenisation' at Morgantina.
24 Snodgrass 1991, 7–11; Martin 1983, Pt. 2, Ch. 1. Bibliography on Crete and the islands is extensive, and the following a brief selection of key discussions: Crete: Myers et al. 1992; Coldstream 1984b; Pendlebury et al. 1937–8; Hayden 1983; Hayden 1988; Gesell et al. 1995; Haggis and Nowicki 1992; Nowicki 1999 and 2000. Chios: Boardman 1967. For the Cyclades, see Gounaris 1999 for an overview of site locations with bibliography. Specific cases include: Andros: Televantou 1999; Cambitoglou et al. 1988. Amorgos (plus fortifications elsewhere): Marangou 1988.
25 Haggis 1996, 408–15; Nowicki 1999.
26 Coldstream 1991.
27 Gounaris 1999; Reger 1997.
28 Lenz 1993, 125–74, acknowledges some of these problems while making extensive use of island evidence alongside the most frequently cited mainland cases (Nichoria, Lefkandi and Eretria).
29 Snodgrass 1987, Ch. 6; the observation (192) that the average life of an EIA site is $c.150$ years rests on evidence from radically different areas and systems.
30 Whitley 1991b, 346–7, although the 'unstable' span of 50–300 years is so wide as to conceal substantial variation. The inclusion of two mainland settlements, Nichoria and Lefkandi, alongside much shorter-lived island sites is also questionable. At Nichoria, the gap between LHIIIB2 and Submycenaean?/Protogeometric habitation remains problematic (McDonald et al. 1983, 318–23; see Mountjoy 1999, 311, on the problems of identifying LHIIIC in Messenia), especially given substantial LBA settlement. Furthermore, the abandonment of the site by the mid-eighth century may be a reponse to the Spartan threat rather than a purely local rhythm of activity (McDonald et al. 1983, 326). At Lefkandi, while settlement traces in particular suggest localized movement within small plots, this is no greater than at many other mainland big sites, and caution is required given the very limited excavation at Xeropolis (noting the longer spans of most local cemeteries).
31 For an eclectic selection from an extensive corpus of work reflecting differing viewpoints, see for example Lenz 1993, 131–42, 154–62. Mazarakis Ainian 1987 (Eretria) and 1997 *passim*. Lefkandi: Morris 2000, 218–37 with bibliography. Nichoria: McDonald et al. 1983, 327–8; Morgan 1990, 65–79.
32 Mazarakis Ainian 1987 with previous bibliography; cf. Bérard 1998. For a review of ninth-century evidence see Blandin 2000.
33 Schmidt 2000–2001, 1–20; Verdan 2000 and 2001; I thank Samuel Verdan and Stephan Schmidt for *in situ* discussion of this new research in August 2001.
34 Evidence from Macedonia is much richer throughout the Late Bronze and Early Iron Ages. See e.g. Hänsel 1989 on Kastanas, and the annual excavation reports on Toumba Thessalonikis published in *AEMΘ*.
35 Mazarakis Ainian 1997, 164–6, 323; Morgan and Hall 1996, 171–3, noting that Bammer forthcoming (see also Bammer 1998, 202–3) rejects both cult

activity at 'Temple A' and Alzinger's reconstruction of the succeeding Temple B, leaving no identifiable temple building on the acropolis in the early Archaic period. Tripod: Alzinger 1981–2, fig. 12.
36 Morris 1991, 29–34.
37 Grove 1972 for a review.
38 Grove 1972; Smith 1972.
39 Gamble 1982; Morgan and Coulton 1997, 91–9; Fletcher 1995, Pt. 1.
40 Fletcher 1995, Ch. 1.
41 Hansen 1997b, 20–2. For discussion in the context of the Southern Argolid Survey, see Jameson et al. 1994, 252–7.
42 A selection of Greek case studies includes Rihll and Wilson 1991; Sanders and Whitbread 1990; Renfrew and Wagstaff 1982, 136–60 (Wagstaff and Cherry); Bintliff 1999; Decourt and Darmezin 1999.; Cavanagh 1991, 110–14.
43 Patras: Morgan and Hall 1996, 182–3. Larisa: see pp. 55, 89–91.
44 McDonald et al. 1983, xxvii–xxix, 4–5.
45 Pfaff forthcoming.
46 Williams 1978, Ch. 1, noting that the locations of many of the cults prominent in literary, epigraphical and iconographical sources have yet to be discovered; Morgan 1999a, appendix 4, site 11 for a summary of LBA and EIA remains from the city centre.
47 Morgan 1999a, appendix 4 for a gazetteer of LBA and EIA sites in the Corinthia as known prior to 1998. The main area newly settled in the eighth century (MG/LG) is the Perachora peninsula: Fossey 1987–8; Fossey 1990b, 209, figs 3 and 4. Preliminary reports of the Eastern Korinthia Archaeological Survey (http://eleftheria.stcloudstate.edu/eks consulted on 21 July 2001) highlight the rarity of Geometric material in surface scatters and do not alter the picture outlined in 1999.
48 Morgan forthcoming a; Wiseman 1978, 66 (Archaic settlement); Rihll and Wilson 1991, 80–1. The EKAS preliminary report for 2000 notes Geometric pottery at Kromna (see note 47 above).
49 EIA burials at Krommyon (Ag. Theodoroi): Morgan 1999a, 476 site 33; Dickey 1992, A102–5.
50 Agathon Kromnites: Wiseman 1978, 10. Timos Teneos: *Ergon* 1961, 209, fig. 224; Wiseman 1978, 14, note 8.
51 On palaeotopography: Hayward forthcoming b. Archaeological evidence is summarized in Williams 1978, Ch. 1; Morgan forthcoming a. Demeter and Kore: Pfaff 1999.
52 Morgan 1999a, 472–3, for bibliography. Potters' Quarter: Stillwell 1948, 6–15, noting no direct evidence for pottery production during this period. Panayia Field; Sanders 1999, 443; *AR* 1998–9, 22, for mention of LBA and EPG finds; G. Sanders pers. comm., notes that early evidence may have been lost in the cutting back of the slope for the construction of a Roman bath.
53 Robinson 1976b, pl. 56 (c, d=eighth-century), p.211 for construction (Corinth Lots 6420, 6421, 6426). I thank Julie Bentz for discussion of early pottery from Temple Hill.
54 See most recently Malkin 1994.
55 For analogous reflections on Eretria, see Mazarakis Ainian 1987.
56 Polignac 1995, Ch. 2; Morgan 1999a, 410–15.

57 Citizen cemeteries: Morris 1987, 185–6 (emphasizing the North Cemetery). Only a fraction has been excavated of the very large North Cemetery which extends along a long-established road towards Cheliotoumylos (*Delt* 21 B [1966] 123, pl. 122γ); nonetheless, PG and G pottery has been found in the fill between graves: Blegen et al. 1964, 13–14; Dickey 1992, 9. Dickey 1992, A-98, CO-11, A-132, no. 7, notes an EIA grave (grave 1930-97) in the otherwise Roman cemetery 800 m from the edge of the excavated area of the North Cemetery, plus an LG krater (T2041) which may have held a burial or marked a grave. Tumulus: Rutter 1990, 455–8; Dickey 1992, 128–9.
58 Brookes 1981; Dickey 1992, 24–36; Rhodes 1987.
59 Wheatley 1972, 612–13.
60 Morris 1991, 29, suggests *c*.200 ha. Whitley 1991a, 61–4, 201–8 for summary list of graves; Morris 1987, 64, fig. 17. Parlama and Stampolidis 2000, 21, 44–50, 162–5, 265–90.
61 Touchais and Divari-Valakou 1998, 14–18, summarise settlement evidence; Piteros 1998 on topography; Hägg 1982; Hall 1997, fig. 11, for distribution of shrines (noting now Barakari-Gleni and Peppa-Papaioannou 1999), figs 13–15 for graves. Aupert 1982, 22–4. Plans of excavation plots: Pariente and Touchais 1998, pls. IX (EIA), X (Archaic).
62 Morgan and Coulton 1997, 107–9.
63 Corinth: Williams 1970, 32–9. Sparta: Waywell 1999, 8–10 noting alternative views and arguing for a location below the acropolis; Kourinou 2000, 99–129, map 2, favouring the Palaiokastro acropolis. Pherai: Dougleri Intzesiloglou 1994, 81, fig. 2 (Hellenistic city).
64 Hägg 1982, 302, thus concludes that, at least in the first quarter of the century, Argos did not have an 'agora' as such; Morris 1987, 184 remarks on the wealth of the seventh-century graves here, perhaps implying the burial ground of a leading lineage.
65 Barakari-Gleni and Pariente 1998, 165–8 (with bibliography); Pariente et al. 1998, 212–13, fig. 2. See also Courtils 1992; *BCH* 93 (1969) 994–1003; *BCH* 98 (1974) 761 (late sixth-century portico SE of Aphrodision); Bommelaer and Grandjean 1972, 168–77; *BCH* 111 (1987) 591 (lead weights from Archaic level south of Classical portico); *BCH* 106 (1982) 640 (Archaic road by theatre); *BCH* 102 (1978) 783 (mid-sixth-century fill south of Classical portico); *BCH* 91 (1967) 802–8 (Archaic drainage system in Kypseli). For the location of excavation plots see Aupert 1982, fig. 1. Shrines: Hall 1997, fig. 11; Pièrart 1991, 141–2 on *heroon* with mid-sixth-century inscription. Archaic (*c*.550 onwards) terracotta workshop in theatre area: Guggisberg 1988, 226–7.
66 Brann 1960; Papadopoulos 1996a; Monaco 2000, Pt. 1.1; Camp 1999, 260–7. On the extent of the Kerameikos in Greek sources, see Wycherley 1957, 221–4; Siewert 1999.
67 Morris 1987, 67–9. In support of this, Morris (67) cites Snodgrass 1983, 170, although Snodgrass is here equivocal if not negative (cf. Snodgrass 1980, 154–7, although his position is reversed in Snodgrass 1991, 11).
68 J. Papadopoulos pers. comm. Building A: Thompson 1940, 3–7.
69 Papadopoulos 1996a, 112 (roads), 124–6 stressing that the number of wells full of potters' debris indicates that the area was probably not heavily settled. Monaco 2000, Pt. 1 presents evidence highlighting the expansion of pottery

production sites to locations beyond the agora excavation area (and much of the intervening land between the agora and Kerameikos excavations lies unresearched beneath the modern city).
70 Ammerman 1996. Forum romanum: Cornell 1995, 93–4; Ammerman 1990.
71 Camp 1986, 33. Papadopoulos 1996a, 116, 123 stressing the presence of workshop debris and doubting the connection with normal settlement.
72 Camp 1994 (*contra* Miller 1995, 224 note 4); Shear 1994. For the state of the agora at the Persian sack, see Shear 1993; Thompson 1940, 8–44, 106–11; Camp 1986, 38–57. Altar of the Twelve Gods: *IG* II2, 2640.
73 Dontas 1983, 62–3 (see note 44 for bibliography); Shear 1994, 225–8; Robertson 1998; Miller 1995.
74 Gauss and Ruppenstein 1998; Glowacki 1998; Touloupa 1972.
75 Seventh-century evidence is assembled by Glowacki 1998. Winter 1993, 213–14 dates the earliest roof *c*.590–580 (see 215–16 and note 30 for affirmation of a date of *c*.570 for the sima Acropolis K11–13, 18 which, together with the antefix K230, 10124 and BPer.327, formed the basis for the 'late seventh-century' predecessor of the Old Temple of Athena suggested by Travlos 1971, 53).
76 Raubitschek 1949, 350–8, nos. 326–8.
77 Raubitschek 1949, 455–9 for summary. Cf. Athena Nike: Mark 1993, 24–8, 31–5. Agora sculpture: Harrison 1965, 1–13.
78 Asea: Forsén and Forsén 1997. Tegea: K. Ødegard pers. comm. (reporting the findings of the NAS up to and including the 2000 season).
79 Summaries of evidence are provided by Morgan and Hall 1996, 171–4 (Aegira, noting the important reappraisal of early architectural evidence in Bammer forthcoming), 176–7 (Aigion, see also Papakosta 1991), 183–94 (Boline, modern Drepanon). Rhypes: Vordos forthcoming.
80 Morgan and Hall 1996, 168–70, 193–7.
81 Morgan and Coulton 1997, 128–9.
82 See Morgan and Coulton 1997, 120–9 for a review.
83 Hansen 1996, 10, 34–6.
84 Jones 1987, 11–12 argues generally that of all the civic divisions attested across Greece, only the *phyle* is likely to be of substantial antiquity. Nonetheless, direct evidence from our regions is late (Jones 1987, 79–81 on third-century Thessaly, 130–2 on third-century Dyme, 132–42 on fourth-century and later Arkadia). Jones' suggestion (92) that the institution of territorial units might be linked to tyranny and the need to enfranchise more distant followers is interesting, and finds echoes in arguments about the relationship between power and territory raised especially with regard to Thessaly. Note also the distinct but related issue of dependent poleis. For Achaia, see Morgan and Hall 1996, 170–1; in the case of Patrees, a number of settlements identified with those named in later synoikisms and dioikisms have produced eighth-century evidence, but their status at this time is unknown (and there is no obvious reason to doubt their independence: Petropoulos 1991; Morgan and Hall 1996, 181–6). Similar issues arise over other rare instances of eighth- and seventh-century rural sites, such as the 'polisma' of Phelloe (Seliana Aigialeias) which has been seen as a deme of synoikized Aigeira: Alzinger et al. 1986, 319–26; Dekoulakou 1982, 229–31; *Delt* 51 B (1996) 252.

85 The case has been most fully argued by S. Morris 1992, 110–15, 123–4.
86 S. Morris 1992, 124; Effenterre 1985a.
87 For example, Snodgrass 1993; Morris 1991 also points to the immediate post Bronze Age history of many of the material developments associated with the polis, but argues for key points of change around 950, 800, and 750, the last coincident with the emergence of the true citizen state.
88 Polignac 1995, xiv. A comparable debate surrounding the origins of the Minoan palaces, and the existence and timing of critical points of transformation in their nature and function, took place some twenty years ago, and a reprise for Early Iron Age poleis would be unproductive: Cherry 1983.
89 Morris 1991, 34–6; Garnsey 1988, 69–86; Garnsey and Morris 1998. Finley 1985b, Ch. V; Humphreys 1978b; Weber 1924, 6, 13.
90 Foxhall pers. comm. (I am grateful to Prof. Foxhall for a copy of her unpublished manuscript 'Cultures, landscapes and identities in the Mediterranean world'); see also Boyd and Jameson 1981 on land divisions, emphasizing evidence from Archaic and later Halieis.
91 Finley 1981, for example, 12–13.
92 Fischer-Hansen 2000 offers analogous reflections on western Greek workshops with primary reference to Archaic and Classical data.
93 See papers in Blondé and Perreault 1992; Cook 1961, 65–6; Despoini 1982, 80–1; Papadopoulos 1989, 43–4; Papadopoulos 1994b, 151–3.
94 Dodona: *PAE* 1967, 40–2. Torone: Papadopoulos 1989. Miletos: von Graeve 1992, 103–4. Miletos and Ephesos: Akurgal et al. forthcoming, Ch. 3.2 (M. Kerschner; I thank Dr Kerschner for sight of his manuscript in advance of publication).
95 For a general review, see Monaco 2000; Rombos 1988, 357–62. Agora: Papadopoulos 1996a. Athens: Baziotopoulou-Valavani 1994.
96 Mazarakis Ainian 1998, 202–3; *PAE* 1998, 51–81. Lefkandi: *Lefkandi* I, 17, 93–7, 279 (Xeropolis bronze foundry); see also *Lefkandi* II.2, 74–6 (kiln fragments associated with the Toumba building). Eretria: Themelis 1983b (eighth-century goldworking).
97 Nichoria: McDonald et al. 1983, 325. Argos: Courbin 1963, 98–100; *BCH* 83 (1959) 755, fig. 3.
98 Pherai: Dougleri Intzesiloglou 1994, 78, fig. 8. Aigion: *Delt* 40B (1985) 120–3: Papakosta 1991, 236.
99 Morris 1991, 38–40.
100 Weber 1978, *passim*.
101 The argument evolves through Durkheim 1964; specific comments, with particular reference to Rome, are made in the preface to the 2nd edition. I do not, however, accept his evaluation of religion per se as the social binding force.
102 Murray 1991, 6, rejects the suggestion that the models of Durkheim and Weber describe successive Archaic and Classical stages on the grounds that there is no evidence for such an evolutionary scheme. While such *a priori* evolutionary assumptions fall foul of the problems with cultural evolution noted in Chapter 1, this is not the same as suggesting that with hindsight they may best describe the circumstances of two rather different data sets.
103 Ducrey 1995; Snodgrass 1986.
104 Coulton 1976, 26–38 (rightly doubting the identification of eighth-century

stoas beneath the Temple of Apollo at Eretria), see also 215, 217 (Argive Heraion, shrines of Aphrodite and Apollo), 285 (Sparta, cf. Kourinou 2000, 98). The Stoa Basileus in the Classical agora of Athens, with a ceramic date of c.500, is at present the earliest well-dated and obviously civic stoa: Shear 1994, 237–9.
105 Polignac 1995, for example the introduction.
106 Hansen and Fischer Hansen 1994.
107 Gneisz 1990, 316, no. 18; Hansen and Fischer Hansen 1994, 39. Rougemont 1980, 102 for a review of scholarship on the building, noting the lack of direct evidence for its identification or date.
108 Walter 1993, 119; cf. Hansen and Fischer Hansen 1994, 86–9. On the date of the bouleuterion: Coulton 1976, 266.
109 Noting also Olympia's wider role in guaranteeing other (especially western Greek) cities' treaties: e.g. Effenterre and Ruzé 1994, nos 17 (re exiles from Selinous), 42 (c.500, Sybaris and the Serdaioica), 58 (c.500–494, Zancle and a neighbouring city).
110 Kraay 1976, 104
111 Morgan and Coulton 1996, 112–14.
112 Eder and Mitsopoulos-Leon 1999 review the archaeological evidence. For inscriptions, see Siewert 2001; Eder and Mitsopoulos-Leon 1999, 23–4.
113 Roy 1997, although he allows a potentially greater role for Olympia in Elean state politics prior to synoikism than I. I am sympathetic to the suggestion offered by Thomas Heine Nielsen (pers. comm.) that Elis may have found it advantageous to blur the distinction between herself and Olympia (no trivial undertaking since she had not always controlled the sanctuary), and may thus have directed at least some public affairs in such a way as 'Eleanize' perceptions of Olympia.
114 Meiggs and Lewis 1988, no. 2 with discussion and bibliography.
115 Effenterre and Ruzé 1994, no. 98. Minon 1994 includes a review of the border inscriptions.
116 A point shared within the various perspectives taken by: Thomas 1996, 116; Detienne 1988; Davies 1996a; Hölkeskamp 2000.
117 Lenz 1993, 228–31, 257–303.
118 SEG 30.380, 34.296. Thomas 1996, 19–25.
119 Thomas 1996, 16–17, 26–8.
120 The Spartan Great Rhetra thus represents the ultimate in divine insurance: Effenterre and Ruzé 1994, no. 61.
121 Thür and Taeuber 1994, no. 21; Effenterre and Ruzé 1994, no. 57, Jeffery 1990, 222–4, no. 8.
122 In this light one might also consider the often political role played by seers, of whom a number came from ethne (e.g. Tellias of Elis who advised the Phokians during their successful campaign to expel the Thessalians, see p. 132).
123 Hölkeskamp 1992a.
124 Waisglass 1956.
125 Effenterre and Ruzé 1994, no. 56.
126 See Davies 1996a for a recent review.
127 Thür and Taeuber 1994, no. 20.
128 Thür and Taeuber 1994, no. 1 (ANM X8165), both faces of tablet inscribed in

Arkadian script (= Effenterre and Ruzé 1995, nos 59, 60; Taeuber 1987–8, 355–6).
129 Thür and Taeuber 1994, no. 7.
130 Thür and Taeuber 1994, no. 8, Effenterre and Ruzé 1995, no. 2; Taeuber 1987–8, 354–5.
131 Early Thessalian inscriptions have recently been fully treated in the PhD thesis of Dr A. Dougleri Intzesiloglou (Aristotelean University of Thessaloniki), publication of which is awaited.
132 Jeffery 1990, 99, no. 6.
133 Jeffery 1990, 97–8, no. 1,
134 Jeffery 1990, 97, 99, no. 2; Masson 1968.
135 As is the kind of public dedication represented by an inscribed statue base from the Halai acropolis: Jeffery 1990, 108, no. 11.
136 Robinson 1976a, 248–50, fig. 11.
137 Hölkeskamp 1992b also emphasizes the significance of the display of written law in sanctuaries, but treats the shrine and the agora as parallel contexts within poleis and focuses on the interplay between them, whereas I emphasize the potential distinction between the two constituencies. From a different perspective, in her discussion of the *theodorokia*, Perlman 2000, 33, notes that the toponyms listed were not formal civic sub-units at the time of the list's composition; in other words, the decisions of sanctuary authorities concerning appropriate and interested parties did not correspond with local judgements about political status.
138 Effenterre and Ruzé 1994, no. 36.
139 Effenterre and Ruzé 1994, no. 4, although doubt remains over whether the *xenos* here refers to the sanctuary or the state (see nos 37, 38 re Lakedaimonian *proxenoi* of the Eleans).
140 Effenterre and Ruzé 1994, no. 108.
141 For example, Roy and Schofield 1999. Effenterre and Ruzé 1994, nos 21 (Khaladrioi and Deucalion), 51 (Anaitioi and Metapoioi). On the 'alliance' see Siewert 1994.
142 For example, Effenterre and Ruzé 1994, nos 23 (re 'Patrias'), 24 (guarantees for magistracies).
143 For the latter suggestion, see Roy 1997.
144 For reviews with extensive bibliography, see Martin 1985, Ch. 1; Martin 1995 (noting, 275–7, that this circumvents what is for nationalist approaches the problem of those poleis that failed to coin but used other state issues). For analogous reflections on the role of coinage in the Archaic Cyclades, see Sheedy 1997.
145 For a review of the attribution of this issue, often assigned to Aigion, see Kroll 1996, 52 note 14.
146 Their absence from the Asyut hoard (Price and Waggoner 1975) is a useful benchmark.
147 Kraay 1976, 115.
148 Martin 1985, 34–5.
149 Martin 1985, 36–8.
150 Kraay 1976, 115; Martin 1995, 36–7.
151 Kraay 1976, 116 (assigning the Thessalian coins to Pherai); *contra* Franke 1970.

152 Franke 1970, 91–3. Martin 1985, 38, 41–2 (noting also the absence of Thessalian coins from the two known fifth-century Thessalian hoards: *IGCH* 21, near Trikkala, *c*.450–440; *CH* 1.25/5.11, Karditsa/Myrina, *c*.440, both savings hoards).
153 Kraay 1976, 95–6; Williams 1970.
154 Williams 1965; Kraay 1976, 97–101; for a review of chronological arguments, see now Psoma 1999, 82–4.
155 Heine Nielsen 1996b (see 41–2 note 15 for previous rejections of the coinage as evidence for a federal state).
156 Psoma 1999, 85–7; cf. Heine Nielsen 1996b, 51 who notes that the dating of these mints has itself been coloured by the interpretation of the Arkadikon coinage.
157 *IvO* 9: see pp. 47, 60 and note 13 above.
158 Head 1911, 449.
159 Williams 1965, 8–15; *contra* Kraay 1976, 98; Heine Nielsen 1996b, 52–3; Psoma 1999, 83.
160 Head 1911, 444; Heine Nielsen 1996b (a tentative conclusion in an article intended primarily as a critique of the federal thesis). Psoma 1999, 87–91, criticizing the idea of a sanctuary issue rather than city issues pertaining (perhaps in a propagandistic fashion) to the festival.
161 Morgan 1999b, 386, 407–8 for a review.
162 Williams 1965, 18–19.
163 Psoma 1999.
164 Heine Nielsen 1996b, 54–5.
165 Williams 1972, 10–18 for types down to *c*.478; McInerney 1999, 178–9. Kase et al. 1991, 86–8, 112 (Szemler) on the location of Lilaia, which was probably by-passed by the Persians due to its strategic unimportance.
166 Svonoros 1896, 11–12.
167 Archibald 2000.
168 For example Jones 1987, 79–81, also highlighting the late date of much evidence for public magistracies.
169 Archibald 2000; Helly 1991, 32–3; Auda et al. 1990, 113 note 35.
170 As has long been observed, see, for example, Kahrsted 1924.
171 Archibald 2000, 215.
172 Morgan 2001a, 30–4; see also Chapter 4 below.
173 Attested on a mid-sixth-century stele from the precinct of Apollo at Korope: Jeffery 1990, Thessaly cat. 1.
174 Jeffery 1990, Thessaly cat. 2 (*SEG* XVII, 287); Masson 1968.
175 Katakouta and Touphexis, 1994, 198. Published remains of the early city are otherwise mainly burials on the lower slopes below the acropolis: *RE* supp. XII *s.v.* Pharsalos (Béquignon), 1039–46; see also *Ergon* ΥΠΠΟ 1 (1997) 100 (SM/PG, tholos tomb); *Delt* 19 B (1964) 260–1 (Fetihye mosque, three PG cists); *Delt* 20 B (1965) 319 (Archaic tomb); *Delt* 43 B (1988), 271–4 (late sixth- to fifth-century votives from a later domestic context); *Delt* 51 B (1996) 373–9 (Archaic building among mostly Hellenistic finds); *PAE* 1954, 153–9 and *PAE* 1955, 140–9, especially 142–3, pl. 45b (Archaic tholoi, the latter of the late sixth century, within an elite Archaic-Classical cemetery west of the settlement). Further west, three Archaic tombs discovered close to Stavros form

part of the cemetery of an unidentified settlement. *Ergon* ΥΠΠΟ 2 (1998) 112. Publication and restudy of finds from the early excavations (directed by Arvanitopoulos) is badly needed.
176 Béquignon 1932, 90–119: the settlement dates from EH, with continuous activity SM–sixth century, including PG tombs (Verdelis 1958, 3). Despite the apparent prosperity of the site (where finds include the celebrated dinos by Sophilos), it was on present evidence abandoned in the sixth century. The date of the fortification is uncertain.
177 Intzesiloglou 2000.
178 For catalogues, see Brommer 1940 (207–8 for the unprovenanced kouros in Volos Museum); Biesantz 1965, 29; Floren 1987, 322.
179 Ploughing near this village revealed an eclectic collection of 242 artefacts, including a Mycenaean figurine and bronzes of the Geometric and later periods, perhaps from a shrine in the vicinity: *Delt* 43 B (1988) 258.
180 Skiatha: Biesantz 1957, 57, searching for a possible temple to house this piece, noted a large foundation but pottery only from the fifth century. For a review of the latest Archaic-early Classical Thessalian style, see Bakalakis 1973.
181 Biesantz 1965, 31–2. Brommer 1940, 111–13, lists 24 reliefs of the fifth century, of which seven come from the Larisa area; these are most common in, but not confined to, eastern Thessaly (one comes from Palama-Karditsa). Funerary inscriptions are equally rare before the fifth century: Lorenz 1976 lists one (cat. 1, from Spalauthra and Olizon) of the last quarter of the sixth century, and notes (cat. 2) the epitaph of Pyrrhiadas from Kierion, for which the consensus date is the start of the fifth century (although opinions vary from seventh/sixth to the end of the fifth); similarly controversial are his cats 3 (epitaph of Diokleas from Pharsalos) and 4 (*polyandrion* inscription from the foot of Mt. Ossa, which he dates *c*.480/479?).
182 Brommer 1940, pl. 72; Biesantz 1965, 31 cat. 43. The earliest examples of smaller-scale work are the sixth-century terracotta relief pinakes from the shrine of the Nymphs at Koukouvaia west of Pharsalos:
183 Ridgway 1993, 403 note 9.12, 410–11 note 9.30.
184 Biesantz 1965, 31, cat. 44.
185 Corinth: Bookidis 1995; see also Bookidis 2000 for discussion (with previous bibliography) of aspects of the larger terracotta corpus, much of which was exported.
186 Evidence is summarized in Morgan 1999b, 426 *et passim*.
187 Gallis 1992, while focused on prehistoric settlement in eastern Thessaly includes details of later finds on prehistoric sites. Surveys in individual city territories include: Halos: Efstathiou et al. 1990. Pharsalos: Béquignon 1932. Pherai: Salvatore 1994. Gonnoi: Helly 1973, 51–4, 72–4.
188 The following sites are located around the acropolis of Krannon and in the neighbouring area: *Delt* 38 B (1983) 204–8 (Girlenia); *Delt* 25 B (1970) 279–82 (Sarmanitsa, two Geometric vessels in fill of later tumulus). Gallis 1992, *s.v.* Kambos 2 and Krannon 3.
189 Tziaphalias 1994b, 153–4.
190 Milojcic 1960, 173–4; Tziaphalias 1995, 69–76. The EIA pit grave cemetery discovered at Pineias during the widening of the road between Larisa and Trikala may be related: *Ergon* ΥΠΠΟ 1 (1997) 101.

191 *BCH* 55 (1931) chronique, 493; Béquignon 1932, 121–91.
192 Desborough 1964, 133–4; Milojcic 1955, 192–4, fig. 15; Milojcic 1957; Kilian 1975a, 3.
193 Tziaphalias 1994b for a systematic review of evidence (155 and fig. 2 for Geometric house); Gallis 1992 *s.v.* Larisa I (Phrourio). *Delt* 31 B (1976) 184; *Delt* 34 B (1979) 221; *Delt* 35 B (1980) 287–8; *Delt* 42 B (1987) 289 reports PG and G pottery in the collection of Anna Angelidou of Larisa. Desborough 1952, 133, notes a pendant semi-circle skyphos. The central *plateia* of the modern city is a likely candidate for the later Eleuthere Agora and probably the gymnasium, but further investigation to locate the early agora is needed. While generally in agreement with Helly 1987, I differ from his interpretation of evidence from Larisa (p. 154), which relies too heavily on the lack of evidence from the Ag. Achilleas acropolis and does not take into account the loose structuring of most Early Iron Age settlements.
194 Located on Od. Giorgios B' 36–8: *Delt* 34 B (1979) 221.
195 Tziaphalias 1994b, 155; Rakatsanis and Tziafalias 1997, 13–15.
196 A point echoed in the analysis of Helly 1987, who argues for a relatively late date for the construction of the city's territory (cf. Helly 1984) which he describes as determined by pre-existing constraints.
197 Helly 1984.
198 *Delt* 38 B (1983) 204–8. Tziaphalias and Zaouri 1999, 144, 146–8, fig. 2, noting that the Kastri burials are inhumations.
199 Sarmanitsa: *Delt* 25 B (1970) 279–82. Ag. Georgios: Tziaphalias 1994a, 179.
200 Gallis 1992, *s.v.* Krannon 3.
201 Tziafalias 1990 and 1994a; Morgan 2001a, 32–4.
202 *Delt* 47 B (1992) 229–34, 237 fig. 8; *Delt* 48 B (1993) 239–40; Malakasioti 1997a. Further evidence from this site will be presented in the proceedings of the 1998 Volos conference (*1η Επιστημονική Συνάντηση γιά το Εργο των Εφορειών Αρχαιοτήτων της Θεσσαλίας*).
203 Chasambali: Theochari 1962, 44–7. Marmariani: *Delt* 39 B (1984) 151; Heurtley and Skeat 1930–1. Bunar Baschi: Kilian 1976, 69–71; Helly 1984, 220, noting also Archaic and later occupation. For a general review of Thessalian tholoi, see Arachoviti 1994, 134–7 (adding a further PG example from Koutsames in the area of Argyroupoli: *Delt* 51 B [1996] 372–3).
204 Platykambos: Theochari 1966, 37–47. Mesorachi: Tziaphalias and Zaouri 1999, 145–6; *Delt* 38 B (1983) 203–4.
205 Helly 1984 (his model would give a maximum distance of 8 km from centre to periphery and the hypothetical extent of the territory thus defined coincides with an area of rich alluvial soil); see also Helly 1987, 131.
206 For a review of research, see Dougleri Intzesiloglou 1994, 71–3.
207 *RE* Supp.VII, *s.v.* Pherai (E. Kirsten); Béquignon 1937a. The following summary is based on the detailed accounts offered by: Apostolopoulou Kakavoyianni 1992; Dougleri Intzesiloglou 1990 and 1994; *Delt* 46 B (1991) 211–16; *Delt* 45 B (1990) 201–3; *Delt* 44 B (1989) 219–20; *Delt* 43 B (1988) 243–9; *Delt* 42 B (1987) 255–61; *Delt* 40 B (1985) 191–3; *Delt* 39 B (1984) 144; *Delt* 38 B (1983) 193–5; *Delt* 37 B (1982) 221; *Delt* 36 B (1981) 249; *Delt* 35 B (1980) 269; *Delt* 32 B (1977) 123–4; *Ergon ΥΠΠΟ* 1 (1997) 92.

208 Aerinos: *AR* 1998–9, 69; *Ergon* ΥΠΠΟ 1 (1997) 93, PG tholos (containing inhumations) within a Mycenaean (tholos and chamber tomb) cemetery, plus a separate Geometric-Classical and Roman cemetery. Compare the results of survey in these areas: Salvatore 1994, 112, table 1.
209 Kakavoyiannis 1977; Apostolopoulou Kakavoyianni 1979; Dougleri Intzesiloglou 1994, 76–7, figs 1 and 2.
210 Dougleri Intzesiloglou 1994, 78.
211 Béquignon 1937a, 43–7; Salvatore 1982.
212 Kalligas 1992, 300, fig. 1.
213 At least some of the many small bronzes from the area of Velestino which lack precise provenance could have been grave offerings rather than votives, but the lack of such finds in context is suggestive (see also the related discussion in Chapter 3, pp. 137–8).
214 *Ergon* ΥΠΠΟ 1 (1997) 92.
215 Arachoviti 1994; *Ergon* ΥΠΠΟ 3 (1999) 118. Pyre pit: *Ergon* ΥΠΠΟ 1 (1997) 92; *Delt* 51 B (1996) 342–4.
216 Adrymi (Sismani) 1983; Dougleri Intzesiloglou 1994, 78–9 (see note 44).
217 Apostolopoulou Kakavoyianni 1992, 319, pl. 74a (BE 1703).
218 Apostolopoulou Kakavoyianni 1992, 318.
219 See Intzesiloglou 1994 for a review with bibliography.
220 Arachoviti 1994, 134; *PAE* 1965, 7–8; Theochari 1966, 50, fig. 18.
221 Marzolff 1980, 22, commenting on Desborough's (1952, 133, 153) note of two Protogeometric vessels published by Apostolides 1912, 36, fig. 2, pl. VIII (who reports that they were collected by him in this area: cf. Tsountas in *PAE* 1957, 55). I exclude here the more remote sites on the east coast of the Pelion peninsula, i.e. Theotokou (PG/G tombs: Wace and Droop 1906–7) and Lestiani (Geometric tholoi: *PAE* 1911, 292–4, listed as Geometric by Arachoviti 1994, 135, fig. 2).
222 Ninth- to eighth-century tombs from Sesklo: Tsountas 1908, 115–16; *PAE* 1911, 294–300, between the prehistoric acropolis and the site of Pyrgos, extensive traces of numerous small tholoi extending up to Dimini of which five were excavated.
223 Milojcic 1955, cols. 221–31; *Delt* 16 B (1960) 194. New evidence from excavations preparatory to the re-establishment of Lake Karla will be published in the proceedings of the 1998 Volos conference (*1η Επιστημονική Συνάντηση γιά το Έργο των Εφορειών Αρχαιοτήτων της Θεσσαλίας*).
224 Melies: *PAE* 1906, 125–6; *PAE* 1910, 226. Argolasti: *PAE* 1910, 221. Both sites noted as Geometric by Arachoviti 1994, 135, fig. 13.
225 Papahatzis 1960; see note 173 above for sixth-century inscription.
226 Theocharis 1959, 37, 40 (noting the presence of Mycenaean sherds to LHIIIB, see pp. 60–4, but adding that post-prehistoric remains were not systematically investigated during that campaign); *Delt* 16 B (1960) 170; *Delt* 42 B (1987) 255.
227 *PAE* 1907, 166–9; *PAE* 1908, 176, 193; Desborough 1952, 133.
228 *Delt* 48 B (1993), 236–7.
229 See note 187 above; Wace and Thompson 1911–12; Dyer and Haagsma 1993.
230 See Feuer 1983, 1992 and 1994 for reviews of data and arguments (with previous bibliography); Halstead 1977, 23; Mountjoy 1999, 822–4.

231 I discount here Petra, the date of which remains unclear: Bintliff 1977a, 62.
232 See Malakasioti 1994 (cf. Adrymi 1994b, 17–19) for a review of research (p. 53 on the plan of Theocharis' 'palace' and the nature of the destruction). Reports of Theocharis' campaigns: *PAE* 1956, 126–7; *PAE* 1957, 54–69; *PAE* 1960, 49–59; *PAE* 1961, 45–54.
233 Adrymi 1994a and 1994b; *Delt* 51 B (1996) 330–1. Kiln: Adrymi 1999.
234 Batziou-Eustathiou 1992; Batziou-Eustathiou 1994, 60–5 with previous bibliography. Late Bronze Age finds from the German campaigns at Pefkakia Magoula are noted by Milojcic 1972, 65–6, with full publication planned in *Pevkakia* IV.
235 Adrymi 1994b, 36–8. A full account of Mycenaean Dimini is given in Dr Adrymi Sismani's PhD thesis (Aristotelean University of Thessaloniki); she identifies an anaktoron, although as yet no archive has been discovered.
236 Halstead 1977, esp. figs 3, 9–11; explored further by Feuer 1983, 41–7. Long term development is summarized by Gallis 1992, 226–40; Halstead 1994.
237 See also Mountjoy 1999, 819, 822–4.
238 Adrymi 1994b, 41; Intzesiloglou 1994. On coastline change, see Kambouroglou 1994.
239 See Malakasioti 1994 for a summary. PG pottery and associated stratigraphy: Sipsie-Eschbach 1991, although on SM see Mountjoy 1999, 826 and note 109 (*contra* Sipsie-Eschbach 1991, 185–90), 856–7. Transitional period burials: Batziou-Efstathiou 1999. Crop storage: Jones 1982.
240 *PAE* 1960, pl. 35; see Papadopoulos 1994a, 494–5 for a review in the context of EIA potters' marks.
241 Malakasioti 1994, 52; Theochari 1966, 47–53; *Delt* 18 B (1963) 140–1; *Delt* 36 B (1981) 252; *Delt* 37 B (1982) 225–6; *Delt* 38 B (1983) 197; *Delt* 39 B (1984) 140–2; *Delt* 42 B (1987) 254.
242 Paspalia: *AE* 1914, 14; *PAE* 1909, 159–62; Arachoviti 1994, 134. Kapakli 2: *AE* 1915, 157–9; *AE* 1914, 141; Coldstream 1968, 161–3, placing the later material from the tholos contemporary with Attic MG and LG. Od Kolokotroni: *Delt* 48 B (1993) 231–2.
243 Corvisier 1991, 29–41; an approach also criticized by Helly 1995, 79.
244 As also emphasized from a slightly different standpoint by Helly 1995, 76–9.
245 Kirk 1985, 48. Helly 1995, 74–5 takes a similar view with explicit reference to Thessaly.
246 See Crielaard 1995 for a review of scholarship; Dickie 1995, 36–8, argues for a seventh-century date for the *Catalogue*.
247 Willcock 1978, 205, although I reject his view that its reflects a 'pre-Dorian' world, as does Kirk 1985, 178–9, and Anderson 1995 (who describes it as an eighth-century Boiotian composition).
248 Kirk 1985, 48–9, 168–70.
249 See most recently Anderson 1995.
250 Hence, for example, Corvisier's (1991, 139–43) argument that it reflects a fundamentally 'pre-Thessalian' situation (dating the arrival of the Thessalians to the mid-twelfth century).
251 Morgan 1999a, 349–50.
252 Corvisier 1991, 39.
253 Corvisier 1991, 41, 142–3. Helly 1995, 78–9 note 25, takes the absence of the

Thessalians as evidence for the relative dates of the *Catalogue* and the settlement of Thessalians on the plain.
254 This is not the Larisa later mentioned as 'deep-soiled' (*Iliad* 2.841; 17.301), which should probably be located in the Troad: Kirk 1985, 257.
255 Corvisier 1991, 142–3.
256 On problems surrounding these ethnics, see Kirk 1985, 229; Willcock 1978, 211.
257 Cf. Helly 1995, 76–8.
258 *Contra* Auda et al. 1990, 103–4, who date the *Catalogue* to the Late Bronze Age, not least to accommodate their view of the ninth–seventh centuries as a key phase in the emergence of city territories.
259 Chiefly due to the work of the CNRS Thessaly team based at Lyon, reviewed by Auda et al. 1990; Helly 1994; see also Bakhuizen 1994.
260 Helly 1991, 35–43, cf. Helly 1995, 79–96; Auda et al. 1990 for case studies. Many of these issues are raised in the case of Larisa by Helly 1984.
261 Auda et al. 1990, 112–14.
262 Helly 1995, 86–93.
263 Morgan 2001a, 31.

3 Communities of cult

1 Demakopoulou 1982: Felsch 1999; Jacob-Felsch 1996, esp. 102–5; Eder 2001a; Moschonissioti 1998; Morgan 1999a, Ch. III.2.
2 Among extensive literature, see for example, Lebessi 1981; Hayden 1991.
3 On the mainland, what is at present exceptional evidence for the post-Bronze Age continuation of the uplifted arm gesture consists of three handmade figurines in Tomb LVIII at Elateia (associated with a probably PG burial, the figurines could be as early as LHIIIC or as late as PG): Alram-Stern 1999, 216–20.
4 The status of Mycenaean pottery from the sanctuary of Athena Alea at Tegea, especially that from the bottom of the *bothros* deposit which contains large quantities of PG and G material, has yet to be evaluated: Voyatzis 1999, 131–2, 143. The situation at Philia is equally complicated: Pilali-Papasteriou and Papaeuthimiou-Papanthimiou 1983. Excavation of a very small (and in places disturbed) area has revealed a few LHIIIB sherds and figurines chiefly in the lowest level (IV) where they were mixed with PG-Roman sherds (thus the building remains related to this level, characterized by Theocharis as Mycenaean, are not securely datable). Mycenaean finds have been regarded as the earliest sanctuary evidence (which is plausible, although given the limited extent of excavation, it is unclear whether proper evaluation is yet possible). Nonetheless, the question of the longevity of LHIIIB in this area (both in terms of the style per se and the use of particular objects), and thus the absolute date of the shrine's establishment, remains problematic.
5 These issues have been most fully considered in the case of Olympia: Eder 2001a; Morgan forthcoming a. For a preliminary notice of a study by Paul Halstead and Valasia Isaakidou indicating the practice of burnt animal sacrifice in the palace at Pylos, see *Nestor* 28(4) (2001), 3354.
6 Sourvinou Inwood 1988; Sourvinou Inwood 1995, 18–32.

7 Notably (among extensive literature): Snodgrass 1980, 33–4, 52–65; Polignac 1995; *contra* Sourvinou-Inwood 1993.
8 Morgan 1999a, 369–72.
9 In central Greece, the possible exception is Thermon: see note 178 below. Further north, in Chalkidike, see Mende-Poseidi Building Στ: Moschonissioti 1998, 265–7.
10 Set out fully by Mazarakis Ainian 1997, 270–6, 287–357.
11 Tegea: Østby et al. 1994, 98–103; Østby 1997. Asine: Wells 1988 and 1990. Ano Mazaraki: Petropoulos 1996–7 and forthcoming. Kalapodi: Felsch et al. 1987, 11, fig. 3. Mazarakis Ainian 1997, 137–8.
12 Daverio Rocchi 1993, 108, Beloch 1890, 557; Francotte 1907, 101, 150. Cf. Gernet 1982, 29–82, for the view that religious festivals were primitive meetings for local groups (phratries?). A more nuanced and cautious approach to the problem is taken by Parker 1998, appendix.
13 Morgan 1997; Morgan 1999a, 379–86, 389–91; Eder 2001b.
14 Morgan 1999a, 315–38, 373–9, 386–9, 392–429.
15 Stroud 1968, with previous bibliography.
16 Morgan 1994.
17 Morgan 1998b.
18 In addition to the general remarks in Morgan 1994, see for Perachora: Menadier 1995, section II. Solygeia: Verdelis 1962, 184–92; Lorandou-Papantoniou 1999, 23–36. Corinth: Pfaff 1999, 119–20; Bookidis and Stroud 1997, 15–17. Isthmia Rachi: Anderson-Stojanovic 2001.
19 For instance, Osborne 1996, 97–8.
20 Morgan 1999a, 293–4, 336.
21 Morgan 1999a, 291–3.
22 Rolley 1992a, 41–3; Morgan 1999a 326–8, 405–6, with bibliography.
23 Pfaff 1999, 113–15.
24 Calligas 1992 (although I follow the views of Demakopoulou and Cartledge amongst others on the history of the shrine before the late ninth century: Morgan 1999a, 296, 382–4, 390; Demakopoulou 1982; Cartledge 1979, 79–100); Cartledge 1992.
25 For example, Arkadia: Jost 1990; 1994. The polis-centred, but more nuanced critique offered by Malkin 1994 is also relevant.
26 See Morgan 1997 for a preliminary review of these issues.
27 McInerney 2001, 63–7.
28 Morgan 1990, Chs 4, 5 (see note 60 below for more recent studies).
29 Sourvinou-Inwood 1990; McInerney 1999, 62–6.
30 *RE* IX, *s.v.* Hyampolis (F. Bölte); McInerney 1999, 288–9.
31 Ellinger 1993; McInerney 1999, 102–9, 165–78.
32 Principal preliminary reports: Felsch 1981, 1983, 1991 and 1999; Felsch et al. 1987; Felsch et al. 1980. Summary history and topographical discussion: Ellinger 1993, 22–32.
33 Ellinger 1993, 34–6. Polignac 1995, 28–30, acknowledging changes in material form and practices at the shrine as evidence for shift in its role. The origin of the notion of rural rallying points is to be found in Gernet 1982, 21–61.
34 Morgan 1997, 175–9.
35 See note 37 below; Hope Simpson 1981, 78–81; Felsch 1981, 81–2; Dasios

1992. Smixi: *Delt* 34 B (1979) 186; *Delt* 51 B (1996) 316–17. Pictorial: Dakoronia 1987; Felsch et al. 1987, figs 50 and 51.

36 Dakoronia 1992b and 1993b; Jalkotzy and Dakoronia 1990; Jalkotzy 1999a.

37 Amphikleia: *Delt* 25 B (1970) 237–40; *Delt* 26 B (1971) 231–2; *Delt* 50 B (1995) 342–3. Modi: *Delt* 44 B (1989) 173–5; *Delt* 45 B (1990) 175–6; *Delt* 46 B (1991) 193; *Delt* 48 B (1993) 206; *Delt* 50 B (1995) 343–4. Elateia: *Delt* 40 B (1985) 171; *Delt* 41 B (1986) 65–78; *Delt* 42 B (1987) 231–4; *Delt* 44 B (1989) 175–7; *Delt* 45 B (1990) 183–4; *Delt* 46 B (1991) 196–8; *Delt* 47 B (1992) 207; Dakoronia 1992b; Dakoronia 1993b. Zeli: *Delt* 32 B (1977) 104; *Delt* 33 B (1978) 139; *Delt* 34 B (1979) 186; *Delt* 35 B (1980) 240–2; *Delt* 37 B (1982) 189; *Delt* 40 B (1985) 171–3; *Delt* 46 B (1991) 193–4. Exarchos (Vrysi-Sykia): *Delt* 33 B (1978) 140–1. Golemi: *Delt* 40 B (1985) 169–70; *Delt* 41 B (1986) 68; *Delt* 42 B (1987) 234; *Delt* 43 B (1988) 223–4; *Delt* 44 B (1989) 170–1; *Delt* 51 B (1996) 322–3. Agnandi: *Delt* 25 B (1970) 235–7. Pyrgos: *Delt* 48 B (1993) 218–19; *Delt* 47 B (1992) 208–11; *Delt* 46 B (1991) 194–5; *Delt* 45 B (1990) 177–8; *Delt* 44 B (1989) 171–2; *Delt* 43 B (1988) 223–4; *Delt* 42 B (1987) 234; *Delt* 41 B (1986) 68–9; *Delt* 40 B (1985) 173–4; *Delt* 34 B (1979) 186–7; Dakoronia 1993a, 125–6 (noting also *Delt* 50 B (1995) 338–9). Schachermeyr 1980, 319–22. Figured pottery: Mountjoy 1999, fig. 325, nos. 27, 28. The association of pictorial from Kynos and Kalapodi is conjectural pending the results of fabric analysis.

38 *AR* 1982–3, 32. Kroll 1993, focusing on LHIIIC-MG levels and noting (table 3) a marked reduction in the range of species thereafter (especially during the eighth and seventh centuries). As Kroll notes, the LHIIIC plant and seed record is best paralleled at northern Greek farming sites such as Assiros Toumba and Kastanas: his detailed analysis of the representation of both cultivated and wild plants rests largely on a thick, burnt MPG-LPG layer close to the temple, which also contained large storage vessels. As he argues, such pithoi and plant remains must have served a ritual purpose, although it is impossible to discriminate between possible explanations for the fact that they were not burnt as offerings (perhaps being a distinct form of offering or stored provision for sacral meals).

39 Felsch 1999, 166–9; Stanzel 1991, 153–67, tables 48–50; Ellinger 1993, 27, 33.

40 Morris 1990; as she points out, there is a close conceptual link between sacrifice, hunting, feasting and masculine status. See also Mountjoy 1999, fig. 325, no. 28 for a hunt scene on an LHIIIC Middle krater from Kalapodi.

41 Felsch 2001 (reviewing the persona of Artemis as represented in the votive record).

42 Felsch 1999, 165–6 (summarizing evidence to be published by Felsch, Schmitt and Prange in *Kalapodi* II).

43 Dakoronia 1992a; Felsch et al. Schuler 1980, 54.

44 Felsch et al. 1987, figs 55 and 56; I am grateful to Dr Dakoronia and Prof. Jalkotzy for showing me some of the pottery from the Elateia cemetery.

45 Felsch et al. 1980, 46–7; Felsch 1981; Felsch et al. 1987, 3–5, 26–40.

46 Modi (Ag. Athanasios): *Delt* 47 B (1992) 200–1, 212 (LPG, noting also an Archaic pithos burial *c*.2 km NW of Modi); *Delt* 48 B (1993) 205–6 (LPG). Agnandi: *Delt* 25 B (1970) 235–7. Amphikleia: Dasios 1992, site 12; there are no reports of PG here. From west of the village of Kalapodi comes a chance find of an LPG child burial in a cist tomb: *Delt* 42 B (1987) 234–5.

47 *Delt* 29 B (1973–4) 582–3; *Delt* 34 B (1979) 193–4; *Delt* 43 B (1988) 233; *Delt* 36 B (1981) 221–2; *Delt* 48 B (1993) 210–11; Paris 1892 for limited investigations on the acropolis and at the Temple of Athena Kranaia *c*.3 km south-east of the city, where the earliest ceramic and bronze finds are Late Geometric (284–6, 292–5).
48 Tragana: Onasoglou 1981; *Delt* 41 B (1986) 74; *Delt* 38 B (1983) 157; sherd scatter 1.5 km north of Tragana village, on the Mitro peninsula, Fossey 1990a, 50–1. Atalante: *Delt* 42 B (1987) 226–8; Dakoronia 1993a, 19–20; Fossey 1990a, 68–74. Veryki Megaplatanou: *Delt* 39 B (1984) 135–6. See Stiros and Rondogianni 1985; Stiros and Dakoronia 1989, 428–32 for tectonic activity and coastline change in the Atalante area.
49 Megaplatonos: *Delt* 36 B (1981) 221; *Delt* 33 B (1978) 140; Dakoronia 1993a, 123–4; Fossey 1990a, 79–80. Fossey 1990a, 22–6 (Kastri), 33–5 (Martinon), 44–5 (Khiliadou, ancient Boumeliteia). Kyparissi: *Delt* 34 B (1979) 187; *Delt* 33 B (1978) 139–40; Fossey 1990a, 62–5; Blegen 1926; Dakoronia 1993a, 117–19; Dakoronia 1990, 175–80. Halai: Goldman 1940; Goldman and Jones 1942; Coleman 1992; Goldman 1930; *Delt* 42 B (1987) 228–31; *Delt* 44 B (1989) 178–83. As Dakoronia (1993a) emphasizes, many of the eight Lokrian cities mentioned in the *Catalogue of Ships* (*Iliad* 2.531–3) remain to be found.
50 Onasoglou 1981, for example 15–23 (36–8 on pendant semi-circle skyphoi, 47–51 on phialai).
51 Parallel strands in myth-history may reflect aspects of this process. Strabo (9.425) preserves a tradition whereby the settlement of East Lokris was attributed to Phokian expansion northwards from Elateia towards Daphnous. By contrast, the Lokrian king lists emphasize local (specifically Opountian) toponyms, and a tradition of a border dispute between the Hyampolitans and their Lokrian neighbours is reported in scholia to the *Iliad* (Erbse 1969, at *Iliad* 2.517b) and Euripides' *Orestes* (Schwartz 1891, at *Orestes* 1094): Oldfather 1908, 411–72; Fossey 1990a, 7.
52 Felsch et al. 1980, 47–63; Felsch et al. 1987, 5–13. For a summary of the building sequence, see Mazarakis Ainian 1997, 137–40.
53 Kearsley 1989, 35; Felsch et al. 1980, 48 (comparison with Lefkandi); Felsch et al. 1987, 41–9 (A. Nitsche); Felsch 1983, figs 9 and 10 illustrates a local oinochoe and a Thapsos krater (for which he adduces parallels at Delphi).
54 Felsch et al. 1980, 65; Stanzel 1991, table 48.
55 Felsch et al. 1980, 54–63; Felsch 1983; Felsch et al. 1987, figs 13–19.
56 Felsch 1983, 123–4; Risberg 1992, 36, 39–40. Cf. Philia: Kilian 1983. Itinerant production: Morgan 1990, 35–47. For evidence of a sanctuary workshop within a settlement, see Huber 1991.
57 Morgan 2001a, *passim*.
58 Compare Felsch 1998 who emphasizes similarities (chiefly in Archaic building programmes) between north and south.
59 Müller 1992 (475–86 on cult); as she notes, the figurines cited as evidence of cult in the Marmaria, which were regrouped in the Archaic period, may have come from local tombs. On interconnections in the area of the Corinthian gulf during this period, see Eder forthcoming.
60 Delphi: Lerat 1961, figs 40 and 41; *BCH* 117 (1993) 619–31; see also *BCH*

116 (1992) 694–8 (eighth-century). Rolley forthcoming, offers an overview of recent research.
61 Felsch 1981, 84 compares certain pithoi, for example. Pendent semi-circle skyphoi: Kearsley 1989, 25–8, 35.
62 Vatin 1969; Morgan 1990, 118–26: much of this extensive site, including the acropolis, remains to be explored.
63 Such as jugs with cut-away necks: for example, Vatin 1969, fig. 72 (LG).
64 Snodgrass 1971, 85, figs 42–4; Vatin 1969, fig. 59; Morgan 1986, 27–8 suggesting an Ithakan origin.
65 Salmon 1984, 82–4. Otranto: D'Andria 1995.
66 Morgan 1990, 125–6.
67 Themelis 1983a, 219, 221; Vatin 1969, 29–30, fig. 27; Morgan 1990, 123–4.
68 Antonaccio 1997, 133–5.
69 Themelis 1983a, 221–2; among the earliest finds see fig. 8 for a local LG krater from cist grave 12. For activity in the area, see Dasios 1992, sites 100–5.
70 See note 60 above; Neeft 1981, 59–65, fig. 15.
71 Rolley forthcoming.
72 Jacquemin 1993, 217–18; de la Coste Messelière 1969, 730–40, fig. 1.
73 Jacquemin 1993, 222–3.
74 Comparable problems surround the date of the first temple of Athena, whose cult has been linked to the role of an amphictyony at Delphi: Jacquemin 1993, 221–2; Sordi 1958, 41.
75 Laroche and Nenna 1993, 228 note at least eleven limestone treasury foundations securely datable between 600 and 548, with a further twelve from the period 548–500.
76 Jacquemin 1993, 224–5.
77 Herrmann 1972.
78 Felsch 1983.
79 Rolley 1969, *passim*; Perdrizet 1908, Pt. 2. It is important to note the disagreement, acknowledged and discussed by Rolley, over the origin (Peloponnesian or northern Greek) of some forms, notably bird figurines. Since style is the only basis for judgement here, it is impossible to trace the origin of every figurine; nonetheless, this cannot account for overall differences in assemblages.
80 Rolley 1977, Boiotian cats 267–8, 271; Amandry 1987 for seventh-century and later tripods. Kalapodi: Felsch et al. 1980, 60–2, figs 33–5.
81 Amandry 1944–5; Italian imports: Rolley 1969, cat. 118; Kilian 1977. Perachora: Kilian-Dirlmeier 1985, 225–30; Kilian-Dirlmeier 1985–6. Corinthian Gulf: Morgan 1998a, 290–2.
82 Perdrizet 1908, 133–40; Amandry 1938, 317–31; Amandry 1944–5, 36–7, 52–5; Lerat 1961. For the presence at Delphi of the impressed pottery of Aigion, see Morgan and Hall 1996, 178 and note 70; Gadolou forthcoming reviews the ceramic repertoire of Ano Mazaraki noting parallels from Delphi.
83 Davies 1994; as he notes, the trend to literal reading dates back to Busolt 1893, 698–700. See also Sanchez 2001, 58–73; McInerney 1999, 165–72, 310–12; Lehmann 1980; Robertson 1978; Morgan 1990, 135–6. Forrest 1956 highlights similarities with alliances attested for the Lelantine war. Following decades of French research in the area, the Pleistos valley has also been the subject of close attention by the Archaeological Service: Skorda 1992 (45 on

Submycenaean evidence from Ag. Giorgios Chryso, 42–3 on Kirrha, where the largest body of post-Bronze Age evidence dates from the second half of the sixth century, as do the earliest votives at the shrine of an unknown deity: Luce 1992). A peribolos (among a large number of walls) at Ag. Varvara, between Delphi and the modern village of Chryso, has been partially excavated and may date soon after 700 (on the basis of associated pottery); it may have delimited some form of religious structure. The site, which seems to have been a substantial settlement, has been tentatively identified with Krisa: Skorda 1992, 50–3, 62–5; Skorda 1998–9, 16–17; *Delt* 49 B (1994) 319–20. Both Gla and Moulki have produced Late Archaic and Classical pottery after a post-prehistoric gap (Themelis 1983a, 223–4), but there are no convincing alternative Geometric sites in this area.

84 McInerney 1999, 168.
85 A point recalled in my previous remark (Morgan 1990, 135) that if the first sacred war did not happen, it would be necessary to invent it.
86 *CID* I.I, 9; Effenterre and Ruzé 1994, no. 71; McInerney 1999, 106–7. See also Effenterre and Ruzé 1994, no. 72, *c*.500, which refers to the presentation of accounts by fifty of the Labyades presided over by Thrasymachos and I[ami]adas during the archonship of Trichas.
87 Morgan 1990, 144–5, Robertson 1978, 49–50; Davies 1994, 203, noting that the last lines of the *Hymn*, with the warning to the Cretan priests, may have been an addendum (relevant especially if the *Hymn* predated a real sacred war). It is also possible to see the institution of the Pythian games in a similar light: Mosshammer 1982.
88 Jacquemin 1993. Peribolos: *BCH* 116 (1992), 693–4.
89 Morgan 1990, 134–7; Sanchez 2001, 58–60, for a review of scholarship focusing on inter-state political interests.
90 Morgan 1990, 144–6.
91 McInerney 1998, 91–108.
92 Cemetery: Themelis 1983a, 232–7; Threpsiades 1972; Morgan 1990, appendix 3. A fortified settlement of the same period (LG onwards) lies on the acropolis of Ag. Athanasios: Baziotopoulou and Valavanis 1993, 198–207. The twenty-eight locations given in the much later inscription, *SIG* 2.III.826–7, constitute the principal evidence for the area of the sacred precinct; see also Rousset 1991 on the division between sacred and public land in this area. For a review for later, chiefly epigraphical, evidence for exploitation of the plain, see Isager 1992, 16–17.
93 Jacquemin 1993.
94 Laroche and Nenna 1993; E. Hansen 2000, 205, 208–10; C. Hayward pers. comm. (drawing on his continuing study of the quarrying, usage and export of Corinthian limestone).
95 *Antre Corycien* I; *Antre Corycien* II. In addition, a dedication to Athena and Hera found at the site of Mycenaean Krisa, dating *c*.600–550 (and perhaps not Phokian) implies a shrine somewhere in the area: Jeffery 1990, 103 no. 1; a bronze votive wheel bearing a dedicatory inscription of Phalas to Apollo in (Opountian) Lokrian script is said to come from Galaxidi: Jeffery 1990, 108 no. 17.
96 *Antre Corycien* II, 262–3, fig. 2 no. 2 (Corinthianizing horse, dated by Rolley

c.720–700, i.e. later than its Corinthian prototypes of *c*.720), fig. 3 no. 3 (bird dated to the seventh century by Rolley on the basis of Spartan prototypes), 263, fig.7 no. 7 (northern Greek/Balkan style ring with bird, second half eighth century, also paralleled at Tegea), 268–9, fig. 10 no. 21 (fibula akin to Phrygian style, eighth–sixth century).

97 *Antre Corycien* II, 29–30, 92 (pottery), 397 (figurines), 183–90 (rings). Themelis 1983a, 222–3 suggests that at least some of the handmade pottery thought to be prehistoric could be Geometric on analogy with finds from Delphi and Medeon, but there are no securely dated imports of this period.

98 *Antre Corycien* II, 377.

99 *Antre Corycien* II, 272, fig. 21 no. 50, 273–4, 277, figs 25, 26 no. 53 (sixth-century gold disc, Archaic bronze repoussé strips).

100 See *Antre Corycien* I, ch. II for a review of literary testimonia.

101 *Antre Corycien* II, 309–10, cat.7, fig. 4, 310–14, cat.8, figs 5 and 6.

102 Cf. Theopompos *FrGHist* 115f., 168; Hyp. *Epit*.18; Harp. *Pylai*. Sordi 1958, 32–58, for a hypothetical reconstruction of the role of, and relationship between, the two forms of amphictyony. Bürgel 1877 for a review of literary sources. The sanctuary of Demeter at Thermopylae has not been precisely located: Béquignon 1937b, 181–204; Thalmann 1980.

103 Parke and Wormell 1956, CVol. 1, 101–5; Sanchez 2001, 32–41.

104 Jacquemin 1993, 218–19.

105 Gadolou 2001; Kelly 1966.

106 Parke and Wormell 1956, 101–3; cf. Sanchez 2001, 32–7.

107 Robertson 1978, 39; Morgan 1990, 148–90, for discussion of the likely role of the oracle in eighth- and seventh-century decision-making.

108 Plutarch *Moralia*, 492 a-b; Parke and Wormell, 1956, 102. Maurizio 1995, 80 note 70, on the tenuous nature of evidence for cleromancy at Delphi.

109 Sordi 1958, 65–8, 71–2; Helly 1995, 118–24. The case against an early federal authority is discussed in Chapter 2 above.

110 Pausanias 10.8.5 (statue group of Achilles and Patroclos); Daux 1936, 141, 192 notes the absence of material remains; Jacquemin 1999, 51–2.

111 Ridgway 1990, 46–50, for a review of scholarship; Jacquemin 1999, 51–2 noting that the monument is now restored within a *lesche* or treasury-like construction (cf. Bommelaer and Laroche 1991, 200–1).

112 See also Pindar *Paean* 8.58–99 (Snell 1964, fragt. 52i).

113 Sourvinou Inwood 1979 (although her early temple sequence and parallels with Eretria should now be rejected). The cult of Neoptolemos may also be viewed in this light, although as Defradas notes, the treatment of the hero reveals an attitude to Thessaly which seems at best equivocal: Defradas 1954, 146–56.

114 Axenidos 1947, Ch. 3; Robertson 1978, 64–5, suggests that Eurylochos was mentioned (or his importance inflated) to flatter one of Philip II's senior generals of the same name.

115 See, for example, Larsen 1968, 12–13.

116 See, for example, Sordi 1979. I am grateful to J.K. Davies (pers. comm.) for a reminder that evidence such as the use of the term *tagos* in the Labyadai inscription (see note 86 above), and the fact that reference to the boys' *theoria* may may be traced back to Ephoros confirms that any later aggrandizement of myth-history did not occur *ex nihilo*.

117 Felsch et al. 1980, 63–7; Felsch et al. 1987, 13–19; Felsch 1991, 86.
118 *Contra* Ellinger 1993, 33–4. Single cities elsewhere were responsible for larger building programmes, and it is salutary to compare, for example, evidence from Corfu (Ridgway 1993, 276–81) with its six pedimental groups over sixty years in the sixth century), and the Cyclades (Gruben 1988; Gruben 1993; Berranger 1992, 239–45 for Paros).
119 Felsch et al. 1980, 66; Felsch et al. 1987, 54.
120 Ellinger 1993, 34. Isthmia: Gebhard and Hemans 1998, 6–10.
121 The principal accounts are: Herodotos 8.27–8; Plutarch *Moralia* 244b-e; Pausanias 10.1. For full discussion and conflicting analyses of the sources, see Ellinger 1993; Pritchett 1996, ch. II. The term 'Phokian National Saga' was coined by Burn 1960, 204.
122 Ellinger 1993, 18–20 for a review of scholarship on the date. As Ellinger emphasizes (21, citing, most importantly, Brelich 1961, 46–52), the historicity of the events described is less important than the place they came to hold in Thessalian consciousness.
123 Ellinger 1993, 32, citing information from the excavator, Rainer Felsch.
124 Felsch et al. 1980, 67–8, 78–85, 112–14; Felsch et al. 1987, 19–25, 54–5.
125 McInerney 1997.
126 Vanderpool 1964; French and Vanderpool 1963. Ellinger 1987, 98. See also the summary critique by McInerney 1991.
127 Ellinger 1993, 25–6 for review of scholarship.
128 Morgan 1997, 175–84.
129 Ioakimidou 1995, 34–6, 135–43. On the oracular consultation which predicted the Phokian victory, see Pausanias 10.1.4; Parke and Wormell 1956, cat. 68.
130 Ioakimidou 1995, 34–6, 135–43; she also places the second Phokian group early (*c*.480), closer to the end of the Thessalian occupation (37–47, 143–8).
131 Citing unpublished observations by Anne Jacquemin, Ellinger 1993, 234–5, reports that the probable base blocks of two of these monuments date to the late fourth or early third century. Keramopoullos 1907; cf. Daux 1936, 136–40, 144–7.
132 Bourguet 1898, 321.
133 Dasios 1992, sites 51, 90, 100, 115 (site 66, Distomo, has a Naue II type sword which could date anywhere from LHIIIB Geometric); Vatin 1969, 59–68.
134 Site information taken from Dasios 1992 (see also Baziotopoulou and Valavanis 1993, 198–207).
135 Amphikleia: *BCH* 78 (1954) chronique, 132–3: Polydroso (Souvala): Arapogianni-Mazokopaki 1982.
136 Paris 1892, 73–118, 139–77, 257–98. Felsch et al. 1980, 57 for comparison with Paris 1892, 286 no. 8. For the earliest roof elements: Winter 1993, 143 note 29, 202–3 (dating them *c*.500–480).
137 McInerney 1999, 269: *Delt* 27 B (1972) 384–8 (cf. *Delt* 50 B (1995) 357); Themelis 1983a, 226–8.
138 Yorke 1896, 298–302; his identification of this shrine with the reknowned oracle of Apollo was rightly rejected by Philippson 1951, 716–17, and more recently by Felsch et al. 1980, 39, and Ellinger 1993, 25.
139 For a systematic review of the cult, see Chrysostomou 1998 (esp. 24–43, and

noting, 48–50, Enodia's inclusion on the Altar of the Twelve Gods at Pherai); Kraus 1960, 77–83.
140 Béquignon 1937a, 50–5; Kalligas 1992, 300, fig.1, for putative tumulus; Chrysostomou 1998, 35–8. The existence of the late sixth-century temple is attested only by *spolia* (including Corinthian tiles, sima fragments and column capitals) beneath the *krepis* of its successor built *c*.300, perhaps on the same site: Béquignon 1937a, 43–55 (who accepted an earlier attribution of the temple to Zeus Thaulios); Østby 1990; Østby 1992, 86–8; Østby 1994. Frieze fragments: *PAE* 1924, 108; *PAE* 1925, 41; Chrysostomou 1998, 38–41.
141 Morgan 1997, 170; Béquignon 1937a, 87–8, no. 52 noting (50 note 4) as a parallel the way in which the Pompeion covered and protected graves in the Athenian Kerameikos (although the function of the Pompeion was different and the time gap longer).
142 Apostolopoulou Kakavoyianni 1990. Chrysostomou 1998, 43–7 favours Demeter on the basis of a figurine dedication, however as Maria Stamatopoulou points out (pers. comm.), a further figurine of a bearded mature male could represent Zeus Meilichios: since the evidence is slight, neither possibility can be discounted. A further, probably Classical, shrine exists in the north cemetery: Chrysostomou 1998, 47–8.
143 There is no evidence for the small wooden makeshift *naos* suggested by Arvanitopoulos, *PAE* 1925, 41; Chrysostomou 1998, 38.
144 Béquignon 1937a, 57–74; Chrysostomou 1998, 36–7.
145 Béquignon 1937a, 57–74, dating the south *favissa* to the fifth century; Kilian 1975a, 6–8, noting the presence of fourth-century material in both deposits, with a link to the second temple.
146 Kilian 1975a, 170; Dougleri Intzesiloglou 1994, 78; Desborough 1952, 133. A comparable situation is found at, for example, the Argive Heraion: for recent views see Strøm 1988, 174–6; cf. Antonaccio 1992, 90. A similar case of dedication of retrieved Mycenaean material at a later shrine is found in the sanctuary of Athena Pronoia at Delphi: see note 59 above.
147 Béquignon 1937a, 70, pl. XXI, 1 (*protome*), 57–66 (figurines). Dougleri Intzesiloglou 1994, 78 notes the difficulty of identifying Archaic Thessalian pottery.
148 Morgan 1997, 171–2.
149 Béquignon 1937a, 67–72; Kilian 1975a, 168–87; Kilian-Dirlmeier 1985, 216–25; Blinkenberg 1962, esp. 110–28; Kilian-Dirlmeier 1979, *passim*.
150 Kilian 1975a, 8–10, 168–9. As Kilian 1975b, 105–6 points out, a wholly cultic explanation is invalidated by their popularity elsewhere in Thessaly, but shared imagery is a different argument. The only other shrines yet to show the same pattern, again in smaller numbers, are distant Emborio and Lindos.
151 Apostolopoulou Kakavoyianni 1992, 313–17; *Delt* 43 B (1988) 247–9; *Delt* 42 B (1987) 256–8.
152 Chrysostomou 1998, 178–82.
153 Béquignon 1964, 400–12, esp. the Archaic cats. 1 and 2 (=Jeffery 1990, 436–4, nos. 13a [ANM 15.448, *c*.450–25], 15 [ANM 15.446, late fifth-century]).

154 Chrysostomou 1998, 35–6 defines the shrine as international in the sense that not all goods derive from local workshops. Kilian 1973 suggested that many small bronzes may have been dedicated by seasonally migrant pastoralists, noting Macedonian stylistic connections; at present this hypothesis is impossible to test, although the peculiarities of the Pherai cult and shrine may imply primarily local interest. Archaic metalworking at Pherai: Dougleri Intzesiloglou 1994, 78, fig. 8.
155 Kilian-Dirlmeier 1985, 216–25. Chrysostomou 1998, 36 note 46, raises the possibility that this reflects commercial exchange at the festival. I dissent from Klaus Kilian's suggestion (1975a, 186) of a 'regional' role by analogy with Tegea, Sparta, the Argive Heraion and Dodona, as the votive record of Dodona is wholly different, and in the other cases, 'region' must surely be defined as city territory, the role suggested here.
156 The shrine is located in the vicinity of a PG and G cemetery on the hill of Ag. Paraskevi between the church (the former Fetihye mosque) and the spring of Apidanos. Votives are mostly Hellenistic, but architectural debris, tumbled down the slope and reused in the mosque, includes Archaic–early Classical Doric capitals. As at Pherai, the cult of Zeus Thaulios is attested here, but the suggestion that Enodia may also have been worshipped is plausible if unproven. The presence of tombs on and around the acropolis dating from PG is interesting, although there is nothing to indicate cult as early as that at Pherai; Chrysostomou 1998, 60–2; *Delt* 19 B (1964) 261. For architectural terracottas, see Winter 1993, 195–201.
157 Chrysostomou 1998, 53–4 (noting similarities with three bases from Phthiotic Thebes dedicated to Enodia); *IG* IX. 2.575.
158 Dakoronia 2001.
159 Chrysostomou 1998, 58 note 156. See Chrysostomou 1998, 59–60, on the cult of the related Zeus Thaulios and Zeus Tritodios in the west cemetery of Atrax, where Enodia is hypothetically associated by virtue of the shrine location and the presence of a deity with whom she is frequently linked.
160 Chrysostomou 1998, figs 1 and 5.
161 Chrysostomou 1998, 70, Pella 1977/1. Chrysostomou 1998, 120–4, in arguing for Enodia, summarizes the various readings proposed by Lilibaki Akamati, Mastrokostas, Sacco and J. and L. Robert.
162 Wilamowitz Möllendorff 1931, 173–8, treated Enodia as a 'pre-Thessalian' deity, but his argument rests on her 'chthonic' character and the dating of the entry of the Thessalians implied by Thucydides 1.12 and Herodotos 7.176. As argued above, material evidence is insufficient to support cult continuity from the Bronze Age at Pherai. Chrysostomou 1998, 97–103, for review of contrary views.
163 Snodgrass 1989–90. Chrysostomou 1998, 97.
164 Chrysostomou 1998, 104–33 (epithets of Enodia), 187–267 (ties with pantheon), 236–43 (Zeus Thaulios).
165 Morgan 1997, 173.
166 Phthiotic Thebes: *PAE* 1907, 166–9, reports Geometric and Archaic sherds plus many small bronzes (circlets, birds, fibulae, rings and small vessels) found below a Classical temple (to Athena?) on the acropolis above Mikrothivai; *Delt* 49 B (1994) 323–4, reports renewed study of the acropolis and the discovery of an Archaic (sixth-century) *apothetes* deposit. Antonaccio 1995a, 136–7,

considers possible instances of tomb cult at Pteleon and Pharsalos, but the evidence implies tomb reuse rather than cult.
167 Philia: *Delt* 43 B (1988) 256–7: *Delt* 22 B (1967) 295–6; *Delt* 20 B (1965) 311–13; *Delt* 19 B (1964) 244–9; *Delt* 18 B (1963) 135–8; Kilian 1983; Kilian 1975a, 8–10; Kilian 1975b, 105–6; Katarachias and Karafyllis 1992. Pilali-Papasteriou and Papaeuthimiou-Papanthimiou 1983, argue for Mycenaean cult on the basis of sherds, figurines and an orthogonal structure, described as a cult building, dated to this period chiefly by its stratification beneath the ash layer which contains most LG bronzes. As they acknowledge, only a very small area around this structure has been excavated and the stratigraphy is disturbed; systematic evaluation is therefore difficult, and the interpretation hard to test. Athena Itonia: Papahatzis 1981, 36; Papahatzis 1992; Bearzot 1982.
168 The relatively early date of spit dedication is striking: the summary of sanctuary evidence given in Haarer 2000, app. B1 table 2, shows the Philia spits to be the earliest reasonably securely dated dedications on the mainland, in the wider Greek world predated only by evidence from Kition (the mid-eighth-century? date given for Perachora rests on an insecure ceramic date for the start of the so-called Akraia deposit).
169 Kilian 1983, 145–6; Risberg 1992, 36–7, sets this within the wider context of sanctuary metalworking.
170 I stress 'extant', since an excavation of this period may well have overlooked sacrificial and dining debris, assuming that the relevant area was investigated – the long-held assumption of a lack of early pottery at Olympia is salutary (Eder 2001a).
171 Chrysostomou 1998, 48–9; Bakalakis 1973, noting the statue as a pre-Pheidian Promachos type. Altar of the Six Goddesses: Miller 1974.
172 Athena Itonia: Papahatzis 1981 and 1992. Note also the two Subgeometric warrior figurines found elsewhere in the territory of Metropolis (Biesantz 1965, 33, cats 78 and 79), and the funerary stele of the warrior Pyrrhiadas from Kierion (Lorenz 1976, cat. 2) who died in an unknown campaign defending his land; the consensus of opinion on the date (not undisputed) would place it at the start of the fifth century, making it one of the earliest epitaphs so far recovered.
173 Intzesiloglou 2000 and 2002; *Delt* 49 B (1994) 310–33; *Delt* 51 B (1996) 347–8.
174 For a review, see Marzolff 1994, 261–2. Kamila: Mazarakis Ainian 1997, 136–7 with bibliography. Gonnoi: *c*.650–600, apsidal temple on the acropolis, rebuilt on the same plan in the fourth or third century: Helly 1973, 72–4 (who describes the temple at Omolion as similar and near contemporary); Drerup 1969, 30. Dendra (Otzaki Magoula); mid-sixth-century relief fragment: Brommer 1940, 110–11; Biesantz 1965, 117 (fifth-century inscription, Franke 1956, 190–1). Proerna: *Delt* 21 B (1966) 250–1 (Demeter sanctuary, end sixth–early fifth-century 'stoa'?); *Delt* 19 B (1964) 263 (Archaic kore head). Ambelia Pharsalou: Daffa-Nikonanou 1973, 27–8. Amphanes: Milojcic 1974, 65–75; Pharsalos, note also the end sixth/early fifth-century Demeter votive deposit with a stele in Hellenistic house A, at the crossroads of Od. Athinas and Chondropoulou: *Delt* 43 B (1988) 271–4. Koukouvaia: Levi 1923–4, 27–42. Ktouri: *BCH* 55 (1931) chronique, 493; Béquignon 1932, 95–101. Korope:

Papahatzis 1960 (although the elongated ground plan illustrated seems closer to a stoa, and may be a different building); Stillwell et al. 1976 *s.v.* Korope (T.S. MacKay) queries the identification as a temple. Marzolff 1994, 261. Intzesiloglou 2000 and 2002 for an Archaic bronze cult statue of Apollo from ancient Metropolis. Literary references to Thessalian temples; Papahatzis 1959. On possible early Demeter shrines, Daffa-Nikonanou 1973, 261–3.

175 Notably by Eric Østby in his studies of the Pherai temple (1990, 1992 and 1994).
176 Cf. Classical Thessaly: Marzolff 1994, 262. For such links in Archaic Macedonia: Vokotopoulou 1993.
177 At present the striking (if still controversial) Cycladic case is the more or less continuous use of the 'temple' at Ag. Irini, Kea: see Caskey 1981 for a review of the evidence (arguing additionally for continuity in the nature of the cult).
178 Mazarakis Ainian 1997, 125–35; Papapostolou 1990 (see also his subsequent reports in *PAE* 1993, 180–92; *PAE* 1996, 173–209; *PAE* 1998, 129–39; *Ergon* 1999, 61–5).
179 Moschonissioti 1998, 265–7; Mazarakis Ainian 1997, 43–4.
180 Viviers 1994, 244–9.
181 Watrous 1998; Carter 1997, 86–97 (although those parts of her argument which rest on Beyer's reconstruction of the sculptural scheme of Temple A should be tempered by Watrous' critique of this scheme).
182 Mazarakis Ainian 1997, Ch. V offers the most systematic review with full bibliography.
183 Sinn 1992; Isager 1992; Dillon 1997.
184 Romano 1988.
185 Mazarakis Ainian 1988; Mazarakis Ainian 1997, Ch. V.
186 The Aetos sequence is reappraised in Symeonoglou 2002, Ch. 1: I am grateful to her for discussion and permission to summarize her conclusions in Morgan 2001b, 224.
187 Davies 2001b offers analogous reflections in considering the management of the monetary assets of sanctuaries during the Classical period.
188 Demakopoulou 1982, pls 25, 26.
189 Amyklaion: Rolley 1992b, fig. 97. Mantineia: illustrated in Spyropoulos 1991, penultimate page (text unpaginated).
190 Fully reviewed by Donohue 1988.
191 Muss 1999; forthcoming.
192 Mattusch 1988, 176–80; Lapatin 2001, 42–60, for a review of EIA and Archaic ivory work (both extant and as reported in literary sources), noting the sixth-century *floruit* of cult imagery.
193 For a review of key monuments and the processes of artistic innovation and adaptation involved, see Croissant forthcoming.
194 Morgan 1999b, 428 (citing the observations of Dr C. Hayward). Classical Bassai: Papantonopoulos 1995, 203–25; Cooper 1996, 98–107, 115–17, 144–5.
195 Broneer 1971, 33–4.
196 Morgan 2001b, 226, for a review of scholarship. Menadier 1995, 77–8, 93–8, 116–17, 157–8, notes difficulties both with a Geometric date for the supposed first temple of Hera (which Payne regarded as a structure similar to that

represented by votive architectural models), and with the closing date and integrity of Payne's Geometric Deposit within which these models were found.
197 Robinson 1976a, 239–52; Robinson 1976b, 203–35. Robin Rhodes is currently studying the architecture of the first temple (Rhodes forthcoming; see *American School of Classical Studies at Athens Newsletter* 45 [2001], 14, for his proposed reconstruction).
198 See Gebhard 1998 for a full account of the data here considered.
199 Gebhard 1998, 97, 102; Rostoker and Gebhard 1980 (noting that while such scrap is not confined to the temple area, it is largely concentrated in deposits, for example, of fire debris, that can be traced back in some way to the temple); Gebhard and Hemans 1998, 19.
200 See Morgan forthcoming a for a summary review with bibliography; Eder 2001a; Felsch 1999 (see also Jacob-Felsch 1996, 1–213, esp. 102–5 on pottery and cult); Moschonissioti 1998, 265–7. I thank Birgitta Eder for sight of her manuscript on the Olympia EIA pottery which is to appear in an *Olympische Forschungen* volume on the Pelopion excavations. Bone and seed debris is most striking at Kalapodi: see notes 38, 39 and 54 above.
201 Eder 2001a and 2001b; Kyrieleis forthcoming. Pylos bone: see note 5 above.
202 Forstenpointner 1990.
203 *IG* V2, 3.28.
204 Lindenlauf 2001, chs III.2, IV.2.
205 Risberg 1992. As Haarer 2000, 118–19 notes, caution is required in distinguishing what is produced at these workshops from what is present as scrap for the forge.
206 Williams 1978; Bookidis and Stroud 1997 (see Ch. 15 for summary); Anderson-Stojanovic 2001.
207 Kilian-Dirlmeier 1985, 225–30; Kilian-Dirlmeier 1985–6.
208 Bookidis et al. 1999. Perachora: Tomlinson 1977 and 1992; Menadier 1995, 117–20.
209 Morgan 2001b and n.d. I thank Nancy Symeonoglou, Bruno d'Agostino and Mariassunta Cuozzo for discussion of finds from Ithaka, Kephallenia and the area of the bay of Naples. On the Kandyliotis Group potters' marks from Ithaka, certain of which appear on vessels previously considered Corinthian: *PAE* 1992, 294 (I thank Nancy Symeonoglou for sight of this material).
210 D'Andria 1995, 476–7, fig. 13 (I thank Prof. d'Andria for showing me the Otranto material); Whitbread 1995, 3–7.
211 Pemberton 1996 and 1999.
212 Pemberton 2000.
213 Hayward 1996, 1999 and forthcoming a. Hayward's continuing work on this and other aspects of the Corinthian stone industry is to form a volume in the *Corinth* series: I thank him for permission to refer to it here.
214 Rostoker and Gebhard 1981 (on clay, see 226–7); Whitbread 1995, 293–300, table 5.2, 311–12, 324–9, 339–40.
215 Morgan 1995; Morgan 1999c, 217–34; here, as elsewhere, I am indebted to Ian Whitbread for numerous discussions of the problems of Corinthian ceramic production.
216 Rostoker and Gebhard 1981, 224–6.

217 An observation made independently in Hayward forthcoming a.
218 Brookes 1981, 286–9, noting that these blocks were damaged by fire before completion and therefore discarded.
219 Davies 2001a offers analogous reflections over a longer time-perspective in assessing building at Delphi.
220 Dillon 1997.
221 Westover 1999.
222 Lindenlauf 2001. Treatment of weapons at sanctuaries: Morgan 2001a, 27 with bibliography.
223 Strøm 1992; Strøm 1995, esp. 85–92.
224 Polignac 1998, 147–9, 157–8.
225 Andrews 1994, 52–8.
226 Andrews 1994, 110, 117–20.
227 Gebhard 1998, 97; Linders 1989–90.
228 Andrews 1994, 42 note 44, 48–9, 151–8, citing Maass 1978, 130–3, and Heilmeyer 1979, 35.
229 A point echoed by Herrmann 1972, 76–7.
230 Andrews 1994, 158–92.
231 Morgan and Coulton 1997, 99–103 with bibliography; see also Mazarakis Ainian 1998, 202–3.
232 Østby 1995c, 306 note 467; Spyropoulos 1993, 258 (reporting Archaic finds from excavations around Episkopi). The unpublished field report of the 1999–2000 season of the Norwegian Arcadia Survey notes the discovery via georadar of a previously unknown temple *c*.600m west of the agora; while this is undated, the discovery of a Doric capital of the second half of the sixth century *c*.150m north of the agora confirms the existence of a monumental Archaic public building. I am grateful to the Director of the Survey, Prof. Knut Ødegard, for access to this report and for the observation that the Survey's fieldwork to date (1998–2000) which has focused on the central part of the ancient territory of Tegea, including the city site, indicates that the earliest material in any quantity from the city seems to date from the latter half of the sixth century: survey of the southern part of the territory is scheduled for 2002.
233 Metalworking: Østby et al. 1994, 103–4. 'Banking': see Chapter 2 note 128 above. Commodity movement: Kilian-Dirlmeier 1979, 40–1 suggests that stamp pendants (as Voyatzis 1990, 177–83) may have marked a limited range of commodities, although clearly their role in relation to the actions of their dedicators and/or the shrine per se is open to a variety of interpretations.
234 Pallantion: Iozzo 1995; Iozzo and Pagano 1995; Østby 1995a-c; Østby 1999b, 397–400. Asea: Forsén and Forsén 1997; Forsén et al. 1999; Morgan 1999b, 400–3 (I am grateful for Jeannette and Björn Forsén for invaluable discussion of Asean questions *in situ* in the summer of 2000, and for showing me material from their excavations at Ag. Ilias Kantrevas).
235 Jost 1994.
236 Østby 1995c; Forsén et al. 1999, 170–7.
237 Roy 1999; Pikoulas 1999.
238 Knauss 1988; Iozzo 1995, 394–5 (on Stesichoros, see note 832). While the

historicity of the Stesichoros story is, of course, open to severe doubt, the report is accepted by Bowra 1961, 118.
239 Bergquist 1990.
240 Østby 1995a, 54–63; Østby 1995c, 288–90.
241 Østby 1995a, 63–9; Østby 1995c, 291–4.
242 Østby 1995a, 69–88; Østby 1995b; Østby 1995c, 294–9.
243 Østby 1995a, 88–93.
244 Østby 1995c, 286–8; Morgan 1999b, 427–8.
245 Morgan 1999b, 400–2 for a summary with bibliography.
246 Forsén and Forsén 1997, 171; Forsén 1998.
247 Rhomaios 1957, 117–26. Relief (Tegea 1605): Rhomaios 1957, 144–6, fig. 35: Raftopoulou 1993, 1–6, fig. 2 (cf. Mycenae, Athens NM 2869: Klein 1997, 285–8).
248 Rhomaios 1957, 126–63; Østby 1995c, 338–50. Sparta: Dawkins 1929, 21–2, pl. 5.
249 Hagemo: Ridgway 1993, 184; de la Genière 1993, 156; Pikoulas 1988, 58, site 10, note 151. Tripolis 3092: Spyropoulos 1993, 257–8, figs 1–2 (see Pikoulas 1988, note 1 on context); Ridgway 1993, 205 note 5.8; de la Genière 1993, 156 (rejecting an identification with Meter).
250 Forsén et al. 1999, 177–82.
251 Forsén et al. 1999, 185.
252 Heine Nielsen 1999; Morgan 1999b, esp. 425–32.
253 Hübinger 1992 and 1993; Jost 1975 and pers. comm.
254 Orlandos 1967–8, 53–9 identifies two building phases; Østby 1995c, 364–81, argues that all extant remains belong to an early fifth-century structure apart from two fragments of antefix and acrogeison of c.550.
255 On evidence for, and the diachronic development of, an overarching concept of Arkadianness, compare Morgan 1999b with Heine Nielsen 1999, and see Heine Nielsen 2002, esp. Ch. II.
256 Jost 1985 *passim* on local deities and heros (see 532–8 on major hero cults, notably that of Herakles, attested at Tegea in Archaic times by *IG* V2, 95).
257 Freyer-Schauenburg 1974, 106–7, cats 58–63, pls 44–53, 73.
258 Effenterre and Ruzé 1994, no. 69.
259 Ibid. no. 70, with previous bibliography.

4 Territory, power and the ancestors

1 See for example Thomas 1979.
2 See for example Attema 1999.
3 Demand 1990, 7–8.
4 Demand 1990, Ch. 2.
5 Instances where her conclusions should be challenged, as Andros town, reflect what may be one of a number of emerging trajectories in the Cyclades and neighbouring islands, with no implications for the mainland: Reger 1997, 468–71 (especially 469). Compare the fate of the short-lived settlement (c.625–575) at Vroulia on Rhodes: Kinch 1914.
6 Little and Papadopoulos 1998.

7 Coldstream 1996, 139, for example, highlights five burials according to Athenian custom in the Toumba cemetery at Lefkandi.
8 As the diversity of approaches to the Early Iron Age Athenian mortuary record highlights: compare Morris 1987, Pt. 2; Whitley 1991, esp. Chs 3–5; Tarlas 1994, introduction and Pt. 3.
9 Snodgrass 1999, 26–7.
10 But only relative: Mountjoy 1999, introduction (interestingly, she defines eleven regions for analysis).
11 Hägg 1998b.
12 Morgan and Whitelaw 1991.
13 Theocharis 1968; Batziou-Eustathiou 1984.
14 Coldstream 1968, 148–63.
15 Johnston 1999.
16 Jeffery 1990, 221–4, 230–1, 248–62.
17 Coldstream 1968, 2 ; Coldstream 1983.
18 Snodgrass 1999, 28–31.
19 Coldstream 1983, 20–5.
20 Morgan 1999c, 239–41, noting that while the images themselves may be borrowed (initially from the Dipylon style), the syntax within which they are used is distinctive and foreshadows Benson's (1995) reading of Archaic narrative.
21 Morgan 1999c, 241–4.
22 Snodgrass 1980, 25–28; *contra* Crone 1986, note 110; Morgan 1999c, 214–15.
23 Dietler and Herbich 1998; van der Leeuw 1999; cf. Papadopoulos 1997, who stresses above all the role of travelling craftsmen. For a pioneering study of the issues raised by a kiln group, see: Whitbread et al. 1997.
24 For a review, see Cherry 1987.
25 Decourt and Darmezin 1999; Helly 1995, 91–3.
26 Papadimitriou 1998; Verdelis et al. 1975.
27 Klein 1997.
28 Mersch 1997; compare Osborne 1985, Ch. 2.
29 Barth 1970; Cohen 1994.
30 Ehrenberg 1969, 3–25.
31 Snodgrass 1980, 26–7.
32 Daverio Rocchi 1993, 108–11.
33 This is not to deny that piracy was undertaken from regions at some stage constituted as ethne, but there is no evidence that it was a staple activity, nor that the communities which supported it did so *qua* ethne rather than *qua* poleis: Thucydides 2.32, for example, reports pirates sailing against Euboia from Opous (which is attested as a polis) and other parts of Lokris.
34 Dimini: Adrymi 1994b, 38. Iolkos: Jones 1982. Arkadia: Roy 1999, 328–9 (the preliminary report on analysis of pollen cores from Tegea conducted by the Botany Department of the University of Bergen and cited by Roy as Bjune 1997 is no longer posted on the internet).
35 See for example Roy 1967, 302–6; Roy 1972c.
36 Following the definition offered by Cherry 1988, 8 (see also 26–30).
37 McInerney 1999, 92–108.
38 Roy 1999, 331, 344–6; see p. 161 here above.
39 Roy 1999, 321, 349–56.

40 For reviews, see Cherry 1988; Hodkinson 1988.
41 Hodkinson 1988, 51–3; Daverio Rocchi 1988, 220–5. On the second-century adjudication between Hermione and Epidauros, see Jameson et al. 1994, appendix F.
42 Whitehouse and Wilkins 1989.
43 Roy 1999; see also Jameson 1989, and Horden and Purcell 2000, 80–2, for more general reviews.
44 Antonaccio 1994, 81–6. Green and Perlman 1985; Trinkhaus 1984, although concerned with imperial systems, also discusses internal boundaries. On the nature of later city boundaries and marginal territory: Daverio Rocchi 1988, 25–40. Sartre 1979.
45 Bintliff 1977b, 116–17; as he points out, this may result in unexpectedly rich and varied material assemblages in ostensibly remote places.
46 The link between water management of various forms and internal and external power relations is reviewed by Horden and Purcell 2000, 244–55.
47 Auda et al. 1990, 118–22; Helly 1984, 231–2, tentatively supports a Hellenistic date for the events described by Strabo.
48 Hodkinson and Hodkinson 1981, 266–8. See also Ch. 1, note 172.
49 Salowey 1994; Salowey 1995, Pt. II (see also 25–35 on Arkadia).
50 Pikoulas 1999.
51 Østby et al. 1994, 103–4.
52 Purcell 1999 (abstract only; I here refer to the full oral version of this conference paper, and thank Nicholas Purcell for subsequent discussion).
53 Gell 1985 (accepting his critique of the concept of mental maps): see Knapp and Ashmore 1999 for a review of scholarship on such topics. That the landscapes experienced and created by individuals or interest groups within a society are not neutral, but contexts for the constant exercise of, and challenge to, social power has been emphasized from a variety of perspectives by a number of authors, including: Bender 1995; contributors to Bender and Winer 1991; Tilley 1994, 12–27. From a more practical perspective, Foxhall (pers. comm., and argued in her unpublished 'Cultures, landscapes and identities in the Mediterranean world') emphasizes the impact of labour constraints in structuring units of agricultural land holding, with wider implications for approaches to spatial division of other kinds. I will not here deal with the conceptualization of physical marginality (i.e. the *eschatia*) in early sources, since my focus is on the practicalities of landscape ordering. While Plato (*Laws* 8.842E-843A) uses the term *eschatia* in the physical sense of land adjoining a boundary, in early usage, as Casevitz 1995 shows, it generally implies moral separation as conveyed through physical distance, the *eschatia* being the place where a civilized individual would not normally wish to be.
54 Bradley 1993, Chs 3, 4, emphasizes the role of monuments in articulating experience and perception of landscape, and the potential for revision of their role over time. Tegea (*c.*1.5 km east of Parthenion): *Delt* 24 B (1969), 130, pl. 119 (Tripolis Museum 2980).
55 Pikoulas 1995, 105–9.
56 Jacob 1991, Ch. 1.
57 Jacob 1991, Ch. 2; Kahn 1960, 82–4. For a further illustration of the conceptual distinction between the space of language and sequential experience

and the visual space which underpins modern approaches to cartography, see Herodotos 5.49–50. Aristogoras of Miletos, in seeking to persuade Kleomenes of Sparta to join the Ionian struggle against Persia, used a bronze map of the world to reinforce his verbal description of the peoples and riches Kleomenes would encounter. As Hartog observes (1988, 361–2), the map was a kind of wonder designed to cloud the issue by giving visual support to the verbal rhetoric, but Kleomenes was not fooled, and his question in reply (how many days' march from the sea were required) is couched in the conventional terms of practical experience.

58 Herman 1987, appendix A.
59 McInerney 1999, 8–9.
60 For a review of literary and epigraphical evidence and past scholarship, see Moggi 1976.
61 For a summary of viewpoints, see Demand 1990, 14–15 with notes 1–3.
62 For a full treatment (upon which I rely heavily here), see Clarke 1999, Ch. 5.
63 Demand 1990, Ch. 2. Cavanagh 1991, 105–10 is only slightly more optimistic.
64 Hägg 1982, 298; Pièrart 1991, 139.
65 Snodgrass 1987–9; Bintliff and Snodgrass 1988. On a wider renaissance in sixth-century Boiotia: Schachter 1989.
66 Whitelaw 1998, 230–3.
67 Moggi 1991.
68 Moggi 1991, 58–62.
69 Pikoulas 1988, 15–17, 229–30 (*et passim* for Archaic finds); Morgan 1999d. A similar pattern is evident in the results of the Pheneos survey, where Geometric was identified on one site (Erath 1999, 235), and the Norwegian Arkadia Survey, although the area south of Tegea where Geometric finds have previously been made is scheduled for survey in 2002 (K. Ødegard pers. comm.). The Asea Valley Survey produced no Early Iron Age finds, although one should note the nature of the material (mainly tile and badly worn pottery which is generally hard to date) and a problem of soil erosion and redeposition: Forsén et al. 1996, 85, 89; Forsén and Forsén 1997, 166, 173 (171 for possibly Geometric sherds at a sanctuary site). The wider problem of visibility and resulting impressions of an underpopulated early Greece are discussed by Bintliff n.d. (I thank Prof. Bintliff for access to this paper and discussion of these issues).
70 Morgan 1999d, note 32 lists five widely scattered burial sites (excluding those in Azania: Dekoulakou 1982, 228–34) with an unknown number of tombs. Sparta: Raftopoulou 1996–7. The problem of dating is well illustrated by the kind of evidence present even at a well-known site such as Classical Mantineia: Hodkinson and Hodkinson 1981, 291–6.
71 The evidence is assembled in Morgan 1999b, see for example 390, 392, 394, 400, 403 (and 403–6 on south-central Arkadia). Only part of the extensive Asea acropolis has been excavated, with research focused on prehistoric remains, and in many places, Hellenistic structures are cut into prehistoric levels: Holmberg 1944, 7, 112–13, pl. V. Survey of this acropolis has filled many chronological and spatial gaps, but without EIA finds: Forsén and Forsén 1997, 166. Megalopolis: Pikoulas 1988, 229–30; Morgan 1999b, 403–6. Megalopolis Survey: J. Roy pers. comm.
72 Jost 1986.

73 Heine Nielsen 1996c, 290–8.
74 For reviews of the successive periods, see: Morgan 1999b (set out geographically); Jost 1999 (set out by site type).
75 See Heine Nielsen 2002, Ch. V, on securely attested and inferred Archaic poleis.
76 Heine Nielsen 1999, 49–51; Morgan 1999b, for example 403–6; Roy 2000.
77 Compare Heine Nielsen 1996a and Roy 1996.
78 See for example Moggi 1976, 131–9 (Tegea), 140–56 (Mantineia); Hodkinson and Hodkinson 1981, 260–1, 287–91; Demand 1990, 61–2, 65–72. In the case of Mantineia, the terms in which Xenophon (*Hell.* 5.2.1–7) describes the dioikism of 385 may, as Thomas Heine Nielsen points out to me, offer indirect evidence of earlier synoikistic thinking.
79 Karagiorga Stathakopoulou 1989 and 1992–3, noting that this was given over to cult from the late eighth century onwards, and that it remained an important cult site throughout our period and beyond. See Morgan 1999b, 389–92 for a review of evidence.
80 Jost 1986, 155–6; Jost 1985, 132–42.
81 Jost 1986, 156–7; Hodkinson and Hodkinson 1981, 248–52.
82 One might, for example, suggest that the development of much of the Megalopolis area before synoikism comes close to Bintliff and Snodgrass' model B: Pikoulas 1988, 229–32. Achaia: Petropoulos 1991; Petropoulos and Rizakis 1994; Morgan and Hall 1996, 181–6, 189–93, 231.
83 I leave aside the much-cited case of Epirus, since current reappraisal of the ceramic sequence (aiming to refine EIA chronology) and the settlement pattern, including many new data, notably from excavations connected with the Egnatia Odos construction project, should change the picture considerably (according to PhD research conducted by Giorgos Papaioannou of King's College London).
84 Dakoronia 1994.
85 See note 88 below.
86 Petropoulos and Rizakis 1994, 195–7. The evidence is summarized in Morgan and Hall 1996, 181–6, to which add *AD* 48 B (1993) 116 (two Geometric pithos burials at Aguia).
87 Petropoulos 1991, 254; *Delt* 26 B (1971) 185–6; Dekoulakou 1973.
88 For the Patras area, see Petropoulos and Rizakis 1994, 192, 194–8; Petropoulos 1991. For comparison, eighth- to sixth-century evidence from Achaia as a whole is surveyed by Morgan and Hall 1996, 169–93.
89 Morgan 1999a, 349–50.
90 Papadopoulos 1979, 28–32, 44–6, 174; Petropoulos 1990, 504–5; Kolonas 1996–7, 477–9, 483–5. Recently discovered Mycenaean evidence from western Achaia as a whole is reviewed by Moschos forthcoming.
91 *Delt* 19 B (1964) 186.
92 Patras: Petropoulos and Rizakis 1994, 197. Western Achaia: Rizakis 1992, 67–8.
93 Ag. Giorgios: *PAE* 1956, 195–6, pl. 89b (see also pl. 90a). Ai-Lias: *Delt* 46 B (1991) 157.
94 Examples of undated and disputed cases are listed by Morgan and Hall 1996, note 149.
95 For example *PAE* 1930, 85; *PAE* 1952, 401 note 1.
96 Morgan and Hall 1996, 176 and note 59.

97 Starochori: *Delt* 39 B (1984) 103–4; *Delt* 42 B (1987) 163. Fteri: *PAE* 1956, 196–7.
98 28 km: *PAE* 1952, 400–12. Kamini: *Delt* 19 B (1964) 186.
99 *PAE* 1956, 197–201 (on the opposite slope from the pithos burials).
100 *Delt* 17 B (1961–2) 129, pl. 153b.
101 *PAE* 1929, 89–91; *PAE* 1930, 83–5.
102 *PAE* 1957, 117; *Ergon* 1957, 69–70. On chronology, compare Moschos 2000, 20 and note 135, with Papadimitriou 2001, 46–7 note 91, who favours a Mycenaean date.
103 Coldstream 1977, 180 (figurine: *PAE* 1929, 85, fig. 7); Papadimitriou 2001, 49–50; Papadopoulos 1979, 60, also notes chronological problems. Antonaccio 1995a, 66–8; Deoudi 1999, 92.
104 Moschos 2000.
105 In our area, the Early Mycenaean tumulus at Agrapidia Chalandritsas is noteworthy: *PAE* 1930, 85, fig. 10; on the date, see Papadopoulos 1979, 59; Moschos 2000, 9 and note 4.
106 Papadopoulos 1999; Moschos 2000, 12 and note 29 (Portes) and forthcoming (placing greater stress on inherited social structures than refugee movements); Eder forthcoming.
107 *PAE* 1929, 91, pl. 7.
108 *Delt* 17 B (1961–2) 131–2.
109 Kourou 1980.
110 Gadolou 1996–7 (see 57 for a list of tomb finds).
111 Petropoulos 1996–7, 172–5, noting that these routes were probably also used during the Late Bronze Age.
112 Morgan 2001a, 22–3.
113 Tomb B: *PAE* 1952, 403–4, fig. 14. Ag. Basileios: *Delt* 44 B (1989) 136; Petropoulos 1990, 504–5.
114 Stamatopoulou 1999, 39.
115 *Delt* 44 B (1989) 132–3.
116 *Delt* 44 B (1989) 133. It has been suggested that the worship perhaps of Pan took place in the caves of Monastiraki and Pangitsa near Katarraktis. Unfortunately, these caves were cleared in the Middle Ages, and the precise nature, date of commencement and duration of activity cannot be established: *PAE* 1952, 396–8.
117 The Ag. Giorgios pottery includes a few Classical black glaze sherds, although the main area of Classical activity was slightly further west. One Classical pithos burial, containing three pots, was discovered at Rachividi, *c.*1 km outside Katarraktis. This pithos was not covered, and was protected by a chance rockfall; if it was common practice to leave pithoi exposed in this way, this might explain the paucity of burial evidence: *Delt* 39 B (1984) 103; Hatzi Spiliopoulou 1991, note 57.
118 Tritaies is treated even more summarily: Rizakis 1995, 188–9.
119 Shennan 1989, especially 22.
120 McInerney 1999, 76–80; even so, there was long-term change in some parts of the border.
121 Lion: *PAE* 1956, 199–200, fig. 2, pl. 93γ. Fish: *PAE* 1952, 402, 410. Birds: *PAE* 1956, 197–8, fig. 2, pl. 92a. Ano Mazaraki: Gadolou pers. comm. (the fineware repertoire is reviewed in Gadolou forthcoming).

122 Morgan 1999c, 241–3; Morgan 2001c, 87–9 (although overstating the extent of isolation). I thank Anastasia Gadolou for discussion of the Ano Mazaraki material which was the subject of her Athens University doctoral thesis.
123 Shennan 1996; Maschner and Mithen 1996.
124 *PAE* 1952, 410; *PAE* 1956, 200–1; Coldstream 1968, 231–2; Morgan 1988, 326–8.
125 Gadolou forthcoming.
126 Petropoulos 1987–8, 86–7, figs 6–7; Petropoulos 1996–7, 173–4; Schaeur 1996–7, 267–9; Gadoulou forthcoming; Morgan and Hall 1996, 178.
127 Petropoulos 1992–3, 1996–7 and forthcoming; *Delt* 51 B (1996) 237–8.
128 Petropoulos 1987–8, 91, figs 12 and 13; Petropoulos forthcoming.
129 Gadolou 1987–8.
130 Petropoulos forthcoming; *Delt* 51 B (1996) 238; impressed ware, see Petropoulos 1987–8, fig. 7.
131 Recorded in an inscription on a bronze mirror of the first half of the fifth century: *Delt* 51 B (1996), pl. 70γ.
132 The discovery of a second structure is reported in *Delt* 51 B (1996) 237–8, but further excavation is required to determine its chronological and functional relationship to the temple.
133 Morgan 1999b, 417–18.
134 Petropoulos 1996–7, 175–7.
135 Petropoulos 1987–8, 88–90, fig. 9.
136 Jost 1985, 51; Polignac 1995, 36.
137 Tausend 1995, map 1.
138 Schaeur 1996–7.
139 Evidence for eighth-sixth century Lousoi is summarized in Morgan 1999b, 417 with bibliography. Bronzes: Voyatzis 1990, 133–8, 155–6, 178–9, 189, 198, 209, 216–17, 242–4 with previous bibliography, and for the contents of a more recently discovered votive deposit, see Mitsopoulos-Leon and Lädstatter 1996, 44–6; Mitsopoulos-Leon and Lädstatter 1997, 57–63.
140 Morgan 1999b, 417 and note 243. Cult image: Mitsopoulos-Leon 1992 and 1993.
141 Heine Nielsen and Roy 1998, 23–7; Morgan 1999b, 419.
142 On the territorial extent of Azania and identification of Azanian cities, see Pikoulas 1981–2; Heine Nielsen and Roy 1998, 7–12.
143 For summaries of archaeological and topographical research, see Petropoulos 1985. Morgan 1999b, 416–24 summarizes EIA and Archaic evidence. Pheneos survey: Erath 1999, 199–202, 214, 217 on Ag. Charalambos, 262 for a review of Geometric and Archaic sites.
144 *Delt* 42 B (1982) 164–5. The discovery of a bronze horse figurine raises the possibility of a shrine somewhere in the vicinity, as this is not a typical settlement or grave find; at present, this is an isolated chance find.
145 Dekoulakou 1982, 231–2, figs 24–9 (Manesi), 232–4 figs 30–4 (Asani), 234–5, fig. 35 (Flaboura); *AR* 1954, 157 (Kompegadi). Ag. Konstantinos, see note 108 above.
146 *PAE* 1930, 84–5.
147 At least according to the preliminary reports: *Delt* 35 B (1980) 198; *Delt* 33 B (1978) 102.

148 *Delt* 22 B (1967) 217, pl. 156e; Coldstream 1998, 325; Morgan 1986, 42–4.
149 For reviews of stylistic influences, see Dekoulakou 1982, 230–5; Coldstream 1998; Gadolou forthcoming.
150 Morgan and Hall 1996, note 151.
151 Heine Nielsen and Roy 1998, 12–19.
152 On Archaic Azanian city ethnics, see Heine Nielsen 2002, 296.
153 A later parallel for political movement around the Achaian-Arkadian border is provided by Pausanias 6.12.8–9. Commenting on a dedicatory inscription on a victory monument for the boxer Agesarchos of Tritaea at Olympia, he notes that the claim that Tritaea was Arkadian is not now to be believed, but was probably true at the time that the inscription was cut. Heine Nielsen and Roy 1998, 38, date any such union after 146.
154 Clarke 1999, 248–51.
155 The loss of all but four fragmentary lines of a chorus from Achaios' tragedy *The Azanes* (*TrGF* 20, frag.2) is unfortunate, as it would have been a rare fifth-century source (assuming with Heine Nielsen and Roy 1998, 17–18, that the ethnic refers specifically to Azania rather than being a synonym for Arkadian). As they point out, the surviving fragment, usually seen as referring to Lykaion's sacrifice of his own son to Zeus, implies a connection with wider Arkadian, rather than specifically Azanian, myth.
156 Hejnic 1961, 60–5: cf. Heine Nielsen and Roy 1998, 18–39.
157 An obvious example being Triphylia: Heine Nielsen 1997.
158 Hall 1997, 36–7; Weber 1978, 389.
159 Hall 1997, Ch. 3 (quotations p. 4).
160 Morgan 2001c, 83–4.
161 Hall 1997, 51–6.
162 Purcell 1990, 58.
163 Morgan 2001c, 84; Morgan 1999c for a review of comparable colonial circumstances.
164 Reviews: Corvisier 1991, 10–16 (see also 17–19 for discussion of Thessaly); Hall 1997, 82–94, 150–68.
165 An event which Corvisier 1991, 140–2 places in the mid-twelfth century, even though (as he acknowledges) it had little impact on the settlement structure of the region.
166 Hall 1997, 114–28; Morgan 1999a, 362–7, 373–9.
167 A point also stressed by Malkin 1998a, 2–3, 10–31.
168 For example, Hall 1997; McInerney 1999, Ch. 5; McInerney 2001. Heine Nielsen and Roy 1998, 18–28; Antonaccio 2001. On the fragmentary evidence for the construction of regional histories in the Archaic period, see Lasserre 1976.
169 On their possible interpretation see Carter 1988, although she associates masks of widely differing date.
170 Voyatzis 1990, 45, 118–19, pl. 65. Unmasked dance groups are known from a number of other sanctuaries, including Lousoi (Voyatzis 1990, 242–4) and Olympia (*Delt* 18 B [1963] pl. 146).
171 Antonaccio 1995a, Ch. 3 for critical review of claims; on Nemea, see now Miller forthcoming.
172 McInerney 1997; McInerney 1999, 127–49.

173 Jost 1985, *passim*, for discussion of individual cults by city, 462 (Penelope), 534–40.
174 Heine Nielsen 1999.
175 Appadurai 1981.
176 Antonaccio 1995a offers the most comprehensive review both of material evidence and previous scholarship on the subject; see Ch. 2 for tomb cults, Ch. 4 for cults of the dead, 249–51 (cemeteries). Deoudi 1999 presents a less critical review under the broad rubric of hero cult.
177 The preliminary report of the cult structures around Platanos Almyrou Tumulus Γ discussed below appeared too recently to have entered into the secondary literature.
178 Antonaccio 1995a, 68–9; I am if anything more sceptical than she about data from Thessaly, Achaia and Arkadia.
179 *Ergon* ΥΠΠΟ 2 (1998) 107–8 (Georgikon-Xinoneriou).
180 Views are summarized by Antonaccio 1995a, 6–9 (see 259–63 for a critical reappraisal), 143, fig. 13 (distribution), 70–102 (Messenia). Van der Kamp 1996 with previous bibliography (noting Alcock 1991 for broader discussion of post-Classical tomb cult).
181 Snodgrass 1980, 35–40; cf. Whitley 1988.
182 Foxhall 1995.
183 Coldstream 1976, 13–14.
184 Snodgrass 1980, 38.
185 Whitley 1998, 181; Antonaccio 1995a, 253–4.
186 Lotze 1959, 48–53 for a review of sources. Welwei 1977, 5–13 reviews modern scholarly approaches to the problem.
187 Ducat 1994, 75–6, 79–86.
188 Helly 1995, 97–9; *contra* Ducat 1994, 46–8.
189 Sordi 1958, 123, 325–7; Ducat 1994, 88, 118–20. Helly 1995, 185–6, 302–12 (reflecting also on Xenophon 2.3.36) argues strongly against the idea that such passages constitute evidence for private aristocratic armies, something which conflicts with his reconstruction of a federal army based on regional levies. As Ducat (1997) points out, the connection between *penestai* and the land implies that they would somehow be implicated in any regional land reform, although as he notes, one might reasonably question the public–private dichotomy implied by the notion of private armies in the context of Archaic cities. With Ducat, I agree with Helly's opposition to a purely feudal interpretation of the status of the *penestai* (not least because, as Ducat notes, there is no evidence that Thessaly was entirely occupied by great estates), although on the rather different grounds that evidence is too slight and could indeed support a more fluid interpretation of *penestai* as closer to Athenian *thetes* (free men, able to participate in some ways in community life, to fight when needed, but also to chose economic dependency, including acting as a resource to be loaned to a *xenos*). But Helly surely underrates the importance of Theocritos' presentation of *penestai* as a measure of personal wealth.
190 Compare Archemachos *FrGHist* 424F1.
191 Helly 1995, 307–8, is equally opposed to the idea of a 'slave revolt', but sees the *penestai* as a distinctive group in the federal army recruited on that basis by Critias.

192 The sources are discussed by Axenidos 1947, 57–64; Lotze 1959, 48–53; Ducat 1994, Pt. I.
193 Archemachos *FrGHist* 314 Fr 1; 424 Fr 1; cf. Athenaios 6.264 citing (with some disbelief) Philocrates' *Thessalika*.
194 Giles et al. 1977 offer similar observations from the perspective of language.
195 Hall 1997, 28–9, summarizes the argument.
196 Antonaccio 1995a, 254.
197 Antonaccio 1995a, 253–5.
198 Morris 1992, 150.
199 Stamatopoulou 1999, 55–6.
200 Efstathiou et al. 1990, 34; *Delt* 47 B (1992) 236–7. Continuing discovery of later remains is reported in *Delt* 51 B (1996) 361–2.
201 Wace and Thompson 1911–12; cf. Coldstream 1977, 87–8 on dating.
202 *Delt* 47 B (1992) 229–34, 237, fig. 8; *Delt* 48 B (1993) 239–40.
203 *Delt* 48 B (1993) 239–40, pl. 79d.
204 Hägg 1983b.
205 Tziaphalias 1994a.
206 *Delt* 1919, par. 25–33; Béquignon 1937b, 204–30; *Delt* 43 B (1988) 224; *Delt* 44 B (1989) 166; *Delt* 45 B (1990) 174.
207 Houby-Nielsen 1992 and 1995.
208 For example Effenterre and Ruzé 1994, no. 75, *c*.500, recording the prohibition by a syssitia or co-proprietory association in Sikyon on selling equipment (including an oil press) and on its use by non-tax payers or non-residents.
209 For example Morris 1992, 154.
210 *PAE* 1953, 121–5.
211 *Delt* 45B (1990) 204–5: Arachoviti 1994, 134, note 15. It seems to have collapsed during the Classical period, and this may account for the later material found in and over it, since the preliminary report does not indicate later reuse.
212 *PAE* 1953, 125–7.
213 *Delt* 45 B (1990) 205, pl. 99b.
214 Helly 1995, ch. IV.
215 Link 1991, 151–7.
216 Plutarch *Moralia* 492a-b, recounts his selection via a lot oracle of which we know no more.
217 Morgan 2001a, 31 and note 13.
218 Helly 1995, 181–7; Morgan 2001a, 31.
219 Morgan and Hall 1996, 193–9.
220 Hall forthcoming.
221 Ioakimidou 1995, 82–7, 213–25; Morgan and Hall 1996, 199.
222 Heine Nielsen 1999, 22–24.
223 Morgan 2001a, 34–8; Morgan 1999b, 431–2.
224 Snodgrass 1980, 20–5. Discussion of social attitudes to burial has focused on Attica (see note 8 above), and the resulting conclusions are less readily transferrable than their proponents sometimes claim: compare Morris 1987, 183–7, with Dickey 1992, 120–34.
225 In this light, it is interesting to note the Delphic response to Myskellos of Rhypes (Diodoros Siculus 8.17), that he will be granted children only after he has founded Kroton: Anderson 1954, 78; Morgan 1990, 172–3.

226 Dakaris, 1971 134–91; Hammond 1956, Hammond, 1967 427–33; Lepore 1962, 137–40.
227 Morgan and Hall 1996, 202–12; Morgan forthcoming b.
228 Vordos forthcoming; for a preliminary note, see *Delt* 51 B (1996) 240–1.
229 Malkin 1987, 2–7: as he stresses (131–2), these cities are cited simply as the home towns of the oikist and it is on this level that they are relevant to the present argument. Whether they *could* have been formal *metropoleis* of Achaian colonies is another matter – the sources do not present the case thus even though there is in principle no objection to such a tiering of identity in the process of colonization also (*pace* Larsen 1968, 82–3).
230 Morgan and Hall 1996, 186–9; see now also Lakaki-Marchetti 2000; Papagiannopoulos and Zachos 2000.
231 For a preliminary note of PG Kynos, see *Delt* 50 B (1995) 338–9. Strabo 13.1.68 reports that Kynos was involved in colonization.
232 Onasoglou 1981; for the inscribed phiale, see 9, 14–15, 47–51, figs 14–15. pl. 21b-d, noting that the second phiale in the same tomb (of different shape and origin) bears impressions of the textile in which it was wrapped. Anavra: *Delt* 32 B (1977) 104–5, grave IV.
233 A view to which many other objections can be raised: Purcell 1997.
234 Greaves 2002 offers a full review of the problems and evidence: I am grateful to Alan Greaves for discussion of these issues and permission to cite his manuscript before publication.
235 Morgan and Hall 1996, 212–14, and especially Hall forthcoming.
236 See for example Snodgrass 1980, 40–2; Malkin 1994.
237 Morgan 2001a, with a review of previous scholarship in all of these areas. On the social composition of the Athenian army: Wees 2001 with a review of previous scholarship. On warrior status in Homer: Wees 1992.
238 Dougherty 1993.
239 Roy 1967; Morgan 1999b, 231–2.
240 Weber 1978, 901–10; Gellner 1983, 3–4.
241 On borders as locations of conflict, see: Sartre 1979: Daverio Rocchi 1988, 225–40.
242 Foxhall 1997, 119.
243 Frost 1984.
244 Herman 1987, 97–105; Watrous 1982.
245 Forrest 1956 highlights the similarity in the patterns of alliances reported for the Lelantine war and the first sacred war.
246 Morgan 2001a, 29–30, noting that overtly financial terminology, as *misthophoros* (for example Thucydides 1.35), is generally a fifth-century phenomenon, and early 'mercenaries' are more commonly called *epikouroi* (as for example *Iliad* 5.614: Herodotos 1.64).
247 Fields 1994, Ch. 4.
248 Kearsley 1999, 118–26, emphasizes the likely role of Greek (probably Ionian, perhaps also Euboian) mercenaries in the Near East by the seventh century, although their ethnic origins are not usually specified in Assyrian sources.
249 Cooper 1996, 70–3, for a summary; Morgan 1999b, 411, reviews interpretations. On personal and booty dedications elsewhere: Morgan 2001a, 25–6.

250 Fields 1994, 60–1.
251 Callmer 1943, 99.

5 Beyond the polis: political communities and political identities

1 Hansen 1999.
2 Corvisier 1991, 50; Hatzopoulos 1994.
3 Lefèvre 1998, 13.
4 Jeffery 1990, 101, 103 no. 5; Bommelaer and Laroche 1991, 128 (Boiotian Treasury).
5 Morgan and Hall 1996, 214; Morgan forthcoming b.
6 Thessaly: Lorenz 1976, see for example cat. 1 from Argalastos in southern Magnesia, *c*.520, with the addition of a patronymic and probable funerary epigram. Phokis: Jeffery 1990, 437, no. 11a-b (Phokikon; although compare p. 438, B, from the same site, where Mnasixenos is described as 'of Stra[. . . .]'), 103, nos 2 (Stiris), 3 (Abai), 11 (Teithronion). Dedications, see for example Halai: Jeffery 1990, 108, nos. 7 and 8.
7 Heine Nielsen 1999, 23.
8 Herman 1987, 21.
9 Watrous 1982.
10 Dubois 1989, 73.
11 Marcadé 1957, 45.
12 Marcadé 1953, 115.
13 Marcadé 1957, 21–2.
14 The evidence is gathered by Viviers 1992.
15 Robertson 1992, 137; Canciani 1978.
16 Wachter 2001, 259 section 241, COR 18 and 102 (Phryx), COP 63 (Lokris), COR 66l (Argeos), COP App1Ad (Qorinthios).
17 Bechtel 1917, 536–62. The earliest epigraphic attestation of Thessalia within Thessaly, for example, dates *c*.450: Fraser and Matthews 2000, *s.v.* Thessalia (from Olosson).
18 See for example Hall 1997, 142; Jones 1997 offers the fullest critique.
19 Jones 1997, 120.
20 Hall 1997, 142 (his italics).
21 Hall 1997, 142.
22 Antonaccio 2001; Morgan 1999e, 87–92.
23 Foxhall 1997, 114–15.
24 Cohen 1994, for analogous reflections on the internal and external meaning of the concept of boundary.
25 See note 24 above.
26 See Chapter 3, p. 118 and note 48.
27 Freitag 2000 (see ch. II for ancient sources on the region). The area considered by Freitag, which focuses on coastal zones and omits the Ionian islands, is more restricted than that preferred here. As a result, his account, while otherwise thorough and thought-provoking, does not consider the effect of the intersection of land and sea communication in linking interior uplands into wider networks, nor the impact of evolving western connections and colonization.

28 Freitag 2000, 330–68, reviews the strategic military role of the gulf from later Archaic to Roman times.
29 The catalogue of historical-geographical writing on the gulf area in Morgan 1986, bibliography 2, highlights the way in which the regions surrounding the gulf were approached and perceived primarily from a terrestrial viewpoint.
30 Salvator 1876, see especially his preface and introduction.
31 Will 1995 exemplifies this approach.
32 Vokotopoulou 1982; Vokotopoulou 1986, 276–80.
33 *EAA* II supp. 1971–1994, IV *s.v.* Otranto (F. d'Andria); d'Andria 1995; Morgan 1998a, 295–6.
34 I thank Francesco d'Andria and Grazia Semeraro for showing me this material in April 2000; we are fully in accord on the Corinthian provenance (Ithakan imports in the Salento are few and probably later). Vokotopoulou 1986, 272, implies a large body of Epirote imports at Otranto, but this is not securely demonstrated as much is common to the wider Illyrian ambit.
35 Snodgrass 2000, also highlights the separation of this systems of contacts.
36 Single skyphoi from Pontecagnano T4871 and Grotta Gramiccia (Veii) T779: Bailo Modesti and Gastaldi 1999, 18, 36–7, pl. 3.3 (see pl. 4.7 for an Ithakan jug from T3089); d'Agostino and Soteriou 1998, 367 (see generally 363–5 for a review of MGII imports in the Tyrrhenian zone).
37 d'Agostino and Soteriou 1998. Ithakan connection: Morgan 2001b.
38 Vatin 1969, figs 58, 63, 65–6.
39 Morgan 1988 and 1995.
40 Morgan 1995, 333–6; Gadolou forthcoming (noting, for example, the likelihood of a Thapsos-style production in Achaia).
41 Morgan n.d.; Dickey 1992, Ch.3 for a review of grave goods. Pottery: Siegel 1978 (her statistics, derived only from Corinth, remain broadly reliable as few early contexts have been excavated since 1980).
42 Kilian-Dirlmeier 1985–6; Morgan 1998a, 290–2, with previous bibliography.
43 Blackman 1966.
44 Horden and Purcell 2000, 455.
45 Menadier 1995, 173–201; Pemberton 2000, 105–6.
46 Anderson 1954, 79, was open to this idea, but lacked evidence to support anything but a negative conclusion. New research is summarized in Greco forthcoming.
47 See for instance, on Elis: Eder 2001a and b. Western Achaia (LBA): Petropoulos 2000: Kolonas 2000; Moschos forthcoming; Eder forthcoming highlights LHIIIC evidence.
48 Coldstream 1968, Ch. 10.
49 Morton 2001, 45, 85–6.
50 Morton 2001, 90–7.
51 Morton 2001, 110–11, with previous bibliography, 114.
52 Morton 2001, 189–90.
53 See Kase et al. 1991, Ch. 3, on the Great Isthmus Corridor Route, Ch. 8 on Early Iron Age and Archaic remains along this corridor; Morgan 1998a, 288–9. Lemos 1998, 49; see also *BCH* 117 (1993) 619–31; Kearsley 1989, 25–8, 35.
54 For echoes in the ceramic repertoire of Medeon, see Vatin 1969, 59–75.
55 Morgan 1999a, 277–8 (noting that Aetos 163 is Ithakan: Morgan 2001b).

56 Frikes may also have been exploited but has yet to be explored. At Vathy, by contrast, there is no evidence that the harbour was exploited before Hellenistic times, and the shallow anchorages on either side of the Aetos ridge were probably preferred (not least for direct access to the settlement): S. Symeonoglou pers. comm.
57 Robertson 1948, 81–2, cat. 490.
58 Benton 1983–9, 134–4, and 1953; Robertson 1948. On present evidence, there appears to have been at least one settlement centre in the north and the south of the island, each with a sanctuary. Evidence for EIA and Archaic settlement between Stavros and the coast of Polis bay was identified by Sylvia Benton during fieldwalking in 1935–6, and is noted in her unpublished report (BSA archive: *Benton: Misc.notebooks: Stavros 1935–6*). I thank the BSA for permission to consult Benton's papers, and the School Archivist, Amalia Kakissis, for her assistance. Reappraisal and publication of Benton's work in this area is one of the objectives of new collaborative fieldwork to be conducted by the author and Dr A. Soteriou (6th Ephoreia of Prehistoric and Classical Antiquities, Patras) from 2002.
59 Gell 1807, 30–3; Holland 1815, 52; see Horden and Purcell 2000, 381–2, on islands with large populations.
60 See Morgan 1988a, 284 note 25 *re BCH* 89 (1965) 757, fig. 1: what was published as an Argive pyxis from a deposit (probably of disturbed grave offerings) in the area of the later agora at Palaiopolis, Corfu, is more likely Ithakan (and a second 'pyxis', in fact probably a kantharos, shows strong influence). A late seventh-century Corfiote stand is a rare import to Aetos: Robertson 1948, 44–9, no. 225, pl. 15, figs 32–3; cf. Dontas 1968, 336 note 29.
61 Morgan 2001b, includes wider discussion of Ithakan exports and iconography; a study in preparation covers the full repertoire of figured scenes. Kantharoi in the wider Tyrrenhian area: d'Agostino 1994–5, 52, cat. 38, pl. XXXVII. Seals: Boardman and Buchner 1966, 26–8.
62 The shortage of Euboian connections is interesting in this respect: Coldstream 1968, 227–8, lists two imported and one local sherd showing Euboian-Cycladic influence (the picture is unchanged by recent excavations at Aetos), and there is nothing reported from the central gulf at sites like Ano Mazaraki (A. Gadolou pers. comm.). In claiming Euboian presence on Ithaka from *c.*750, Malkin places great emphasis on script and geography. He wrongly claims (Bats and d'Agostino 1998, 403) that Ithakan script is Euboian; in the same volume (Malkin 1988b, 1–3) he cites Jeffery 1990, 230 on the existence of Chalkidian influences which are then treated as evidence of presence. Jeffery, however, states that the Ithakan alphabet is Achaian, with, on one early inscription, instances of the Euboic lambda, exaggerated iota and red chi, which have been interpreted as showing possible, and brief, Chalkidian influence (for which Ithakan contacts with Pithekoussai provide a plausible route of transmission: Morgan 1998a, 299). Malkin 1998a, 8, further ascribes the seventh-century cessation of expensive dedication at Polis Cave to Corinth's opening of the Leukas channel (attested by Strabo): yet this ignores the question of local input into the shrine, and since lavish metal dedications (tripods included) decline across the board in Greek sanctuaries around the mid-seventh century, the Polis

record, which continues to Roman times, follows well-established general trends (Snodgrass 1989–90). Stress on the cave setting of this shrine is also unwise given the archaeological questions that surround the depositional history of these votives within what may be a collapsed rock shelter. I find no evidence in the large body of published evidence to support the claim (Malkin 2001b, 207 note 15) that Eretria had already declined in the seventh century (cf. for example, Bérard 1998).

63 *PAE* 1992, 294; I thank Nancy Symeonoglou for a copy of her article on this material in advance of publication, and permission to discuss it in Morgan 1998a, 291 and Morgan 2001b.
64 Vokotopoulou 1986, 58, 65, 159, 253–4, 286.
65 Coulson 1988.
66 Robertson 1948, cat. 358, pl. 23.
67 Benton 1973, 715.
68 Benton 1953, 778.
69 d'Agostino and Soteriou 1998.
70 Eder forthcoming.
71 Mountjoy 1999, *s.v.* Achaia (LHIIIC); Eder forthcoming; Bejko 1994, 118–19, 122–3.
72 Benzi and Graziado 1996.
73 Papadopoulos 1995. On the role of the Ionian islands, see Souyoudzoglou-Haywood 1999, 141–2.
74 Eder forthcoming. Mountjoy 1999, *s.v.* Achaia (LHIIIC).
75 L. Vagnetti pers. comm.
76 Dekoulakou 1973; Stavropoulou Gatsi 1980; Vokotopoulou 1969. Ionian islands: Souyoudzoglou-Haywood 1999, 142–4.
77 Odos Plastira 6, LG pithos burial: *Delt* 45 B (1990) 137; Petropoulos forthcoming.
78 Gadolou 1996–7.
79 Jeffery 1990, 221–4, 248–51. Corfiote script, by contrast, is Corinthian-derived.
80 Coldstream 1998; Luppino and Tomay forthcoming; Tomay pers. comm. emphasizes that most are local products.
81 Banks 1996, 190.
82 See note 19 above.
83 Nevett 1999, Chs 1, 2. On gender imagery in Early Iron Age art, see for example Langdon 1999 and 2001.
84 Wees 1998.
85 Among a wide range of discussions, see for example: Wees 1992 and 1998; Eder forthcoming.
86 Kilian 1988, 135.
87 Papadopoulos 1999; Eder forthcoming.
88 Eder 2001a and 2001b; Morgan forthcoming a.
89 Bennet n.d.; Davis and Bennet 1999.
90 Gounaris 1999: Reger 1997.
91 Televantou 1999.
92 Cambitoglou et al. 1988, Ch. 3; Mazarakis Ainian 1988, 117 note 43.

BIBLIOGRAPHY

Special abbreviations

Antre Corycien I   *L'Antre Corycien* I (*BCH* supp.7), Athens/Paris: Boccard, 1981.
Antre Corycien II   *L'Antre Corycien* II (*BCH* supp.9), Athens/Paris: Boccard, 1984.
Corinto   Corinto e l'Occidente. Atti del XXXIV Convegno di Studi sulla Magna Grecia, Taranto 7–11 ottobre 1994, Taranto: Istituto per la Storia e l'Archeologia della Magna Grecia, 1995.
CPCActs 1   M.H. Hansen (ed.) *The Ancient Greek City-State. Acts of the Copenhagen Polis Centre* 2, Copenhagen: KDVS, 1993.
CPCActs 2   M.H. Hansen (ed.) *Sources for the Ancient Greek City-State. Acts of the Copenhagen Polis Centre* 2, Copenhagen: KDVS, 1995.
CPCActs 3   M.H. Hansen (ed.) *Introduction to an Inventory of Poleis. Acts of the Copenhagen Polis Centre* 3, Copenhagen: KDVS, 1996.
CPCActs 4   M.H. Hansen (ed.) *The Polis as an Urban Centre and as a Political Community. Acts of the Copenhagen Polis Centre* 4, Copenhagen: KDVS, 1997.
CPCActs 6   T. Heine Nielsen and J. Roy (eds) *Defining Ancient Arkadia. Acts of the Copenhagen Polis Centre* 6, Copenhagen: KDVS, 1999.
CPCPapers 1   D. Whitehead (ed.) *From Political Architecture to Stephanus Byzantius. Sources for the Ancient Greek Polis* (*Historia* Einz.87), Stuttgart: Franz Steiner, 1994.
CPCPapers 2   M.H. Hansen and K. Raaflaub (eds) *Studies in the Ancient Greek Polis* (*Historia* Einz. 95), Stuttgart: Franz Steiner, 1995.
CPCPapers 3   M.H. Hansen and K. Raaflaub (eds) *More Studies in the Ancient Greek Polis* (*Historia* Einz. 108), Stuttgart: Franz Steiner, 1996.
CPCPapers 4   T. Heine Nielsen (ed.) *Yet More Studies in the Ancient Greek Polis* (*Historia* Einz. 117), Stuttgart: Franz Steiner, 1997.
CPCPapers 5   P. Flensted-Jensen (ed.) *Further Studies in the Ancient Greek Polis* (*Historia* Einz. 138), Stuttgart: Franz Steiner, 2000.
Lefkandi I   M. Popham, L. Sackett and P. Themelis (eds) *Lefkandi* I. *The Iron Age*, London: BSA, 1980.
Lefkandi II.2   M. Popham, P. Calligas and L. Sackett (eds) *Lefkandi* II, part 2. *The Excavation, Architecture and Finds*, London: BSA, 1993.
Pallantion Scavi di Pallantion, *ASAtene* 68–9 (51–2), 1990–1 (1995).
ΠΕΡΙΦΕΡΕΙΑ Περιφέρεια του Μυκηναϊκού Κόσμου. Πρακτικά Α᾿ Διεθνές Διεπιστημονικό Συμπόσιο, Λαμία, 25–29 Σεπτεμβρίου 1994, Lamia: ΤΑΡΑ/ΙΔ᾿ ΕΠΚΑ, 1999.

BIBLIOGRAPHY

Praktika Theochari Πρακτικά. Διεθνές Συνεδρίο γιά την Αρχαία Θεσσαλία στη Μνημή του Δημήτρη Ρ. Θεοχάρη, Athens: TAPA, 1992.
ΘΕΣΣΑΛΙΑ 1, 2 ΘΕΣΣΑΛΙΑ Δεκαπέντε χρόνια αρχαιολογικής έρευνας 1975–1990. Αποτελέσματα και προόπτικες, vols. 1, 2, Athens: Kapon, 1994.

References by author

Adrymi (Sismani), V. (1983) 'Τύμβος Φερῶν', AAA 16: 23–42.
—— (1992) 'Μυκηναϊκός οικισμός στο Διμήνι', Praktika Theochari: 272–8.
—— (1994a) 'Ο Μυκηναϊκός οικισμός Διμηνίου', ΘΕΣΣΑΛΙΑ 1: 225–32.
—— (1994b) 'Η Μυκηναϊκή πόλη στο Διμήνι. Νεότερα δεδομένα για την αρχαία Ιωλκό', in Koliou 1994: 17–43.
—— (1999) 'Μυκηναϊκός κεραμικός κλίβανος στο Διμήνι', ΠΕΡΙΦΕΡΕΙΑ: 31–142.
Akurgal, M., Kerschner, M, Mommsen, H. and Niemeier, W.-D. (forthcoming) Töpferzentren der Ostägäis. Archäometrische und archäologische Untersuchungen zur mykenischen, geometrischen und archaischen Keramik aus Fundorten in Westkleiasien (3 Ergänzungsheft der ÖJh).
Albanese Procelli, R.M. (1996) 'Greeks and indigenous peoples in eastern Sicily: forms of interaction and acculturation', in R. Leighton (ed.) Early Societies in Sicily, London: Accordia: 167–76.
Alcock, S. (1991) 'Tomb cult and the post-Classical polis,' AJA 95: 447–67.
—— (1993) Graecia Capta. The Landscapes of Roman Greece, Cambridge: CUP.
Alcock, S. and Osborne, R. (eds) (1994) Placing the Gods. Sanctuaries and Sacred Space in Ancient Greece, Oxford: OUP.
Alram-Stern, E. (1999) 'The Mycenaean figurines of Elateia', ΠΕΡΙΦΕΡΕΙΑ: 215–22.
Alzinger, W. (1983) 'Aigeira-Hyperesia', ÖJh 54, Grab. 1983: 35–40).
Alzinger, W. et al. (1985) 'Aegeira-Hyperesia und die Siedlung Phelloe in Achaia I', Klio 67: 389–451.
—— (1986) 'Aegira-Hyperesia und die Siedlung Phelloe in Achaia II, III', Klio 68: 6–62, 309–47.
Amandry, P. (1938) 'Vases, bronzes et terres cuites de Delphes', BCH 62: 305–11.
—— (1944–5) 'Petits objets de Delphes', BCH 68–9: 36–74.
—— (1987) 'Trépieds de Delphes et du Péloponnèse', BCH 111: 79–131.
Ammerman, A.J. (1990) 'On the origins of the forum romanum', AJA 94: 627–45.
—— (1996) 'The Eridanos valley and the Athenian agora', AJA 100: 699–715.
Anderson, B. (1991) Imagined Communities. Reflections on the Origin and Spread of Nationalism, rev. edn, London/New York: Verso.
Anderson, J.K. (1954) 'A topographical and historical study of Achaia', BSA 59: 72–92.
—— (1995) 'The Geometric Catalogue of Ships', in J. Carter and S. Morris (eds) The Ages of Homer. A Tribute to Emily Townsend Vermeule, Austin: University of Texas Press: 181–91.
Anderson-Stojanovic, V.R. (2001) 'The cult of Demeter and Kore at the Isthmus of Corinth', in R. Hägg (ed.) Peloponnesian Sanctuaries and Cults. Proceedings of the 9th International Symposium at the Swedish Institute at Athens, 11–13 June 1994, Stockholm: Paul Åström: 75–83.

BIBLIOGRAPHY

Andrews, T.K. (1994) 'Bronzecasting at Geometric Period Olympia and Early Greek Metals Sources' (PhD diss., Brandeis University).

Antonaccio, C.M. (1992) 'Terraces, tombs and the early Argive Heraion', *Hesperia* 61: 85–105.

—— (1994) 'Placing the past: the Bronze Age in the cultic topography of early Greece', in Alcock and Osborne 1994: 79–104.

—— (1995a) *An Archaeology of Ancestors*, Lanham: Rowman and Littlefield.

—— (1995b) 'Lefkandi and Homer', in Ø. Andersen and M. Dickie (eds) *Homer's World. Fiction, Tradition, Reality* (Papers from the Norwegian Institute at Athens 3), Bergen: Norwegian Institute at Athens: 5–27.

—— (1997) 'Urbanism at Archaic Morgantina', in Damgard Andersen et al. 1997: 167–93.

—— (2001) 'Ethnicity and colonisation', in Malkin 2001: 113–57.

Apostolides, P. (1912) *Αἱ Παγασαί ἐξεταζούμεναι διὰ τῶν Αἰώνων*, Athens: Estia.

Apostolopoulou Kakavoyianni, O. (1979) 'Τοπογραφία της περιοχής των Φερών Θεσσαλίας κατά την Προϊστορική περίοδο', *Delt* 34 Α: 174–206.

—— (1990) 'Ένα νεό ιερό στις Φερές', in P. Kamilakis and A. Polymerou-Kamilaki (eds) *ΥΠΕΡΕΙΑ Ι. Πρακτικά του Α΄ Συνεδρίου Φεραί – Βελεστίνο – Ρήγας, Βελεστίνο 30–31.5–1.6.86*, Athens: Syllogi Velestinon: 57–70.

—— (1992) 'Ευρήματα της πρωτογεωμετρικής και γεωμετρικής περίοδου από τις Φερες', *Praktika Theochari*: 312–20.

Appadurai, A. (1981) 'The past as a scarce resource', *Man* 16: 201–19.

—— (1986) 'Introduction: commodities and the politics of value', in A. Appadurai (ed.) *The Social Life of Things*, Cambridge: CUP: 3–63.

Arachoviti, P. (1994) 'Θολωτός Πρωτογεωμετρικός τάφος στην περιοχή των Φερών', *ΘΕΣΣΑΛΙΑ* 2: 125–38.

Arafat, K. and Morgan, C. (1994) 'Athens, Etruria and the Heuneburg: mutual misconceptions in the study of Greek-Barbarian relations', in I. Morris (ed.) *Classical Greece: Ancient Histories and Modern Archaeologies*, Cambridge: CUP: 108–34.

Arapogianni-Mazokopaki, X. (1982) 'Γεωμετρικός τάφος Πολύδροσο Παρνασσίδας', *AAA* 15: 76–85.

Archibald, Z. (2000) 'Space, hierarchy and community in Archaic and Classical Macedonia, Thessaly and Thrace', in Brock and Hodkinson 2000: 212–33.

Ardener, E. (1989) 'The construction of history: "vestiges of creation"', in E. Tonkin, M. McDonald and M. Chapman (eds) *History and Ethnicity*, London/New York: Routledge: 22–33.

Asheri, D. (1970) 'I coloni elei ad Agrigento', *Kokalos* 16: 79–88.

Attema, P. (1999) 'Cartography and landscape perception: a case study from central Italy', in M. Gillings, D. Mattingly and J. van Dalen (eds) *Geographical Information Systems and Landscape Archaeology*, Oxford: Oxbow: 23–34.

Auda, Y., Darmezin, L., Decourt, J.-C., Helly, B. and Lucas, G. (1990) 'Espace géographique et géographie historique en Thessalie', in J.-L. Fiches and S.E. van der Leeuw (eds) *Archéologie et espaces*, Juan-les-Pins: APDCA: 87–126.

Aupert, P. (1982) 'Argos aux VIIIe-VIIe siècles: bourgade ou métropole?', *ASAtene* 60: 21–32.

Axenidos, T.D. (1947) *Λάρισα καί ή Ἀρχαία Θεσσαλία* I, Athens: Sideri.
Bailo Modesti, G. and Gastaldi, P. (1999) *Prima di Pithecusa i più antichi materiali greci del golfo di Salerno*, Naples: Museo Nazionale dell'Agro Picentino.
Bakalakis, G. (1973) 'Φεραία 'Αθηνᾶ', *Αρχεῖον θεσσαλικῶν Μελετῶν* 2: 1–24.
Bakhuizen, S.C. (1989) 'The *ethnos* of the Boeotians', in H. Beister and J. Buckler (eds) *BOIOTIKA. Vorträge vom 5 internationalen Böoten Kolloquium zu Ehren von Professor Dr. Siegfried Lauffer*, Munich: Maris: 65–72.
—— (1994) 'Sixty-five years of Magnesian research, 1924–1989', *ΘΕΣΣΑΛΙΑ* 2: 21–30.
Bammer, A. (1998) 'Zur Topographie von Aigeira', in D. Katsonopoulou, S. Soter and D. Schilardi (eds) *Ancent Helike and Aigialeia*, Athens: Helike Society: 199–207.
—— (forthcoming) 'Aigeira-Hyperesia', in Greco forthcoming.
Banks, M. (1996) *Ethnicity: Anthropological Constructions*, London: Routledge.
Barakari-Gleni, K. and Pariente, A. (1998) 'Argos du VIIe au IIe siècle av. J.-C.: synthèse des données archéologiques', in Pariente and Touchais 1998: 165–78.
Barakari-Gleni, K. and Peppa-Papaioannou, E. (1999) 'A new cult place of the Archaic period in Argos', in R. Docter and E. Moormann (eds) *Classical Archaeology towards the Third Millenium. Proceedings of the XVth International Congress of Classical Archaeology, Amsterdam, July 12–17, 1998*, Amsterdam: Allard Pierson Museum: 62–5.
Barker, E. (1946) *The Politics of Aristotle*, Oxford: OUP.
Barth, F. (1970) 'Introduction', in F. Barth (ed.) *Ethnic Groups and Boundaries*, repr. London: George Allen & Unwin: 9–38.
Bats, M. and d'Agostino, B. (1998) *Euboica. L'Eubea e la presenza euboica in Calcidia e in Occidente*, Naples: Centre Jean Bérard coll.15/*AION* Quad.12.
Batziou-Efstathiou, A. (1984) 'Πρωτογεωμετρικά από τη Δυτική Θεσσαλία', *AAA* 17: 74–87.
__(1992) 'Νεότερες Ανασκαφικές Έρευνες στην Ευρύτερη Περιοχή της Μαγούλας –Πευκάκια', *Praktika Theochari*: 279–85.
—— (1994) 'Αποτελέσματα των Πρόσφατων Ανασκαφικών Ερευνών στη Ν. Ιωνία και στην Περιοχή Πευκακίων', in Koliou 1994: 59–70.
—— (1999) 'Το Νεκροταφείο της Νέας Ιωνίας (Βόλου) κατά τη Μετάβαση από την ΥΕ ΙΙΙΓ στην ΠΓ Εποχή', *ΠΕΡΙΦΕΡΕΙΑ* : 117–30.
Baziotopoulou-Valavani, E. (1994) 'Ανασκαφές σε Αθηναϊκά Κεραμικά Εργαστήρια των αρχαϊκών και κλασικών χρόνων', in Coulson et al. 1994: 45–54.
Baziotopoulou, E. and Valavanis, P. (1993) 'Deux acropoles antiques sur les montagnes de Galaxidi', *BCH* 117: 189–209.
Bearzot, C. (1982) 'Atena Itonia, Atena Tritonia e Atena Iliaca', *CISA* 8: 43–60.
Bechtel, F. (1917) *Die historischen Personennamen des Griechischen bis zur Kaiserzeit*, Halle: Max Niemeyer.
Bejko, L. (1994) 'Some problems of the Middle and Late Bronze Age in Albania', *BIA* 31: 105–26.
Beloch, J. (1890) 'Die Dorische Wanderung', *Rheinisches Museum für Philologie*, 45: 555–98.
Bender, B. (1995) 'Introduction. Landscape – meaning and action', in B. Bender (ed.) *Landscape. Politics and Perspectives*, Oxford: Berg: 1–17.

Bender, B. and Winer, M. (eds) (2001) *Contested Landscapes. Movement, Exile and Place*, Oxford: Berg.

Bennet, J. (n.d.) 'The meaning of "Mycenaean". Speculations on ethnicity in the Aegean Late Bronze Age', Mycenaean Seminar delivered at the Institute of Classical Studies, University of London, 5 May 1999.

Benson, J.L. (1995) 'Human figures, the Ajax Painter, and narrative scenes in earlier Corinthian vase painting', in J. Carter and S. Morris (eds) *The Ages of Homer. A Tribute to Emily Townsend Vermeule*, Austin: University of Texas Press: 335–62.

Benton, S. (1934–5) 'Excavations in Ithaca, III. The cave at Polis, I', *BSA* 35: 45–73.

—— (1938–9) 'Excavations in Ithaca, III. The cave at Polis, II', *BSA* 39: 1–51

—— (1953) 'Further excavations at Aetos', *BSA* 48: 255–358.

Benzi, M. and Graziado, G. (1996) 'The last Mycenaeans in Italy', *SMEA* 38: 95–138.

Béquignon, Y. (1932) 'Études Thessaliennes. V (1). Recherches archéologiques dans la région de Pharsale', *BCH* 56: 89–191.

—— (1937a) *Recherches archéologiques à Phères de Thessalie*, Paris: Les Belles Lettres.

—— (1937b) *La vallée du Sperchios des origines au IVe siècle. Études d'archéologie et de topographie*, Paris: Faucheux et fils.

—— (1964) 'Études thessaliennes XI. Inscriptions,' *BCH* 88: 395–412.

Bérard, C. (1998) 'Érétrie géométrique et archaïque. Délimitation des espaces construits: zones d'habitat et zones religieuses', in Bats and d'Agostino 1998: 147–52.

Bergquist, B. (1990) 'The Archaic temenos in western Greece: a survey and two enquiries', in A. Schachter (ed.) *Le sanctuaire grec* (*Entretiens Hardt* 37) Geneva: Vandœuvres: 109–52.

Berranger, D. (1992) *Recherches sur l'histoire et la prosopographie de Paros à l'époque archaïque*, Clermont Ferrand: Faculté des lettres et sciences humaines de l'université Blaise Pascal, fasc. 36.

Biesantz, H. (1957) 'Bericht über Ausgrabungen im Gebiet der Gremnos – Magula bei Larisa im Frühjahr 1958', *AA*: 37–57.

—— (1965) *Die Thessalischen Grabreliefs*, Mainz: von Zabern.

Bintliff, J. (ed.) (1977a) *Mycenaean Geography*, Cambridge: British Association for Mycenaean Studies.

—— (1977b) *Natural Environment and Human Settlement in Prehistoric Greece*, Oxford: BAR.

—— (1999) 'Pattern and process in the city landscapes of Boeotia from Geometric to Late Roman times', in M. Brunet (ed.) *Territoires des cités grecques* (*BCH* supp. 34), Paris/Athens: Boccard/EFA: 15–33.

—— (n.d.) 'The contribution of archaeological survey to our understanding of Archaic Greece', paper delivered to the Oxford University Ancient History Seminar, March 2001.

Bintliff, J., Howard, P. and Snodgrass, A.M. (1999) 'The hidden landscape of prehistoric Greece', *JMA* 12: 139–68.

Bintliff, J. and Snodgrass, A.M. (1988) 'Mediterranean survey and the city', *Antiquity* 62: 57–71.

Blackman, D. (1966) 'The harbour at Perachora', *BSA* 61: 192–4.

Blandin, B. (2000) 'Une tombe du IXe siècle av. J.-C. à Erétrie', *AntK* 43: 134–46.

Blegen, C.C. (1926) 'The site of Opous', *AJA* 30: 401–4.

Blegen, C.C., Palmer, H. and Young, R. (1964) *Corinth* XIII. *The North Cemetery*, Cambridge, Mass: ASCSA.

Blinkenberg, C. (1962) *Fibules grecques et orientales (Lindiaka* V), Copenhagen: Høst.

Blondé, F. and Perreault, J.Y. (eds) (1992) *Les ateliers de potiers dans le monde grec aux époques géométrique, archaïque et classique* (*BCH* supp. 23), Paris: Boccard.

Blum, I., Darmezin, L., Decourt, J.-C., Helly, B. and Lucas, G. (1992) *Topographie antique et géographie historique du pays grec*, Paris: CNRS.

Boardman, J. (1967) *Excavations in Chios 1952–1955. Greek Emporio* (*BSA* supp. 6), London: BSA.

—— (1990) 'Al Mina and history', *OJA* 9: 169–90.

—— (1994) 'Orientalia and orientals in Ischia', in d'Agostino and Ridgway 1994: 95–100.

Boardman, J. and Buchner, G. (1966) 'Seals from Ischia and the Lyre Player Group', *JdI* 81: 1–62

Bommelaer, J.-F. and Grandjean, Y. (1972) 'Recherches dans le quartier sud d'Argos', *BCH* 96: 155–228.

Bommelaer, J.-F., and Laroche, D. (1991) *Guide de Delphes. Le site*, Paris: EFA/Boccard.

Bommeljé, S., Doorn, P., Deylius, M., Vroom, J., Bommeljé, Y., Fagel, R. and van Wijngaarden, H. (1987) *Aetolia and the Aetolians. Towards the Interdisciplinary Study of a Greek Region*, Utrecht: Parnassus.

Bookidis, N. (1995) 'Archaic Corinthian sculpture: a summary', *Corinto*: 231–56.

—— (2000) 'Corinthian terracotta sculpture and the temple of Apollo', *Hesperia* 6: 381–452.

Bookidis, N. and Stroud, R. (1997) *Corinth* XVIII, iii. *The Sanctuary of Demeter and Kore. Topography and Architecture*, Princeton: ASCSA.

Bookidis, N., Hansen, J., Snyder, L. and Goldberg, P. (1999) 'Dining in the sanctuary of Demeter and Kore at Corinth', *Hesperia* 68: 1–54.

Bourguet, E. (1898) 'Inscriptions de Delphes: colonne de droite', *BCH* 22: 320–8.

Bourriot, F. (1976) *Recherches sur la nature du génos*, Paris: Honoré Champion.

Bowra, C.M. (1961) *Greek Lyric Poetry*, 2nd edn, Oxford: OUP.

Boyd, T.D. and Jameson, M.H. (1981) 'Urban and rural land division in ancient Greece', *Hesperia* 50: 327–42.

Boyer, P. (1990) *Tradition as Truth and Communication*, Cambridge: CUP.

—— (1993) 'Cognitive aspects of religious symbolism', in P. Boyer (ed.) *Cognitive Aspects of Religious Symbolism*, Cambridge: CUP: 4–47.

Bradley, R. (1990) *The Passage of Arms*, Cambridge: CUP.

—— (1991) 'Ritual time and history', *WA* 23: 209–19.

—— (1993) *Altering the Earth*, Edinburgh: Society of Antiquaries of Scotland monograph series 8.

Brann, E. (1960) *Agora* VIII. *Late Geometric and Proto-Attic Pottery*, Princeton: ASCSA.

Brather, S. (2000) 'Ethnisch Identitäten als Konstrukte der frühgeschichtlichen Archäologie', *Germania* 78: 139–77.

Brelich, A. (1961) *Guerre, agoni e culti nella Grecia arcaica*, Bonn: Rudolph Habelt.

Brock, R. and Hodkinson, S. (eds) (2000) *Alternatives to Athens*, Oxford: OUP.

Brommer, F. (1940) 'Neue Thessalische Bildwerke vorklassicher Zeit', *AthMitt* 65: 103–19.

Broneer, O. (1971) *Isthmia* I. *The Temple of Poseidon*, Princeton: ASCSA.

Brookes, A.C. (1981) 'Stoneworking in the Geometric period at Corinth', *Hesperia* 50: 285–90.
Bruhns, H. (1987–9) 'Max Weber, Moses I. Finley et le concept de cité antique', *Opus* VI-VIII: 27–42.
Bürgel, H. (1877) *Die Pylaeisch-Delphische Amphiktyonie*, Munich: Ackermann.
Burn, A.R. (1960) *The Lyric Age of Greece*, London: Edward Arnold.
Burrow, J.W. (1966) *Evolution and Society: a Study in Victorian Social Theory*, Cambridge: CUP.
—— (1991) 'Henry Maine and mid-Victorian ideas of progress', in Diamond 1991: 55–75.
Busolt, G. (1893) *Griechische Geschichte* I, Gotha: F.A. Perthes.
Calligas, P.G. (1992) 'From the Amyklaion,' in J.M. Sanders (ed.) *ΦΙΛΟΛΑΚΩΝ. Lakonian Studies in Honour of Hector Catling*, London: BSA: 31–48.
Callmer, C. (1943) *Studien zur Geschichte Arkadiens bis zur Gründung des arkadischen Bundes*, Lund: Gleerupska.
Cambitoglou, A., Birchall, A., Coulton, J.J. and Green, J.R. (1988) *Zagora* II. *Excavation of a Geometric Town on the Island of Andros, Greece*, Athens: Archeological Society of Athens.
Camp, J. (1986) *The Athenian Agora*, London: Thames and Hudson.
—— (1994) 'Before democracy: Alkmaionidai and Peisistratidai', in Coulson et al. 1994: 7–12.
—— (1999) 'Excavations in the Athenian Agora 1996 and 1997', *Hesperia* 68: 255–83.
—— (2000) 'Walls and the Polis', in Flensted-Jensen, Heine Nielsen and Rubinstein 2000: 41–57.
Canciani, F. (1978) 'Lydos, der Sklave?', *AntK* 21: 17–21.
Carlier, P. (1984) *La royauté en Grèce avant Alexandre*, Strasbourg: AECR.
Carr, C. and Neitzel, J.E. (eds) (1995) *Style, Society and Person. Archaeological and Ethnological Perspectives*, New York/London: Plenum.
Carter, J.B. (1988) 'Masks and poetry in early Sparta', in Hägg, Marinatos and Nordquist 1988: 89–98.
—— (1997) '*Thiasos* and *Marzeah*. Ancestor cult in the age of Homer', in S. Langdon (ed.) *New Light on a Dark Age*, Columbia: University of Missouri Press: 72–112.
Cartledge, P. (1979) *Sparta and Lakonia*, London: Routledge.
—— (1992) 'Early Lacedaimon: the making of a conquest-state', in J.M. Sanders (ed.) *ΦΙΛΟΛΑΚΩΝ. Lakonian Studies in Honour of Hector Catling*, London: BSA: 49–55.
—— (1993) *The Greeks*, Oxford: OUP.
—— (1995) 'We are all Greeks'? Ancient (especially Herodotean) and modern contestations of Hellenism', *BICS* 40: 75–82.
Casevitz, M. (1995) 'Sur ἐσχατιά (eschatia). Histoire du mot', in A. Rousselle (ed.) *Frontières terrestres, frontières célestes dans l'antiquité*, Paris: Presses universitaires de Perpignan: 19–30.
Caskey, M.E. (1981) 'Ayia Irini, Keas: the terracotta statues and the cult in the temple', in R. Hägg and N. Marinatos (eds) *Sanctuaries and Cults in the Aegean Bronze Age*, Stockholm: Paul Åström: 127–35.
Cavanagh, W.G. (1991) 'Surveys, cities and synoecism', in Rich and Wallace-Hadrill 1991: 97–118.

Champion, T. (1987) 'The European Iron Age: assessing the state of the art', *Scottish Archaeological Review* 4: 98–108.
Champion, T. and Champion, S. (1986) 'Peer polity interaction in the European Iron Age', in C. Renfrew and J.F. Cherry (eds) *Peer Polity Interaction and Socio-Political Change*, Cambridge: CUP: 59–68.
Chapman, M., McDonald, M. and Tonkin, E. (1989) 'Introduction. History and social anthropology', in E. Tonkin, M. McDonald and M. Chapman (eds) *History and Ethnicity*, London/New York: Routledge: 1–21.
Chapman, R. and Randsborg, K. (1981) 'Approaches to the archaeology of death', in R. Chapman, I. Kinnes and K. Randsborg (eds) *The Archaeology of Death*, Cambridge: CUP: 1–24.
Cherry, J.F. (1983) 'Evolution, revolution and the origins of complex society in Minoan Crete', in O. Krzyszkowska and L. Nixon (eds) *Minoan Society*, Bristol: Bristol Classical Press: 33–53.
—— (1987) 'Power in space: archaeological and geographical studies of the state', in J.M. Wagstaff (ed.) *Landscape and Culture. Geographical and Archaeological Perspectives*, Oxford: Blackwell: 146–72.
—— (1988) 'Pastoralism and the role of animals in the pre- and protohistoric economies of the Aegean', in Whittaker 1988: 6–34.
Childe, V.G. (1929) *The Danube in Prehistory*, Oxford: OUP.
—— (1950) 'The urban revolution', *Town Planning Review* 21: 9–16.
Chrysostomou, P. (1998) *Η Θεσσαλική Θεά Εν[ν]οδία ή Φεραια Θεά*, Athens: TAPA.
Clarke, D. (1978) *Analytical Archaeology* 2nd edn, London: Methuen.
Clarke, K. (1999) *Between Geography and History. Hellenistic Constructions of the Roman World*, Oxford: OUP.
Cohen, A.P. (1985) *The Symbolic Construction of Community*, London: Routledge.
—— (1994) 'Boundaries of consciousness, consciousness of boundaries. Critical questions for anthropology', in H. Vermeulen and C. Govers (eds) *The Anthropology of Ethnicity: Beyond "Social groups and Boundaries"*, Amsterdam: Het Spinhuis: 59–79.
Cohen, R. and Schlegel, A. (1968) 'The tribe as a socio-political unit: a cross-cultural examination', in Helm 1968: 120–49.
Coldstream, J.N. (1968) *Greek Geometric Pottery*, London: Methuen.
—— (1976) 'Hero cults in the age of Homer', *JHS* 106: 8–17.
—— (1977) *Geometric Greece*, London: Ernest Benn.
—— (1983) 'The meaning of the regional styles in the eighth century B.C.', in Hägg 1983a: 17–25.
—— (1984a) 'The formation of the Greek *polis*: Aristotle and archaeology', *Rheinisch-Westfälische Akademie Vorträge* G272, Düsseldorf: Westdeutsche Verlag: 7–22.
—— (1984b) 'Dorian Knossos and Aristotle's villages', in C. Nicolet (ed.) *Aux origines de l'Hellenisme: hommages à Henri von Effenterre*, Paris: Centre Gustav Glotz: 311–22.
—— (1989) 'Early Greek visitors to Cyprus and the eastern Mediterranean', in V. Tatton-Brown (ed.) *Cyprus and the Eastern Mediterranean in the Iron Age*, London: British Museum Press: 90–6.
—— (1991) 'Knossos: an urban nucleus in the Dark Age?', in D. Musti et al. (eds) *La Transizione dal Miceneo all'alto Arcaismo*, Rome: CNR: 287–99.

—— (1994) 'Propectors and pioneers: Pithekoussai, Kyme and central Italy', in G.R. Tsetskhladze and F. de Angelis (eds) *The Archaeology of Greek Colonization*, Oxford: OUCA: 47–59.

—— (1996) 'Knossos and Lefkandi: the Attic connections', in D. Evely, I.S. Lemos and S. Sherratt (eds) *Minotaur and Centaur. Studies in the Archaeology of Crete and Euboea Presented to Mervyn Popham*, Oxford: BAR: 133–45.

—— (1998) 'Achaean pottery around 700 B.C., at home and in the colonies', in D. Katsonopoulou, S. Soter and D. Schilardi (eds) *Helike* II. *Ancient Helike and Aigialeia*, Athens: Helike Society: 323–34.

Coleman, J. (1992) 'Excavations at Halai, 1990–1991', *Hesperia* 61: 265–77.

Collini, S., Winch, D. and Burrow, J. (1983) *That Noble Science of Politics: a Study in Nineteenth Century Intellectual History*, Cambridge: CUP.

Conkey, M. and Hastorf, C. (eds) (1990) *The Uses of Style in Archaeology*, Cambridge: CUP.

Cook, R.M. (1961) 'The 'double stoking tunnel' of Greek kilns', *BSA* 56: 64–7.

Cooper, F. (1996) *The Temple of Apollo Bassitas* I. *The Architecture*, Princeton: ASCSA.

Cornell, T.J. (1995) *The Beginnings of Rome. Italy and Rome from the Bronze Age to the Punic Wars (c.1000–264 BC)*, London: Routledge.

Cornell, T.J. and Lomas, K. (1995). *Urban Society in Roman Italy*, London: UCL Press.

Corvisier, J.N. (1981) 'Entre l'esclavage et la liberté, un cas peu connu: les Pénestes thessaliens', *L'information historique* 43: 115–18.

—— (1991) *Aux origines du miracle grec. Peuplement et population en Grèce du Nord*, Paris: Presses Universitaires de France.

—— (1993) 'Quelques remarques sur la mise en place de l'urbanisation en Illyrie du sud et en Epire', in P. Cabanes (ed.) *L'Illyrie méridionale et l'Épire dans l'antiquité* II, Paris: Boccard: 85–9.

Coulson, W.D.E. (1988) 'Geometric pottery from Volimedia', *AJA* 92: 53–74.

Coulson, W.D.E., Palagia, O., Shear T.L. Jnr., Shapiro, H.A. and Frost F.J. (eds) (1994) *The Archaeology of Athens and Attica under the Democracy*, Oxford: Oxbow.

Coulton, J.J. (1976) *The Architectural Development of the Greek Stoa*, Oxford: OUP.

Courbin, P. (1963) 'Stratigraphie et stratigraphie', *Etudes archéologiques*, 59–102.

Courtils, J. de. (1992) 'L'architecture et l'histoire d'Argos dans la première moitié du Ve siècle avant J.C.', in M. Pièrart (ed.) *Polydipsion Argos (BCH* supp. 22), Paris/Athens: Boccard: 241–51.

Crielaard, J.-P. (1995) 'Homer, history and archaeology: some remarks on the date of the Homeric world', in J.-P. Crielaard (ed.) *Homeric Questions*, Amsterdam: Gieben: 201–88.

—— (1999) 'Early Iron Age pottery in Cyprus and North Syria: a consumption-oriented approach', in J.-P. Crielaard, G.-J. van Wijngaarden and V. Stissi (eds) *The Complex Past of Pottery*, Amsterdam: Gieben: 261–90.

Croissant, F. (forthcoming) 'On the diffusion of certain Corinthian stylistic models in the colonial world of the second half of the seventh century BC', *RA*, forthcoming.

Crone, P. (1986) 'The tribe and the state', in J. Hall (ed.) *States in History*, Oxford: Blackwell: 48–77.

Csapo, E. (1991) 'An international community of traders in late 8th-7th c. B.C. Kommos in southern Crete', *ZPE* 88: 211–16.

—— (1993) 'A postscript to "An international community of traders in late 8th-7th c. B.C. Kommos"', *ZPE* 96: 235–6.
Csapo, E., Johnston, A.W. and Geagan, D. (2000) 'The Iron Age inscriptions', in J.W. and M.C. Shaw (eds) *Kommos* IV. *The Greek Sanctuary*, Princeton: PUP: 101–34.
Daffa-Nikonanou, A. (1973) 'Θεσσαλικά Ιερά Δημήτρας και Κοροπλαστικά Αναθήματα' (PhD thesis, University of Thessaloniki).
d'Agostino, B. (1994–5) 'La "Stipe dei Cavalli" di Pitecusa', *Atti e Memorie della Società Magna Grecia,* 3rd ser. 3: 9–91.
d'Agostino, B. and Ridgway, D. (eds) (1994) *APOIKIA. Scritti in onore di Giorgio Buchner* (*AION* n.s. 1), Naples: Istituto Universitario Orientale.
d'Agostino, B., and Soteriou, A. (1998) 'Campania in the framework of the earliest Greek colonisation in the west', in Bats and d'Agostino 1998: 355–68.
Dakaris, S. (1971) *Cassopaia and the Elean Colonies* (*Ancient Greek Cities* 4), Athens: Athens Centre of Ekistics.
—— (1987) 'Organisation politique et urbanistique de la ville dans l'Épire antique', in P. Cabanes (ed.) *L'Illyrie méridionale et l'Épire dans l'antiquité*, Clermont-Ferrand: Adosa: 71–80.
Dakoronia, F. (1987) 'War-ships on sherds of LHIIIC kraters from Kynos', in H. Tzalas (ed.) *2nd International Symposium on Ship Construction in Antiquity* (*Tropis* II), Delphi: Hellenic Institute for the Preservation of Nautical Tradition: 117–22.
—— (1990) 'Αρχαϊκές Κεραμίδες απο την Ανατολική Λοκρίδα', *Hesperia* 59: 175–80.
—— (1991) 'Late Helladic III, Submycenaean and Protogeometric finds in the Sperchios Valley', in Kase et al. 1991: 70–3.
—— (1992a) 'Χρήση και Προέλευση Μακρών Περονών ΥΜ και ΠΓ εποχής', *Praktika Theochari*: 292–7.
—— (1992b) 'Ελάτεια', *Αρχαιολογία* 45: 20.
—— (1993a) 'Homeric towns in East Lokris. Problems of identification', *Hesperia* 62: 115–27.
—— (1993b) 'Ελάτεια', *Φώκικα Χρονικά* 5: 25–39.
—— (1994) 'Sperchios Valley and the adjacent area', *ΘΕΣΣΑΛΙΑ* 1: 233–42.
—— (2001) 'Αρτέμις – Ασπασίας', in A. Alexandri and I. Levendi (eds) ΚΑΛΛΙΣΤΕΥΜΑ. Μελέτες προς Τιμήν Ολγας Τζάχου-Αλεξανδρής, Athens: ΥΠΠΟ/ICOM: 403–409.
Dakoronia, F. and Tziafalias, A. (1991) 'La Thessalie à l'époque géométrique', *Les Dossiers d'Archaeologie*: 20–5.
Dalongeville, R. (2000) 'L'Achaïe: une région aux paysages fragiles et instabiles', in Rizakis 2000: 11–20.
Damgard Andersen, H, Horsnæs, H.W., Houby-Nielsen, S. and Rathje, A. (eds) (1997) *Urbanisation in the Mediterranean in the 9th to 6th Centuries BC* (*Acta Hyperborea* 7), Copenhagen: Museum Tusculanum Press.
D'Andria, F. (1995) 'Corinto e l'occidente: la costa Adriatica', *Corinto*: 457–508.
Danner, P. (1997) 'Megara, Megara Hyblaea and Selinus: the relationship between the town planning of a mother city, a colony and a sub-colony in the Archaic period', in Damgard Andersen et al. 1997: 143–65.
Darby, H.C. (1953) 'On the relations of geography and history', *TIBG* 19: 1–11.
Dasios, Ph. (1992) 'Συμβολή στην Τοπογραφία της Αρχαίας Φωκίδας', *Φώκικα Χρονικά* 4: 18–97.

Daux, G. (1936) *Pausanias à Delphes*, Paris: Picard.
Daverio Rocchi, G. (1988) *Frontiera e confini nella Grecia antica*, Rome: Bretschneider.
—— (1993) *Città-Stato e Stati federali della Grecia Classica. Lineamenti di Storia delle Istituzioni Politiche*, Milan: LED.
Davies, J.K. (1994) 'The tradition about the First Sacred War', in S. Hornblower (ed.) *Greek Historiography*, Oxford: OUP: 193–210.
—— (1996a) 'Deconstructing Gortyn: when is a code a code?', in Foxhall and Lewis 1996: 33–56.
—— (1996b) 'Strutture e suddivisioni delle <poleis> arcaiche. Le ripartzioni minori', in S. Settis (ed.) *I Greci. Storia, Cultura, Arte, Società* 2. *Una Storia Greca* 1. *Formazione*, Turin: Giulio Einauldi: 599–652.
—— (1997) 'The "origins of the Greek *polis*". Where should we be looking?' in Mitchell and Rhodes 1997: 24–38.
—— (2001a) 'Rebuilding a temple: the economic effects of piety', in D.J. Mattingley and J. Salmon (eds) *Economies beyond Agriculture in the Classical World*, London: Routledge: 209–29.
—— (2001b) 'Temples, credit, and the circulation of money', in A. Meadows and K. Shipton (eds) *Money and its Uses in the Ancient Greek World*, Oxford: OUP: 117–28.
Davis, J. and Bennet, J. (1999) 'Making Mycenaeans: warfare, territorial expansion, and representations of the other in the Pylian kingdom', in Laffineur 1999: 107–20.
Dawkins, R.M. (1929) *The Sanctuary of Artemis Orthia at Sparta*, London: SPHS.
Decourt, J.-Cl. (1990) *La vallée de l'Énipeus en Thessalie (BCH supp. 21)*, Athens/Paris: Boccard.
Decourt, J.-Cl. and Darmezin, L. (1999) 'Modèle, limites géographiques, limites historiques: cités et territoires en Thessalie', in M. Brunet (ed.) *Territoires des cités grecques (BCH supp. 34)*, Paris/Athens: Boccard/EFA: 79–97.
Defradas, J. (1954) *Les thèmes de la propagande delphique*, Paris: C. Klincksieck.
Dekoulakou, I. (1973) 'Γεωμετρικοί Ταφικοί Πίθοι ἐξ 'Αχαΐας', *AE* chronika: 15–29.
—— (1982) 'Κεραμεική 8ου και 7ου αἰ. π.χ. από Τάφους της Αχαΐας και της Αιτωλίας', *ASAtene* 60: 219–35.
de la Coste Messelière, P. (1969) 'Topographie delphique', *BCH* 93: 730–58.
de la Genière, J. (1993) 'Statuaire archaïque de la Mère des dieux en Arcadie et en Laconie', in Palagia and Coulson 1993: 153–8.
Demakopoulou, K. (1982) 'Το Μυκηναΐκο Ιερο στο Αμυκλαίο και ἡ ΥΕΙΙΙΓ Περίοδος στη Λακωνία' (PhD thesis, University of Athens).
Demand, N.H. (1990) *Urban Relocation in Archaic and Classical Greece. Flight and Consolidation*, Norman/London: University of Oklahoma Press.
Deoudi, M. (1999) *Heroenkulte in homerische Zeit*, Oxford: BAR.
Desborough, V.R.d'A. (1952) *Protogeometric Pottery*, Oxford: OUP.
—— (1964) *The Last Mycenaeans and their Successors. An Archaeological Survey c.1200–1000 BC*, Oxford: OUP.
Despoini, A. (1982) 'Κεραμεικοί Κλίβανοι Σίνδου', *AE*: 61–84.
Detienne, M. (1988) 'L'espace de la publicité: ses opérateurs intellectuels dans la cité', in M. Detienne (ed.) *Les savoirs de l'écriture. En Grèce ancienne*, Arras: Presses universitaires de Lille: 29–81.

Diamond, A. (ed.) (1991) *The Victorian Acheivement of Sir Henry Maine: a Centennial Reappraisal*, Cambridge: CUP.
Dickey, K. (1992) 'Corinthian Burial Customs, ca.1100–500BC' (PhD diss., Bryn Mawr College).
Dickie, M. (1995) 'The geography of Homer's world', in Ø. Andersen and M. Dickie (eds) *Homer's World. Fiction, Tradition, Reality*, (*Papers from the Norwegian Institute at Athens* 3), Bergen: Norwegian Institute at Athens: 29–56.
Dietler, M., and Herbich, I. (1998) '*Habitus*, techniques, style: an integrated approach to the social understanding of material culture and boundaries', in M.T. Stark (ed.) *The Archaeology of Social Boundaries*, Washington and London: Smithsonian Institution Press: 232–63.
Dillon, M. (1997) 'The ecology of the Greek sanctuary,' *ZPE* 118: 113–30.
Docter, R.F. and Niemeyer, H.-G. (1994) 'Pithekoussai: the Carthaginian connection. On the archaeological evidence of Euboeo-Phoenician partnership in the 8th and 7th centuries B.C.', in d'Agostino and Ridgway 1994: 101–15.
Donlan, W. (1985) 'The social groups of Dark Age Greece', *CP* 80: 293–308.
—— (1989) 'The pre-state community in Greece', *SO* 64: 5–29.
Donohue, A. (1988) *Xoana and the Origins of Greek Sculpture*, Atlanta: Scholars' Press.
Dontas, G. (1968) 'Local imitation of Corinthian vases of the later seventh century B.C. found in Corfu', *Hesperia* 37: 331–7.
—— (1983) 'The true Aglaurion', *Hesperia* 52: 48–63.
Dougherty, C. (1993) 'It's murder to found a colony,' in C. Dougherty and L. Kurke (eds) *Cultural Poetics in Archaic Greece. Cult, Performance, Politics*, Cambridge: CUP: 178–98.
Dougleri Intzesiloglou, A. (1990) 'Φεραί', *Αρχαιολογία* 34: 58–64.
—— (1994) 'Οι Νεότερες Αρχαιολογικές Έρευνες στην Περιοχή των Αρχαίων Φερών', *ΘΕΣΣΑΛΙΑ* 2: 71–92.
Drerup, H. (1969) *Griechische Baukunst in geometrischer Zeit*, (*Archaeologia Homerica* II, O.F. Matz and H.-G. Buchholz eds), Göttingen: Vandenhoeck and Ruprecht.
Drews, R. (1981) 'The coming of the city to central Italy', *AJAH* 6: 133–65.
Dubois, L. (1989) *Inscriptions grecques dialectales de Sicile. Contributions à l'étude du vocabulaire grec colonial*, Rome: Coll. EFR 119.
Ducat, J. (1994) *Les Pénestes de Thessalie* (*Annales littéraires de l'université de Besançon* 512).
—— (1997) 'Bruno Helly et les pénestes', *TOPOI* 7: 183–9.
Ducrey, P. (1995) 'La muraille est-elle un élément constitutif d'une cité?,' *CPCActs* 2: 245–56.
Dunnell, R.C. (1980) 'Evolutionary theory and archaeology', in M.B. Schiffer (ed.) *Advances in Archaeological Method and Theory* 3, New York: Academic Press: 35–99.
Durkheim, E. (1964) *The Division of Labour in Society* (trans. G. Simpson): Free Press of Glencoe: Collier/Macmillan.
Dyer, C., and Haagsma, M. (1993) 'A Geometric krater from New Halos. Results of the 1992 Halos study season', *Pharos* 1: 165–74.
Eder, B. (2001a) 'Continuity of Bronze Age cult at Olympia? The evidence of the Late Bronze Age and Early Iron Age pottery', in R. Laffineur and R. Hägg (eds) *POTNIA. Deities and Religion in the Aegean Bronze Age. Proceedings of the 8th International Aegean Conference, Göteborg 12–15 April 2000* (*Aegaeum* 23): 201–9.

—— (2001b) 'Die Anfänge von Elis und Olympia: zur Siedlungsgeschichte der Landschaft Elis am Übergang von der Spätbronze-zur Früheisenzeit', in V. Mitsopoulos-Leon (ed.) *Forschungen in der Peloponnes. Akten des Symposions zur 100-Jahr-Feier des Österreichischen Archäologischen Instituts Athen, Athens 5–7.3 1998,* Athens: Österreichisches Archäologisches Institut: 233–43.

—— (forthcoming) 'Patterns of contact and communication between the regions south and north of the Corinthian Gulf in LHIIIC,' *The Periphery of the Mycenaean World: 2nd International Interdisciplinary Colloquium, Lamia 26–30 Sept. 1999,* Lamia: ΤΑΡΑ/ΙΔ' ΕΠΚΑ.

Eder, B. and Mitsopoulos-Leon, V. (1999) 'Zur Geschichte der Stadt Elis vor dem Synoikismos von 471 v. Chr.', *ÖJh* 68: 1–39.

Effenterre, H. van. (1985a) 'Il problema delle istituzioni doriche', in D. Musti (ed.) *Le origini dei Greci: Dori e mondo egeo,* Rome: Laterza: 293–312.

—— (1985b) *La cité grecque,* Paris: Hachette.

—— (1990) 'La notion de 'ville' dans la préhistoire Égéenne', in P. Darcque and R. Treuil (eds) *L'habitat Égéen préhistorique* (*BCH* supp. 19), Paris: Boccard: 485–91.

Effenterre, H. van and Ruzé, F. (1994) *Nomima. Recueil d'inscriptions politiques et juridiques de l'archaïsme grec* I, Rome: EFR.

—— (1995) *Nomima. Recueil d'inscriptions politiques et juridiques de l'archaïsme grec* II, Rome: EFR.

Efstathiou, A., Malakasioti, Z. and Reinders, R. (1990) 'Halos archaeological field survey project. Preliminary report of the 1990 campaign', *Netherlands Institute at Athens Newsletter* 3: 31–7.

Ehrenberg, V. (1969) *The Greek State.* 2nd edn, London: Methuen.

Ellinger, P. (1987) 'Hyampolis et le sanctuaire d'Artémis Elaphébolos dans l'histoire, la légende et l'éspace de la Phocide', in Felsch et al. 1987: 88–99.

—— (1993) *La légende nationale Phocidienne* (*BCH* supp. 27), Paris/Athens: Boccard.

Erath, G. (1999) 'Archäologische Funde im Becken von Pheneos', in K. Tausend (ed.) *Pheneos und Lousoi. Untersuchungen zu Geschichte und Topographie Nordostarkadiens,* Frankfurt a.M.: Peter Lang: 199–237.

Erbse, H. (1969) *Scholia graeca in homeri iliadem* (*scholia vetera*) I, Berlin: de Gruyter.

Felsch, R.C.S. (1981) 'Mykenischer Kult in Heiligtum bei Kalapodi', in R. Hägg and N. Marinatos (eds) *Sanctuaries and Cults in the Aegean Bronze Age,* Stockholm: Paul Åström: 81–9.

—— (1983) 'Zur Chronologie und zum Stil geometrischen Bronzen aus Kalapodi', in Hägg 1983a: 123–9.

—— (1991) 'Tempel und Altäre im Heiligtum der Artemis Elaphebolos von Hyampolis bei Kalapodi', in R. Etienne and M.T. le Dinahet (eds) *L'espace sacrificiel dans les civilisations Méditerranéennes de l'antiquité,* Paris/Lyons: Boccard: 85–91.

—— (1998) 'Kalapodi und Delphi – zur Frühzeit des Apollonkultes in Mittelgriechenland,' *Joachim Jungius-Ges.Wiss. Hamburg* 87: 219–36.

—— (1999) 'Το Μυκηναϊκό Ιερό στο Καλαπόδι: Λατρεία και Τελετουργικό', *ΠΕΡΙΦΕΡΕΙΑ:* 163–70.

—— (2001) 'Opferhandlungen des Alltagslebens im Heiligtum der Artemis Elaphebolos von Hyampolis in den Phasen SHIIIC-Spätgeometrisch', in R. Laffineur and R. Hägg (eds) *POTNIA. Deities and Religion in the Aegean Bronze Age. Proceedings of the 8th International Aegean Conference, Göteborg 12–15 April 2000* (*Aegaeum* 23): 193–200.

Felsch R.C.S., Kienast, H.J. and Schuler, H. (1980) 'Apollon und Artemis oder Artemis und Apollon? Bericht von der Grabungen im neu Entdeckten Heiligtum bei Kalapodi, 1973–1977', *AA*: 38–123.
Felsch R.C.S. et al. (1987) 'Bericht über die Grabungen im Heiligtum der Artemis Elaphebolos und des Apollon von Hyampolis 1978–1982', *AA*: 1–99.
Feuer, B. (1983) *The Northern Mycenaean Border in Thessaly*, Oxford: BAR.
—— (1992) 'Mycenaean Thessaly: our present state of knowledge', *Praktika Theochari*: 286–7.
—— (1994) 'Mycenaean Thessaly', *ΘΕΣΣΑΛΙΑ* 1: 211–14.
Fields, N. (1994) 'The Anatomy of a Mercenary: from Archilochos to Alexander' (PhD thesis, University of Newcastle upon Tyne).
Finley, M.I. (1981) 'The ancient city, from Foustel de Coulanges to Max Weber and beyond', in B.D. Shaw and R.P. Saller (eds) *Economy and Society in Ancient Greece*, Harmondsworth: Penguin: 3–23.
—— (1985a) *Ancient History. Evidence and Models*, London: Chatto & Windus.
—— (1985b) *The Ancient Economy* 2nd ed., London: Hogarth Press.
Fischer-Hansen, T. (1996) 'The earliest urbanisation of the Sicilian colonies with special regard to Gela', *CPCActs* 3: 317–73.
—— (2000) '*Ergasteria* in the western Greek world', in Flensted-Jensen, Heine Nielsen and Rubinstein 2000: 91–120.
Flensted-Jensen, P, Heine Nielsen, T., and Rubinstein, L. (eds) (2000) *Polis and Politics. Studies in Ancient Greek History Presented to Mogens Herman Hansen on his Sixtieth Birthday, August 20, 2000*, Copenhagen: Museum Tusculanum Press.
Fletcher, R. (1995) *The Limits of Settlement Growth. A Theoretical Outline*, Cambridge: CUP.
—— (1996) 'Organized dissonance. Multiple code structures in the replication of human culture', in H. Maschner and S. Mithen (eds) *Darwinian Archaeologies*, New York and London: Plenum: 61–86.
Floren, J. (1987) *Die Griechische Plastik I. Die geometrische und archaische Plastik*, Munich: C.H. Beck.
Forrest, G. (1956) 'The first sacred war', *BCH* 80: 33–52.
Forsén, J. (1998) 'The discovery of an Archaic sanctuary in the Asea valley in Arcadia', *AJA* 102: 370.
Forsén, J. and Forsén, B. (1997) 'The *polis* of Asea. A case-study of how archaeology can expand our knowledge of the history of a *polis*', *CPCPapers* 4: 163–76.
Forsén, J., Forsén, B. and Lavento, M. (1996) 'The Asea Valley survey: a preliminary report on the 1994 season', *OpAth* 21: 73–97.
Forsén, J., Forsén, B. and Østby, E. (1999). 'The sanctuary of Agios Elias – its significance, and its relations to surrounding sanctuaries and settlements', *CPCActs* 6, 169–91.
Forstenpointner, G. (1990) 'Tierknochenfunde aus der arkadischen Ansiedlung Lousoi: Erste Ergebnisse', *ÖJh* 60, Grab. 37–47.
Fossey, J.M. (1987–1988) 'Η Εξέλιξις της Αρχαίας Κατοικησέως της Χερσόνησου Περαχώρας', *Πρακτικά Γ' Διεθνους Συνέδριου Πελοποννησιακών Σπουδών* II, Athens: Society for Peloponnesian Studies: 421–6.
—— (1990a) *The Ancient Topography of Opountian Lokris*, Amsterdam: Gieben.
—— (1990b) 'The Perakhorá peninsula survey', *EMC* 34 (9): 201–11.

Fox, R. (1967) *Kinship and Marriage*. Penguin: Harmondsworth.
Foxhall, L. (1995) 'Bronze to iron: agricultural systems and political structures in Late Bronze Age and Early Iron Age Greece', *BSA* 90: 239–50.
—— (1997) 'A view from the top. Evaluating the Solonian property classes', in Mitchell and Rhodes 1997: 113–36.
Foxhall, L. and Lewis, A.D.E. (eds) (1996) *Greek Law in its Political Setting*, Oxford: OUP.
Francotte, H. (1907) *La Polis grecque* (*Studien zur Geschichte und Kultur des Altertums* 1907), Paderborn: Schöningh.
Franke, P.R. (1956) 'Drei neue Inschriften aus Thessalien', *AA*: 183–91.
—— (1970) 'ΦΕΘΑΛΟΙ-ΦΕΤΑΛΟΙ-ΠΕΤΘΑΛΟΙ-ΘΕΣΣΑΛΟΙ. Zur Geschichte Thessaliens im 5. Jahrhundert v. Chr.', *AA*: 85–93.
Fraser, P.M. and Matthews, E. (2000) *A Lexicon of Greek Personal Names* vol. IIIB. *Central Greece from the Megarid to Thessaly*, Oxford: OUP.
Freitag, K. (2000) *Der Golf von Korinth. Historisch-topographische Untersuchungen von der Arkaik bis in das 1.Jh. v. Chr.*, Munich: Tuduv.
French, E. and Vanderpool, E. (1963) 'The Phokikon', *Hesperia* 32: 213–25.
Freyer-Schauenburg, B. (1974) *Samos* XI. *Bildwerke der archaischen Zeit und des strengen Stils*, Bonn: Rudolf Habelt.
Frost, F.J. (1984) 'The Athenian military before Cleisthenes', *Historia* 33: 283–94.
Funke, P. (1993) 'Stamm und *polis*. Überlegungen zur Entstehung der griechischen Staatenwelt in den "Dunklen Jahrhunderten"', in J. Bleicken (ed.) *Colloquium aus Anlass des 80. Geburtstages von Alfred Heuss*, Kallmünz: *FAS* 13: 29–48.
—— (1997) 'Polisgenese und Urbanisierung in Aitolien im 5. und 4. Jh. v. Chr.', *CPCActs* 4: 145–88.
Furtwangler, A. (1884) 'Archaischer Goldschmuck', *Arch.Zeitung* 42: 99–114.
Fustel de Coulanges, N.D. (1864) *La cité antique. Étude sur le culte, le droit, les institutions de la Grèce et de Rome*, Paris: Hachette.
Gadolou, A. (1996–1997) 'Χάλκινα και Σιδερένια ῞Οπλα από το Ιερό στο Ανω Μαζαράκι (Ρακίτα) Αχαΐας. Μια Πρώτη Παρουσίαση', *Πρακτικά του Ε' Διεθνους Συνέδριου Πελοποννησιακῶν Σπουδῶν, 6–10 Σεπτ 1995*, Athens: Society for Peloponnesian Studies: 51–72.
—— (2001) 'The formation of sacred landscapes of the Eastern Argolid, 900–700BC. A religious, social and political survey', in R. Hägg (ed.) *Peloponnesian Sanctuaries and Cults. Proceedings of the 9th International Symposium at the Swedish Institute at Athens, 11–13 June 1994*, Stockholm: Paul Åström: 37–43.
—— (forthcoming) 'The pottery fabrics and workshops from Ano Mazaraki', in Greco forthcoming.
Gallis, K. (1979) 'A short chronicle of Greek archaeological investigations in Thessaly from 1881 until the present day', in Helly 1979: 1–30.
—— (1992) *Ατλας Προϊστορικῶν Οικισμῶν της Ανατολικής Θεσσαλικής Πεδιάδας*, Larissa: Society for Research in the History of Thessaly.
Gamble C. (1982) 'Animal husbandry, population and urbanisation', in Renfrew and Wagstaff 1982: 161–71.
Ganas, A. and Buck, V. (1998) 'A model for the tectonic subsidence of the Allai archaeological site, Lokris', *Bulletin of the Geological Society of Greece* 32(1): 181–7.
Garnsey, P. (1988) *Famine and Food Supply in the Graeco-Roman World*, Cambridge: CUP.

Garnsey, P. and Morris, I. (1988) 'Risk and the *polis*: the evolution of institutionalised responses to food supply problems in the early Greek state', in P. Halstead and J. O'Shea (eds) *Cultural Responses to Uncertainty*, Cambridge: CUP: 98–105.
Garnsey, P., Gallant, T. and Rathbone, D. (1984) 'Thessaly and the grain supply of Rome during the second century B.C.', *JRS* 74: 30–44.
Gauss, W. and Ruppenstein, F. (1998) 'Die Athener Akropolis in der frühen Eisenzeit', *AthMitt* 113: 1–60.
Gawantka, W. (1985) *Die sogenannte Polis. Entstehung, Geschichte und Kritik der modernen althistorischen Grundbegriffe der griechische Staat, die griechische Staatsidee, die Polis*, Stuttgart: Steiner.
Gebhard, E. (1998) 'Small dedications in the Archaic temple of Poseidon at Isthmia', in Hägg 1998a: 91–115.
Gebhard, E. and Hemans, F. (1998) 'University of Chicago excavations at Isthmia 1989: II', *Hesperia* 67: 1–63.
Gehrke, H.-J. (1986) *Jenseits von Athen und Sparta: das dritte Griechenland und seine Staatenwelt*, Munich: Beck.
—— (2000) '*Ethnos, phyle, polis*. Gemäßigt unorthodoxe Vermutungen', in Flensted-Jensen, Heine Nielsen and Rubinstein 2000: 160–76.
Gell, A. (1985) 'How to read a map: remarks on the practical logic of navigation', *Man* 20: 271–86.
Gell, W. (1807) *The Geography and Antiquities of Ithaca*, London: Longman, Hurst, Rees and Orme.
Gellner, E. (1983) *Nations and Nationalism*, Oxford: Basil Blackwell.
—— (1987) *Culture, Identity and Politics*, Cambridge: CUP.
Gernet, L. (1982) *L'anthropologie de la Grèce antique*, Paris: Maspero.
Gesell, G., Day, L.P. and Coulson, W.D.E. (1995) 'Excavations at Kavousi, Crete, 1989 and 1990', *Hesperia* 64: 67–120.
Giles, H., Bourhis, R.Y. and Taylor, D.M. (1977) 'Towards a theory of language and ethnic group relations', in H. Giles (ed.) *Language, Ethnicity and Inter-group Relations*, London/New York: Academic Press: 307–48.
Giovannini, A. (1971) *Untersuchungen über die Natur und die Anfänge der bundesstaatlichen Sympolitie in Griechenland*, Göttingen: Vandenhoeck and Ruprecht.
Glowacki, K.T. (1998) 'The Acropolis of Athens before 566 B.C.', in K.J. Hartswick and M.C. Sturgeon (eds) *ΣΤΕΦΑΝΟΣ. Studies in Honor of Brunilde Sismondo Ridgway*, Philadelphia: University of Pennsylvania Museum: 79–88.
Gneisz, D. (1990) 'Das antike Rathaus. Das griechische Bouleuterion und die frühromische Curia' (PhD thesis, University of Vienna).
Gogos, S. (1986–7) 'Kult und Heiligtümer der Artemis von Aegeira', *ÖJh* 57: cols. 108–39.
Goldman, H. and Jones, F. (1942) 'Terracottas from the necropolis at Halae', *Hesperia* 11: 365–421.
Goldman, H.B. (1930) 'Some votive offerings from the acropolis of Halae', in *Festschrift für James Loeb, zum sechzigsten Geburtstag gewidmet von seinen archäologischen Freunden in Deutschland und Amerika*, Munich: Bruckmann: 67–72.
—— (1940) 'The acropolis of Halae', *Hesperia* 9: 381–514.
Gounaris, A.P. (1999) Ἔρευνες Οικιστικής των Πρωτογεωμετρικών – Γεωμετρικών Κυκλάδων και τα ζητούμενα της Κυκλαδικής Πρωτοϊστορίας',

in N. Stampolidis (ed.) *ΦΩΣ ΚΥΚΛΑΔΙΚΩΝ. Μνήμη Νικόλαου Ζαφειρόπουλου*, Athens: N.P. Goulandris Foundation: 96–113.
Graeve, V. von (1992) 'Milet 1991', *IstMitt* 42: 97–134.
Graham, A.J. (1983) *Colony and Mother City in Ancient Greece* 2nd edn, Chicago: Ares.
—— (1986) 'The historical interpretation of Al Mina', *DHA* 12: 51–65.
Greaves, A.M. (2002) *Miletos: a History*, London: Routledge.
Greco, E. (ed.) (forthcoming) *Gli Achei a l'Identità etnica degli Achei d'Occidente*, Paestum: Fondazione Paestum.
Green, S.W. and Perlman, S.M. (eds) (1985) *The Archaeology of Frontiers and Boundaries*, Orlando: Academic Press.
Grote, G. (1854) *History of Greece* III 4th edn, London: John Murray.
Grove, D. (1972) 'The function and future of urban centres', in Ucko, Tringham and Dimbleby 1972: 559–65.
Gruben, G. (1988) 'Fundamentierungsprobleme der ersten archaischen Grossbauten', in H. Büsing and F. Hiller (eds) *Bathron. Beiträge zur Architektur und verwandten Künsten für Heinrich Drerup zu seinem 80 Geburtstag von seinen Schülern und Freunden*, Saarbrücken: Saarbrückner Druckerei und Verlag: 159–72.
—— (1993) 'Die inselionische Ordnung', in J. des Courtils and J.-C. Moretti (eds) *Les grands ateliers d'architecture dans le monde egéen du VIe siècle av. J.C. (Actes du colloque d'Istanbul, 23–25 mai 1991)*, Paris: Boccard: 97–109.
Gschnitzer, F. (1955) 'Stammes- und Ortsgemeinden im alten Griechenland', *Wiener Studien* 68: 120–44.
—— (1960) *Gemeinde und Herrschaft: von den Grundformen griechischer Staatsordnung*, Graz: Hermann Böhlaus.
—— (1971) 'Stadt und Stamm bei Homer', *Chiron* 1: 1–17.
Guggisberg, M. (1988) 'Terrakotten von Argos. Ein Fundkomplex aus dem Theater', *BCH* 112: 167–234.
Haarer, P. (2000) 'Οβελοί and Iron in Archaic Greece' (DPhil thesis, University of Oxford).
Hägg, R. (1982) 'Zur Stadtwerdung des dorischen Argos', in D. Papenfuss and V.M. Strocka (eds) *Palast und Hütte*, Mainz: von Zabern: 297–307.
—— (1983a) *The Greek Renaissance of the Eighth Century BC. Tradition and Innovation*, Stockholm: Paul Åström.
—— (1983b) 'Funerary meals in the Geometric necropolis at Asine', in Hägg 1983a: 189–93.
—— (ed.) (1998a) *Ancient Greek Cult Practice from the Archaeological Evidence*, Stockholm: Paul Åström.
—— (1998b) 'Argos and its neighbours: regional variations in the burial practices in the Protogeometric and Geometric periods', in Pariente and Touchais 1998: 131–5.
Hägg, R., Marinatos, N. and Nordquist, G.C. (eds) (1988) *Early Greek Cult Practice. Proceedings of the Fifth International Symposium at the Swedish Institute at Athens, 26–29 June, 1986*, Stockholm: Paul Åström.
Haggis, D. (1996) 'Archaeological survey at Kavousi, east Crete. Preliminary report', *Hesperia* 65: 373–432.
Haggis, D. and Nowicki, K. (1992) 'Khalasmeno and Katalimata: two Early Iron Age settlements in Monastiraki, East Crete', *Hesperia* 62: 303–37.
Hall, J.M. (1995a) 'Approaches to ethnicity in the Early Iron Age of Greece', in N.

Spencer (ed.) *Time, Tradition and Society in Greek Archaeology*, London: Routledge: 6–17.
—— (1995b) 'The role of language in Greek ethnicity', *PCPS* 41: 83–100.
—— (1997) *Ethnic Identity in Greek Antiquity*, Cambridge: CUP.
—— (2000) 'Sparta, Lakedaimon and the nature of perioikic dependency', *CPCPapers* 5: 73–89.
——(2001) 'Contested ethnicities: perceptions of Macedonia within evolving definitions of Greek identity', in Malkin 2001: 159–86.
—— (forthcoming) 'Myths of Greek colonialism: the case of south Italy and Achaean identity', in C. Morgan and G. Tsetskhladze (eds) *Art and Myth in the Colonial World*, Brill: Leiden.
Halstead, P. (1977) 'Prehistoric Thessaly: the submergence of civilisation', in Bintliff 1977a: 23–9.
—— (1994) 'The north-south divide: regional paths to complexity in prehistoric Greece', in C. Mathers and S. Stoddart (eds) *Development and Decline in the Mediterranean Bronze Age*, Sheffield: Collis: 195–219.
Hammond, N.G.L. (1956) 'The colonies of Elis in Cassopaea', in Ἀφιέρωμα εἰς τήν Ἤπειρον εἰς μνήμην Χρίστου Σουλή *(1892–1951)*, Athens: Myrtidi: 26–36.
—— (1967) *Epirus*, Oxford: OUP.
Handler, R. (1994) 'Is 'identity' a useful cross-cultural concept?', in J.R. Gillis (ed.) *Commemorations. The Politics of National Identity*, Princeton: PUP: 27–41.
Hänsel, B. (1989) *Kastanas. Ausgrabungen in einem Siedlungshügel der Bronze- und Eisenzeit Makedoniens, 1975–1979: Die Grabung und der Baubefund* (PAS 7), Berlin: Volker Speiss.
Hansen, E. (2000) 'Delphes et la travaille de la pierre', in A. Jacquemin (ed.) *Delphes cent ans après la Grande Fouille. Essai de bilan (BCH* supp. 36), Paris/Athens: Boccard/EFA: 201–13.
Hansen, M.H. (1995a) 'The "autonomous city-state". Ancient fact or modern fiction?', *CPCPapers* 2: 21–43.
—— (1995b) 'Boiotian *poleis* – a test case', *CPCActs* 2: 13–63.
—— (1996) ΠΟΛΛΑΧΩΣ ΠΟΛΙΣ ΛΕΓΕΤΑΙ (Arist.*Pol.* 1267a23). The Copenhagen inventory of *poleis* and the *lex hafniensis de civitate*', *CPCActs* 3: 7–72.
—— (1997a) 'Πόλις as the generic term for state', *CPCPapers* 4: 9–15.
—— (1997b) 'The polis as an urban centre. The literary and epigraphical evidence', *CPCActs* 4: 9–86.
—— (1997c) 'A typology of dependent poleis', *CPCPapers* 4: 29–37.
—— (1997d) 'The Copenhagen inventory of poleis and the *lex hafniensis de civitate*', in Mitchell and Rhodes 1997: 9–23.
—— (1999) 'Aristotle's reference to the Arkadian Federation at *Pol.* 1261a29', *CPCActs* 6: 80–8.
Hansen, M.H. and Fischer Hansen, T. (1994) 'Monumental political architecture in Archaic and Classical Greek *poleis*. Evidence and historical significance', *CPCPapers* 1: 23–90.
Harke, H. (1982) 'Early Iron Age hill settlement in west central Europe: patterns and developments', *OJA* 1: 187–211.
Harrison, E.B. (1965) *Agora* XI. *Archaic and Archaistic Sculpture*, Princeton: ASCSA.

BIBLIOGRAPHY

Hartog, F. (1988) *The Mirror of Herodotos. The Representation of the Other in the Writing of History*, Berkeley/London: University of California Press.

Hatzi Spiliopoulou, G. (1991) 'Ταφικοί Πίθοι στην Ηλεία κατά τον 4ου αι. π.χ. και τους Ελληνιστικούς Χρόνους', in Rizakis 1991b: 351–63.

Hatzopoulos, M. (1994) 'Thessalie et Macédoine: affinités et convergences', *ΘΕΣΣΑΛΙΑ* 2: 249–54.

Hayden, B. (1983) 'New plans of the Early Iron Age settlement of Vrokastro', *Hesperia* 52: 367–87.

—— (1988) 'Fortifications of postpalatial and Early Iron Age Crete', *AA*: 1–21.

—— (1991) 'Terracotta figures, figurines, and vase attachments from Vrokastro, Crete', *Hesperia* 60: 103–44.

Hayward, C.L. (1996) 'High-resolution provenance determination of construction-stone: a preliminary study of Corinthian oolitic limestone quarries at Examilia', *Geoarchaeology* 11: 215–34.

—— (1999) 'First results from a high resolution study of ancient construction-stone quarries of the Corinthia, southern Greece', in M. Schvoerer (ed) *Archaeomateriaux: marbres et autres roches. ASMOSIA IV. Actes de la IVème conference internationale, Bordeaux, France, octobre 1995*, CRPAA: Université Michel de Montaigne, Bordeaux 3/CNRS: 91–100.

—— (forthcoming a) 'Geology of Corinth: study of a basic resource', *Corinth* XX. *Corinth: the Centenary, 1896–1996*, Princeton: ASCSA: 15–42.

—— (forthcoming b) 'The pre-eighth century palaeotopography of Corinth', *Geoarchaeology*.

Head, B.V. (1911) *Historia numorum. A Manual of Numismatics* 2nd edn, Oxford: OUP.

Hedeager, L. (1992) *Iron Age Societies: from Tribe to State in Northern Europe 500BC to AD 700*, Oxford: Blackwell.

Heilmeyer, W.D. (1979) *Olympische Forschungen* XII. *Frühe olympische Bronzefiguren, die Tiervotive*, Berlin: de Gruyter.

Heine Nielsen, T. (1996a) 'Arkadia. City ethnics and tribalism', *CPCActs* 3: 117–63.

—— (1996b) 'Was there an Arkadian confederacy in the fifth century B.C.?', *CPCPapers* 3: 39–61

—— (1996c) 'A survey of dependent poleis in Classical Arkadia', *CPCPapers* 3: 63–105.

—— (1997) '*Triphylia*. An experiment in ethnic construction and political organisation', *CPCPapers* 4: 129–62.

—— (1999) 'The concept of Arkadia – the people, their land, and their organisation', *CPCActs* 6: 16–79.

—— (2000) 'Epiknemidian, Hypoknemidian, and Opountian Lokrians. Reflections on the political organisation of East Lokris in the Classical period', *CPCPapers* 5: 91–120.

—— (2002) *Arkadia and its Poleis in the Archaic and Classical Periods* (*Hypomnemata* 140), Göttingen: Vandenhoeck and Ruprecht.

Heine Nielsen, T. and Roy, J. (1998) 'The Azanians of northern Arkadia', *ClMed* 49: 5–44.

Hejnic, J. (1961) *Pausanias the Perieget and the Archaic History of Arcadia*, Prague: Czech Academy of Sciences.

Helly, B. (1973) *Gonnoi* I. *La cité et son histoire*, Amsterdam: Hakkert.

—— (ed.) (1979) *La Thessalie. Actes de la table-ronde 21–24 Juillet 1975, Lyon*, Lyon/Paris: Maison de l'Orient/Boccard.

—— (1984) 'Le territoire de Larisa: ses limites, son extension, son organisation', *Ktêma* 9: 213–34.

—— (1987) 'Le "Dotion Pedion", Lakéreia et les origines de Larisa', *Journal des Savants*: 127–58.

—— (1991) 'Les cités antiques de la Thessalie', *Les Dossiers d'Archaeologie*: 30–43.

—— (1994) 'Quinze années de géographie historique en Thessalie', *ΘΕΣΣΑΛΙΑ* 2: 13–20.

—— (1995) *Aleuas le Roux, les tétrades et les Tagoi*, Lyon: Collection de la Maison de l'Orient Méditerranéen.

—— (1997) 'Arithmétique et histoire. L'organisation militaire et politique des Ioniens en Achaïe à l'époque archaique', *TOPOI* 7: 207–62.

Helm, J. (ed.) (1968) *Essays on the Problem of the Tribe (Proceedings of the 1967 Annual Spring Meeting of the American Ethnological Society)*, Seattle/London: University of Washington Press.

Herman, G. (1987) *Ritualised Friendship and the Greek City*, Cambridge: CUP.

Herrmann, H.-V. (1972) *Olympia: Heiligtum und Wettkampfstätte,* Munich: Hirmer.

Heurtley, W.A. and Skeat, T.C. (1930–1) 'The tholos tombs of Marmariane', *BSA* 31: 1–55.

Hignett, C. (1952) *A History of the Athenian Constitution*, Oxford: OUP.

Hiller von Gärtringen, F. (1890) 'Das Königtum bei den Thessalern,' *Aus der Anomia*, Berlin: Weidmann: 1–16.

Hobsbawm, E. (1992) 'Ethnicity and nationalism in Europe today', *Anthropology Today* 8: 3–8.

Hodder, I. (1978) 'Simple correlations between material culture and society: a review', in I. Hodder (ed.) *The Spatial Organization of Culture*, London: Duckworth: 3–24.

—— (ed.) (1987) *Archaeology as Long-Term History*, Cambridge: CUP.

—— (1991) *Reading the Past* 2nd edn, Cambridge: CUP.

Hodkinson, S. (1988) 'Animal husbandry in the Greek polis', in Whittaker 1988: 35–74.

Hodkinson, S. and Hodkinson, H. (1981) 'Mantineia and the Mantinike: settlement and society in a Greek polis', *BSA* 76: 239–96.

Hoffman, G. (1997) *Imports and Immigrants. Near Eastern Contacts with Iron Age Crete*, Ann Arbor: University of Michigan Press.

Hölkeskamp, K.-J. (1992a) 'Arbitrators, lawgivers and the 'codification of law' in Archaic Greece', *Metis* 7: 49–81.

—— (1992b) 'Written law in Archaic Greece', *PCPS* 38: 87–117.

—— (2000) '(In-)Schrift und Monument. Zum Begriff des Gesetzes im archaischen und klassischen Griechenland', *ZPE* 132: 73–96.

Holland, H. (1815) *Travels in the Ionian islands, Albania, Thessaly, Macedonia during the years 1812 and 1813*, London: Longman, Hurst, Rees, Orme and Brown.

Holmberg, E. (1944) *The Swedish Excavations at Asea in Arcadia*, Lund: Gleerup.

Hope Simpson, R. (1981) *Mycenaean Greece*, Park Ridge, NJ: Noyes.

Horden, P. and Purcell, N. (2000) *The Corrupting Sea. A Study of Mediterraean History*, Oxford: Blackwell.

Horowitz, D.L. (1975) 'Ethnic identity', in N. Glazer and D. Moynihan (eds)

Ethnicity. Theory and Experience, Cambridge, Mass./London: Harvard University Press: 111–40.

Houby-Nielsen, S. (1992) 'Interaction between chieftains and citizens? 7th cent. B.C. burial customs in Athens', *Acta Hyperboreia* 4: 343–74.

—— (1995) '"Burial language" in Archaic and Classical Kerameikos', *Proceedings of the Danish Institute at Athens* I: 129–91.

Huber, S. (1991) 'Un atelier de bronzier dans le sanctuaire d'Apollon à Érétrie?', *AntK* 34: 137–54.

Hübinger, U. (1992) 'On Pan's iconography and the cult in the sanctuary of Pan on the slopes of Mount Lykaion', in R. Hägg (ed.) *The Iconography of Greek Cult in the Archaic and Classical Periods* (*Kernos* supp.1), Athens/Liège: Kernos: 189–212.

—— (1993) 'Überlegungen zu den Bronzestatuetten aus dem 'Pan'-Heiligtum am Südabhang des Lykaion', in Palagia and Coulson 1993: 25–31.

Humphreys, S.C. (1978a) 'Anthropology and the Classics', in S.C. Humphreys (ed.) *Anthropology and the Greeks*, London: Routledge: 17–30.

—— (1978b) 'Town and country in ancient Greece', in S.C. Humphreys (ed.) *Anthropology and the Greeks*, London: Routledge: 130–5.

—— (1978c) 'Structure, context and communication. Part II. Kinship in Greek society, c.800–300 B.C.', in S.C. Humphreys (ed.) *Anthropology and the Greeks*, London: Routledge: 193–202.

Huntington, R. and Metcalf, P. (1979) *Celebrations of Death*, Cambridge: CUP.

Huxley, G.L. (1980) 'Aristotle on the origins of the polis', *ΣΤΗΛΗ. Τόμος εἰς μνήμην Νικολάου Κοντολέοντος*, Athens: Σωματείο Φίλων Νικ. Κοντολέοντος: 258–64.

Intzesiloglou, B.G. (1994) 'Ἱστορικὴ Τοπογραφία τῆς Περιοχῆς τοῦ Κόλπου τοῦ Βόλου', *ΘΕΣΣΑΛΙΑ*: 2: 31–56.

—— (2000) 'A newly discovered Archaic bronze cult statue from the ancient city of Metropolis in Thessaly', in C.C. Mattusch, A. Brauer and S.E. Knudsen (eds) *From the Parts to the Whole I. Acta of the 13th International Bronze Congress held at Cambridge, Massachussets, May 28–June 1 1995* (*JRA* supp.39), Portsmouth, Rhode Island: 65–8.

—— (2002) 'The Archaic temple of Apollo in ancient Metropolis (Thessaly)', in M. Stamatopoulou and M. Yerolanou (eds) *Excavating Classical Culture: Recent Archaeological Discoveries in Greece. Proceedings of an International Symposium, University of Oxford 24–26 March 2001*, Oxford: Beazley Archive/Archaeopress: 109–15.

Ioakimidou, C. (1995) *Die Statuenreihen griechischer Poleis und Bünde aus spätarchaischer und klassischer Zeit*, Munich: Tuduv.

Iozzo, M. (1995) 'Sintesi storica', *Pallation*: 393–403.

Iozzo, M. and Pagano, M. (1995) 'Cataloghi degli oggetti', *Pallation*: 19–280.

Isaacs, H.R. (1975) 'Basic group identity', in N. Glazer and D. Moynihan (eds) *Ethnicity. Theory and Experience*, Cambridge, Mass./London: Harvard University Press: 29–52.

Isager, S. (1992) 'Sacred animals in Classical and Hellenistic Greece,' in T. Linders and B. Alroth (eds) *Economics of Cult in the Ancient Greek World*, Uppsala: University of Uppsala Press: 15–20.

Jacob, C. (1980–1) 'Paysages hantés et jardins merveilleux: la Grèce imaginaire de Pausanias', *L'Ethnographie*: 35–67.

—— (1991) *Géographie et ethnographie en Grèce ancienne*, Paris: Armand Colin.

Jacob-Felsch, M. (1996) 'Die spätmykenische bis frühprotogeometrische Keramik', in R.C.S. Felsch (ed.) *Kalapodi* I. *Ergebnisse der Ausgrabungen im Heiligtum der Artemis und des Apollon von Hyampolis in der antiken Phokis*, Mainz: von Zabern: 2–114.

Jacquemin, A. (1993) 'Repercussions de l'éntrée de Delphes dans l'amphictionie sur la construction à Delphes à l'époque archaïque', in J. des Courtils and J.-C. Moretti (eds) *Les grands ateliers d'architecture dans le monde egéen du VIe siècle av. J.C. (Actes du colloque d'Istanbul, 23–25 mai 1991)*, Paris: Boccard: 217–25.

—— (1999) *Offrandes monumentales à Delphes*, Paris/Athens: EFA/Boccard.

Jalkotzy, S. Deger (1999a) 'Elateia and problems of pottery chronology', *ΠΕΡΙΦΕΡΙΑ*: 195–202.

—— (1999b) 'Military prowess and social status in Mycenaean Greece', in Laffineur 1999: 121–31.

Jalkotzy, S. Deger and Dakoronia, F. (1990) 'Elateia (Phokis) und die frühe Geschichte der Griechen. Ein österreichisch-griechisches Grabungsprojekt', *Anzeiger der Österreichische Akademie der Wissenschaften Philosophische-Historische Klasse* 127: 77–86.

Jameson, M.H. (1989) 'Mountains and the Greek city-states', in J.-F. Bergier (ed.) *Montagnes, fleuves, forêts dans l'histoire. Barrières ou lignes de convergence?*, St. Katharinen: Scripta Mercaturae: 7–17.

Jameson, M.H., Runnels, C.N. and van Andel T.H. (eds) (1994) *A Greek Countryside. The Southern Argolid from Prehistory to the Present Day*, Stanford CA: Stanford University Press.

Jeffery, L.H. (1990) *The Local Scripts of Archaic Greece* 2nd edn, rev. A.W. Johnston, Oxford: OUP.

Johnston. A.W. (1999) 'Epichoric alphabets: the rise of the *polis* or a slip of the pen?', in N. Dimoudis (ed.) *The History of the Hellenic Language and Writing*, Altenburg: Verlag für Kultur und Wissenschaft: 419–33.

Johnston, C.N. (1988) *Aristotle's Theory of the State*, Basingstoke: MacMillan.

Jones, C.P. (1996) 'Εθνος and γένος in Herodotus', *CQ* ns 46: 315–20.

Jones, G. (1982) 'Cereal and pulse remains from Protogeometric and Geometric Iolkos, Thessaly', *Ανθροπολογικά* 3: 75–8.

Jones, N. (1987) *Public Organisation in Ancient Greece: a Documentary Study*, Philadephia: American Philosophical Society.

Jones, R.E. (1986) *Greek and Cypriot Pottery. A Review of Scientific Studies* (BSA Fitch Laboratory Occasional Paper 1), Athens/London: Thames & Hudson/BSA.

Jones, S. (1997) *The Archaeology of Ethnicity. Constructing Identities in the Past and Present*, London: Routledge.

Jost, M. (1975) 'Statuette de bronze archaïque provenant de Lykosoura', *BCH* 99: 339–40.

—— (1985) *Sanctuaires et Cultes d'Arcadie*, Paris: Vrin.

—— (1986) 'Villages de l'Arcadie antique', *Ktêma* 11: 145–58.

—— (1990) 'Sanctuaires ruraux et sanctuaires urbains en Arcadie', in A. Schachter (ed.) *Le sanctuaire grec* (Entretiens Hardt 37), Geneva: Vandœuvres: 205–39.

—— (1994) 'The distribution of sanctuaries in civic space in Arkadia', in Alcock and Osborne 1994: 217–30.

—— (1999) 'Les schémas de peuplement de l'Arcadie aux époques archaïque et classique', *CPCActs* 6: 192–247.

Kahn, C. (1960) *Anaximander and the Origins of Greek Cosmology*, New York: Columbia University Press.

BIBLIOGRAPHY

Kahrsted, U. (1924) 'Grundherrschaft, Freistadt und Staat in Thessalien,' *Nachrichten von der Gesellschaft der Wissenschaften zu Göttingen. Philologische-Historische Klasse:* 128–55.

Kakavoyiannis, E. (1977) 'Ανασκαφικές Έρευνες στις Φερές της Θεσσαλίας το 1977', *AAA* 10: 174–87.

Kalligas, P.G. (1992) 'Θεσσαλία και Εύβοια κατά την Πρώιμη Εποχή του Σιδήρου (11ος–9ος αι. π.χ.)', *Praktika Theochari:* 298–307.

Kambouroglou, E.M. (1994) 'Η Γεωμορφολογική Εξέλιξη του Κόλπου του Βόλου από τη Νεολιθική Εποχή μέχρι Σήμερα', *ΘΕΣΣΑΛΙΑ* 1: 41–52.

Karageorghis, V. (1994) *Cyprus in the 11th Century B.C.*, Nicosia: Levendis Foundation.

Karageorghis, V. and Stampolidis, N. (eds) (1998) *Eastern Mediterranean. Cyprus – Dodecanese – Crete 16th–6th century B.C. Proceedings of an International Symposium held at Rethymnon – Crete in May 1997*, Athens: Adam.

Karagiorga Stathakopoulou, T. (1989) 'Πτόλις Μαντινείας', *AAA* 22: 113–22.

—— (1992–3) 'Η Μαντινική Πτόλις', *Πρακτικά του Δ' Διεθνους Συνέδριου Πελοποννησιακών Σπουδών* II, 9–16 Σεπτ 1990 Athens: Society for Peloponnesian Studies: 97–115.

Karamitrou-Mentesidi, G. (1999) *Βοΐον – Νότια Ορεστίς. Αρχαιολογική Ερευνα και Ιστορική Τοπογραφία*, Thessaloniki: Th. Altinzis.

Kase, E.W., Szemler, G.J., Wilkie, N.C. and Wallace, P.W. (1991) *The Great Isthmus Corridor Route. Explorations of the Phokis-Doris Expedition* I, Dubuque: Kendall Hunt.

Katakouta, S. and Touphexis, G. (1994) 'Τα Τείχη του Φαρσάλου', *ΘΕΣΣΑΛΙΑ* 2: 189–200.

Katarachias, K. and Karafyllis, N. (1992) *Αρχαιολογικά Ευρήματα Φιλίας και Αρνής-Κιερίου*, Karditsa: Karditsas.

Kearsley, R. (1989) *The Pendent Semi-Circle Skyphos* (BICS supp. 44), London: ICS.

—— (1999) 'Greeks overseas in the 8th century BC: Euboeans, Al Mina and Assyrian imperialism', in G.R. Tsetskhladze (ed.) *Ancient Greeks West and East*, Leiden: Brill: 109–34.

Kellas, J.G. (1991) *The Politics of Nationalism and Ethnicity*, London: Macmillan.

Kelly, T. (1966) 'The Calaurian Amphictiony', *AJA* 70: 113–21.

Keramopoullos, A. (1907) '*Φωκικὸν ἀνάθημα ἐν Δελφοῖς*', *AE:* cols 91–104.

Kilian, K. (1973) 'Zur eisenzeitlichen Transhumanz in Nordgriechenland', *Archäologisches Korrespondenzblatt* 3: 431–5.

—— (1975a) *Fibeln in Thessalien von der mykenischen bis zur archaischen Zeit* (PBF XIV, ii), Munich: C.H. Beck.

—— (1975b) 'Trachtzubehör der Eisenzeit zwischen Ägäis und Adria', *PZ* 50: 9–140.

—— (1976) 'Der Siedlungshügel Bunar Baschi bei Sikourion', in V. Milojcic et al. *Die deutschen Ausgrabungen auf Magulen um Larisa in Thessalien 1966*, Bonn: Habelt: 65–71.

—— (1977) 'Zwei Italische Kammhelme aus Griechenland', *Etudes Delphiques* (BCH supp. 4), Athens/Paris: Boccard: 429–42.

—— (1983) 'Weihungen aus Eisen und Eisenverarbeitung im Heiligtum zu Philia (Thessalien)', in Hägg 1983a: 131–46.

—— (1988) 'Mycenaeans up to date, trends and changes in recent research', in E. French and K. Wardle (eds) *Problems in Greek Prehistory. Papers Presented at the*

Centenary Conference of the British School of Archaeology at Athens, Manchester, April 1986, Bristol: Bristol Classical Press: 115–52.
Kilian-Dirlmeier I. (1979) *Anhänger in Griechenland von der mykenischen bis zur spätgeometrichen Zeit* (PBF XI, ii), Munich: C.H. Beck.
—— (1985) 'Fremde Weihungen in griechischen Heiligtümern vom 8. bis zum Beginn des 7. Jahrhunderts v. Chr.', *JRGZM* 32: 215–54.
—— (1985–6) 'Αφιερώματα μη Κορινθιακής Προλεύσεως στα Ηραία της Περαχώρας (τέλος 8ου-ἀρχή 7ου αἰ. Π.Χ.)', *Πελοποννη6ιακά* 19: 369–75.
Kinch, K. (1914) *Fouilles de Vroulia: (Rhodes)*, Berlin: G. Reimer.
Kinzl, K.H. (1988) 'Gawantka's *Sogenannte Polis*: and some thoughts *à propos*', *EMC* 7: 403–12.
Kirk, G.S. (1985) *The Iliad: a Commentary* I, Cambridge: CUP.
Klein, N. (1997) 'Excavation of the Greek temples at Mycenae by the British School at Athens', *BSA* 92: 247–322.
Knapp, A.B. and Ashmore, W. (1999) 'Archaeological landscapes: constructed, conceptualized, ideational', in A.B. Knapp and W. Ashmore (eds) *Archaeologies of Landscape. Contemporary Perspectives*, Oxford: Blackwell: 1–30.
Knauss, J. (1988) 'Der Damm im Takka-See beim alten Tegea (Arkadien, Peloponnes)', *AthMitt* 105: 1–52.
—— (1990) 'Der Graben des Herakles im Becken von Pheneos und die Verteibung der Stymphalischen Vögel', *AthMitt* 103: 25–36.
Knauss, J., Heinrich, B. and Kalcyk, H. (1986) 'Der Damm bei Kaphyai und Orchomenos in Arkadien', *AA*: 583–611.
Koerner, R. (1974) 'Die staatliche Entwicklung in Alt-Achaia', *Klio* 56: 457–95.
Koliou, N. (ed.) (1994) *Νεότερα Δεδομένα των Ερευνών γιά την Αρχαία Ιωλκό*, Volos: Demos Volou.
Kolonas, L. (1996–7) 'Νεώτερη μυκηναϊκή τοπογραφία της Αχαΐας', *Πρακτικά του Ε΄ Διεθνους Συνέδριου Πελοποννησιακῶν Σπουδῶν, 6–10 Σεπτ 1995*, Athens: Society for Peloponnesian Studies: 468–96.
—— (2000) 'Μυκηναϊκές Εγκαταστάσεις στην Ορεινή Δυμαία χώρα', in Rizakis 2000: 93–104.
Kopcke, G. and Tokumaru, I. (eds) (1992). *Greece between East and West: 10th-8th Centuries BC*, Mainz: von Zabern.
Kourinou, E. Pikoulas (2000) *Σπάρτη. Συμβολή στὴ Μνημειακη Τοπογραφία της*, Athens: Horos.
Kourou, N. (1980) 'Ταφικὸ Σύνολο ἀπο τήν Περιοχὴ Αἰγίου', *ΣΤΗΛΗ· Τόμος εἰς μνήμην Νικόλαου Κοντολεόντος* Athens: *Σωματείο Φίλων Νικ. Κοντολεόντος*: 303–17.
—— (1990–1) 'Εύβοια και Ανατολική Μεσογείος στις Αρχές της Πρώτες Χιλιετίας (ἡ το Προοίμο τῆς Εμφάνισης του Ελληνικού Αλφαβήτου)', *Αρχείον Ευβοϊκών Μελετών* 29: 237–79.
—— (2000) 'Phoenician presence in east Crete reconsidered', *Actas del IV Congreso des Estudios Fenicios y Púnicos, Cádiz, 2 al 6 de Octubre de 1995* 3, Cádiz: Universidad de Cádiz: 1067–81.
Kraay, C. (1976) *Archaic and Classical Greek Coins*, London: Methuen.
Kraus, T. (1960) *Hekate. Studien zu Wesen und Bild der Göttin in Kleiasien und Griechenland*, Heidelberg: Carl Winter University Press.
Kristiansen, K. (1998) 'The formulation of tribal systems in northern Europe,

4000–500 BC', in K. Kristiansen and M. Rowlands (eds) *Social Transformations in Archaeology. Global and Local Perspectives*, London: Routledge: 70–105.
Kroll, H. (1993) 'Kulturpflanzen von Kalapodi', *AA*: 161–82.
Kroll, J.H. (1996) 'Hemiobols to Assaria: the bronze coinage of Roman Aigion', *NC* 156: 49–78.
Kumar, K. (1991) 'Maine and the theory of progress', in Diamond 1991: 76–87.
Kuper, A. (1982) 'Linear theory: a critical retrospective', *AnnRevAnth* 11: 71–95.
—— (1991) 'The rise and fall of Maine's patriarchal society', in Diamond 1991: 99–110.
Kyrieleis, H. (forthcoming a) 'Zu den Anfängen des Heiligtums von Olympia', in Kyrieleis forthcoming b.
—— (forthcoming b) *Olympia 1875–2000*, Berlin: DAI.
Laffineur, R. (ed.) (1999) *POLEMOS, Le contexte guerrier en égée à l'âge du bronze (Aegaeum 19)*, Liège/Austin: Université de Liège/University of Texas.
Lakaki-Marchetti, M. (2000) 'Σωστικές Ανασκαφές στην Κάτω Αχαγία', in Rizakis 2000: 113–22.
Langdon, S. (1999) 'Figurines and social change: visualizing gender in Dark Age Greece', in N.L. Wicker and B. Arnold (eds) *From the Ground Up: Beyond Gender Theory in Archaeology* , Oxford: BAR: 23–29.
—— (2001) 'Beyond the grave: biographies from early Greece', *AJA* 105: 579–606.
Lapatin, K. (2001) *Chryselephantine Statuary in the Ancient Mediterranean World*, Oxford: OUP.
Laroche, D. and Nenna, M.-D. (1993) 'Etudes sur les trésors en Poros à Delphes', in J. des Courtils and J.-C. Moretti (eds) *Les grands ateliers d'architecture dans le monde egéen du VIe siècle av. J.C. (Actes du colloque d'Istanbul, 23–25 mai 1991)*, Paris: Boccard: 227–45.
Larsen, J.A.O. (1945) 'Representation and democracy in Hellenistic federalism', *ClPh* 40: 65–97.
—— (1966) *Representative Government in Greek and Roman History*, Berkeley/Los Angeles: University of California Press.
—— (1968) *Greek Federal States. Their Institutions and History*, Oxford: OUP.
Lasserre, F. (1976) 'L'historiographie grecque à l'époque archaïque', *Quaderni di Storia* 4: 113–42.
Leach, E. (1989) 'Tribal ethnography: past, present and future', in E. Tonkin, M. McDonald and M. Chapman (eds) *History and Ethnicity*, London/New York: Routledge: 34–47.
Lebessi, A. (1981) 'Η Συνέχεια της Κρητομυκηναϊκής Λατρείας· Επιβιώσεις και Αναβιώσεις,' *AE*: 1–24.
Lefèvre, F. (1998) *L'amphictionie Pyléo-Delphique: histoire et institutions*, Paris/Athens: Boccard/EFA.
Lehmann, G.A. (1980) 'Die 'Erste' Heilige Kreig – eine Fiktion?', *Historia* 29: 242–6.
Lemos, I. (1998) 'Euboea and its Aegean koine', in Bats and d'Agostino 1998: 45–58.
Lenz, J.R. (1993) 'Kings and the Ideology of Kingship (c.1200–700B.C.). Epic, Archaeology and History' (PhD diss., Colombia University).
Lepore, E. (1962) *Ricerche sull'Antico Epiro*, Bari: Vittorio de Falco.
Lerat, L. (1961) 'Fouilles à Delphes, à l'est du grande sanctuaire (1950–1957)', *BCH* 85: 316–66.

Levi, D. (1923–4) 'L'antro delle Ninfe e di Pan a Farsalo in Tessaglia', *ASAtene* 6–7: 27–42.
Lewis, H.S. (1968) 'Typology and process in political evolution', in Helm 1968: 101–10.
Lindenlauf, A. (2001) 'Waste Management in Ancient Greece from the Homeric to the Classical Period: Concepts and Practices of Waste, Dirt, Recycling and Disposal' (PhD thesis, University of London).
Linders, T. (1989–90) 'The melting down of discarded metal offerings in Greek sanctuaries', *Scienze dell'Antichità* 3–4: 281–6.
Link, S. (1991) *Landverteilung und sozialer Frieden im archaischen Griechenland* (Historia Einz. 69), Stuttgart: Franz Steiner.
Little, L.M. and Papadopoulos, J. (1998) 'A social outcast in Early Iron Age Athens', *Hesperia* 67: 375–404.
Lorandou-Papantoniou, R. (1999) *ΣΟΛΥΓΕΙΑ. Η Ανασκαφή του 1957–1958*, Athens: Archaeological Society of Athens.
Lorenz, B. (1976) *Thessalische Grabgedichte vom 6 bis zum 4 Jahrhundert v. Chr.*, Innsbruck: Wagner.
Lotze, D. (1959) *Μεταξύ Ελευθερών και Δούλων. Studien zur Rechtsstellung unfrier Landbervölkerungen in Griechenland bis zum 4. Jahrhundert v. Chr.*, Berlin: Akademie Verlag.
Luce, J.-M. (1992) 'Les terres cuites de Kirrha', in J.-F. Bommelaer (ed.) *Delphes, centenaire de la 'Grande Fouille'*, Leiden: Brill: 263–75.
Luppino, S. and Tomay, G. (forthcoming) 'Sibari e la ceramica di tradizione achea', in Greco forthcoming.
Maass, M. (1978) *Olympische Forschungen X. Die geometrischen Dreifüsse von Olympia*, Berlin: de Gruyter.
McDonald, W., Coulson, W. and Rosser, J. (1983) *Nichoria III. Dark Age and Byzantine Occupation*, Minneapolis: University of Minnesota Press.
MacFarlane, A.D.J. (1991) 'Some contributions of Maine to history and anthropology', in Diamond 1991: 111–42.
McInerney, J. (1997) 'The Phokikon and the hero archegetes', *Hesperia* 66: 193–207.
—— (1999) *In the Folds of Parnassos. Land and Ethnicity in Ancient Phokis*, Austin: University of Texas Press.
—— (2001) 'Ethnos and ethnicity in early Greece', in Malkin 2001: 51–73.
McNairn, B. (1980) *The Method and Theory of V. Gordon Childe*, Edinburgh: Edinburgh University Press.
Maine, H.S. (1861) *Ancient Law*, London: John Murray.
Malakasioti, Z. (1994) 'Νεότερα Δεδομένα για την Αρχαία Ιωλκό στα Παλιά του Βόλου', in Koliou 1994: 47–57.
—— (1997a) 'Ταφικοί Τύμβοι στην Περιοχή Βουλοκαλύβα-Πλατάνου Αλμυρού, *Αχαιοφθιώτικα Β΄. Πρακτικά του Β΄ Συνέδριου Αλμυρωτικών Σπουδών* I, Almyros: Karatasiou: 189–96.
—— (1997b) 'Αρχαιολογικές και Τοπογραφικές Ερευνες στην Τετράδα της Αχαΐας Φθιώτιδας: περιοχή Αλμυρού', *Δελτίο της Φιλαρχαίου Εταιρείας Αλμυρού Όθρυς* 1: 29–53.
Malkin, I. (1987) *Religion and Colonization in Ancient Greece*, Leiden: Brill.
—— (1994) 'Inside and outside: colonization and the formation of the mother city', in d'Agostino and Ridgway 1994: 1–9.

—— (1998a) 'Ithaka, Odysseus and Euboeans in the eighth century', in Bats and d'Agostino 1998: 1–10.
—— (1998b) *The Returns of Odysseus. Colonization and Ethnicity*, Berkeley/London: University of California Press.
—— (ed.) (2001a) *Ancient Perceptions of Greek Ethnicity*, Harvard: Center for Hellenic Studies/Harvard University Press.
—— (2001b) 'Greek ambiguities: "Ancient Hellas" and "Barbarian Epirus"', in Malkin 2001a: 187–212.
Marangou, L. (1988) 'Τειχισμένοι Οἰκισμοὶ τῶν Γεωμετρικῶν Χρόνων (9ος-8ος π.Χ. αἰωνας', *Πρακτικά της Ακαδημίας Αθηνών*: 80–94.
Marcadé, J. (1953) *Recueil des signatures de sculpteurs grecs* I, Paris: Boccard.
—— (1957) *Recueil des signatures de sculpteurs grecs* II, Paris: Boccard.
Mark, I. (1993) *The Sanctuary of Athena Nike in Athens. Architectural Stages and Chronology* (*Hesperia* supp. 26), Princeton: ASCSA.
Martin, R. (1983) *L'urbanisme dans la Grèce antique* 2nd edn, Paris: Picard.
Martin, T. (1985) *Sovereignty and Coinage in Classical Greece*, Princeton: PUP.
—— (1995) 'Coins, mints, and the polis', *CPCActs* 2: 257–91.
Marx, K. (1857–8) 'Pre-capitalist economic formations', manuscript published in E. Hobsbawm (ed.) (1961) *Pre-Capitalist Economic Formations: Karl Marx*, New York: International Publishers: 67–120.
Marzolff, P. (1980) *Demetrias* III. *Demetrias und seine Halbinsel*, Bonn: Habelt.
—— (1994) 'Antike Städtebau und Architektur in Thessalien', *ΘΕΣΣΑΛΙΑ*: 2: 255–76.
Maschner, H. and Mithen, S. (eds) (1996) 'Darwinian archaeologies: an introductory essay', in H. Maschner (ed.) *Darwinian Archaeologies*, New York/London: Plenum: 3–14.
Masson, O. (1968) 'Une inscription Thessalienne archaïque relative à la construction d'un édifice', *BCH* 92: 97–102.
Mattusch, C. (1988) *Greek Bronze Statuary. From the Beginnings through the Fifth Century BC*, Ithaka/London: Cornell University Press.
Maurizio, L. (1995) 'Anthropology and spirit possession: a reconsideration of the Pythia's role at Delphi', *JHS* 105: 69–86.
Mazarakis Ainian, A. (1987) 'Geometric Eretria', *AntK* 30: 3–24.
—— (1988) 'Early Greek temples: their origin and function', in Hägg, Marinatos and Nordquist 1988: 105–9.
—— (1996) 'Ανασκαφή Σκάλας Οροποῦ (1985–87, 1996)', *PAE*: 21–124
—— (1997) *From Rulers' Dwellings to Temples. Architecture, Religion and Society in Early Iron Age Greece (1100–700 B.C.)*, Jonsered: Paul Åström.
—— (1998) 'Oropos in the Early Iron Age', in Bats and d'Agostino 1998: 179–215.
Meiggs, R. and Lewis, D. (eds) (1988) *A Selection of Greek Historical Inscriptions* rev. edn, Oxford: OUP.
Melas, E.M. (1989) 'Emics, etics and empathy in archaeological theory', in I. Hodder (ed.) *The Meaning of Things. Material Culture and Symbolic Expression*, London: Unwin Hyman: 137–55.
Menadier, B. (1995) 'The Sixth Century BC Temple and the Sanctuary and Cult of Hera Akraia, Perachora' (PhD diss., University of Cincinatti).
Mersch, A. (1997) 'Urbanization of the Attic countryside from the late 8th century to the 6th century BC', in Damgard Andersen et al. 1997: 45–62.

Miller, S.G. (1974) 'The altar of the six goddesses in Thessalian Pherai', *CSCA* 7: 231–56.
—— (1995) 'Architecture as evidence for the identity of the early *polis*', *CPCActs* 2: 201–44.
—— (forthcoming) 'The shrine of Opheltes and the earliest stadium of Nemea,' in Kyrieleis forthcoming b.
Milojcic, V. (1955) 'Vorbericht über die Ausgrabungen auf den Magulen von Otzaki, Arapi und Gremnos bei Larisa 1955', *AA*: 182–231.
—— (1957) 'Bericht über die ausgrabungen auf der Gremnos-Magula bei Larisa 1956', *AA*: 141–83.
—— (1960) 'Bericht über die Ausgrabungen und Arbeiten in Thessalien im Herbst 1959', *AA*: 150–78.
—— (1972) 'Neue deutsche Ausgrabungen in Demetrias/Thessalien, 1967–1972', *Jahrbuch der Heidelberger Akademie der Wissenschaften*: 61–84.
—— (1974) 'Bericht über die Deutschen archäologischen Ausgrabungen in Thessalien 1973', *AAA* 7: 43–75.
Minon, S. (1994) 'Les tablettes éléenes du VIe et du Ve siècle: étude dialectologique et historique' (thèse de doctorat, École Pratique des Hautes Études, Paris). [Non vidi].
Mitchell, L. and Rhodes, P.J. (eds) (1997) *The Development of the Polis in Archaic Greece*, London: Routledge.
Mitsopoulos-Leon, V. (1992) 'Artémis de Lousoi: les fouilles autrichiennes', *Kernos* 5: 97–108.
—— (1993) 'The statue of Artemis at Lousoi: some thoughts', in Palagia and Coulson 1993: 33–9.
Mitsopoulos-Leon, V. and Lädstatter, G. (1996) 'Lousoi', *JOAI* 65 Grab.: 40–6.
—— (1997) 'Lousoi', *JOAI* 66 Grab.: 57–64.
Moggi, M. (1976) *I Sinecismi Interstatali Greci I. Dalle origini al 338 a.c.*, Pisa: Marlin.
—— (1991) 'Processi di urbanizzazione nel libro di Pausania sull'Arcadia', *RFIC* ns 119: 46–62.
Momigliano, A.D. (1932) 'Tagia e tetrarchia in Tessaglia', *Athenaeum* 10: 47–54.
—— (1994) 'The ancient city of Fustel de Coulanges', reprinted in G.W. Baverstock and T.J. Cornell (eds) *A.D. Momigliano. Studies on Modern Scholarship*, Berkeley: University of California Press: 162–78.
Monaco, M.C. (2000) *Ergasteria. Impianti artigianali ceramici ad Atene ed in Attica dal Protogeometrico alle soglie dell'Ellenismo*, Rome: Bretschneider.
Morgan, C.A. (1986) 'Settlement and Exploitation in the Region of the Corinthian Gulf, ca.1000–700 BC' (PhD thesis, University of Cambridge).
—— (1988) Corinth, the Corinthian Gulf and western Greece during the eighth century BC', *BSA* 83: 313–38.
—— (1990) *Athletes and Oracles. The Transformation of Olympia and Delphi in the Eighth Century BC*, Cambridge: CUP.
—— (1991) 'Ethnicity and early Greek states; historical and material perspectives', *PCPS* 37: 131–63.
—— (1994) 'The evolution of a sacral "landscape": Isthmia, Perachora, and the early Corinthian state', in Alcock and Osborne 1994: 105–42.
—— (1995) 'Problems and prospects in the study of Corinthian pottery production', *Corinto*: 313–44.

—— (1997) 'The archaeology of sanctuaries in Early Iron Age and Archaic ethne: a preliminary view', in Mitchell and Rhodes 1997: 168–98.
—— (1998a) 'Euboians and Corinthians in the area of the Corinthian Gulf?', in Bats and d'Agostino 1998: 281–302.
—— (1998b) 'Ritual and society in the Early Iron Age Corinthia', in Hägg 1998: 73–90.
—— (1999a) *Isthmia* VIII. *The Mycenaean Settlement and Early Iron Age Sanctuary*, Princeton: ASCSA.
—— (1999b) 'Cultural subzones in Early Iron Age and Archaic Arkadia?', *CPCActs* 6: 382–456.
—— (1999c) 'Some thoughts on the production and consumption of Early Iron Age pottery in the Aegean', in J.-P. Crielaard, G.-J. van Wijngaarten and V. Stissi (eds) *The Complex Past of Pottery*, Amsterdam: Gieben: 213–59.
—— (1999d) 'The human figure in eighth century Corinthian vase painting', in M.-C. Villaneuva Puig, F. Lissarague, P. Rouillard and A. Rouveret (eds) *Céramique et peinture grecques. Modes d'emploi*, Paris: La documentation française: 279–87.
—— (1999e) 'The archaeology of ethnicity in the colonial world of the eighth to sixth centuries BC: approaches and prospects', *Frontieri e Confini. Atti della 37o Convegno internazionale di studi sulla Magna Grecia, Taranto Ott. 1997*, Taranto: Istituto per la Storia e l'Archeologia della Magna Grecia: 85–145.
—— (2000) 'Politics without the polis: cities and the Achaean ethnos, c.800–500 BC', in Brock and Hodkinson 2000: 189–211.
—— (2001a) 'Symbolic and pragmatic aspects of warfare in the Greek world of the 8th-6th centuries BC', in L. Hannestad and T. Bekker Nielsen (eds) *War as a Cultural and Social Force. Essays on Warfare in Antiquity*, Copenhagen: KDVS: 20–44.
—— (2001b) 'Figurative iconography from Corinth, Ithaka and Pithekoussai: Aetos 600 reconsidered', *BSA* 96: 195–227.
—— (2001c) 'Ethne, ethnicity and early Greek states, ca.1200–480: an archaeological perspective', in Malkin 2001: 75–112.
—— (forthcoming a) 'The origins of the Isthmian festival: points of comparison and contrast,' in Kyrieleis forthcoming b.
—— (forthcoming b) 'Ethnicity: the example of Achaia,' in Greco forthcoming.
—— (n.d.) 'Wealthy Corinth revisited', Lecture delivered at the British School at Athens, January 2000.
Morgan, C. and Coulton, J.J. (1997) 'The polis as a physical entity', *CPCActs* 4: 87–144.
Morgan, C. and Hall, J.M. (1996) 'Achaian poleis and Achaian colonisation', *CPCActs* 3: 164–232.
—— (forthcoming) 'An inventory of Achaian poleis in the Archaic and Classical periods,' in M.H. Hansen (ed.) *An Inventory of Greek Poleis in the Archaic and Classical Periods*, Oxford: OUP.
Morgan, C. and Whitelaw, T. (1991) 'Pots and politics: ceramic evidence for the rise of the Argive state', *AJA* 95: 79–108.
Morris, C.E. (1990) 'In pursuit of the white-tusked boar: aspects of hunting in Mycenaean society', in R. Hägg and G. Nordquist (eds) *Celebrations of Death and Divinity in the Bronze Age Argolid*, Stockholm: Paul Åström: 149–55.
Morris, I. (1987) *Burial and Ancient Society*, Cambridge: CUP.

—— (1991) 'The early *polis* as city and state', in Rich and Wallace-Hadrill 1991: 25–57.
—— (1992) *Death Ritual and Social Structure*, Cambridge: CUP.
—— (2000) *Archaeology as Cultural History*, Oxford: Blackwell.
Morris, S.P. (1984) *The Black and White Style*, New Haven/London: Yale University Press.
—— (1992) *Daidalos and the Origins of Greek Art*, Princeton: PUP.
Morton, J. (2001) *The Role of the Physical Environment in Ancient Greek Seafaring*, Leiden: Brill.
Moschonissioti, S. (1998) 'Excavation at ancient Mende', in Bats and d'Agostino 1998: 255–71.
Moschos, I. (2000) 'Prehistoric tumuli at Portes in Achaea. First preliminary report', *Proceedings of the Danish Institute in Athens* 3: 9–49.
—— (forthcoming) 'L'Acaia Micenea attraverso le ricerche archeologiche più recenti', in Greco forthcoming.
Mosshammer, A. (1982) 'The date of the first Pythiad – again', *GRBS* 23: 15–30.
Mountjoy, P.A. (1999) *Regional Mycenaean Decorated Pottery*, Rahden Westfalen: Marie Leidorf.
Müller, C. (1878) *Fragmente historicorum graecorum* II, Paris: Firmin-Didot.
Müller, S. (1992) 'Delphes et sa région à l'époque mycénienne', *BCH* 116: 445–96.
Mullings, L. (1994) 'Ethnicity and representation', in G.C. Bond and A. Gilliam (eds) *Social Construction of the Past. Representation as Power*, London: Routledge: 25–8.
Murray, O. (1990) 'Cities of reason', in Murray and Price 1990: 1–25.
Murray, O. and Price, S. (eds) (1990) *The Greek City from Homer to Alexander*, Oxford: OUP.
Muss, U. (1999) 'Zur Dialetik von Kultstatue und Statuetten im Artemision von Ephesos', in H. Friesinger and F. Krinzinger (eds) *100 Jahre Österreichischei Forschungen im Ephesos*, Vienna: Österreichische Akademie der Wissenschaften: 597–603.
—— (forthcoming) 'Die Kleinplastik aus dem Artemision von Ephesos', in J. Cobet, V. v. Graeve, W.-D. Niemeier and K. Zimmerman (eds) *Frühes Ionien: Eine Bestandsaufnahme, Akten des Symposions am Panionion 26.9–1.10. 1999* (*Milesische Forschungen* 4).
Myers, J.W., Myers, E. and Cadogan, G. (1992) *The Aerial Atlas of Ancient Crete*, London: Thames and Hudson.
Nagy, G. (1987) 'The Indo-European heritage of tribal organisation: evidence from the Greek *polis*', in S. Nacev Skomal and E. Polomé (eds) *Proto-Indo-European: the Archaeology of a Linguistic Problem. Studies in Honour of Marija Gimbutas*, Washington DC: Institute for the Study of Man: 245–66.
Neeft, C. (1981) 'Observations on the Thapsos class', *MEFRA* 93: 7–88.
Nevett, L.C. (1999) *House and Society in the Ancient Greek World*, Cambridge: CUP.
Nicholls, R.V. (1958–9) 'Old Smyrna: the Iron Age fortifications and associated remains on the city perimeter', *BSA* 53–4: 35–137.
Nippel, W. (1987–9) 'Finley and Weber. Some comments and theses', *Opus* 6–8: 43–50.
Nowicki, K. (1992) 'Fortifications in Dark Age Krete', in S. van der Maele and J. Fossey (eds) *Fortificationes antiquae*, Amsterdam: Gieben: 53–76.

—— (1999) 'Economy of refugees: life in the Cretan mountains at the turn of the Bronze and Iron Age', in A. Chaniotis (ed.) *From Minoan Farmers to Roman Traders. Sidelights on the Economy of Ancient Crete*, Stuttgart: Franz Steiner: 145–71.

—— (2000) *Defensible Sites in Crete c.1200–800 B.C.* (Aegaeum 21), Liège/Austin: Université de Liège/University of Texas.

Oldfather, W. (1908) 'Lokrika', *Philologus* 677: 411–72.

Onasoglou, A. (1981) 'Οι Γεωμετρικοί Τάφοι της Τραγάνας στην Ανατολική Λοκρίδα', *Delt* 36 A: 1–57.

Oommen, T.K. (1994) 'State, nation and ethnie: the processual linkages', in P. Ratcliffe (ed.) *"Race", Ethnicity and Nation. International Perspectives on Social Conflict*, London: UCL Press: 26–46.

Orlandos, A.K. (1967–1968) *Η Αρκαδική Αλίφειρα καί τά Μνημεῖα της*, Athens: Archaeological Society of Athens.

Osborne, R. (1985) *Demos: the Discovery of Classical Attika*, Cambridge: CUP.

—— (1996) *Greece in the Making*, London: Routledge.

Østby, E. (1990) 'Ο Ναός Διός Θαυλίου – τά Θεμέλια καί ή 'Αναπαράστασις', in P. Kamilakis and A. Polymerou-Kamilaki (eds) *ΥΠΕΡΕΙΑ* I. *Πρακτικά του Α΄ Συνεδρίου – Φεραί – Βελεστίνο – Ρήγας ῇ, Βελεστίνο 30–31.5–1.6.86*, Athens: Syllogi Velestinon: 101–8.

—— (1992) 'Der dorische Tempel von Pherai', *OpAth* 19: 85–113.

—— (1992–3) 'The temples of Pallantion and Archaic temple architecture of Arcadia', *Πρακτικα του Δ΄ Διεθνους Συνέδριου Πελοποννησιακῶν Σπουδῶν, 9–16 Σεπτ. 1990*, Athens: Society for Peloponnesian Studies: 65–75.

—— (1994) 'A reconsideration of the Classical temple at Pherai', *ΘΕΣΣΑΛΙΑ* 2: 139–42.

—— (1995a) 'I Templi di Pallantion', *Pallation*: 53–93.

—— (1995b) 'Il Tempio C: riconstruzione e interpretazione', *Pallation*: 109–18.

—— (1995c) 'Templi di Pallantion e dell'Arcadia', *Pallation*: 285–391.

—— (1997) 'Early Iron Age in the sanctuary of Athena Alea at Tegea. Recent excavations,' *Acta ad archaeologiam et artium historiam pertinentia* 9: 79–107.

Østby, E., Luce, J.-M., Nordquist, G., Tarditi, C. and Voyatzis, M.E. (1994) 'The sanctuary of Athena Alea at Tegea: first preliminary report (1990–1992)', *OpAth* 20: 89–141.

Palagia, O. and Coulson, W.D.E. (eds) *Sculpture from Arcadia and Laconia. Proceedings of an International Conference held at the American School of Classical Studies at Athens, April 10–14, 1992*, Oxford: Oxbow.

Papadimitriou, A. (1998) 'Η Οικιστική Εξέλιξη της Τίρυνθας μετά τη Μυκηναϊκή Εποχή. Τα Αρχαιολογικά Ευρήματα και η Ιστορική Ερμηνεία τους', in Pariente and Touchais 1998: 117–30.

Papadimitriou, N. (2001) *Built Chamber Tombs of Middle and Late Bronze Age Date in Mainland Greece and the Islands*, Oxford: BAR.

Papadopoulos, A. (1979) *Mycenaean Achaea*, Göteborg: Paul Åström.

—— (1995) 'A Late Mycenaean koine in western Greece and the adjacent Ionian islands', in C. Morris (ed.) *Klados. Essays in Honour of J.N. Coldstream* (BICS 63), London: ICS: 201–8.

—— (1999) 'Warrior graves in Achaean Mycenaean cemeteries', in Laffineur 1999: 267–74

Papadopoulos, J. (1989) 'An Early Iron Age potter's kiln at Torone', *MeditArch* 2: 9–44.
—— (1994a) 'Early Iron Age Potters' marks in the Aegean', *Hesperia* 63: 437–507.
—— (1994b) 'Review of N. Cuomo di Caprio, *Fornaci e Officine da Vasaia Tardo-Ellenistiche*', *CR* 44: 151–5.
—— (1996a) 'The original Kerameikos of Athens and the siting of the Classical Agora', *GRBS* 37: 107–28.
—— (1996b) 'Euboians in Macedonia? A closer look,' *OJA* 15: 151–81.
—— (1997) 'Innovations, imitations and ceramic style: modes of production and mode of dissemination', in R. Laffineur and P.B. Betancourt (eds) *TEXNH Craftsmen, Craftswomen and Craftsmanship in the Aegean Bronze Age* (*Aegaeum* 16), Liège/Austin: Université de Liège/University of Texas: 449–62.
Papagiannopoulos, K. and Zachos, G. (2000) 'Εντατική Επιφανειακή Έρευνα στη Δυτική Αχαΐα· μια άλλη προσέγγιση', in Rizakis 2000: 139–53.
Papahatzis, N. (1959) 'Η Σημερινή Θέση της Τοπογραφικής Μελέτης της Αρχαίας Θεσσαλίας', *Θεσσαλικά* 2: 5–21.
—— (1960) 'Η Κορόπη και το Ιερό του Απόλλωνα', *Θεσσαλικα* 3: 3–24.
—— (1981) 'Προθεσσαλικές Λατρείες στη Θεσσαλία των Ιστορικών Χρόνων', *Ανθρωπολογικά* 2: 33–7.
—— (1992) 'Η Φύση και η Καταγωγή της Θεσσαλικής Ιτωνίας και της Πανελλήνιας Αθηνάς', *Praktika Theochari*: 321–5.
Papakosta, L. (1991) 'Παρτηρήσεις σχετικά με την Τοπογραφία του Αρχαίου Αιγίου', in Rizakis 1991b: 235–40.
Papantonopoulos, K. (1995) *Ναός Επικούριου Απόλλωνος Βασσών, Μελέτη Δομικής Αποκαταστάσεως* 1. Athens: Ministry of Culture.
Papapostolou, I. (1990) 'Ζητήματα των Μεγαρών Α και Β του Θερμοῦ', *AE*: 191–200.
Papastamataki, A., Demetriou, D. and Orphanos, B. (1994) 'Mining and metallurgical activity in Pelasgia. The production of copper in antiquity', *ΘΕΣΣΑΛΙΑ*: 1: 243–8.
Pariente, A., Pièrart, M. and Thalmann, J.-P. (1998) 'Les recherches sur l'agora d'Argos: résultats et perspectives', in Pariente and Touchais 1998: 211–31.
Pariente, A. and Touchais, G. (eds) (1998) *Argos et l'Argolide. Topographie et urbanisme (Actes de la Table Ronde internationale Athènes-Argos 28/4–1/5 1990)*, Paris: Boccard.
Paris, P. (1892) *Elatée. La ville, le temple d'Athéna Cranaia*, Paris: Thorin.
Parke, H. and Wormell, D. (1956) *The Delphic Oracle*, Oxford: Blackwell.
Parker, R. (1998) *Cleomenes on the Acropolis. An Inaugural Lecture delivered before the University of Oxford on 12 May 1997*, Oxford: OUP.
Parlama, L. and Stampolidis, N. (2000) *Η Πόλη κάτω από την Πόλη*, Athens: Ministry of Culture/Goulandris Foundation.
Patterson, O. (1975) 'Context and choice in ethnic allegiance: a theoretical framework and Caribbean case study', in N. Glazer and D. Moynihan (eds) *Ethnicity. Theory and Experience*, Cambridge, Mass./London: Harvard University Press: 305–49.
Pearson, L. (1962) 'The pseudo-history of Messenia and its authors', *Historia* 11: 397–426.
Pemberton, E.G. (1996) 'Weathy Corinth: the archaeological evidence for cult

investment at Greek Corinth,' in M. Dillon (ed.) *Religion in the Ancient World. New Themes and Approaches*, Amsterdam: Hakkert, 353–66.

―― (1999) 'Wealthy Corinth: the archaeology of a Classical city', *Proceedings 1998 of the Australian Academy of the Humanities, Canberra*: 138–65.

―― (2000) 'Wine, women and song: gender roles in Corinthian cult,' *Kernos* 13: 85–106.

Pendlebury, H., Pendlebury, J. and Money-Coutts, M. (1937–8) 'Excavations in the plain of Lasithi III. Karphi: a city of refuge of the Early Iron Age in Crete', *BSA* 38: 57–145.

Perdrizet, P. (1908) *Fouilles de Delphes* V i. *Monuments figurés, arts mineurs*, Paris: Boccard.

Perlman, P. (1996) 'Πόλις Υπήκοος. The dependent *polis* and Crete', *CPCActs* 3: 233–87.

―― (2000) *City and Sanctuary in Ancient Greece. The Theodorokia in the Peloponnese*, Göttingen: Vandenhoeck and Ruprecht.

Petronotis, A. (1973) 'Αρχιτεκτονικά και Οικιστικά Μνημεία και Ιστορικές Θέσεις του Νομού Φωκίδος', *Επετηρίς Εταιρείας Στερεοελλαδικών Μελετών* 4: 93–132.

Petropoulos, M. (1985) 'Τοπογραφικά Βόρεας Αρκαδίας', *ΗΟΡΟΣ* 3: 63–73.

―― (1987–8) 'Τρίτη Ανασκαφική Περίοδος στο Ανω Μαζαράκι (Ρακίτα) Αχαΐας', *Πρακτικά του Γ' Διεθνούς Συνέδριου Πελοποννησιακών Σπουδών* II, Athens: Society for Peloponnesian Studies: 81–96.

―― (1990) 'Αρχαιολογικές Έρευνες στην Αχαΐα', *Τόμος Τιμητικός Κ.Ν. Τριανταφύλλου* I, Patras: G. Petraki: 495–537.

―― (1991) 'Τοπογραφικά της Χώρας των Πατρέων', in Rizakis 1991b: 249–58.

―― (1992–3) 'Περίπτερος Αψίδωτος Γεωμετρικός Ναός στὸ Ἀνω Μαζαράκι (Ρακίτα) Πατρῶν', *Πρακτικά του Δ' Διεθνούς Συνέδριου Πελοποννησιακών Σπουδών* II, 9–16 Σεπτ 1990, Athens: 141–58.

―― (1996–7) 'Νεώτερα Στοιχεία από την Ανασκαφή Γεωμετρικοῦ Ναοῦ στο Ανω Μαζαράκι (Ρακίτα) Πατρῶν', *Πρακτικά του Ε' Διεθνους Συνέδριου Πελοποννησιακών Σπουδών, 6–10 Σεπτ 1995*, Athens: Society for Peloponnesian Studies: 165–92.

―― (2000) 'Μυκηναϊκό Νεκροταφείο στα Σπαλιαρεϊκα των Λουσικῶν', in Rizakis 2000: 65–92.

―― (forthcoming) 'The sanctuary of Ano Mazaraki,' in Greco forthcoming.

Petropoulos, M. and Rizakis, A. (1994) 'Settlement patterns and landscape in the coastal area of Patras. Preliminary report', *JRA* 7: 183–207.

Pfaff, C. (1999) 'The Early Iron Age pottery from the sanctuary of Demeter and Kore at Corinth,' *Hesperia* 68: 55–134.

―― (forthcoming) 'Corinthian architecture of the sixth century B.C.', *Corinth* XX. *Corinth: the Centenary, 1896–1996*, Princeton: ASCSA.

Philippson, A. (1897) *Thessalien und Epirus. Reisen und Forschungen im nördlichen Griechenland*, Berlin: Kühl.

Philippson, A. (1950) *Die Griechischen Landschaften* I, 1, Frankfurt am Main: Vittorio Klostermann.

―― (1951) *Die Griechischen Landschaften* I, 2, Frankfurt am Main: Vittorio Klostermann.

—— (1959) *Die Griechischen Landschaften* III, 1, Frankfurt am Main: Vittorio Klostermann.
Pièrart, M. (1991) 'Aspects de la transition en Argolide', in D. Musti et al. (eds) *La transizione dal Miceneo all'alto arcaismo*, Rome: CNR: 133–44.
Pikoulas, Y. (1981–2) 'Η Αρκαδική Αζάνια', Πρακτικά του Β΄ Διεθνούς Συνέδριου Πελοποννησιακῶν Σπουδῶν, Πάτραι 25–31 Μαίου 1980, II, Athens: Society for Peloponnesian Studies: 269–81.
—— (1988) *Η Νότια Μεγαλοπολιτική Χώρα από τον 8ο π.χ. ως τον 4ο μ.χ. αιώνα. Συμβολή στην Τοπογραφία της*, Athens: Horos.
—— (1995) *Οδικό Δίκτυο και Αμυνα. Από την Κόρινθο στο Αργος και την Αρκαδία*, Athens: Horos.
—— (1999) 'The road-network of Arkadia', *CPCActs* 6: 248–319.
Pilali-Papasteriou, A. and Papaeuthimiou-Papanthimiou, K. (1983) 'Νέα Ανασκαφική Έρευνα στο Ιερό της Φιλίας', *Ανθρωπολογικά* 4: 49–67.
Piteros, C. (1998) 'Σύμβολη στην Αργειακή Τοπογραφία. Χώρος, Οχυρώσεις, Τοπογραφία και Προβλήματα' in Pariente and Touchais 1998: 179–210.
Polignac, F. de. (1992) 'Influence extérieure ou évolution interne? L'innovation cultuelle en Grèce géométrique et archaïque', in Kopcke and Tokumaru 1992: 114–27.
—— (1995) *Cults, Territory and the Origins of the Greek City-State*, Chicago: University of Chicago Press.
—— (1998) 'Cité et territoire à l'époque géométrique: un modèle argien?', in Pariente and Touchais 1998: 145–62.
Popham, M. (1994) 'Precolonization: early Greek contact with the East', in G.R. Tsetskhladze and F. de Angelis (eds) *The Archaeology of Greek Colonization*, Oxford: OUCA: 11–34.
Popham, M. and Lemos, I. (1995) 'A Euboean warrior trader', *OJA* 14: 151–7.
Pretzler, M. (1999) 'Myth and history at Tegea – local tradition and community identity', *CPCActs* 6: 89–129.
Price, M. and Waggoner, N. (1975) *Archaic Greek Coinage. The Asyut Hoard*, London: Vecchi.
Pritchett, W.K. (1996) *Greek Archives, Cults and Topography*, Amsterdam: Gieben.
Psoma, S. (1999) ''Αρκαδικόν,' *ΗΟΡΟΣ* 13: 81–96.
Purcell, N. (1990) 'Mobility and the *polis*', in Murray and Price 1990: 29–58.
—— (1997) 'Review of G. Tsetskhladze and F. de Angelis (eds) *The Archaeology of Greek Colonisation: Essays Dedicated to Sir John Boardman*', *Antiquity* 71: 500–2.
—— (1999) 'Mobilità e Magna Grecia', *Frontieri e Confini. Atti della 37o Convegno internazionale di studi sulla Magna Grecia, Taranto Ott. 1997*, Taranto: Istituto per la Storia e l'Archeologia della Magna Grecia: 573–80.
Raaflaub, K. (1993) 'Homer to Solon. The rise of the *polis*. The written sources', *CPCActs* 1: 41–105.
Raftopoulou, E.G. (1993) 'Sur certains archétypes de thèmes iconographiques provenant du centre du Péloponnèse', in Palagia and Coulson 1993: 1–12.
Raftopoulou, S. (1996–7) 'Ταφές της Εποχής του Σιδήρου στη Σπάρτη', Πρακτικά του Ε΄ Διεθνους Συνέδριου Πελοποννησιακῶν Σπουδῶν, 6–10 Σεπτ 1995, Athens: Society for Peloponnesian Studies: 272–82.
Rakatsanis, K., and Tziafalias, A. (1997) *Λατρείες και Ιερά στην Αρχαία Θεσσαλία* A, *Pelasgiotis* (*Dodoni* supp. 63), Ioannina: University of Ioannina Press.

Raubitschek, A. (1949) *Dedications from the Athenian Acropolis*, Cambridge, Mass.: AIA.
Reger, G. (1997) 'Islands with one *polis* versus islands with several *poleis*', *CPCActs* 4: 450–92.
Renfrew, C. and Wagstaff, M. (1982) *An Island Polity. The Archaeology of Exploitation in Melos*, Cambridge: CUP.
Rhodes, P. (1995) 'Epigraphical evidence: laws and decrees', *CPCActs* 2: 91–112.
Rhodes, R. (1987) 'Early stoneworking in the Corinthia', *Hesperia* 56: 229–32.
—— (forthcoming) 'The seventh century temple and the earliest Greek architecture at Corinth', *Corinth* XX. *Corinth: the Centenary, 1896–1996*, Princeton: ASCSA.
Rhomaios, K. (1957) 'Ἱερόν Ἀθηνᾶς Σωτείρας καί Ποσειδῶνος κατά τήν ἀρκαδικήν 'Ασέαν', *AE*: 114–63.
Rich, J. and Wallace-Hadrill, A. (eds) (1991) *City and Country in the Ancient World*, London: Routledge.
Ridgway, B.S. (1990) *Hellenistic Sculpture I. The styles of ca.331–200 BC*, Madison: University of Wisconsin Press.
—— (1993) *The Archaic Style in Greek Sculpture* 2nd ed., Chicago: Ares.
Ridgway, D. (1994) 'Phoenicians and Greeks in the west: a view from Pithekoussai', in G. Tsetskhladze and F. de Angelis (eds) *The Archaeology of Greek Colonization*, Oxford: OUCA: 35–46.
Rihll, T. and Wilson, A. (1991) 'Modelling settlement structures in ancient Greece: new approaches to the *polis*', in Rich and Wallace-Hadrill 1991: 59–95.
Risberg, C. (1992) 'Metal-working in Greek sanctuaries', in T. Linders and B. Alroth (eds) *Economics of Cult in the Greek World*, Uppsala: Acta Universitatis Upsaliensis: 33–40.
Rizakis, A (1991a) 'Ἀχαϊκή Ιστοριογραφία. Ἀπολογισμός καί Προοπτικές της Έρευνας', in Rizakis 1991b: 51–60.
—— (ed.) (1991b) *Αρχαια Αχαϊα και Ηλεία*, KERA/Boccard: Athens/Paris.
—— (ed.) (1992) *Paysages d'Achaïe I. Le bassin du Peiros et la plaine occidentale*, Athens: KERA/Boccard.
—— (1995) *Achaïe I. Sources textuelles et histoire regionale*, Athens: KERA/Boccard.
—— (1998) *Achaïe II. La cité de Patras: épigraphie et histoire*, Athens: KERA/Boccard.
—— (ed.) (2000) *Paysages d'Achaïe II. Dymé et son territoire*, Athens: KERA/Boccard.
Robertson, G.C. (1997) 'Evaluating the citizen in Archaic Greek lyric, elegy and inscribed epigram', in Mitchell and Rhodes 1997: 148–57.
Robertson, M. (1948) 'Excavations in Ithaca, V: the Geometric and later finds from Aetos. The pottery', *BSA* 43: 9–124.
—— (1992) *The Art of Vase-Painting in Classical Athens*, Cambridge: CUP.
Robertson, N. (1978) 'The myth of the first Sacred War', *CQ* 72: 38–73.
—— (1998) 'The city centre of Archaic Athens', *Hesperia* 67: 283–302.
Robinson, H. (1976a) 'Temple Hill, Corinth', in U. Jantzen (ed.) *Neue Forschungen in griechischen Heiligtümern*, Tübingen: Wasmuth: 239–60.
—— (1976b) 'Excavations at Corinth: Temple Hill 1968–1972', *Hesperia* 45: 203–39.
Rolley, C. (1969) *Fouilles de Delphes* V, ii. *Les statuettes de bronze*, Paris: Boccard.
—— (1977) *Fouilles de Delphes* V, iii. *Les trépieds à cuve clouée*, Paris: Boccard.
—— (1992a) 'Argos, Corinthe, Athènes. Identité culturelle et modes de développement', in M. Pièrart (ed.) *Polydipsion Argos* (*BCH* supp. 22), Paris/Athens: Boccard: 37–49.

—— (1992b) *La sculpture grec* I. *Des origines au milieu du Ve siècle*, Paris: Picard.
—— (forthcoming) 'Delphes de 1500 à 575 av. J.-C. Nouvelles données sur le problème "ruptures et continuité"', in Kyrieleis forthcoming b.
Romano, I.B. (1988) 'Early Greek cult images and cult practices,' in Hägg, Marinatos and Nordquist 1988: 127–33.
Rombos, T. (1988) *The Iconography of Attic LGII Pottery*, Jonsered: Paul Åström.
Rostoker, W. and Gebhard, E. (1980) 'The sanctuary of Poseidon at Isthmia: techniques of metal manufacture', *Hesperia* 49: 347–63.
—— (1981) 'The reproduction of rooftiles for the Archaic temple of Poseidon at Isthmia, Greece', *JFA* 8: 211–27.
Rougemont, G. (1980) 'Un atlas delphique', *RA*: 97–104.
Roussel, D. (1976) *Tribu et cité: études sur les groupes sociaux dans les cités grecques aux poques archaïque et classique*, Paris: Annales littéraires de l'université de Besançon/Les Belles Lettres.
Rousset, D. (1991) 'Autour de Delphes: territoire d'Apollon et territoire de la cité', *REG* 104: xv-xvii.
—— (1999) 'Centre urbain, frontière et espace rural dans les cités de Grèce centrale', in M. Brunet (ed.) *Territoires des cités grecques* (*BCH* supp. 34), Paris/Athens: Boccard/EFA: 35–77.
Rowlands, M. (1998) 'Kinship, alliance and exchange in the European Bronze Age', in K. Kristiansen and M. Rowlands (eds) *Social Transformations in Archaeology. Global and Local Perspectives*, London: Routledge: 142–82.
Rowlett, R. (1989) 'Detecting political units in archaeology – an Iron Age example', in S. Shennan (ed.) *Archaeological Approaches to Cultural Identity*, London: Unwin Hyman: 219–30.
Roy, J. (1967) 'The mercenaries of Cyrus', *Historia* 16: 287–323.
__(1972a) 'An Arcadian League in the earlier fifth century B.C.?', *Phoenix* 26: 334–41.
—— (1972b) 'Tribalism in southwestern Arcadia in the Classical period', *Acta Antiqua* 20: 43–51.
—— (1972c) 'Arcadian nationality as seen in Xenophon's *Anabasis*', *Mnemosyne* 25: 129–36.
—— (1996) 'Polis and tribe in Classical Arcadia', *CPCPapers* 3: 107–12.
—— (1997) 'The perioikoi of Elis', *CPCActs* 4: 282–320.
—— (1999) 'The economies of Arkadia', *CPCActs* 6: 320–81.
—— (2000) 'The frontier between Arkadia and Elis in Classical antiquity', in Flensted-Jensen, Heine Nielsen and Rubinstein 2000: 133–56.
Roy, J. and Schofield, D. (1999) '*IvO* 9: a new approach,' ΗΟΡΟΣ 13: 155–65.
Roymans, N. (1990) *Tribal Societies in Northern Gaul. An Anthropological Perspective*, Amsterdam: University of Amsterdam.
Runciman, W.G. (1990) 'Doomed to extinction: the *polis* as an evolutionary deadend', in Murray and Price 1990: 347–67.
Ruschenbusch, E. (1978) *Untersuchungen zu Staat und Politik in Griechenland von 7–4 Jh. v. Chr.*, Bamberg: Fotodruck.
Rutter, J. (1990) 'Pottery groups from Tsoungiza of the end of the Middle Bronze Age', *Hesperia* 59: 375–458.
Sahlins, M.D. (1968) *Tribesmen*, New Jersey: Prentice-Hall.
Sakellariou, M. (1989) *The Polis-State. Definition and Origin*, Paris: Boccard.

Salmon, J. (1984) *Wealthy Corinth*, Oxford: OUP.
Salowey, C. (1994) 'Herakles and the waterworks: Mycenaean dams, Classical fountains, Roman acqueducts', in K. Sheedy (ed.) *Archaeology in the Peloponnese. New Excavations and Research*, Oxford: Oxbow: 77–94.
—— (1995) 'The Peloponnesian Herakles: Cults and Labors' (PhD diss., Bryn Mawr College).
Salvator, L. (1876) *Eine Spazierfahrt im Golfe von Korinth*, Prague: Mercy.
Salvatore, M. di. (1982) 'La citta tessala di Fere in epoca classica' (PhD thesis, University of Milan).
—— (1994) 'Ricerche sul territorio di Pherai. Insediamente, difese, vie e confine', *ΘΕΣΣΑΛΙΑ*: 1: 93–124.
Sanchez, P. (2001) *L'Amphictionie des Pyles et de Delphes. Recherches sur son rôle historique des origines au IIe siècle de notre ère* (*Historia* Einz. 148), Stuttgart: Franz Steiner.
Sanders, G.D.R. (1999) 'A late Roman bath at Corinth. Excavation in the Panayia field, 1995–1996', *Hesperia* 68: 441–80.
Sanders, G.D.R. and Whitbread, I.K. (1993) 'Central places and major roads in the Peloponnese', *BSA* 85: 333–61.
Sanderson, S.K. (1990) *Social Evolutionism. A Critical History*, Oxford/Cambridge Mass.: Blackwell.
Sapouna-Sakellaraki, E. (1998). 'Geometric Kyme. The excavation at Viglatouri, Kyme, on Euboia', in Bats and d'Agostino 1998: 59–104.
Sartre, M. (1979) 'Aspects économiques et aspects religieus de la frontière dans les cités grecques', *Ktêma* 4: 213–24.
Schachermeyr, F. (1980) *Die ägäische Frühzeit IV. Griechenland im Zeitalter der Wanderungen*, Vienna: Öst. Akad. der Wissenschaften.
Schachter, A. (1989) 'Boiotia in the 6th century B.C.', in H. Beister and J. Buckler (eds) *BOIOTIKA. Vorträge vom 5 internationalen Böoten Kolloquium zu Ehren von Professor Dr. Siegfried Lauffer*, Munich: Maris: 73–86.
Schaeur, C. (1996–7) 'Κεραμεικὴ ἀπὸ το Ἀρχαϊκὸ Ἱερὸ τῆς Ἀρτέμιδος στοὺς Λουσοὺς', *Πρακτικά του Ε´ Διεθνοῦς Συνέδριου Πελοποννησιακῶν Σπουδῶν, 6–10 Σεπτ 1995*, Athens: Society for Peloponnesian Studies: 257–71.
Schmidt, S.G. (2000–1) 'Zwischen Mythos und Realität. Neue Forschungen zum geometrischen und archaischen Eretria', *Nürnberger Blätter zur Archäologie* 17, 1–20.
Schober, F. (1925) *Phokis*, Jena: Richard Zeidler.
Schwartz, E. (1891) *Scholia in Euripidem*, Berlin: Reimer.
Service, E.R. (1975) *Origins of the State and Civilisation: the Process of Cultural Evolution*, New York: Norton.
Shanks, M. and Tilley, C. (1987) *Social Theory and Archaeology*, Cambridge: Polity.
Shear, T.L. Jnr. (1993) 'The Persian destruction of Athens. Evidence from Agora deposits', *Hesperia* 62: 83–482.
—— (1994) 'Ἰσονόμους τ᾽ Ἀθήνας ἐποιησάτην: the Agora and democracy', in Coulson et al. 1994: 225–48.
Sheedy, K. (1997) 'Late Archaic hoards in the Cyclades and some thoughts on a regional pattern of trade', in K. Sheedy and C. Papageorgiadou-Banis (eds) *Numismatic Archaeology. Archaeological Numismatics*, Oxford: Oxbow: 107–17.

Shennan, S. (1978) 'Archaeological "cultures": an empirical investigation', in I. Hodder (ed.) *The Spatial Organization of Culture*, London: Duckworth: 113–39.

—— (1989) 'Introduction: archaeological approaches to cultural identity', in S. Shennan (ed.) *Archaeological Approaches to Cultural Identity*, London: Unwin Hyman: 1–32.

—— (1996) 'Foreword,' in H. Maschner (ed.) *Darwinian Archaeologies*, New York/London: Plenum: ix-xiii.

Sherratt, A. and Sherratt, S. (1992) 'The growth of the Mediterranean economy in the early first millenium BC', *WA* 24: 361–78.

Shils, E. (1991) 'Henry Sumner Maine in the tradition of the analysis of society', in Diamond 1991: 143–78.

Shipley, G. (1997) '"The other Lakedaimonians": the dependent perioikic poleis of Lakonia and Messenia', *CPCActs* 4: 189–281.

Siegel, L.J. (1978) 'Corinthian Trade in the Ninth through Eighth Centuries BC' (PhD diss., Yale University).

Siewert, P. (1994) 'Symmachien in neuen Inschrften von Olympia', in L.A. Foresti, A. Barzanò, C. Bearzot, L. Prandi and G. Zecchini (eds) *Federazioni e federalismo nell'Europa antica*, Milan: LED: 257–64.

—— (1999) 'Literarische und epigraphische Testimonien über "Kerameikos" und "Kerameis"', *AthMitt* 114: 1–8.

—— (2001) 'Inschriften und Geschichte der Stadt Elis,' in V. Mitsopoulos-Leon (ed.) *Forschungen in der Peloponnes. Akten des Symposions zur 100-Jahr-Feier des Österreichischen Archäologischen Instituts Athen, Athens 5–7 March 1998*: Athens: Österreichisches Archäologisches Institut: 245–52.

Silverman, E.K. (1990) 'Clifford Geertz; towards a more "thick" understanding?', in C. Tilley (ed.) *Reading Material Culture*, Oxford: Blackwell: 121–59.

Sinn, U. (1992) 'The "Sacred Herd" of Artemis at Lusoi', in R. Hägg (ed.) *The Iconography of Greek Cult in the Archaic and Classical Periods* (Kernos supp. 1), Athens/Liège: Kernos: 177–87.

Sipsie-Eschbach, M. (1991) *Protogeometrische Keramik aus Iolkos*, Mainz: Volker Spiess.

Sivignon, M. (1975) *La Thessalie. Analyse géographique d'une province grecque*, Lyon: Audin.

Skorda, D. (1992) 'Recherches dans la vallée du Pléistos,' in J.-F. Bommelaer (ed.) *Delphes, centenaire de la 'Grande Fouille'*, Leiden: Brill: 39–66.

—— (1998–9) 'Η Κοιλάδα του Πλειστού. Η Περιοχή των Δελφών με τους Δρόμους, τους Οικισμούς και τις Οχυρώσεις της', *Φωκικά Χρόνικα* 7-8: 11–18.

Smith, A.D. (1986) *The Ethnic Origins of Nations*, Oxford: Blackwell.

Smith, M.J. (1972) 'Complexity, size and urbanization', in Ucko, Tringham and Dimbleby 1972: 567–74.

Snell, B. (ed.) (1964) *Pindari carmina cum fragmentis* 2, 3rd edn, Leipzig: Teubner.

Snodgrass, A.M. (1971) *The Dark Age of Greece*, Edinburgh: Edinburgh University Press.

—— (1980) *Archaic Greece. The Age of Experiment*, London: Dent.

—— (1983) 'Two demographic notes', in Hägg 1983a: 167–71.

—— (1986) 'The historical significance of fortification in Archaic Greece', in P. Lerich and H. Tréziny (eds) *La fortification dans l'histoire du monde grec*, Paris: CNRS: 125–31.

—— (1987) *An Archaeology of Greece. The Present State and Future Scope of a Discipline*, Berkeley: University of California Press.
—— (1987–9) 'The rural landscape and its political significance', *Opus* 6–8: 53–65.
—— (1989–90) 'The economics of dedication at Greek sanctuaries', *Scienze dell'Antichità* 3–4: 287–94.
—— (1991) 'Archaeology and the study of the Greek city', in Rich and Wallace-Hadrill 1991: 1–23.
—— (1993) 'The rise of the *polis*. The archaeological evidence', in M.H. Hansen (ed.) *The Ancient Greek City-State*, Copenhagen: KDVS: 30–40.
—— (1994) 'A new precedent for westward expansion: the Euboeans in Macedonia', in d'Agostino and Ridgway 1994: 87–93.
—— (1999) 'Centres of pottery production in Archaic Greece', in M.-C. Villaneuva Puig, F. Lissarague, P. Rouillard and A. Rouveret (eds) *Céramique et peinture grecques. Modes d'emploi*, Paris: La documentation française: 25–33.
—— (2000) 'Prehistoric Italy. A view from the sea', in D. Ridgway, F. Serra Ridgway, M. Pearce, E. Herring, R.D. Whitehouse and J.B. Wilkins (eds) *Ancient Italy in its Mediterranean Setting*, London: Accordia Research Institute: 171–7.
Sordi, M. (1958) *La lega Tessala fino ad Alessandro Magno*, Rome: Istituto Italiano per la Storia Antica.
—— (1979) 'Aspetti della propaganda Tessala a Delfi', in Helly 1979: 157–64.
—— (1992) 'Η Θεσσαλία στην Περίοδο της Ανεξαρτησίας', Θεσσαλικό Ημερολόγιο 22: 209–24.
Sørensen, L.W. (1997) 'Travelling pottery connections between Cyprus, the Levant and the Greek world in the Iron Age', in S. Swiny, R. Hohlfelder and H. Swiny (eds) *Res Maritimae. Cyprus and the Eastern Mediterranean from Prehistory to Late Antiquity*, Atlanta: Scholars' Press: 285–99.
Sourvinou Inwood, C. (1979) 'The myth of the first temples at Delphi', *CQ* 29: 231–51.
—— (1988) 'Further aspects of polis religion,' *AION*: 259–74.
—— (1990) 'What is *polis* religion? in Murray and Price 1990: 295–322.
—— (1993) 'Early sanctuaries, the eighth century and ritual space: fragments of a discourse', in R. Hägg and N. Marinatos (eds) *Greek Sanctuaries. New Approaches*, London: Routledge: 1–17.
—— (1995) *"Reading" the Greek Discourse of Death. To the End of the Classical Period*, Oxford: OUP.
Souyoudzoglou-Haywood, C. (1999) *The Ionian Islands in the Bronze Age and the Early Iron Age, 3000–800 BC*, Liverpool: Liverpool University Press.
Spencer, N. (1995) 'Multi-dimensional group definition in the landscape of rural Greece', in N. Spencer (ed.) *Time, Tradition and Society in Greek Archaeology*, London: Routledge: 28–42.
Spyropoulos, T. (1991) *Monuments archéologiques et musées d'Arcadie*, Tripolis: Tripolis Museum.
Spyropoulos, T. (1993) 'Νέα Γλυπτά Αποκτήματα του Αρχαιολογικού Μουσείο Τριπόλεως', in Palagia and Coulson 1993: 257–66.
Stählin, F. (1924) *Das hellenische Thessalien*, Stuttgart: J. Engelhorn.
Stamatopoulou, M. (1999) 'Burial Customs in Thessaly in the Classical and Hellenistic Periods' (DPhil thesis, University of Oxford).
Stanzel, M. (1991) 'Die Tierreste aus dem Artemis-/Apollon-Heiligtum bei Kalapodi

in Böotien, Griechenland' (PhD thesis, Ludwig Maximilians Universität, Munich).
Stavropoulou Gatsi, M. (1980) 'Πρωτογεωμετρικό Νεκροταφείο Αιτωλίας', *Delt* 30 A: 102–30.
Stillwell, A.N. (1948) *Corinth* XV, i. *The Potters' Quarter*, Princeton: ASCSA.
Stillwell, R, MacDonald, W. and McAllister, M. (eds) (1976) *The Princeton Encyclopedia of Classical Sites*, Princeton: PUP.
Stiros, S. and Dakoronia, F. (1989) 'Ruolo storico e identificazione di antiche terremoti nei siti della Grecia', in E. Guidoboni (ed.) *Terremoti prima del Mille in Italia e nell'area Mediterranea*, Bologna: ING: 422–39.
Stiros, S. and Papagiorgiou, S. (1992) 'Σύμβολη στην Παλαιογεωγραφία Μαγνησίας-Φθιώτιδας', *Praktika Theochari*: 217–25.
—— (1994) 'Post Mesolithic evolution of the Thessalian landscape', *ΘΕΣΣΑΛΙΑ*:1: 29–36.
Stiros, S. and Rondogianni, T. (1985) 'Recent vertical movement across the Atalandi fault-zone (central Greece)', *Pageoph*. 123: 837–48.
Strøm, I. (1988) 'The early sanctuary of the Argive Heraion and its external relations (8th–early 6th cent. B.C.)', *Acta Archaeologia* 59: 173–203.
—— (1992) 'Evidence from the sanctuaries', in Kopcke and Tokumaru 1992: 46–60.
—— (1995) 'The early sanctuary of the Argive Heraion and its external relations (8th-early 6th cent. B.C.). The Greek Geometric bronzes', *Proceedings of the Danish Institute at Athens* 1: 37–127.
Stroud, R. (1968) 'Tribal boundary markers from Corinth,' *CSCA* 1: 233–42.
Svonoros, J. (1896) 'Νομισματική των Δελφών', *BCH* 20: 1–54.
Swinton, A.M. (1996) 'Religion and Ancient Society: the Development of Public Cult in Cyprus from Late Cypriot I – Cypro-Archaic I' (PhD thesis, University of Cambridge).
Symeonoglou, N.E.W. (2002) 'The Early Iron Age pottery and development of the sanctuary at Aetos, Ithaka' (PhD diss., Washington University in St Louis).
Taeuber, H. (1987–8) 'Arcadian inscriptions as a source for ancient Greek law', *Πρακτικά του Γ΄ Διεθνούς Συνέδριου Πελοποννησιακών Σπουδών*, II: Athens, Society for Peloponnesian Studies: 353–8.
Tarlas, S. (1994) 'Social Change, Organisation and Cremation in Prehistoric Greece' (PhD thesis, University of Liverpool).
Tausend, K. (1995) 'Von Artemis zu Artemis? – Der antike Weg von Lousoi nach Pheneos?', *JOAI* 64: 1–19.
—— (1999) *Pheneos und Lousoi. Untersuchungen zu Geschichte und Topographie Nordostarkadiens*, Frankfurt a.M: Peter Lang.
Televantou, C. (1999) 'Άνδρος. Το Ιερό της Υψηλής', in N. Stampolidis (ed.) *ΦΩΣ ΚΥΚΛΑΔΙΚΩΝ. Μνήμη Νικόλαου Ζαφειρόπουλου*, Athens: N.P. Goulandris Foundation: 132–9.
Thalmann, J.-P. (1980) 'Recherches aux Thermopyles', *BCH* 104: 757–60.
Themelis, P.G. (1983a) 'Δελφοί και Περιοχή τον 8ο. και 7ο. π.Χ. αιώνα', *ASAtene* 61: 213–55.
—— (1983b) 'An 8th century goldsmith's workshop at Eretria', in Hägg 1983a: 157–65.
Theochari, M.D. (1962) 'Δοκιμαστική Ανασκαφή εις Χασάμβαλι Λαρίσης', *Θεσσαλικά* 4: 35–50.

―― (1966) 'Πρωτογεωμετρικά Θεσσαλίας', Θεσσαλικά 5: 37–53.
Theocharis, D. (1959) 'Πύρασος', Θεσσαλικά 2: 29–68.
―― (1968) 'Ο Τύμβος του Εξαλόφου και η Εισβολή των Θεσσαλών', ΑΑΑ 1: 290–5.
Thomas, C.G. (1979) 'The territorial imperative of the polis', *Ancient World* 2: 35–39.
Thomas, R. (1996) 'Written in stone? Liberty, equality, orality and the codification of law', in Foxhall and Lewis 1996: 9–31.
―― (2000) *Herodotos in Context. Ethnography, Science and the Art of Persuasion*, Cambridge: CUP.
Thompson, H.A. (1940) *The Tholos of Athens and its Predecessors* (*Hesperia* supp. 4), Princeton: ASCSA.
Threpsiades, I. (1972) 'Ἀνασκαφὴ Γαλαξιδίου', *AE*: 184–207.
Thür, G. and Taeuber, H. (1994) *Prozessrechtliche Inschriften der Griechischen Poleis: Arkadien*, Vienna: Österreichischen Akademie der Wissenschaften.
Tilley, C. (1994) *A Phenomenology of Landscape. Places, Paths and Monuments*, Oxford: Berg.
Tomlinson, R. (1977) 'The upper terraces at Perachora', *BSA* 72: 197–202.
―― (1992) 'Perachora', in A. Schachter (ed.) *Le Sanctuaire Grec* (*Entretiens Hardt* 37), Geneva: Vandœuvres: 321–46.
Touchais, G. and Divari-Valakou, N. (1998) 'Argos du néolithique à l'époque géométrique: synthèse des données archéologiques', in Pariente and Touchais 1998: 9–21.
Touloupa, E. (1972) 'Bronzebleche von der Akropolis in Athen. Gehämmerte geometrische Dreifüße', *AthMitt* 87: 57–76.
Travlos, J. (1971) *Pictorial Dictionary of Ancient Athens*, London: Thames and Hudson.
―― (1988) *Bildlexikon zur Topographie des antiken Attika*, Tübingen: Wasmuth.
Tréziny, H. (1997) 'On equality of lot division at Megara Hyblaia in the eighth century BC', *AJA* 101: 381.
Trigger, B. (1972) 'Determinants of urban growth in pre-industrial societies', in Ucko, Tringham and Dimbleby 1972: 575–99.
―― (1980) *Gordon Childe: Revolutions in Archaeology*, London: Thames & Hudson.
―― (1989) *A History of Archaeological Thought*, Cambridge: CUP.
Trinkhaus, K.M. (1984) 'Boundary maintenance strategies and archaeological indicators', in S. de Atley and F. Findley (eds) *Exploring the Limits. Frontiers and Boundaries in Prehistory* (*BAR* IS 223), Oxford: BAR: 35–49.
Tritsch, F. (1929) 'Die Stadtbildungen des Altertums und die griechische *polis*', *Klio* 22: 1–83.
Tsountas, C. (1908) *Αἱ Προϊστορικαί Ἀκροπόλεις Διμηνίου καί Σέσκλου*, Athens: Sakellariou.
Tziaphalias, A. (1990) 'Άγιος Γεώργιος Λάρισας', *Αρχαιολογιά* 34: 44–9.
―― (1994a) 'Άγιος Γεώργιος Λάρισας', *ΘΕΣΣΑΛΙΑ*: 2: 179–88.
―― (1994b) 'Δεκαπέντε Χρόνια Ανασκαφών στην Αρχαία Λάρισα', *ΘΕΣΣΑΛΙΑ*: 2: 153–78.
―― (1995) 'Αρχαίος Άτραξ· Ιστορία – Τοπογραφία – Πολιτισμός', *ΤΡΙΚΑΛΙΝΑ* 15: 69–96.
Tziaphalias, A. and Zaouri, A. (1999) 'Από τη Βόρεια Περραιβία ως την

Αρχαία Κραννώνα: Νεκροταφεία της Πρωιμής Εποχής του Σιδήρου', *ΠΕΡΙΦΕΡΕΙΑ*: 143–52.
Ucko, P.J., Tringham, R. and Dimbleby, G.W. (eds) (1972) *Man, Settlement and Urbanism*, London: Duckworth.
Vallois, R. (1926) 'Le théâtre de Tégée', *BCH* 50: 135–73.
Van Andel, T. and Runnels, C. (1995) 'The earliest farmers in Europe,' *Antiquity* 69: 481–500.
van der Kamp, J.S. (1996) 'Anonymous tomb cults in western Messenia. The search for a historical explanation', *Pharos* 4: 63–88.
van der Leeuw, S. (1999) 'Exchange and trade in ceramics: some notes from the potter's point of view', in J.-P. Crielaard, G.-J. van Wijngaarten and V. Stissi (eds) *The Complex Past of Pottery*, Amsterdam: Gieben: 115–36.
Vanderpool, E. (1964) 'More inscriptions from the Phokikon', *Hesperia* 33: 84–5.
Vatin, C. (1969) *Médéon de Phocide*, Paris: Boccard.
Veit, U. (1989) 'Ethnic concepts in German prehistory: a case study on the relationship between cultural identity and archaeological objectivity', in S. Shennan (ed.) *Archaeological Approaches to Cultural Identity*, London: Unwin Hyman: 35–56.
Verdan, S. (2000) 'Fouilles dans le sanctuaire d'Apollon Daphnéphoros', *AntK* 43: 128–30.
—— (2001) 'Fouilles dans le sanctuaire d'Apollon Daphnéphoros', *AntK* 44: 84–7.
Verdelis, N.M. (1958) *Ο Πρωτογεωμετρικός Ρυθμός της Θεσσαλίας*, Athens: Archaeological Society of Athens.
—— (1962) 'A sanctuary at Solygeia,' *Archaeology* 15: 184–92.
Verdelis, N., Jameson, M. and Papachristodoulou, I. (1975) ''Αρχαϊκὴ Ἐπιγραφαὶ ἐκ Τίρυνθος', *AE*: 150–205.
Vink, M.C.V. (1997) 'Urbanization in Late and Sub-geometric Greece: abstract considerations and concrete case studies of Eretria and Zagora c.700 BC', in Damgard Andersen et al. 1997: 111–41.
Viviers, D. (1992) *Recherches sue les atéliers de sculpteurs et la cité d'Athènes à l'époque archaïque*, Gemblous: Académie royale de Belgique.
—— (1994) 'La cité de Dattalla et l'expansion territoriale de Lyktos en Crète centrale,' *BCH* 118: 229–59.
Vlachos, G. (1974) *Les sociétés politiques Homériques*, Paris: Presses Universitaires de France.
Vokotopoulou, I. (1969) 'Πρωτογεωμετρικά 'Αγγεῖα ἐκ τῆς Περιοχῆς Ἀγρινίου', *Delt* 24 A: 79–94.
—— (1982) 'Η ῎Ηπειρος στον 8ο και 7ο Αἰώνα π.χ.', *ASAtene* 60: 77–98.
—— (1986) *Βίτσα. Τα Νεκροταφεία μίας Μολοσσικής Κώμης*, Athens: TAPA.
—— (1993) 'Nouvelles données sur l'architecture archaïque en Macedoine centrale et en Chalcidique', in J. des Courtils and J.-C. Moretti (eds) *Les grands ateliers d'architecture dans le monde egéen du VIe siècle av. J.C. (Actes du colloque d'Istanbul, 23–25 mai 1991)*, Paris: Boccard: 85–95.
Vordos, A. (forthcoming) 'Rhypes: à la recherche de la métropole achéenne', in Greco forthcoming.
Voyatzis, M. (1990) *The Early Sanctuary of Athena Alea at Tegea and Other Archaic Sanctuaries in Arcadia*, Göteborg: Paul Åström.
—— (1999) 'The role of temple building in consolidating Arkadian communities,' *CPCActs* 6: 130–68.

Wace, A. and Droop, J. (1906–7) 'Excavations at Theotokou, Thessaly', *BSA* 13: 309–27.
Wace, A. and Thompson, M. (1911–12) 'Excavations at Halos', *BSA* 18: 1–29.
Wachter, R. (1989) 'Zur Vorgeschichte des griechischen Alphabets', *Kadmos* 28: 19–78.
—— (2001) *Non-Attic Greek Vase Inscriptions*, Oxford: OUP.
Wade-Gery, H. (1924) 'Jason of Pherae and Aleuas the Red', *JHS* 44: 55–64.
Waisglass, A. (1956) 'Demonax ΒΑΣΙΛΕΥΣ ΜΑΝΤΙΝΕΩΝ', *AJP* 77: 167–76.
Walbank, F.W. (1972) *Polybius*, Berkeley: University of California Press.
—— (1985) 'Were there Greek federal states?,' in F.W. Walbank, *Selected Papers. Studies in Greek and Roman History and Historiography*, Cambridge: CUP: 20–37.
—— (2000) 'Hellenes and Achaians. Greek nationality revisited', *CPCPapers* 5: 19–33.
Walter, U. (1993) *An der Polis teilhaben* (*Historia* Einz. 83), Stuttgart: Franz Steiner.
Waterhouse, H. (1996) 'From Ithaca to the Odyssey', *BSA* 91: 301–17.
Watrous, L.V. (1982) 'The sculptural programme of the Siphnian Treasury at Delphi', *AJA* 86: 159–73.
—— (1998) 'Crete and Egypt in the seventh century BC: Temple A at Prinias', in W.G. Cavanagh and M. Curtis (eds) *Post-Minoan Crete. Proceedings of the First Colloquium on Post-Minoan Crete held by the British School at Athens and the Institute of Archaeology, University College London, 10–11 November 1995*, London: British School at Athens: 75–9.
Waywell, G.B. (1999) 'Sparta and its topography', *BICS* 43: 1–26.
Weber, M. (1924) 'Agrarverhältnisse im Altertum', in M. Weber, *Gesammelte Aufsätze zur Sozial- und Wirtschaftgeschichte*, Tübingen: J.C.B. Mohr: 1–288.
—— (1978) *Economy and Society: an Outline of Interpretative Sociology*, G. Roth and C. Wittich (eds), Berkeley/London: University of California Press.
Wees, H. van (1992) *Status Warriors. War, Violence and Society in Homer and History*, Amsterdam: Gieben.
—— (1998) 'A brief history of tears: gender differentiation in Archaic Greece', in L. Foxhall and J. Salmon (eds) *When Men were Men. Masculinity, Power and Identity in Classical Antiquity*, London: Routledge: 10–53.
—— (2001) 'The myth of the middle-class army: military and social status in ancient Athens', in L. Hannestad and T. Bekker Nielsen (eds) *War as a Cultural and Social Force. Essays on Warfare in Antiquity*, Copenhagen: KDVS: 45–71.
Wells, B. (1988) 'Early Greek building sacrifices', in Hägg, Marinatos and Nordquist 1988: 259–66.
—— (1990) 'The Asine sima', *Hesperia* 59: 157–61.
Wells, P.S. (1980) *Culture Contact and Culture Change: Early Iron Age Central Europe and the Mediterranean World*, Cambridge: CUP.
—— (1984) *Farms, Villages and Cities: Commerce and Urban Origins in Late Prehistoric Europe*, Ithaca, NY: Cornell University Press.
Welwei, K.-W. (1977) *Unfrieie im antiken Kriegsdienst 2*, Wiesbaden: Franz Steiner.
—— (1983) *Die griechische Polis*, Stuttgart: Kohlhammer.
—— (1988) 'Ursprünge genossenschaftlicher Organisationsformen in der archaischen *polis*', *Saeculum* 89: 12–23.
—— (1992) *Athen. Vom neolithischen Siedlungsplatz zur archaischen Grosspolis*, Darmstadt: Wissenschaftliche Buchgesellschaft.

Westover, S.B. (1999) 'Smelting and sacrifice: comparative analysis of Greek and Near Eastern cult sites from the Late Bronze through the Classical periods,' in S. Young, M. Pollard, P. Budd and R. Ixer (eds) *Metals in Antiquity*, Oxford: BAR: 86–90.
Wheatley, P. (1972) 'The concept of urbanism', in Ucko, Tringham and Dimbleby 1972: 601–37.
Whitbread, I.K. (1995) *Greek Transport Amphorae. A Petrological and Archaeological Study* (BSA Fitch Laboratory Occasional Paper 4), Athens/London: BSA.
Whitbread, I.K., Jones, R.E. and Papadopoulos, J.K. (1997) 'The Early Iron Age kiln at Torone, Greece: geological diversity and the definition of control groups', in A. Sinclair, E. Slater, and J. Gowlett (eds) *Archaeological Sciences 1995*, Oxford: BAR: 88–91.
Whitehouse, R. and Wilkins, J. (1989) 'Greeks and natives in south-east Italy', in T. Champion (ed.) *Centre and Periphery: Comparative Studies in Archaeology*, London: Unwin Hyman: 102–26.
Whitelaw, T. (1998) 'Colonisation and competition in the *polis* of Koressos: the development of settlement in north-west Keos from the Archaic to the Late Roman periods', in L.G. Mendoni and A. Mazarakis Ainian (eds) *Kea-Kythnos: History and Archaeology*, Athens/Paris: KERA/Boccard: 227–57.
Whitley, A.J.M. (1988) 'Early states and hero cults: a reappraisal', *JHS* 108: 173–82.
—— (1991a) *Style and Society in Dark Age Greece*, Cambridge: CUP.
—— (1991b) 'Social diversity in Dark Age Greece', *BSA* 86: 341–65.
—— (1998) 'From Minoans to Eteocretans: the Praisos region, 1200–500 BC', in Cavanagh and Curtis 1998: 27–39.
Whittaker, C.R. (ed.) (1988) *Pastoral Economies in Classical Antiquity* (PCPS supp. 14), Cambridge: Cambridge Philological Society.
Wilamowitz Möllendorff, U. von. (1931). *Der Glaube der Hellenen* I, Berlin: Weidmann.
Will, E. (1995) 'Corinthe, la richesse et la puissance', *Corinto*: 13–28.
Willcock, M. (1978) *A Commentary on Homer's Iliad. Books I-IV*, London: Macmillan.
Williams, C.K. II. (1970) 'Corinth, 1969: forum area', *Hesperia* 39: 1–39.
—— (1978) 'Pre-Roman Cults in the Area of the Forum of Ancient Corinth' (PhD diss., University of Pennsylvania).
Williams, R. (1965) *The Confederate Coinage of the Arcadians in the Fifth Century* (The American Numismatic Society Notes and Monographs 155), New York: ANS.
—— (1970) 'The Archaic coinage of Arcadian Heraea', *American Numismatic Society Museum Notes* 16: 1–12.
—— (1972) *The Silver Coinage of the Phokians*, London: Royal Numismatic Society.
Winter, N. (1993) *Greek Architectural Terracottas from the Prehistoric to the end of the Archaic Period*, Oxford: OUP.
Wiseman, J. (1978) *The Land of the Ancient Corinthians*, Göteborg: Paul Åström.
Woolf, G.D. (1998) *Becoming Roman. The Origins of Provincial Civilisation in Gaul*, Cambridge: CUP.
Wycherley, R.E. (1957) *The Athenian Agora III. Literary and Epigraphical Testimonia*, Princeton: ASCSA.
Yorke, V.W. (1896) 'Excavations at Abae and Hyampolis in Phocis', *JHS* 16: 291–312.

INDEX

Achaia: burial 177, 179–80, 190, 220, 224; ethnic 196–7, 213; external relations 3, 121, 129, 216–17, 219–22; hero cult 162, 189; lack of inscriptions 77–8; polis centres 69–70; pottery 181–5; script 166, 221; settlement and region 31–8, 46, 199–200, 234 n.165; *see also* Aegira; Aigion; Ano Mazaraki; Azanes; coinage; colonization; Dyme; Patras; Pharai valley; pottery; Rhypes
Aegira 52–4, 69, 201, 215
Aeschylus 128
Aetolia 7, 216, 218, 220
Ag. Georgios *see* Krannon cemeteries
Aigion: external relations 183, 213, 215, 221; settlement 46, 69, 177, 181, 183, 199, 217; pottery 73, 182; *see also* Ano Mazaraki; colonization
Aleuas the Red 22, 130
Alipheira 161
Almyros *see* Halos
amphictyony *see* Delphi; Kynourian amphictyony; Pylaean amphictyony
Amyklaion 107–9, 113, 144, 149
Anaximander 171
ancestor cult 188–90, 102; Achaia 179; Arkadia 189; Medeon 122; Thessaly 192
Ano Mazaraki 74, 108, 180, 182–5, 215, 221
Antikyra 122, 125
Argissa Magoula 89–90; in Homer 103–4
Argive Heraion 112, 153
Argos 46; settlement 61–4, 66, 68, 74, 92, 172; territory 167; *see also* Argive Heraion
Aristophanes 191
Aristotle: Arkadia 69; community of place 47; law 78; *penestai* 190; settlement 172; state forms 8–9, 206; territory 164
Arkadia: borders, 47; burials 174, 184–5; coinage 82–4, 185–6, 207; economy 160–1; ethnos 161–2, 185–6, 197; inscriptions 79; region 38–42, 160–1; sculpture 159–60, 185; settlement 69, 181, 173–5; shrines 155–62, 188, 208; territory and land maintenance 155, 168–70; tribes 12, 39–40; *see also* Alipheira; ancestor cult; Asea; Azanes; Bassai; Berekla; Heraia; Kleitor; Lousoi; Lykaion; Mantineia; mercenaries; Pallantion; Pastoralism; Tegea; Thelpousa; trade
Asea 38, 155, 157, 159–60, 170, 174, 184
Asine: burial cult 194; shrine 108.
Athens: acropolis 68–9; agora 2, 64–9; burial 195; territory 167; settlement 61; tribes 14; *see also* metalworking; names, personal; pottery; war; *xenia*
Atrax 79, 89–91, 140
autochthony 3
autonomia 5–6, 187
Azanes 42, 77–8, 175, 177, 180–6, 212

Bacchylides 184
basileus see ruler
Bassai 144, 157, 204
Berekla 128, 161, 168
Boiotia survey 172–3, 175
Boline *see* Patras
Bordieu, Pierre 211
bouleuteria 75
Bronze Age/Iron Age transition 223–4

Chaleion *see* Galaxidi
city *see* polis, settlement, urbanization
coinage 81–5, 207; *see also* Arkadia; Elis

322

INDEX

colonization 197–8; Achaian 37–8, 184, 188, 196, 198–202, 221; economies 169; from ethne 201–2; Lokrian 30, 198, 200–1; temples 155; town planning 49; *see also* Elis
community 11–12, 165
Copenhagen Polis Centre 5–6, 45, 173, 201, 212
Corfu: external relations 3, 219; Heraion 144
Corinth: external relations 4, 121–2, 198–9, 214–16, 220–2; in Homer 103, 177; settlement 55–61, 63, 68, 92; shrines 57, 59, 74, 109, 144, 146, 150–2; stone industry 60–1, 126, 150–2; *see also* Corinthian gulf; Isthmia; law; lawgivers; names, personal; Perachora; pottery
Corinthian gulf 167, 177, 213–22; *see also* Achaia; Delphi; Ithaka; Phokis
Corycaean Cave 127–9
Crete 183; Achaia 221; Delphi 125; immigrants 4; sanctuaries 107, 143; sites and planning 2, 49–50, 63; *see also* Kommos; law; lawgivers; *perioikoi*
cultures archaeological 17–18, 165–7, 229 n.64
Cyclades 224; town planning 49–50, 224; sanctuaries 143, 224

Delphi: amphictyony and first sacred war 23, 114, 123–6, 129–31, 207; bouleuterion 75; early settlement and shrine 24–5, 114, 120–3, 129; external connections 123–4, 129, 182, 213, 215, 217–18, 220; oracle 77, 196; polis 85, 124–5, 153; Phokis 131, 133–4, 181. Thessaly 129–31; *see also* Corycaean Cave; Homer; Kynourian amphictyony; Pylaean amphictyony; sculpture.
Demosthenes, pseudo 198–9
Dimini 95–102, 168
Dionysus of of Halikarnassus 191
Dodona 72, 103–4
drainage 38, 57, 155, 169–70, 176
Durkheim, Emile 73–4
Dyme 47, 77, 177, 199–200

Ehrenberg, Victor 6, 9, 46, 168
Elateia 24, 115, 118, 133–4, 190, 220
Elis 47, 216; borders 175, 208; coinage 75; colonization 198–9; external relations 219; pre-synoikism 75–6; *see also* Olympia; *perioikoi*
Enodia 92–3, 95, 135–40; *see also* Thessaly
Ephesos 72, 144
Ephoros 131, 199, 204
Eretria 50–2, 73
ethnicity 10–12, 222; and archaeology 16–18, 211–12
ethnos: ancient perceptions 7, 9–10; death of 186; ethnos (ethnogenesis) 47, 188, 202; modern scholarship, 5–7, 9, 168, 206–7; tiered political identity 1, 8, 12, 196, 206–13, 222; towns in, 69–70, 212–13, sanctuaries in 108–9, 113; *see also* ancestor cult; colonization; ethnicity; myth-history; names, personal; *xenia*
Euboia: external relations 3, 119, 121, 142, 166, 201, 214, 223, 276–7 n.62; Kyme 2; *see also* Eretria; Lefkandi
Euhydrion (Ktouri) 87, 89, 142
Euphorion 8

feudalism 24
Finley, Moses 14, 71–2
fortification 45, 50, 74, 87, 89, 92
Foustel de Coulanges, Numa 47

Galaxidi 30, 80, 125–6
Gell, William 219
gender 223; *see also* war; mercenaries
geneaology *see* myth-history
Gonnoi 23, 89, 141–2, 203
Grote, George 14

Halos 91, 96, 193–4; in Homer 103
Hellanikos of Mytilene 22
Hellenic identity 2–3, 15
Herodotos: Achaia 37, 176–7, 196–7; agoras 69; Argos 190; arbitration (Kyrene) 78; Arkadia 42, 175, 186, 196–7, 204; autochthony 187; Delphi 126–7, 130, 196; Phokis 26, 133; Thessaly 23, 105, 203
Heraia 82–3
Hippokrates 203
Holland, Henry 219
Homer: burial 195; *Catalogue of Ships* 13, 39, 91, 102–5, 167, 171, 175, 177, 185, 204, 207; crafts 72; ethne 9–10; ethnics 166; journeys 171; kinship terminology 13; polis 7; Scheria 164

323

INDEX

Homeric hymns: to Hermes 128–9; to Pythian Apollo 125, 131
Hyampolis *see* Kalapodi

identity 222–5; outsider 171, 202–3, 205, 213–14; Delphi 203, 208–9; script 30, 166, 210, 221; *see also* Achaia; Arkadia; Korope; law; names, personal; Olympia; pottery; sculpture
Iolkos 23, 96, 99, 101–3, 105; *see also* Dimini; Volos-Palia
Isokrates 124
Isthmia 2; EIA 55, 107–13, 149; Archaic temple 74, 132, 144–8, 150–2, 154
Italy 3, 122, 150, 214–15, 218–20; *see also* colonization
Ithaka 3, 121, 182; Aetos shrine 143; external connections 215, 218–21; Polis Cave 107

Kalapodi 24, 107–9, 114–19, 131–3, 141; and Delphi 121
kinship *see* tribes
Kirrha *see* Krisa
Kleitor 79, 83–4, 184, 186
Kommos 3–4, 210
Korope: sacral inscription 79, 87; shrine 96, 142
Krannon 22, 81, 86; cemeteries 89–91, 180, 194–5, 202
Krisa 124–6
Kromna 57
Kynos 30, 115, 201
Kynourian amphictyony 129

Larisa 22, 55, 169, 196; cult 135, 139–40; in Homer 102–4; sculpture 88, 131; settlement 89–91
Larsen, Frederick 7, 9, 30
law, written display and guarantee of 75–81; Dreros 76
lawgivers 78
Lefkandi 2, 50, 73, 201, 237 n.30
Lilaia 85
Lokris, East 28–31, 223; early burials and settlement 115, 118, 200–1, 214; *see also* colonization; Kalapodi; Kynos; myth-history; names, personal; Naupaktos; Opous
Lousoi 38, 149, 180, 182–4; sacred law 77–9, 182–4
Lykaion, Mt. 74

Maine, Henry Sumner 13–15
Mantineia: coinage 83–4; cult of Penelope 189; land 169–70; Ptolis 70, 144, 174–5; war 204; *see also* law; lawgivers
maps 170–1
Marx, Karl 231 n.88
Medeon 25, 121–2, 125, 215, 217, 220
Megalopolis 172–4, 186
Megara 46
Melitaia 139–40
Mende-Poseidi 107, 143, 149
mercenaries 23, 84, 168, 197, 203–4; and sanctuaries 120, 142, 204
meros 37
metalworking: in sanctuaries 119–20, 148–9, 152–5, 170, 184; in settlements 64, 72
Metropolis: ancestor cult 192; Apollo shrine 87, 141–2
migration *see* mobility, human; myth-history
Miletos 72, 201
mobility, human 3–4, 101–2, 164, 171, 187–8, 196–205; craftsmen 209–10
Morgan, Lewis Henry 15
myth-history 46–7, 113, 161–2, 187–8, 202, 222, 252 n.51

names, personal 6, 23, 57, 196–7, 208–11
Naupaktos 30, 198, 200
Nichoria 50, 55, 73, 143, 237 n.30

Oiti, Pyra Herakleous 194–5
Olympia 2, 107–9; EIA origins 149, 224; Elean political centre 75–6, 80, 125, 143; epigraphy 80; metal dedications 112, 153–4, 184; *see also* Arkadia; Elis; sculpture; war
Opous 30
Oropos 2, 73

Pallantion 74, 143, 155–7
pastoralism 168–9; *see also* Berekla; mobility, human
Patras 36, 55, 176–7, 180, 199, 214; Boline 69, 176
patriotism 1
patronymics 6
Patterson, Orlando 10–11
Pausanias: Achaia 39, 176, 196–7, 199, 214; Arkadia 173–5, 186, 189, 204; Olympia 196, 204; Phokis 188; Thessaly and Delphi 131, 133

INDEX

Pefkakia 96, 98
Peisistratids 23, 67, 203, 209
Pellene 8, 177
penestai 190–2, 196
Perachora 57, 124, 146, 150, 157, 215–17, 219
perioikoi 6, 11, 23, 76, 102
Pharai valley 36, 166, 176–87, 198
Pharsalos 8, 20, 22, 81, 87–8, 139, 142, 180, 203
Pherai: settlement 22, 46, 63, 89, 92–5; bronzeworking 73; cemeteries 93–5, 138, 195; Homer 102–3; sculpture 88, 138; shrines 92, 95, 135–41
Philia 87, 119, 135, 141, 149, 249 n.4
Phokis: burials 190; coinage 84, 132; economy 125–6, 134, 168; Phokikon 26, 133, 162, 188–9; region 24–7, 196, 213–14; shrines 114, 134, 162, 208; Thessaly 26–7, 47, 131–4; *see also* Delphi; Elateia; ethnos (ethnogenesis); Kalapodi; myth-history; names, personal
Pindar 77, 86–7, 196, 203, 209
Plato 87, 191
Plint the Elder 201
Plutarch 130, 203
polis; Aristotle 9; definition, 5; in ethne 1, 45–6, 212; towns 69–71, 201; *see also* Copenhagen Polis Centre; settlement
Polis Cave *see* Ithaka
Pollux 191
Polyaenus 140
Polybios 37, 109
pottery: painters 210; potters' marks 219; production 64–5, 72–3, 152; style 165–7, 181–4; visibility 173–4
Pylaean amphictyony 129–30
Pylos *see* Olympia, EIA origins

Rhianos of Bene 8
Rhypes 36, 69, 182, 199
roads 38, 55, 57, 61, 64–6, 72, 94–5, 97, 109, 135, 138–40, 146, 152, 155, 159, 170
rulers: and customary law 77; foci of identity 54, houses 50, 52, 143; *see also* colonization; mercenaries; war

Salvator, Ludwig 214
sanctuaries: divine oikos 143–4; economies 135, 149–55; equipment 79; group dedications 163; location 74, 108; longevity 107–8; political function 74–6, 105, 143; temple buildings 142–4; *see also* ancestor cult; ethnos; Isthmia; metalworking; sculpture
sculpture 163; cult statues 143–4; historical 8, 131, 133–4, 186, 196–7; stoneworkers 209–10; *see also* Arkadia; Thessaly
Sesklo 95–6, 101–2
settlements: economic and political role 71–4, 105–6; planning 49–54; public space 63–9, 74, 92; size 54–5
Sparta 11, 63, 74, 159–61, 169–70, 174–5, 188–9, 202–3; *see also* Amyklaion; Tegea
Stesichoros 155
Strabo: Achaia 176, 199, 214; Arkadia 42, 186; Peloponnese 171–2; Thessaly 104, 169, 203
synoikism 45, 164, 171–6

tageia see Thessaly
Tegea: Aristotlean constitution 8; economy 168–70; sanctuary 108, 149, 155, 170, 184, 249 n.4; settlement 174–5; silver deposit 79, 148; Sparta 196
temples *see* Arkadia; Isthmia; Phokis; sanctuaries; Thessaly
territory 164–8; *see also* synoikism
Thelpousa 76
Theocritos 191
Theopompos 198
Thermon 109, 143
Thessaly: burials 90–1, 93–5, 101, 138, 180, 190, 193–5; *Catalogue of Ships*, 102–3; coinage 81–2; geography and settlement 18–24, 85–9, 95–6, 98–9, 104–5, 167–9, 176, 188, 196; land and warfare 196; rulers 77, 86–7, 131, 196; sculpture 87–8, 138; *tageia* 24; temples/shrines 87, 141–2; tomb cult 189; unification 206; *see also* Aleuas the Red; Argissa Magoula; Atrax; Delphi; Dimini; Enodia; Euhydrion; Gonnoi; Halos; Homer; Iolkos; Korope; Krannon; law; Melitaia; Metropolis; Pefkakia; *penestai*; *perioikoi*; Pharsalos; Pherai; Philia; Phokis; pottery; Sesklo; Volos-Palia
Thucydides: Achaia 214; Athens 23, 67, 172, 209; colonization 201; Corinthian gulf 217; ethne 7–8, 49, 168, 223; mercenaries 84; Sicily 211; Thessaly 188

325

INDEX

torone 72
trade: marble 160, 170, 209–10; metals 170; wine 215; *see also* Corinth; Ithaka; metalworking
Trapeza Hill *see* Rhypes
tribes 6–7, 12–16, 188, 211–12; *see also* Arkadia; myth-history

unfree labour *see penestai*
urbanism 46–9, 105–6; relocation 164.

village residence 7, 69, 168, 173–4

Volos-Palia 22, 88, 89, 95–102, 168

war: armies 196, 202, 271 n.189; in burial 90–1, 180, 185, 194–5, 202, 220, 223–4; ethne as warlike 7–8; and gender 223; in sanctuaries 119–20, 132–4, 149, 204; *see also* Phokis; mercenaries
Weber, Max 12, 71, 73–4
writing *see* names; law; maps

xenia 1, 23, 163, 171, 203, 209, 218
Xenophon 168, 191, 196